オール

ド

ルーズ戦記

ボーイ

OLDBOY

publisher
MIKE RICHARDSON

editor
CHRIS WARNER

collection designer
DARIN FABRICK

art director
LIA RIBACCHI

English-language version produced by DARK HORSE MANGA.

OLD BOY Vol. 6

© 1997 by GARON TSUCHIYA and NOBUAKI MINEGISHI. All rights reserved. Originally published in Japan in 1997 by FUTABASHA PUBLISHERS CO., LTD, Tokyo. English-language translation rights arranged with FUTABASHA PUBLISH-ERS CO., LTD, Tokyo, through TOHAN CORPORATION, Tokyo. Dark Horse Manga™ is a trademark of Dark Horse Comics, Inc. All rights reserved. No portion of this publication may be reproduced or transmitted, in any form or by any means, without the express written permission of the copyright holders. Names, characters, places, and incidents featured in this publication are either the product of the author's imagination or are used fictitiously. Any resemblance to actual persons (living or dead), events, institutions, or locales, without satiric intent, is coincidental.

Dark Horse Manga
A division of Dark Horse Comics, Inc.
10956 SE Main Street
Milwaukie OR 97222

darkhorse.com

To find a comics shop in your area, call the Comic Shop Locator Service toll-free at 1-888-266-4226

First edition: June 2007
ISBN 978-1-59307-720-4

3 5 7 9 10 8 6 4 2
Printed in Canada

OLDBOY

volume 6

story by
GARON TSUCHIYA

art by
NOBUAKI MINEGISHI

translation
KUMAR SIVASUBRAMANIAN

lettering and retouch
MICHAEL DAVID THOMAS

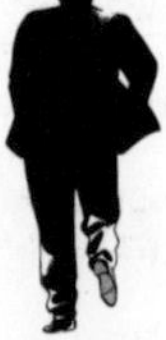

®
DARK HORSE MANGA™

CONTENTS

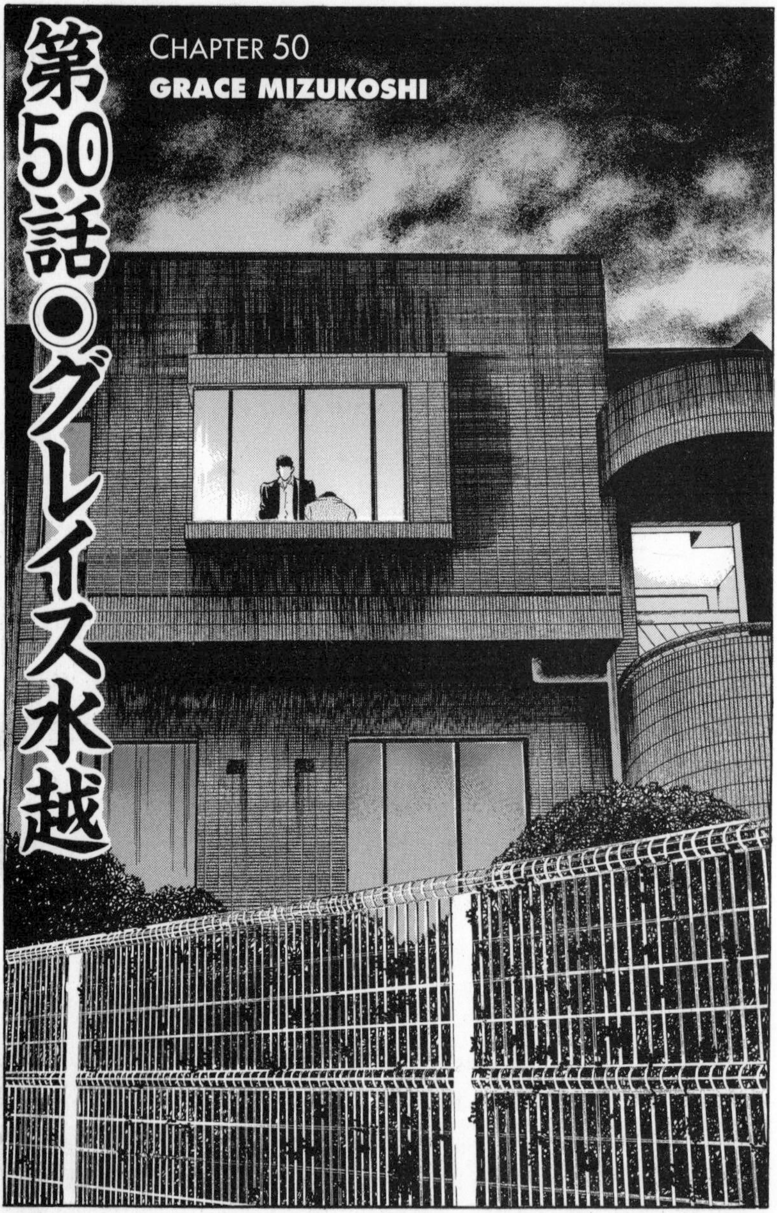
第50話◎グレイス水越
CHAPTER 50
GRACE MIZUKOSHI

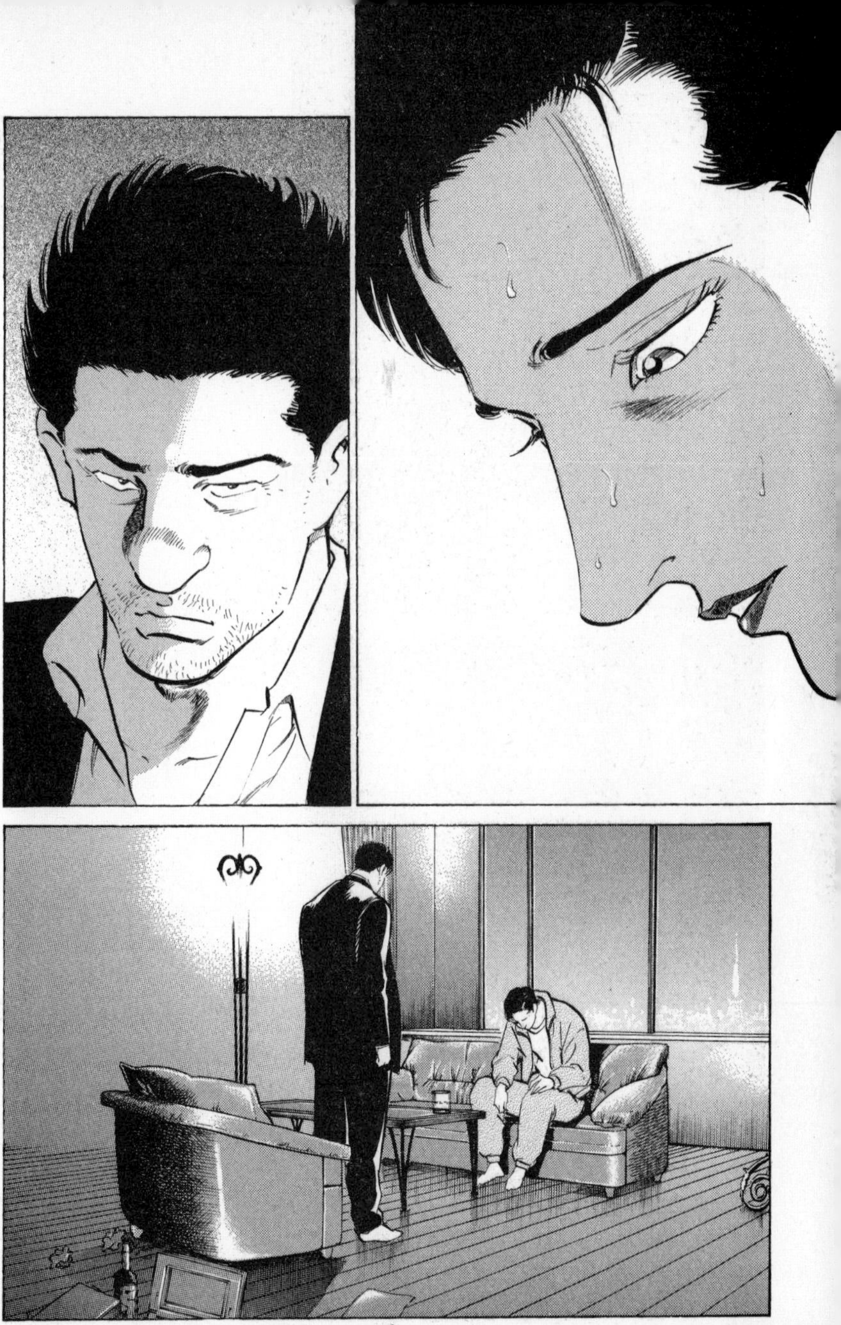

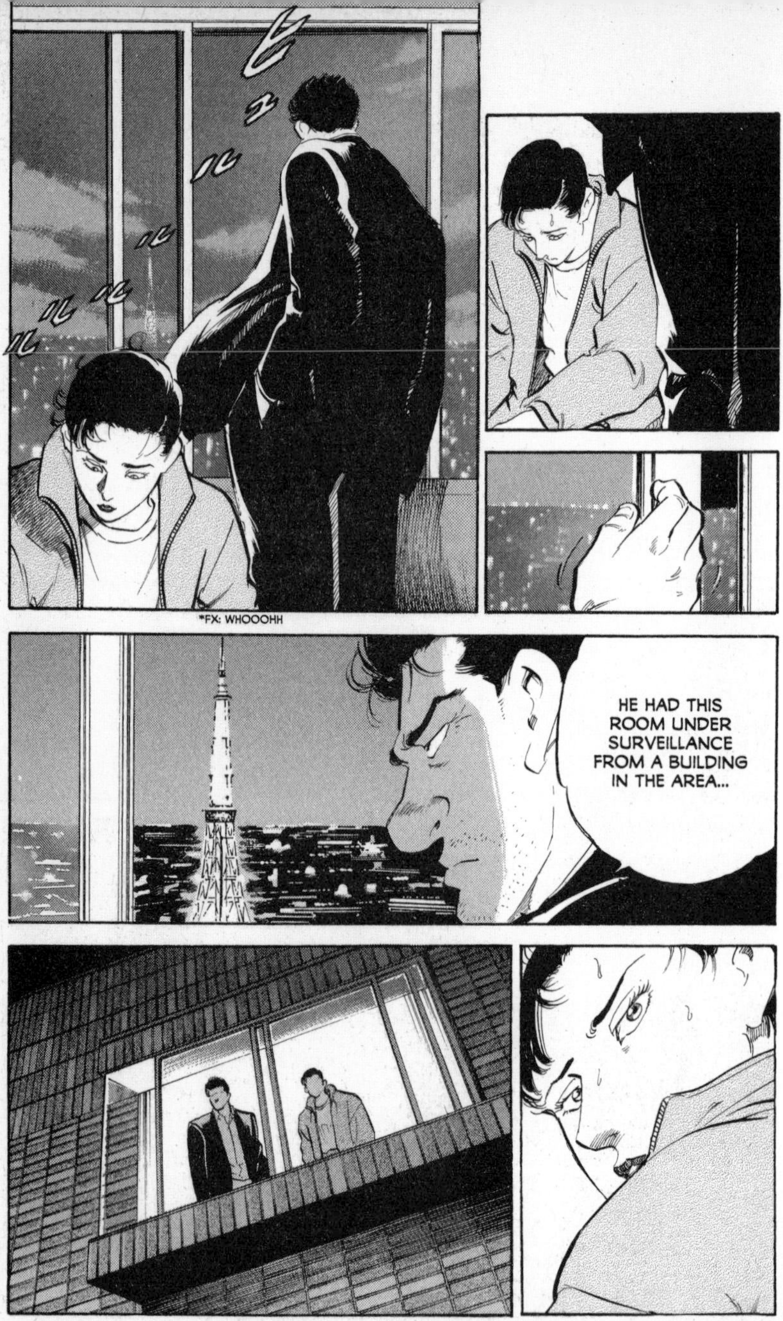
*FX: WHOOOHH
HE HAD THIS ROOM UNDER SURVEILLANCE FROM A BUILDING IN THE AREA...

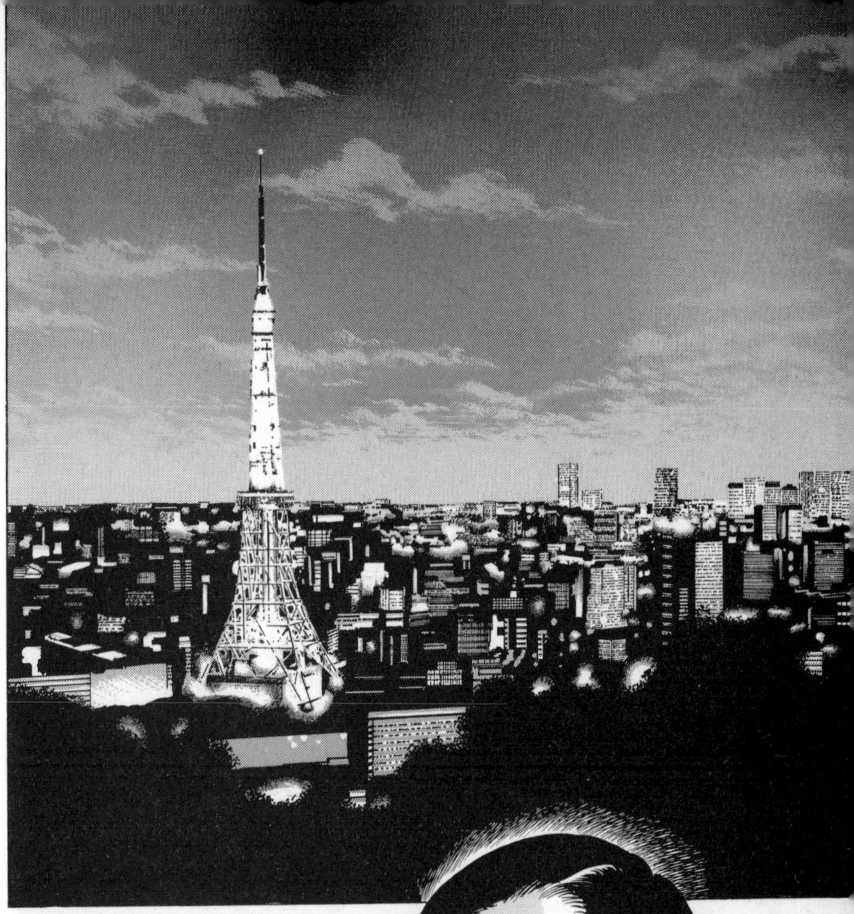
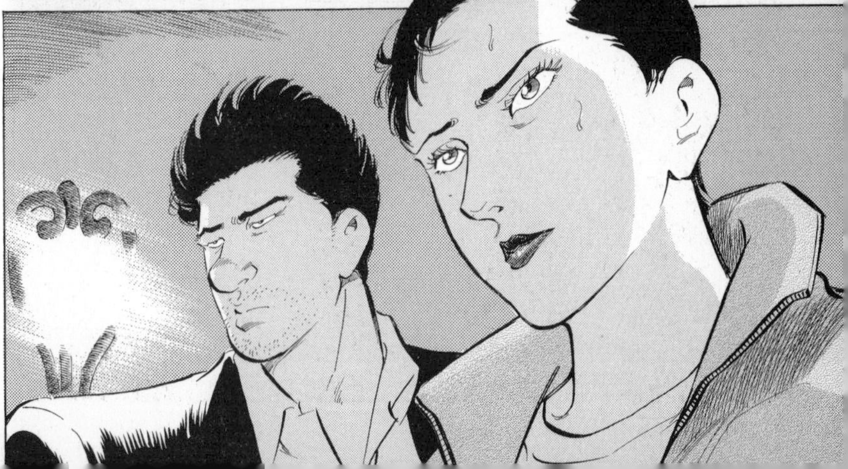

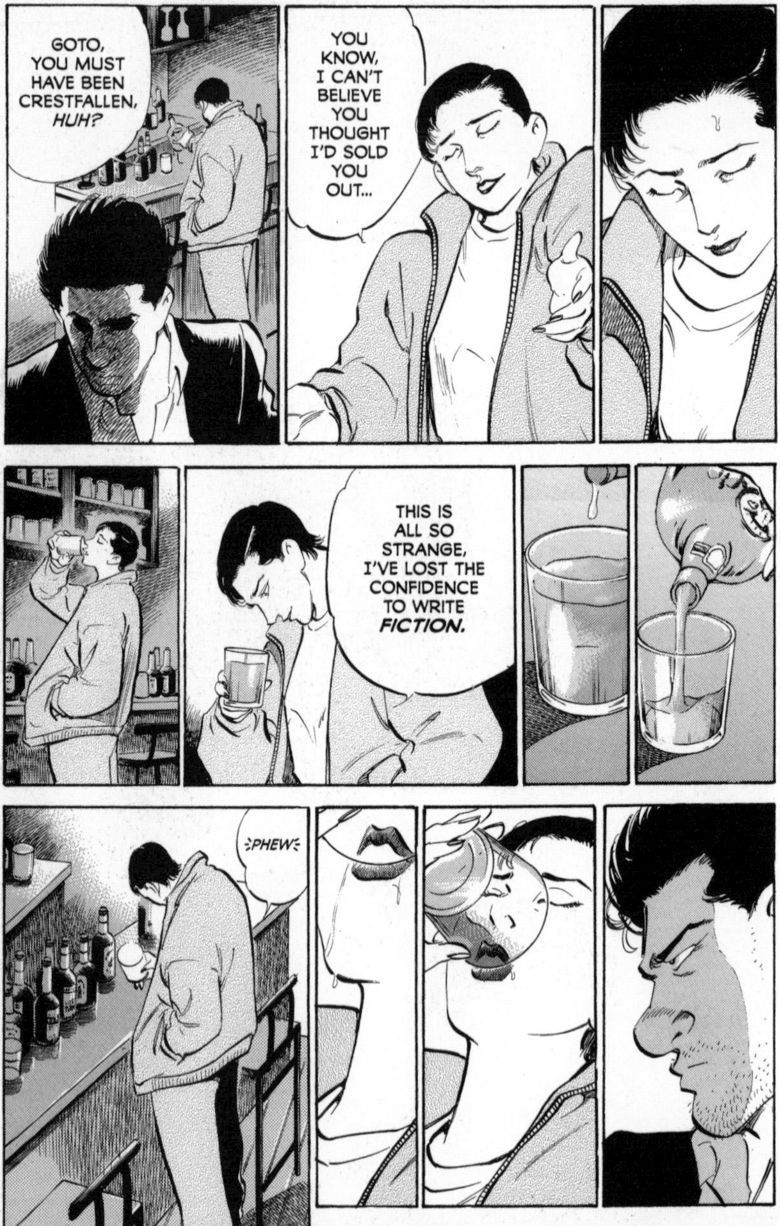
YOU KNOW, I CAN'T BELIEVE YOU THOUGHT I'D SOLD YOU OUT...
GOTO, YOU MUST HAVE BEEN CRESTFALLEN, *HUH?*
THIS IS ALL SO STRANGE, I'VE LOST THE CONFIDENCE TO WRITE ***FICTION.***
PHEW

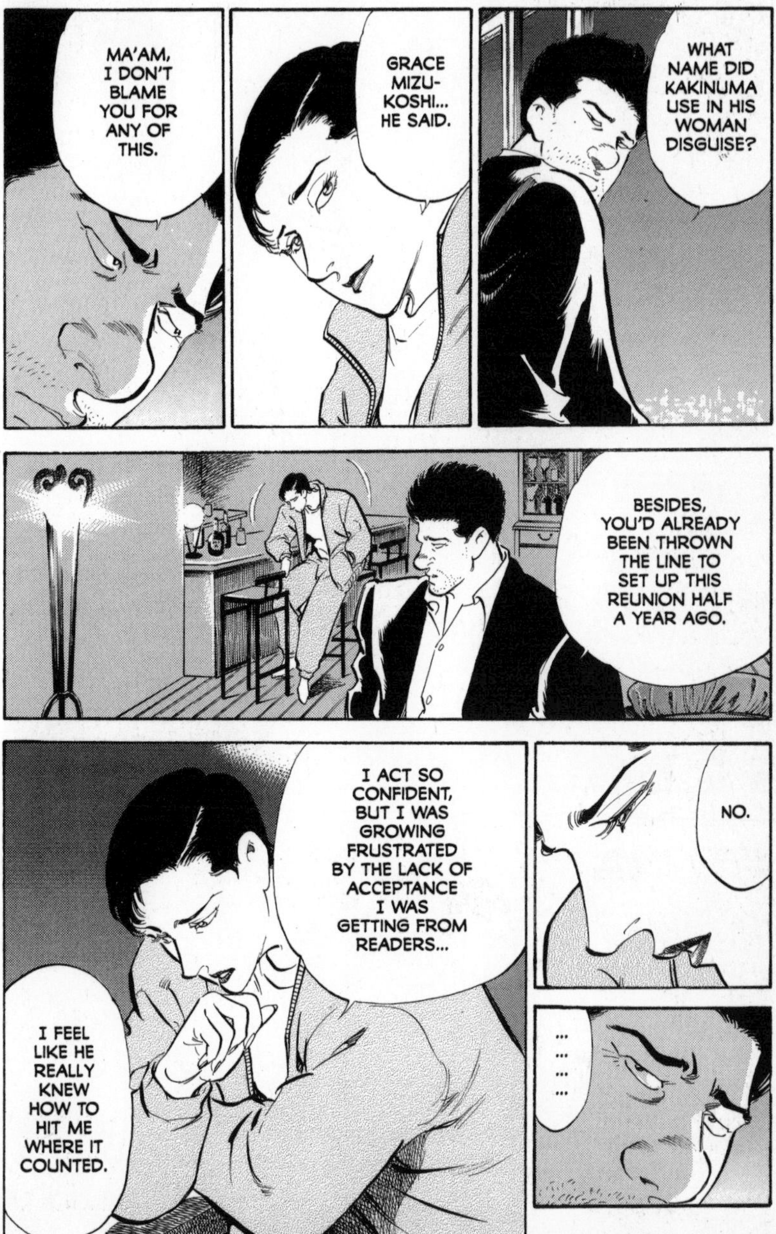
WHAT NAME DID KAKINUMA USE IN HIS WOMAN DISGUISE?
GRACE MIZU-KOSHI... HE SAID.
MA'AM, I DON'T BLAME YOU FOR ANY OF THIS.
BESIDES, YOU'D ALREADY BEEN THROWN THE LINE TO SET UP THIS REUNION HALF A YEAR AGO.
NO.
....
I ACT SO CONFIDENT, BUT I WAS GROWING FRUSTRATED BY THE LACK OF ACCEPTANCE I WAS GETTING FROM READERS...
I FEEL LIKE HE REALLY KNEW HOW TO HIT ME WHERE IT COUNTED.

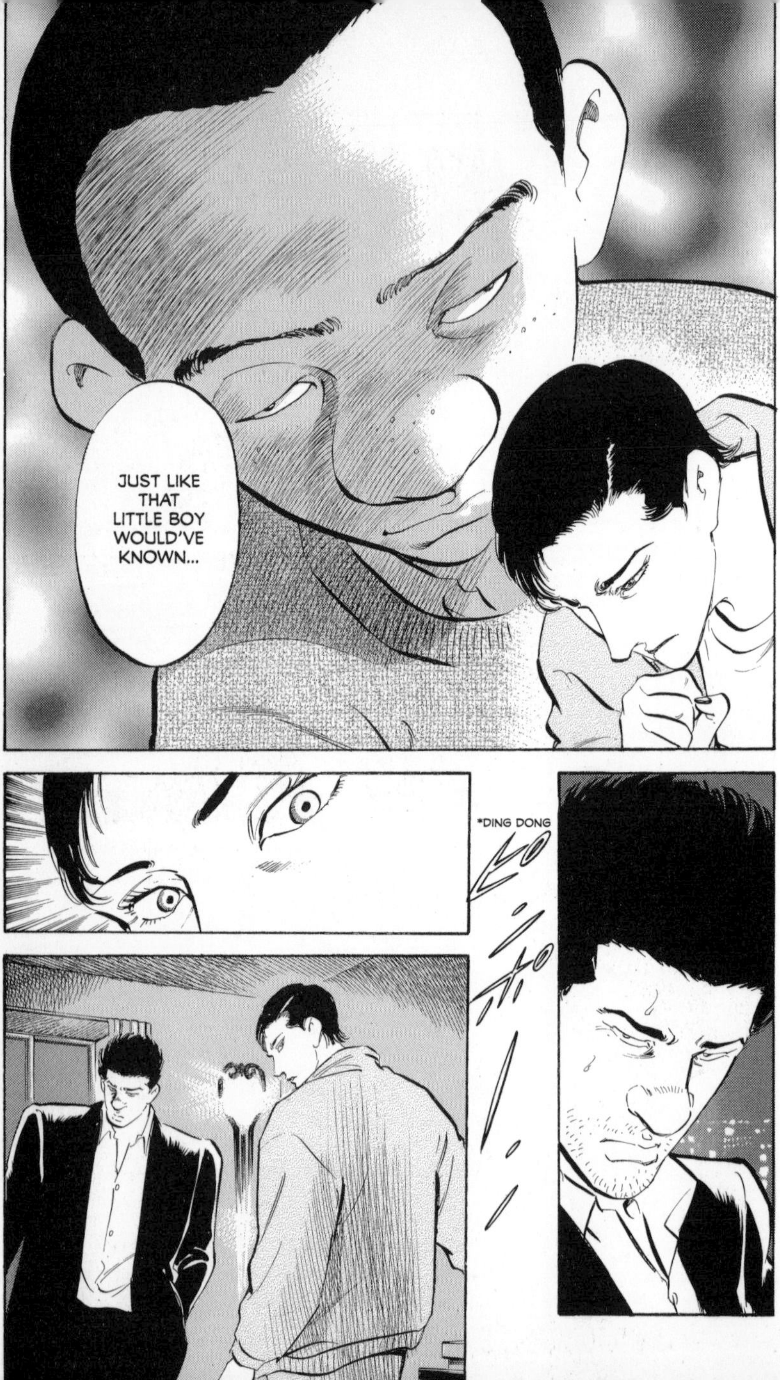
JUST LIKE THAT LITTLE BOY WOULD'VE KNOWN...
*DING DONG

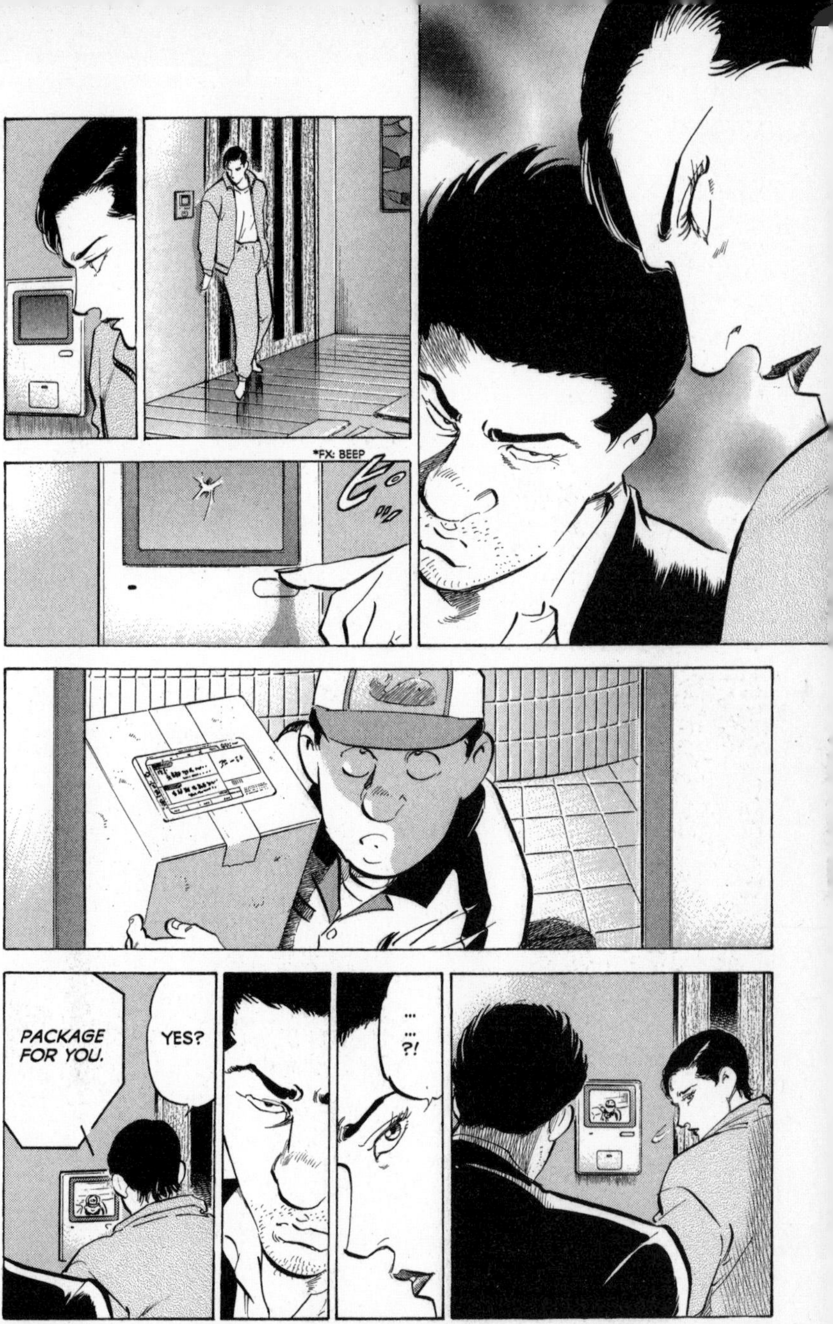
*FX: BEEP
...
...
?!
YES?
PACKAGE FOR YOU.

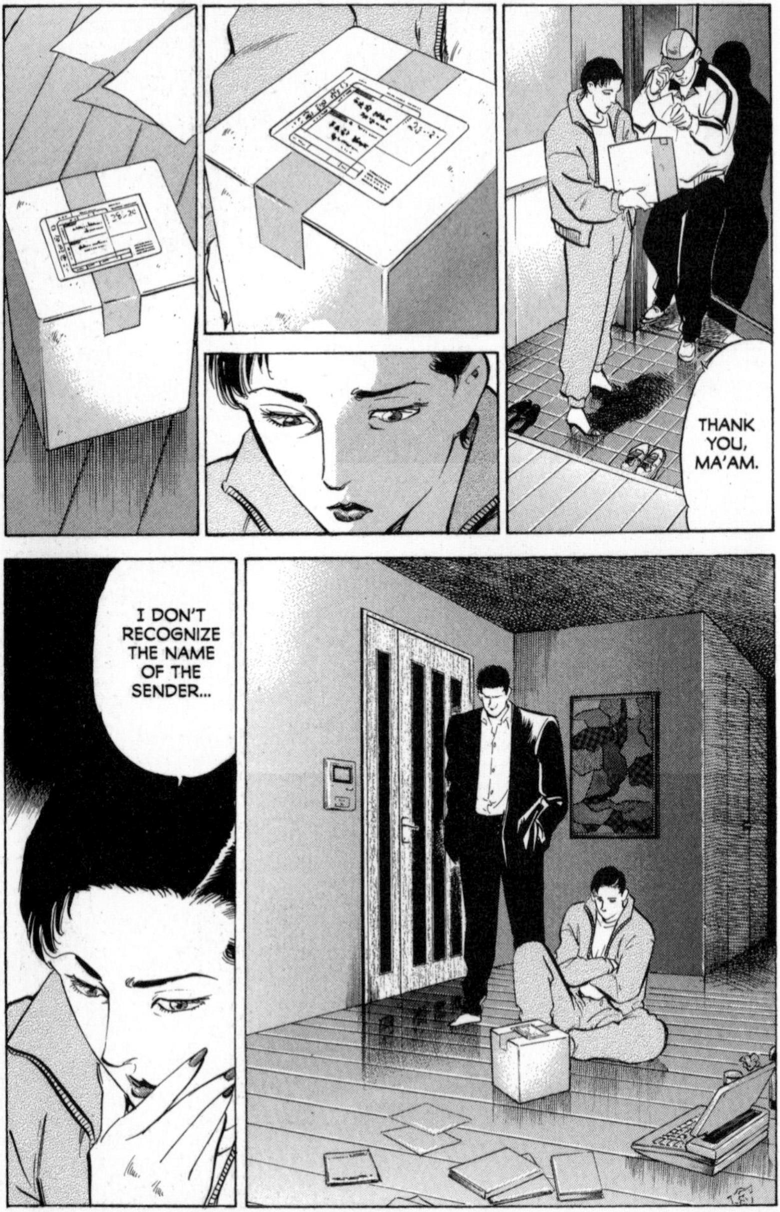
THANK YOU, MA'AM.
I DON'T RECOGNIZE THE NAME OF THE SENDER...

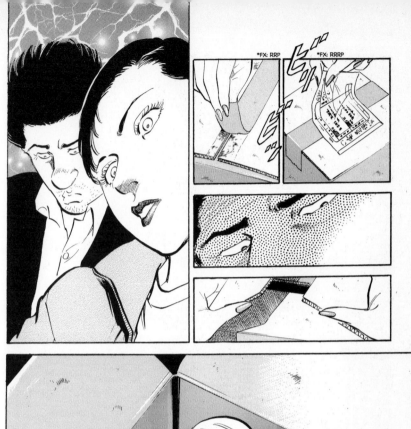

*FX: RRP

*FX: RRRP

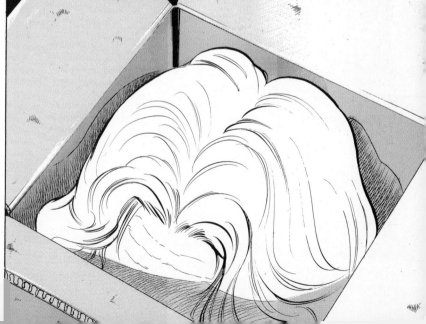

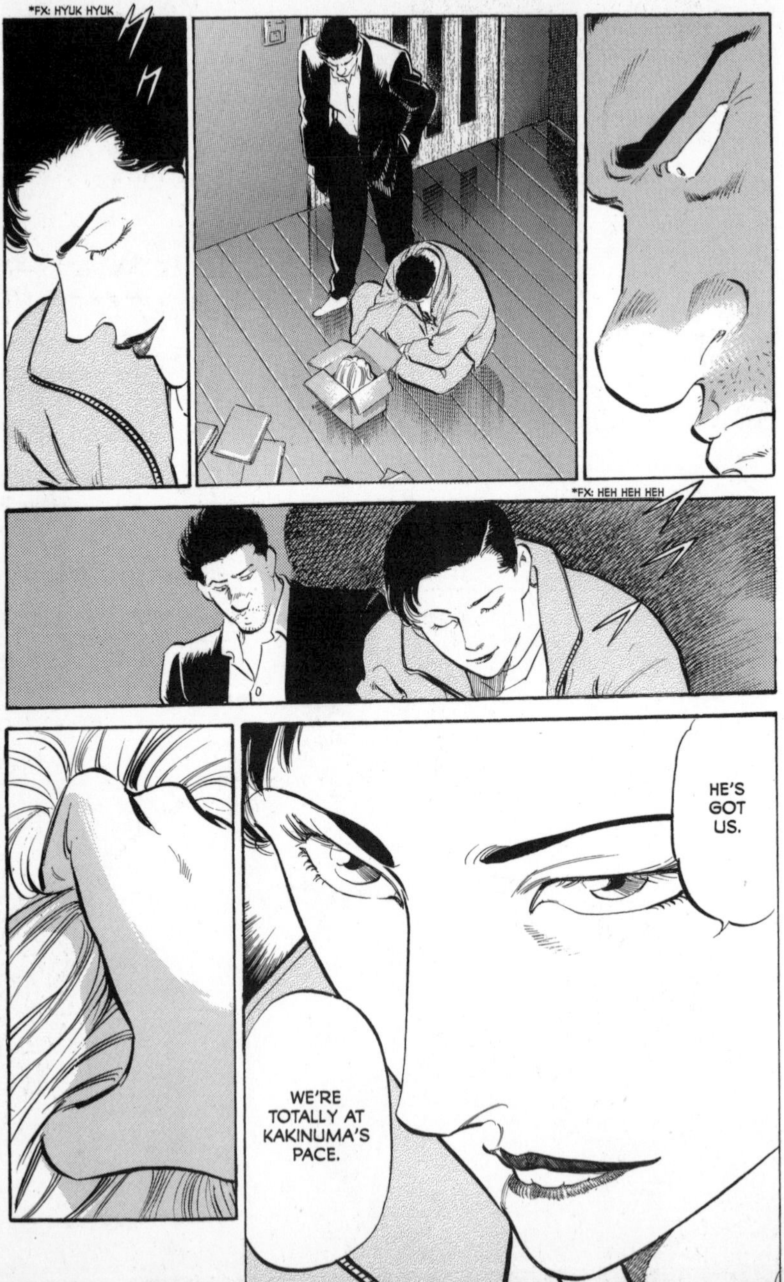
*FX: HYUK HYUK
*FX: HEH HEH HEH
HE'S GOT US.
WE'RE TOTALLY AT KAKINUMA'S PACE.

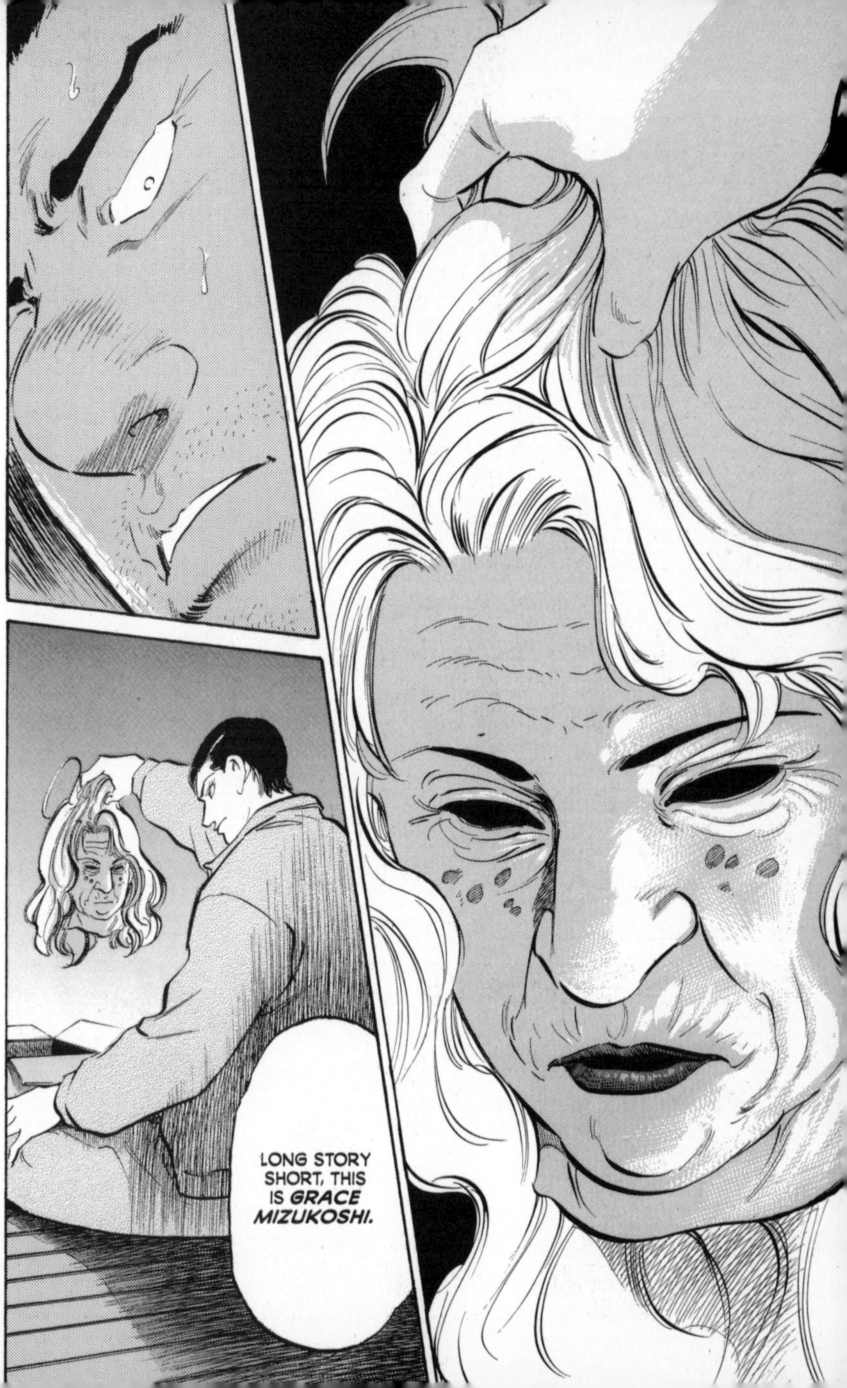
LONG STORY SHORT, THIS IS GRACE MIZUKOSHI.

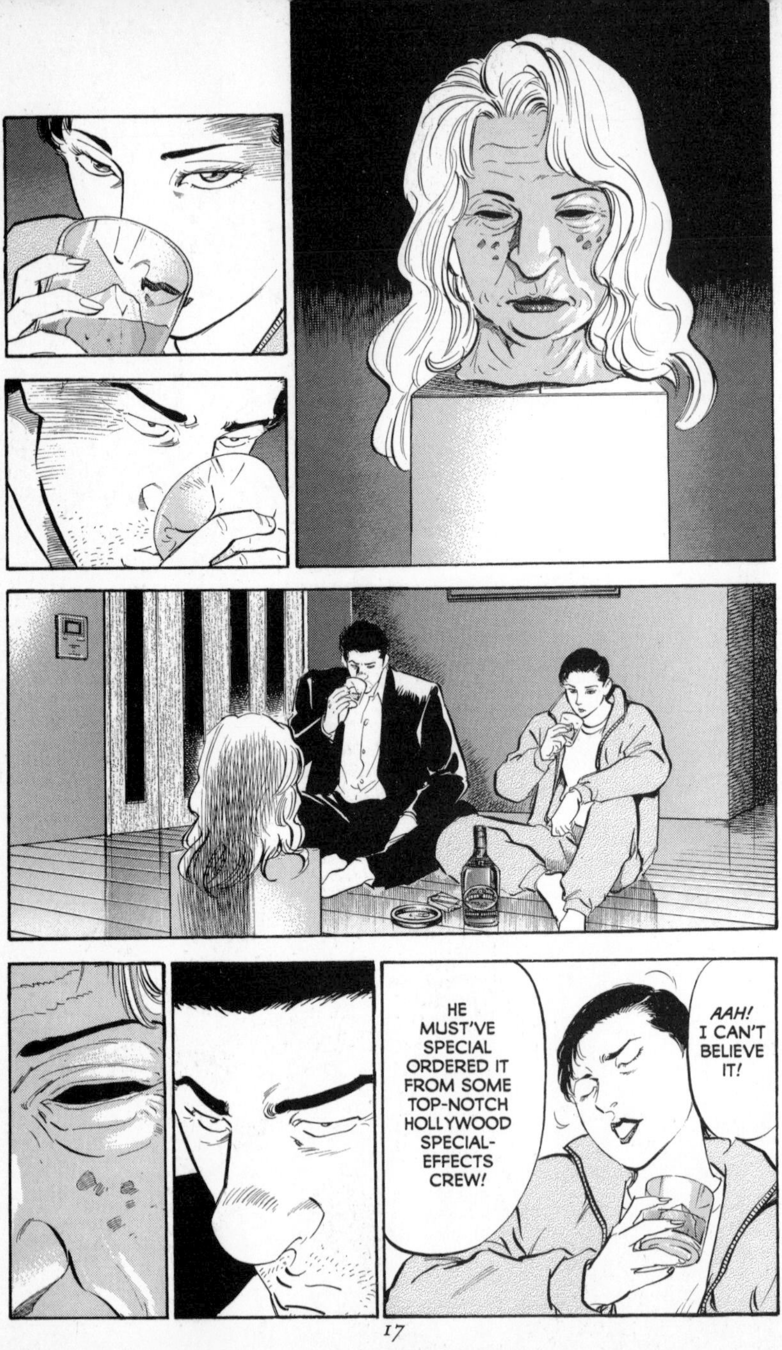
AAH! I CAN'T BELIEVE IT!
HE MUST'VE SPECIAL ORDERED IT FROM SOME TOP-NOTCH HOLLYWOOD SPECIAL-EFFECTS CREW!

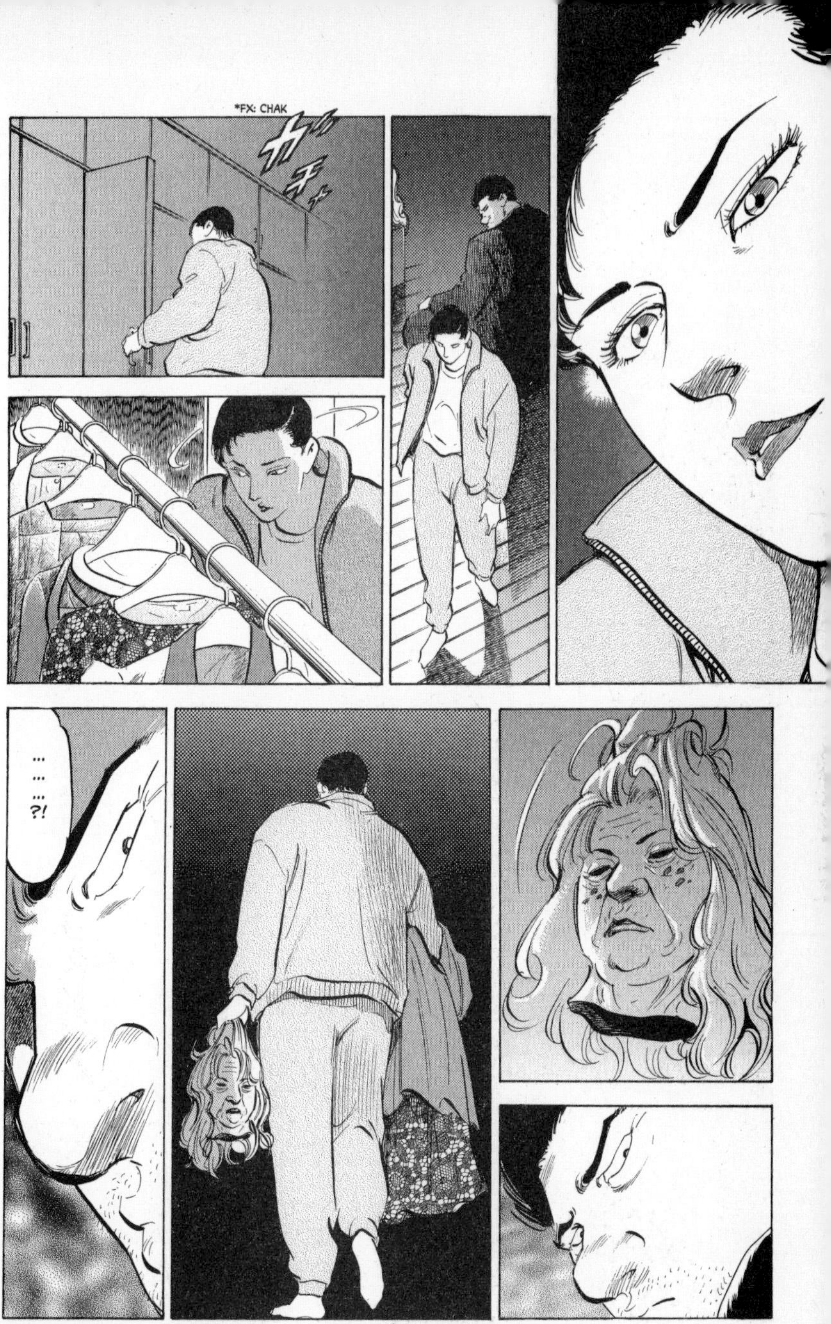

*FX: CHAK
...
...
...
?!

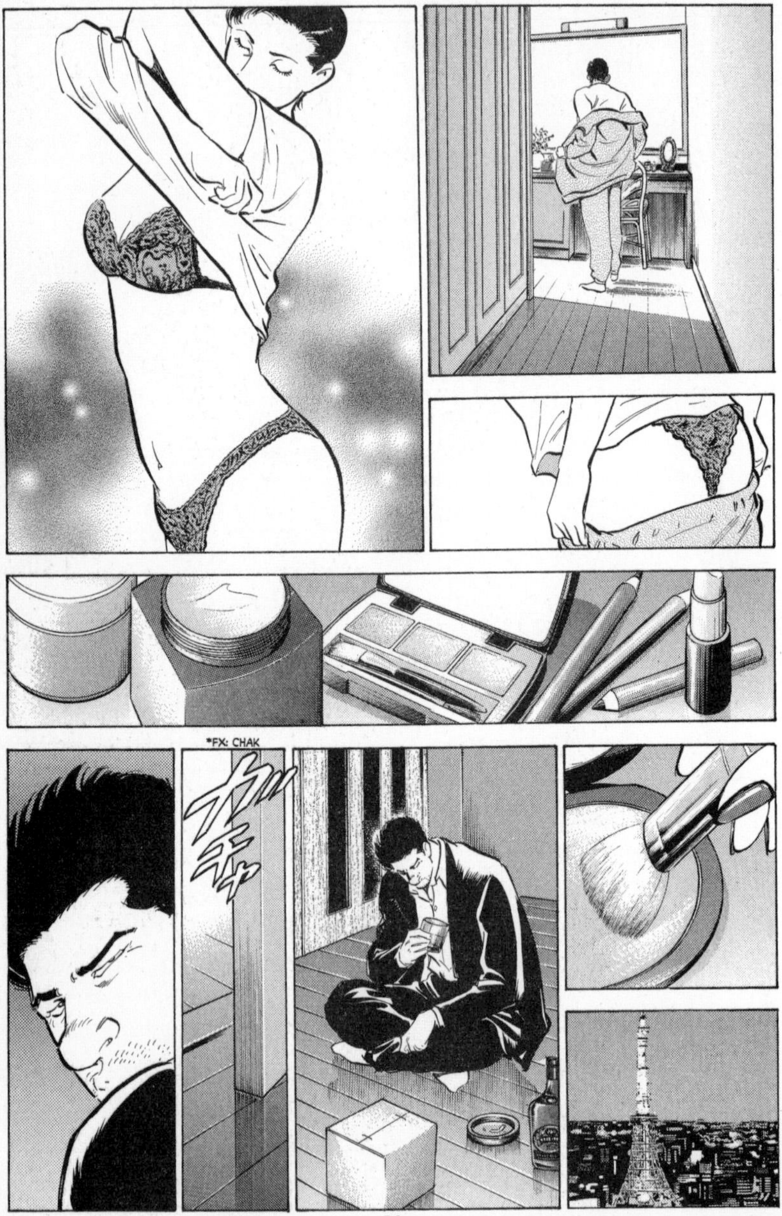
*FX: CHAK
カチャ

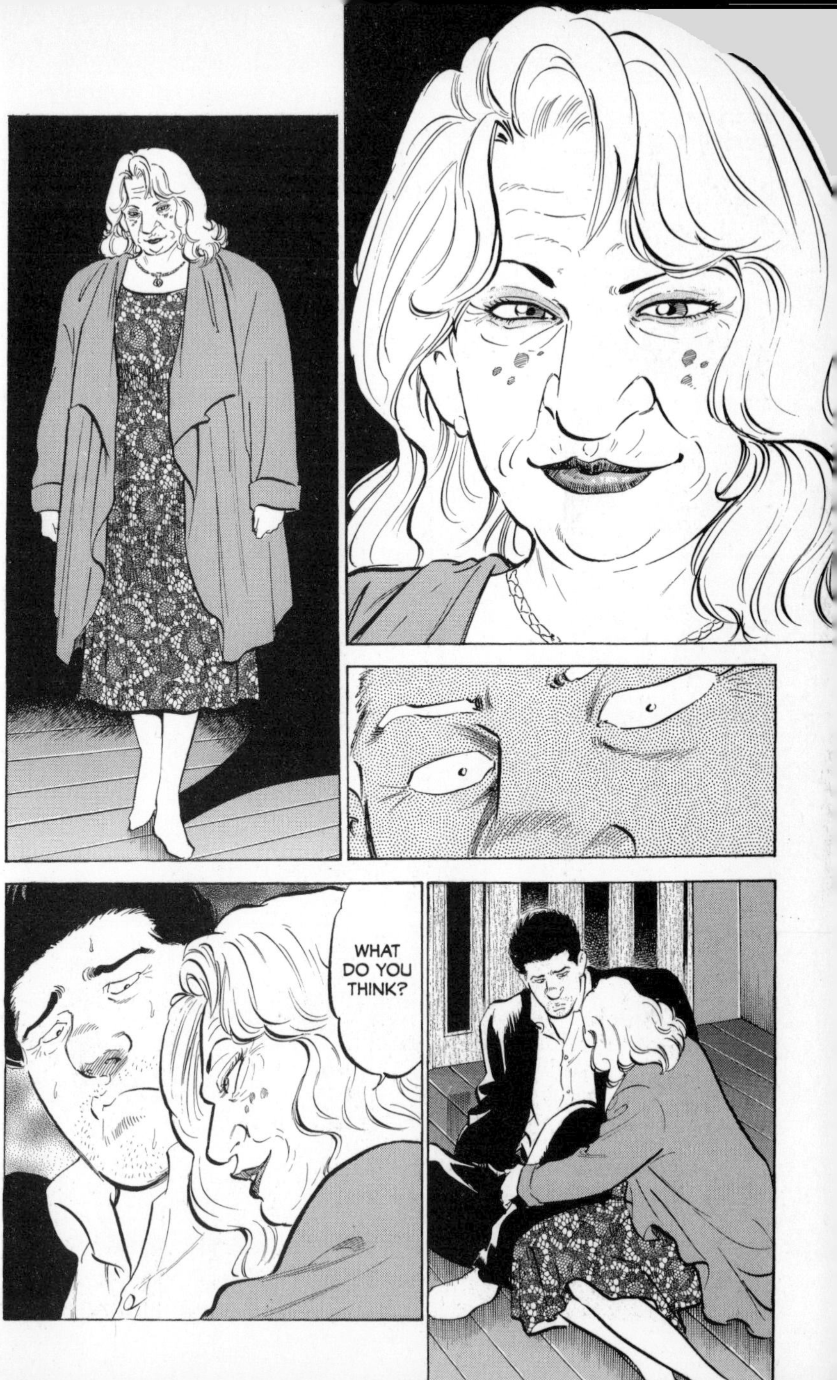
WHAT DO YOU THINK?

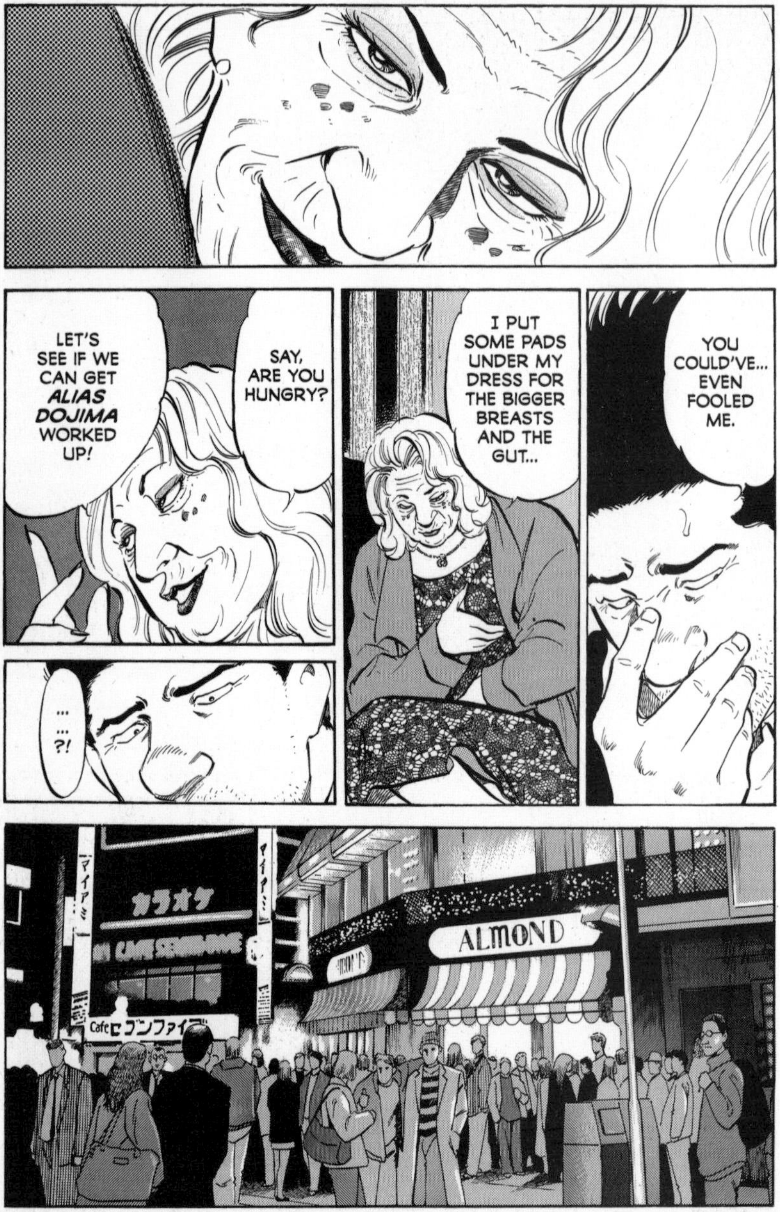

YOU COULD'VE... EVEN FOOLED ME.
I PUT SOME PADS UNDER MY DRESS FOR THE BIGGER BREASTS AND THE GUT...
SAY, ARE YOU HUNGRY?
LET'S SEE IF WE CAN GET *ALIAS DOJIMA* WORKED UP!
...... ?!
マイアミ
カラオケ
マイアミ
Cafe セブンファイブ
ALMOND

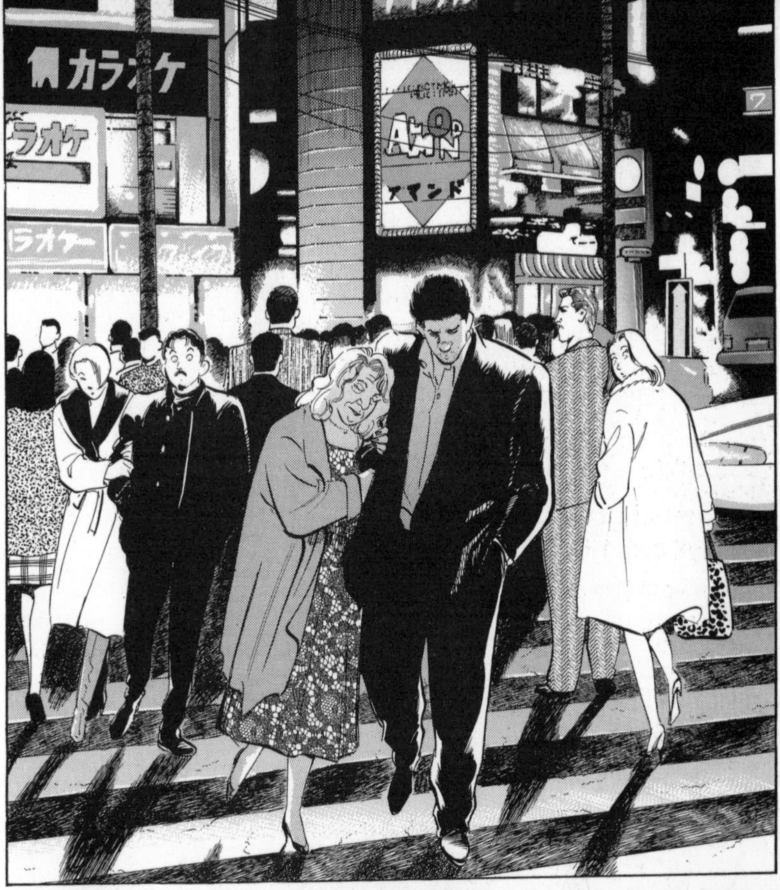
カラオケ
アマンド
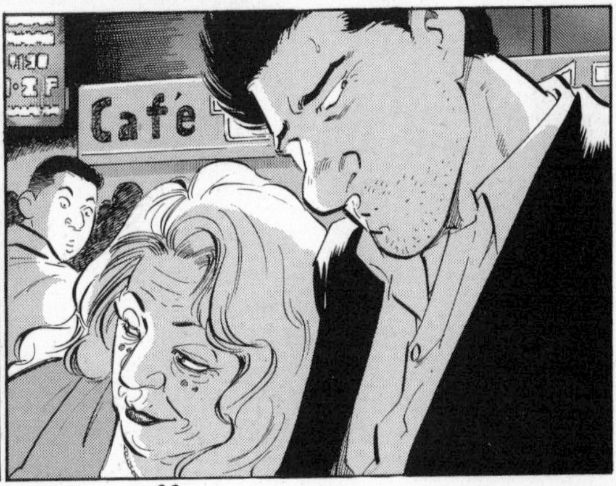
Café
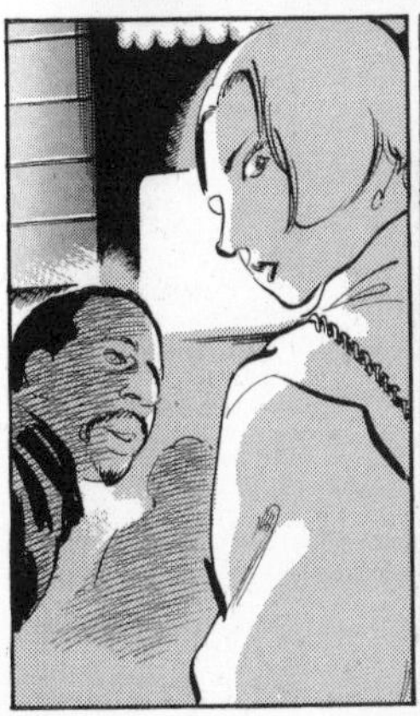

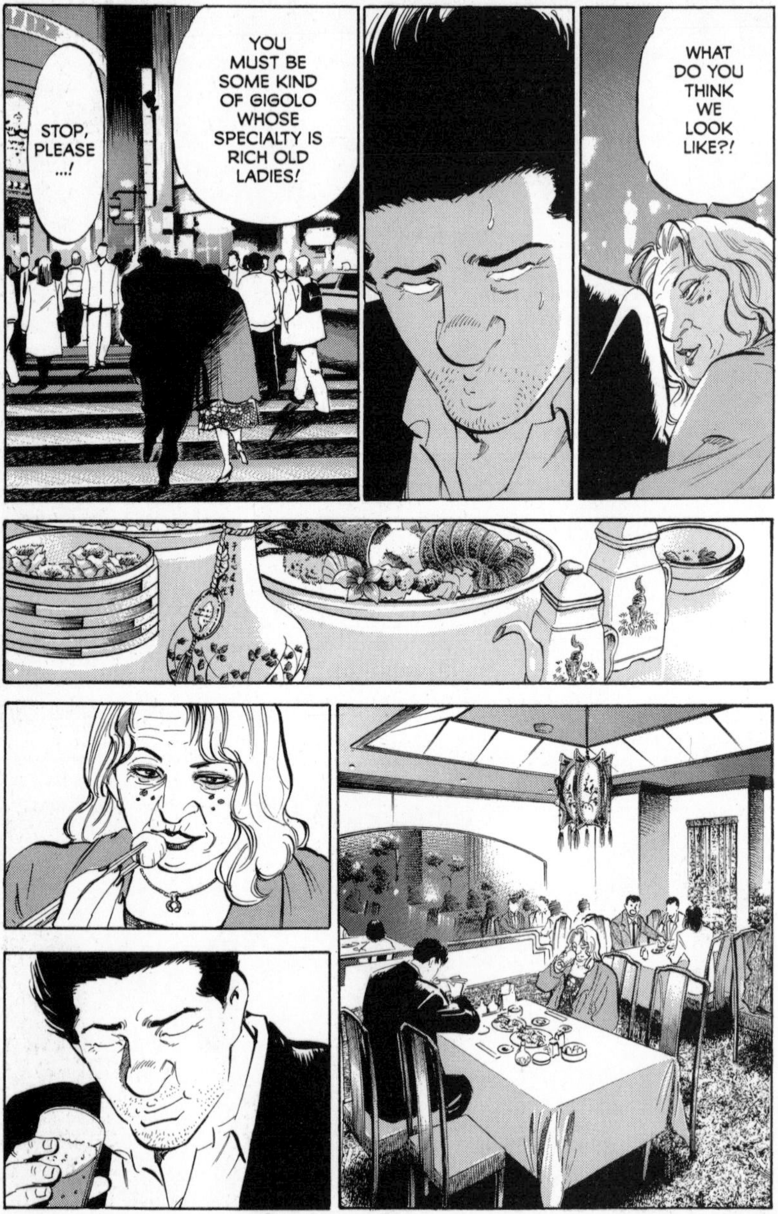
WHAT DO YOU THINK WE LOOK LIKE?!
YOU MUST BE SOME KIND OF GIGOLO WHOSE SPECIALTY IS RICH OLD LADIES!
STOP, PLEASE ...!

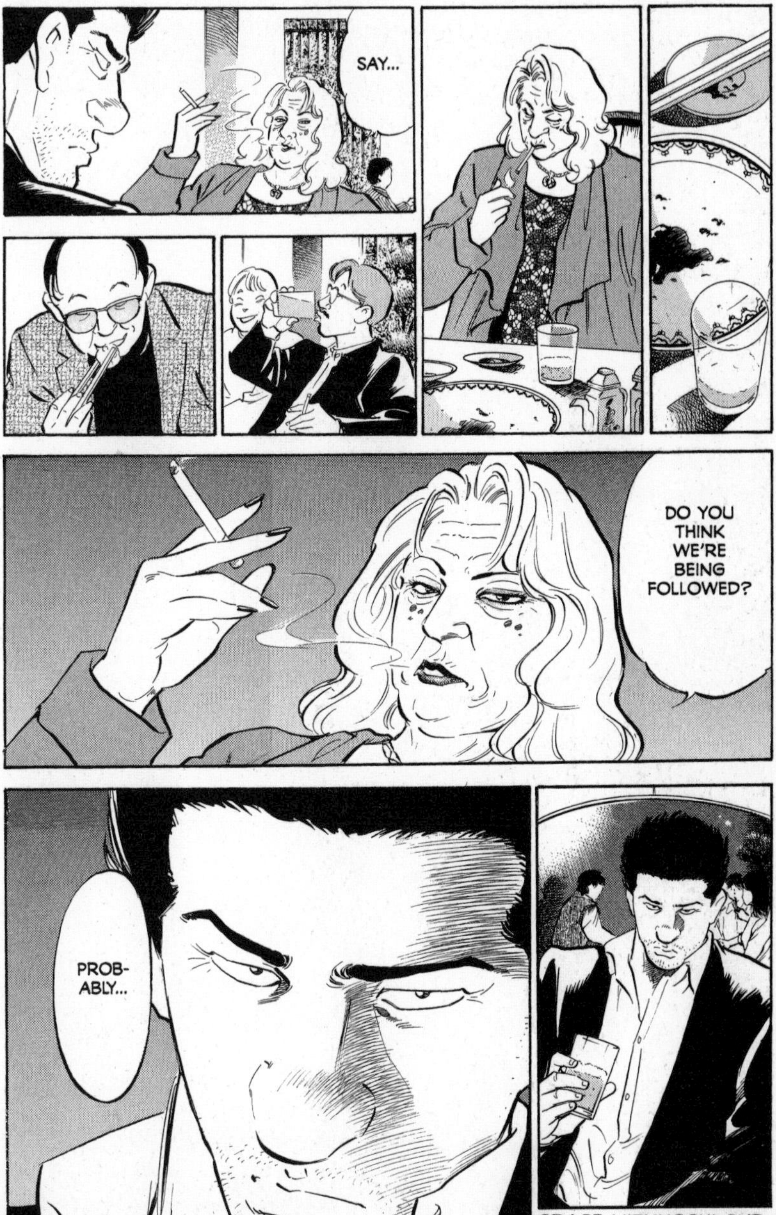
SAY...
DO YOU THINK WE'RE BEING FOLLOWED?
PROB-ABLY...

GRACE MIZUKOSHI: END

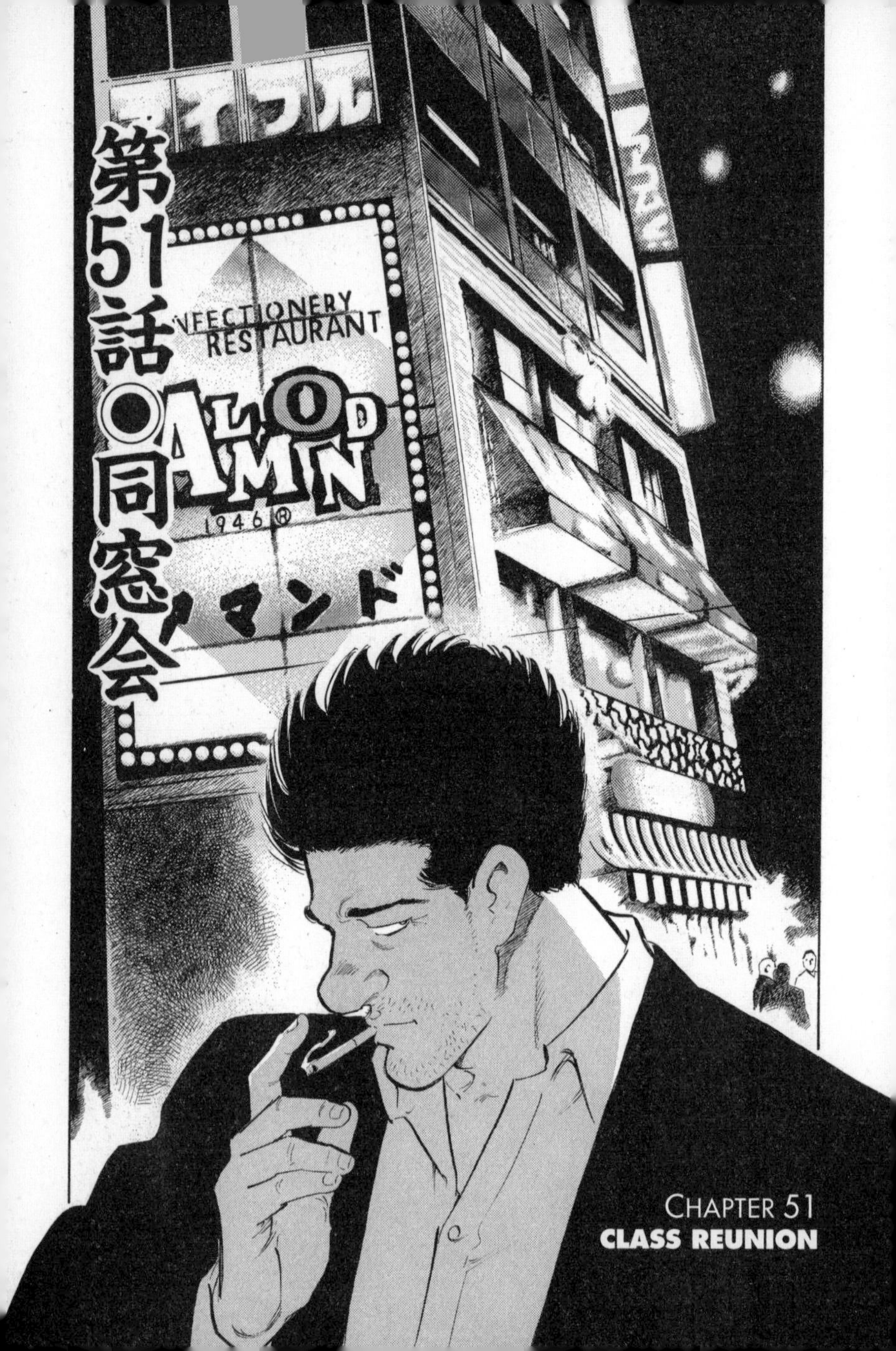
イフル
NFECTIONERY
RESTAURANT
1946
マンド

第51話◎同窓会

CHAPTER 51
CLASS REUNION

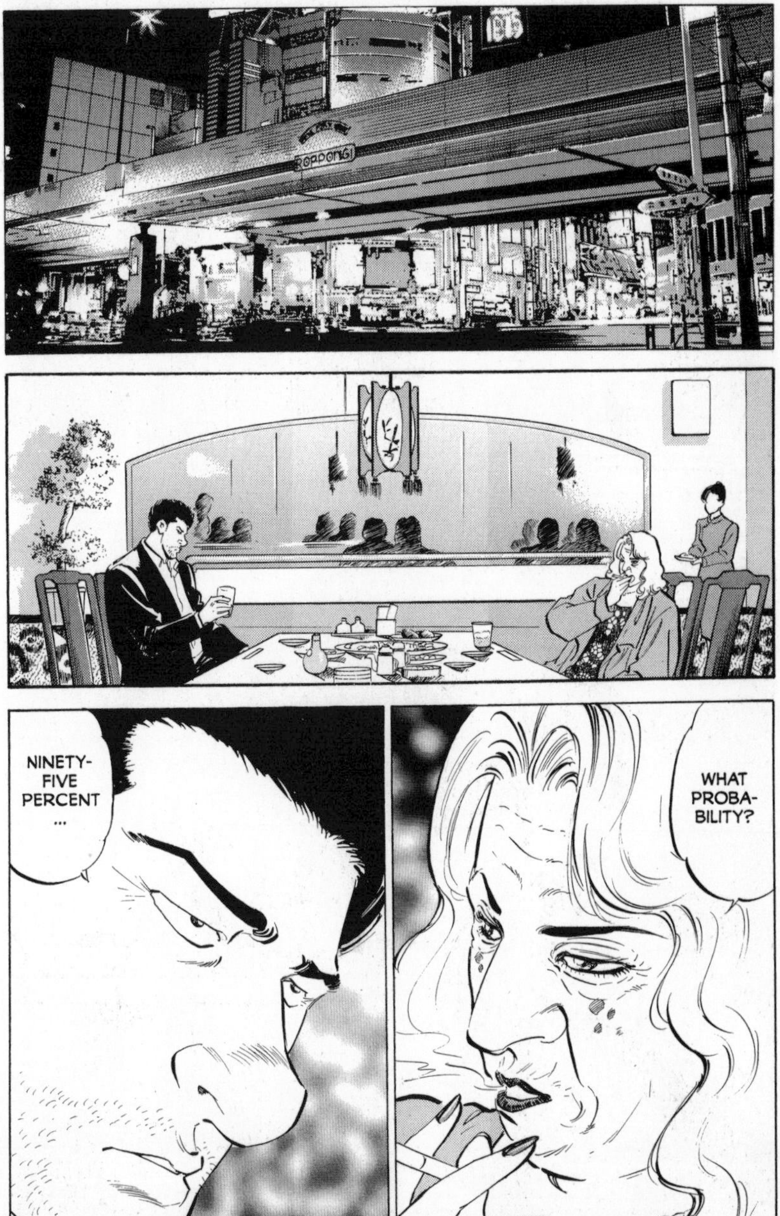
ROPPONGI
WHAT PROBA-BILITY?
NINETY-FIVE PERCENT ...

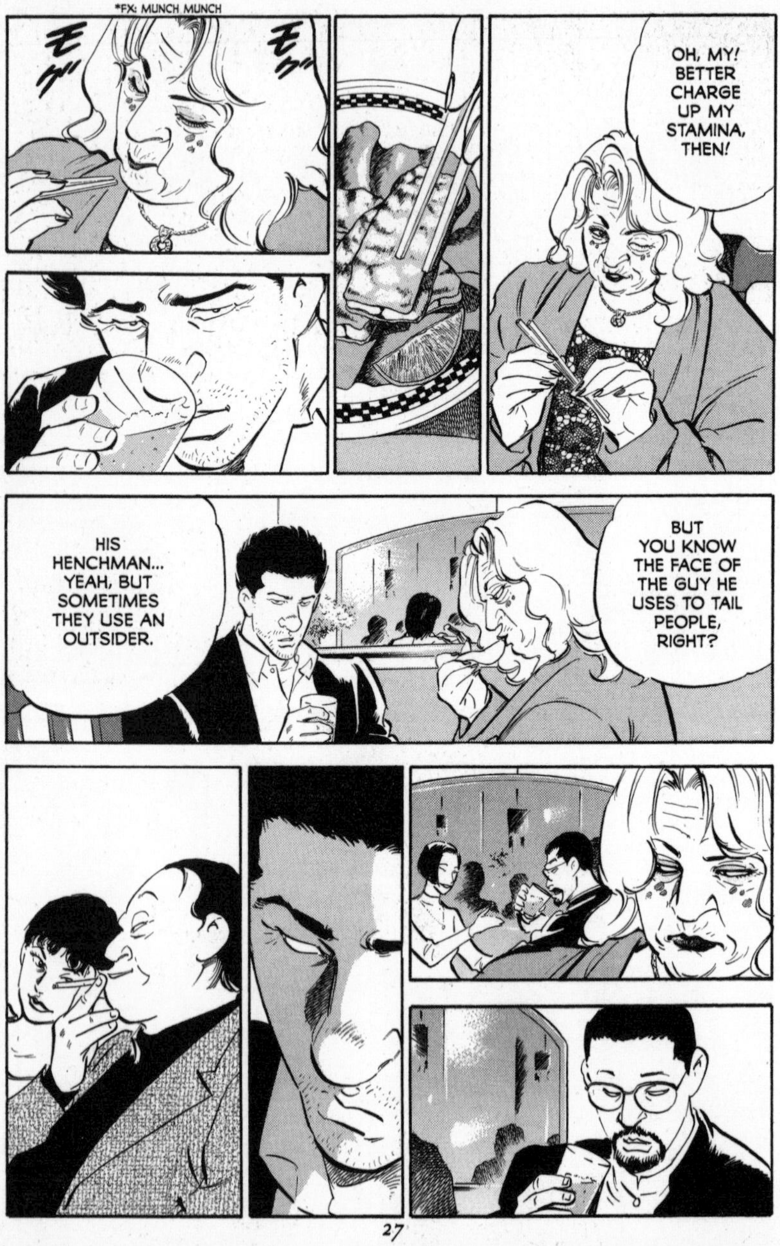
OH, MY! BETTER CHARGE UP MY STAMINA, THEN!
*FX: MUNCH MUNCH
BUT YOU KNOW THE FACE OF THE GUY HE USES TO TAIL PEOPLE, RIGHT?
HIS HENCHMAN... YEAH, BUT SOMETIMES THEY USE AN OUTSIDER.

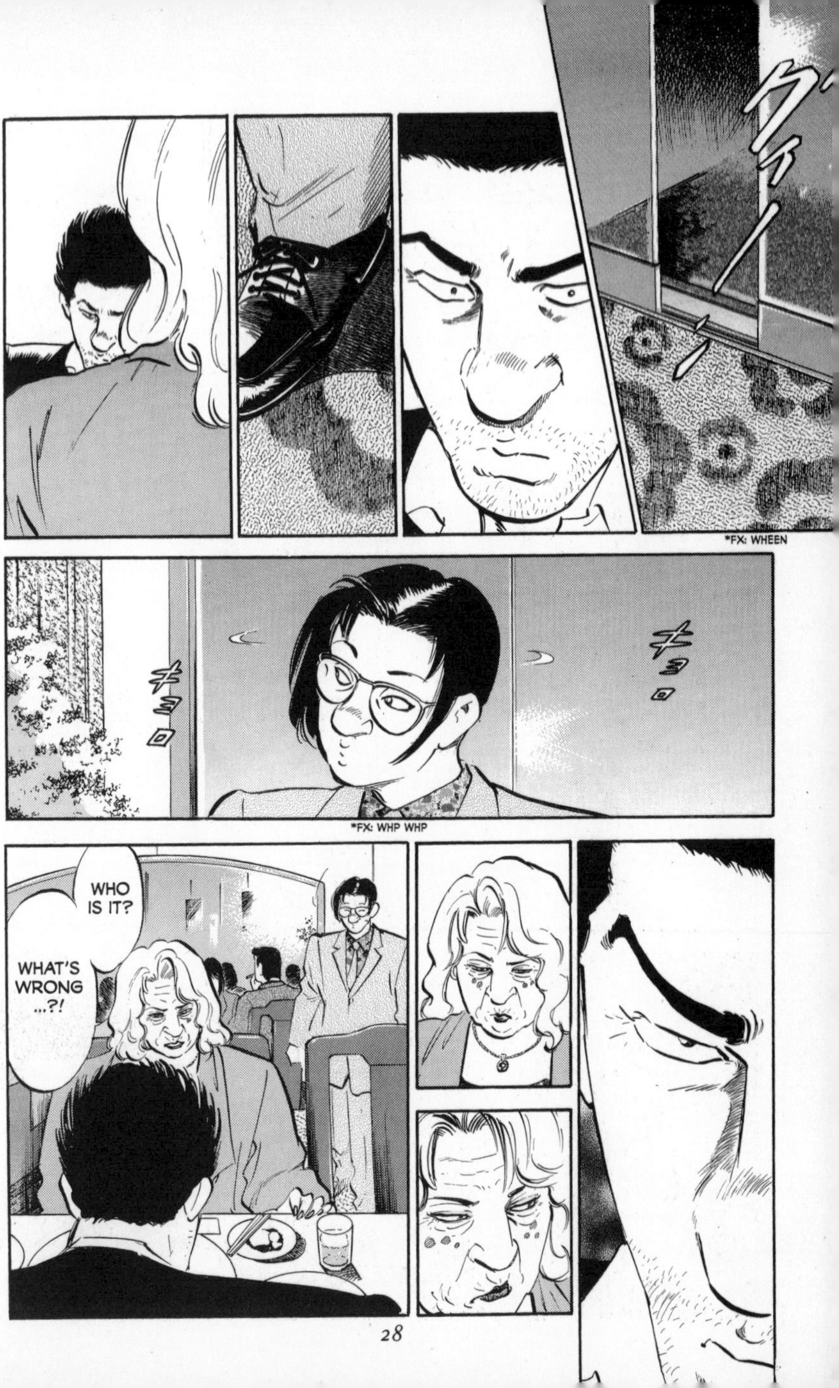
*FX: WHEEN
*FX: WHP WHP
WHO IS IT?
WHAT'S WRONG ...?!

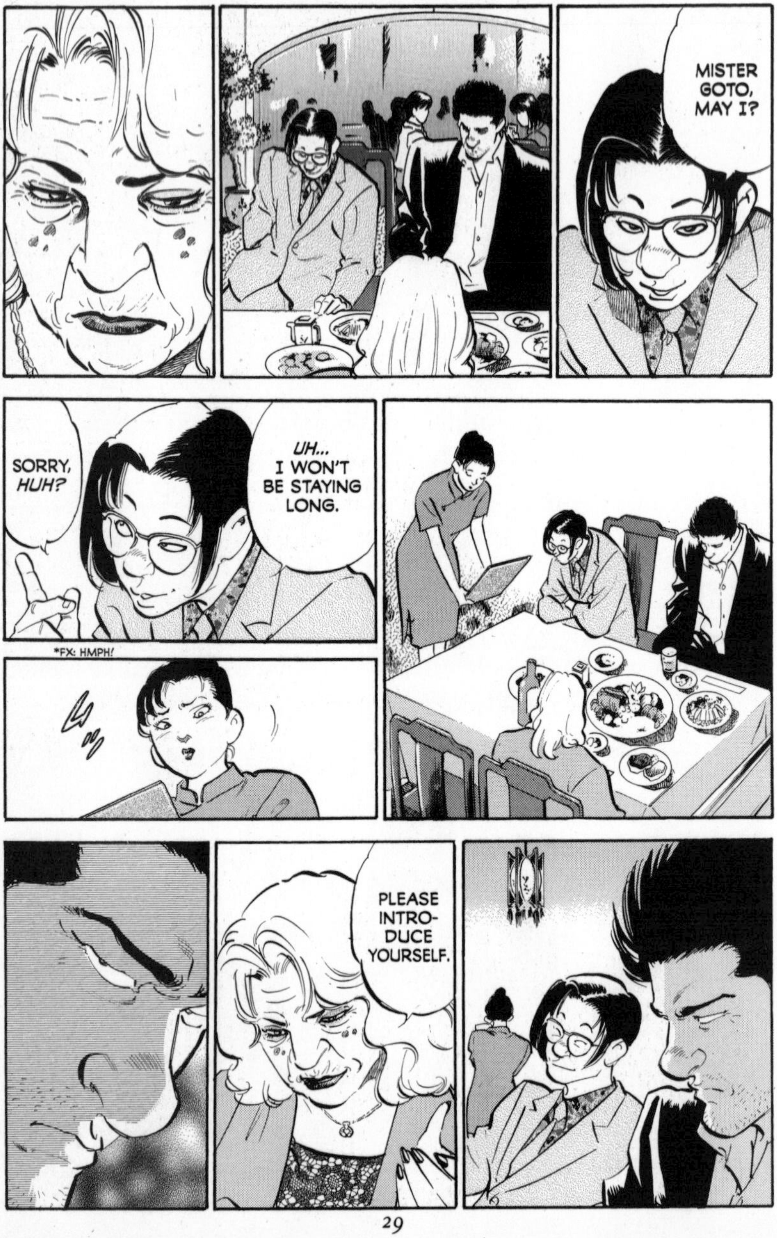
MISTER GOTO, MAY I?
UH... I WON'T BE STAYING LONG.
SORRY, HUH?
*FX: HMPH!
PLEASE INTRO-DUCE YOURSELF.

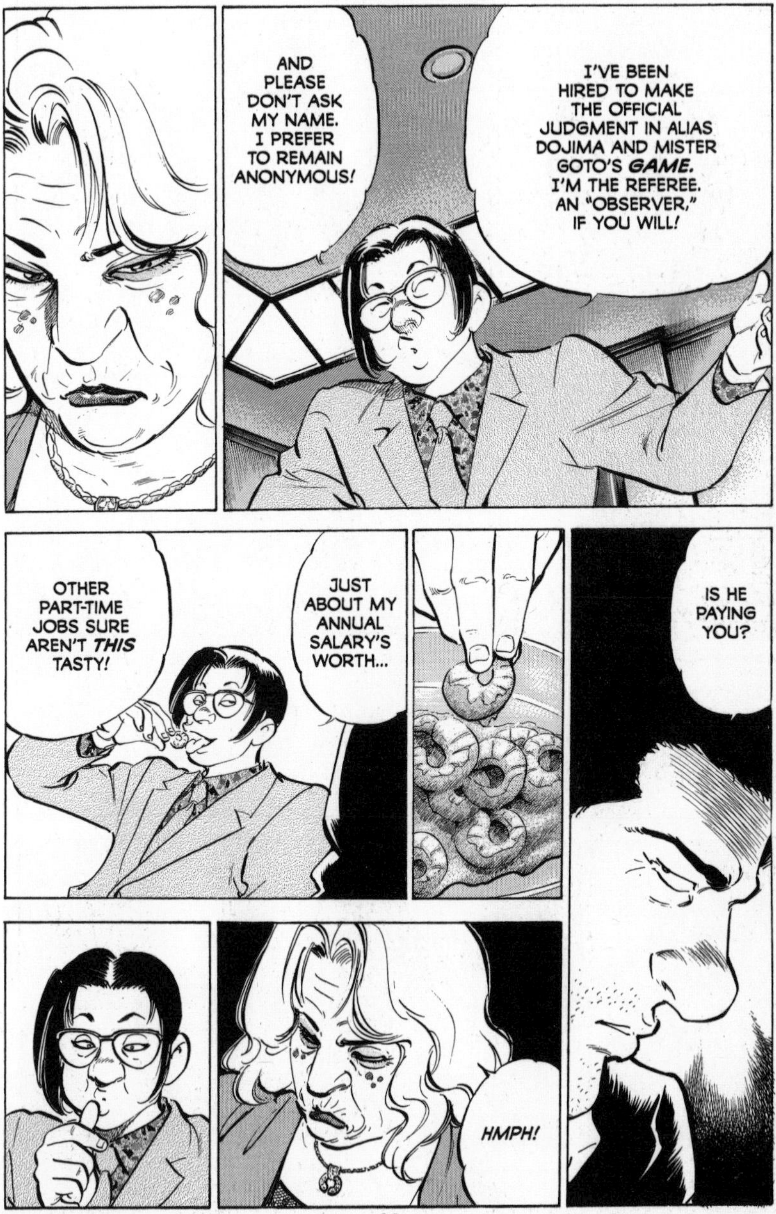
I'VE BEEN HIRED TO MAKE THE OFFICIAL JUDGMENT IN ALIAS DOJIMA AND MISTER GOTO'S *GAME.* I'M THE REFEREE. AN "OBSERVER," IF YOU WILL!
AND PLEASE DON'T ASK MY NAME. I PREFER TO REMAIN ANONYMOUS!
IS HE PAYING YOU?
JUST ABOUT MY ANNUAL SALARY'S WORTH...
OTHER PART-TIME JOBS SURE AREN'T *THIS* TASTY!
HMPH!

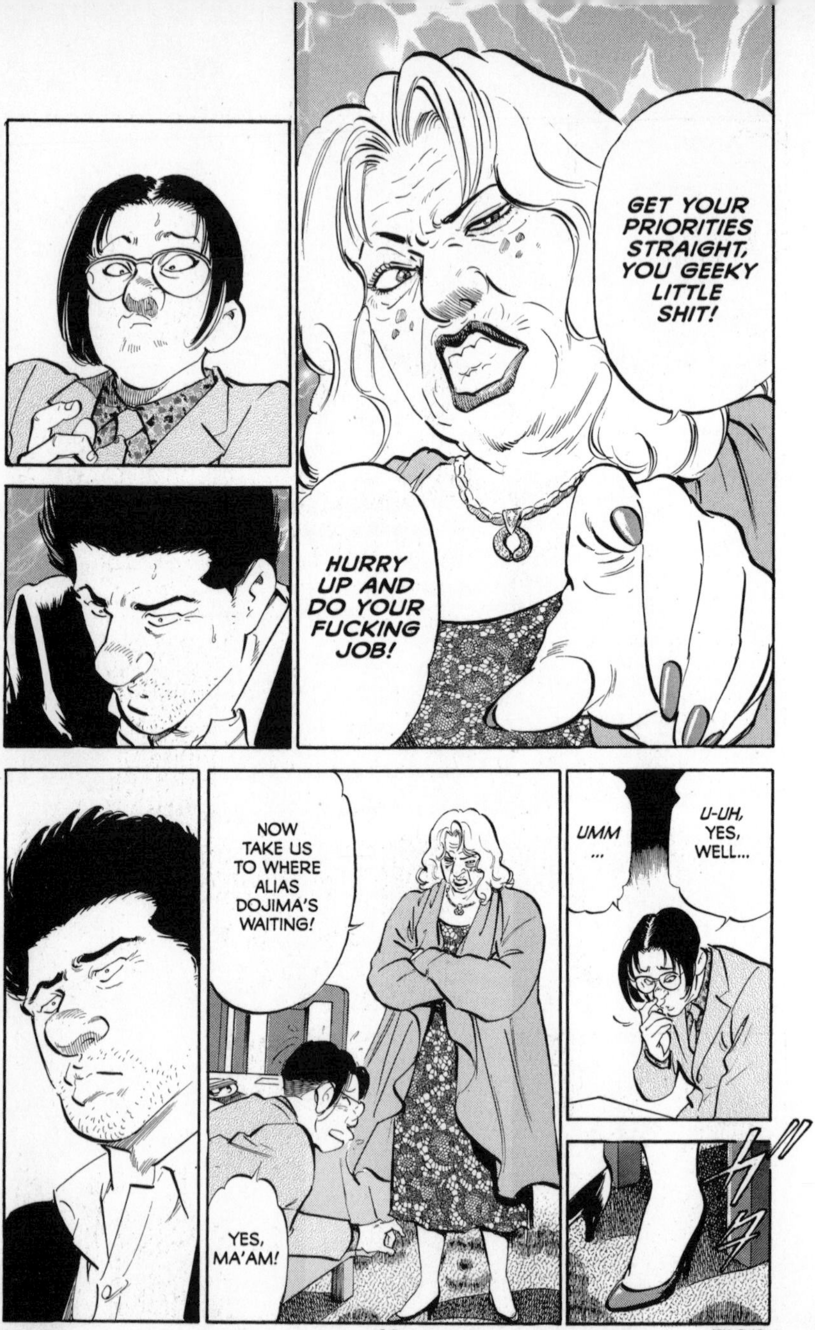
GET YOUR PRIORITIES STRAIGHT, YOU GEEKY LITTLE SHIT!
HURRY UP AND DO YOUR FUCKING JOB!
U-UH, YES, WELL...
UMM ...
NOW TAKE US TO WHERE ALIAS DOJIMA'S WAITING!
YES, MA'AM!

*FX: CLACK

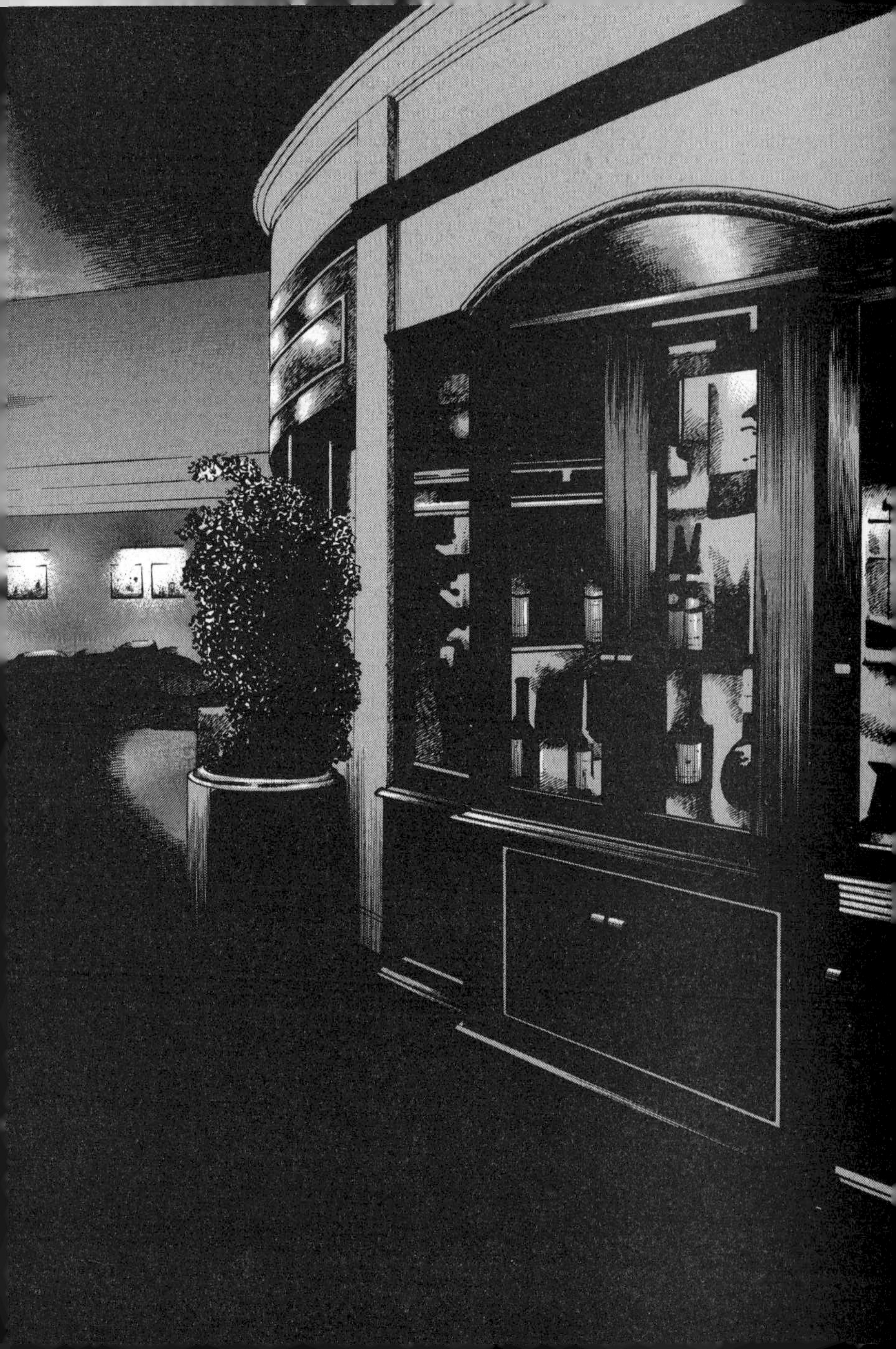

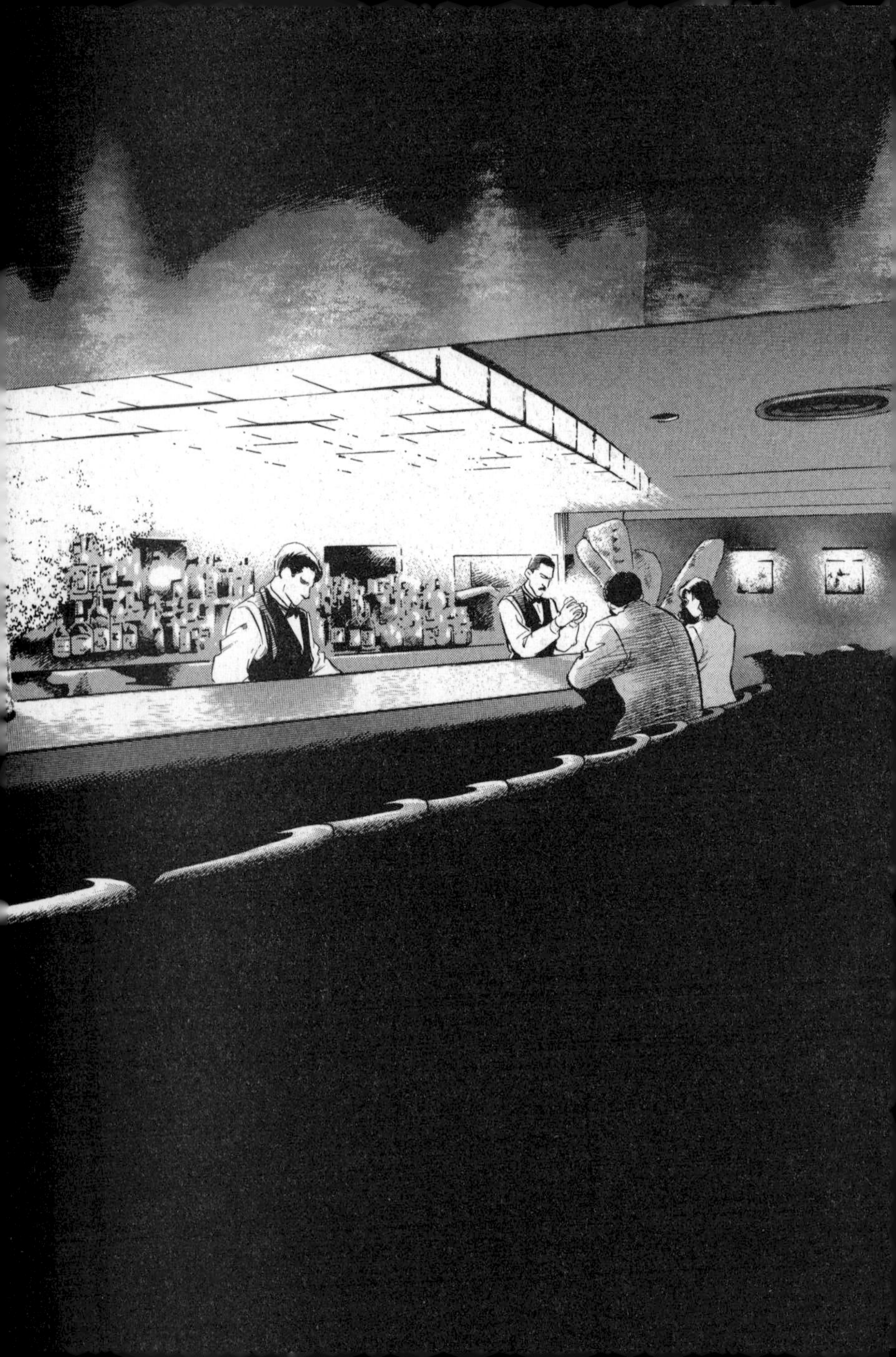

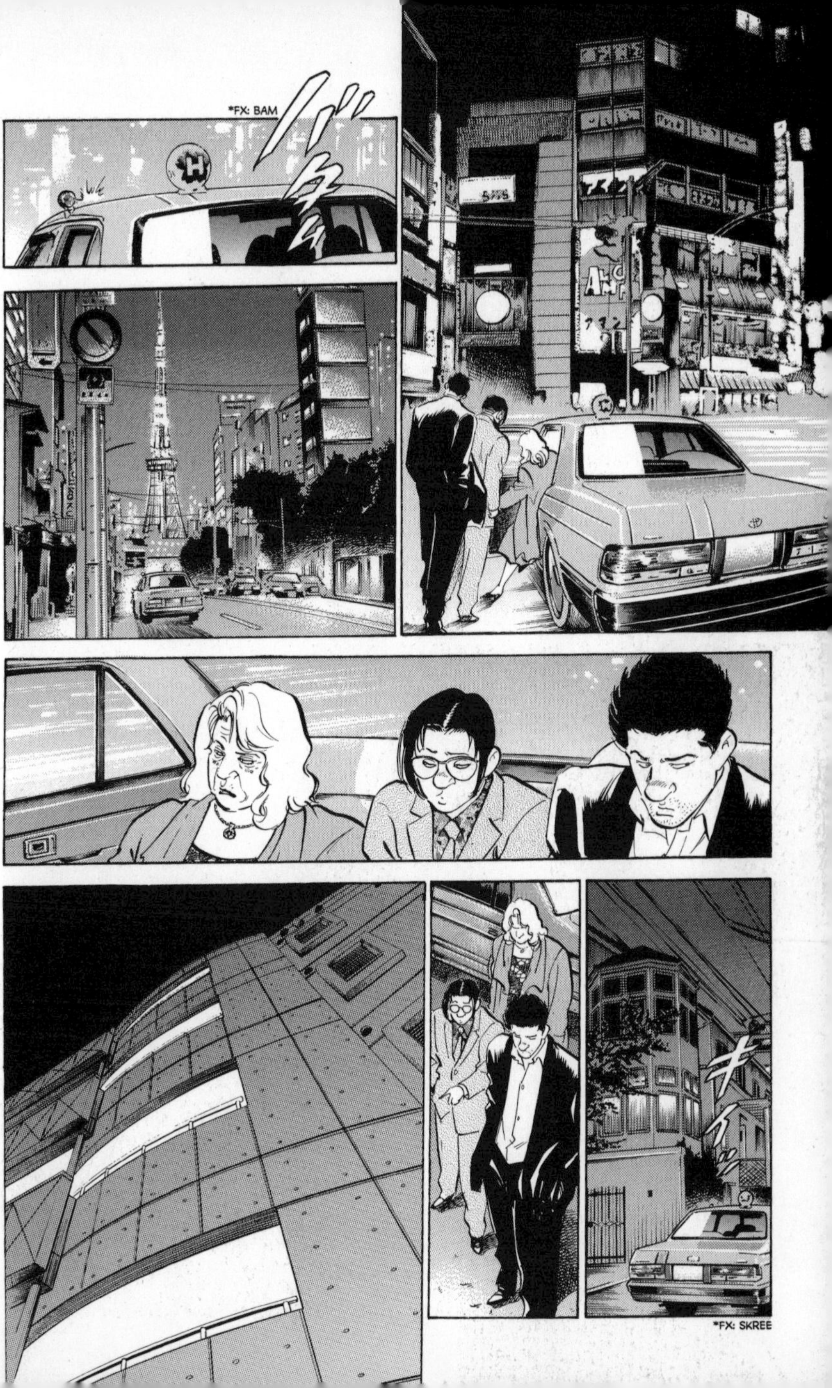
*FX: BAM
*FX: SKREE

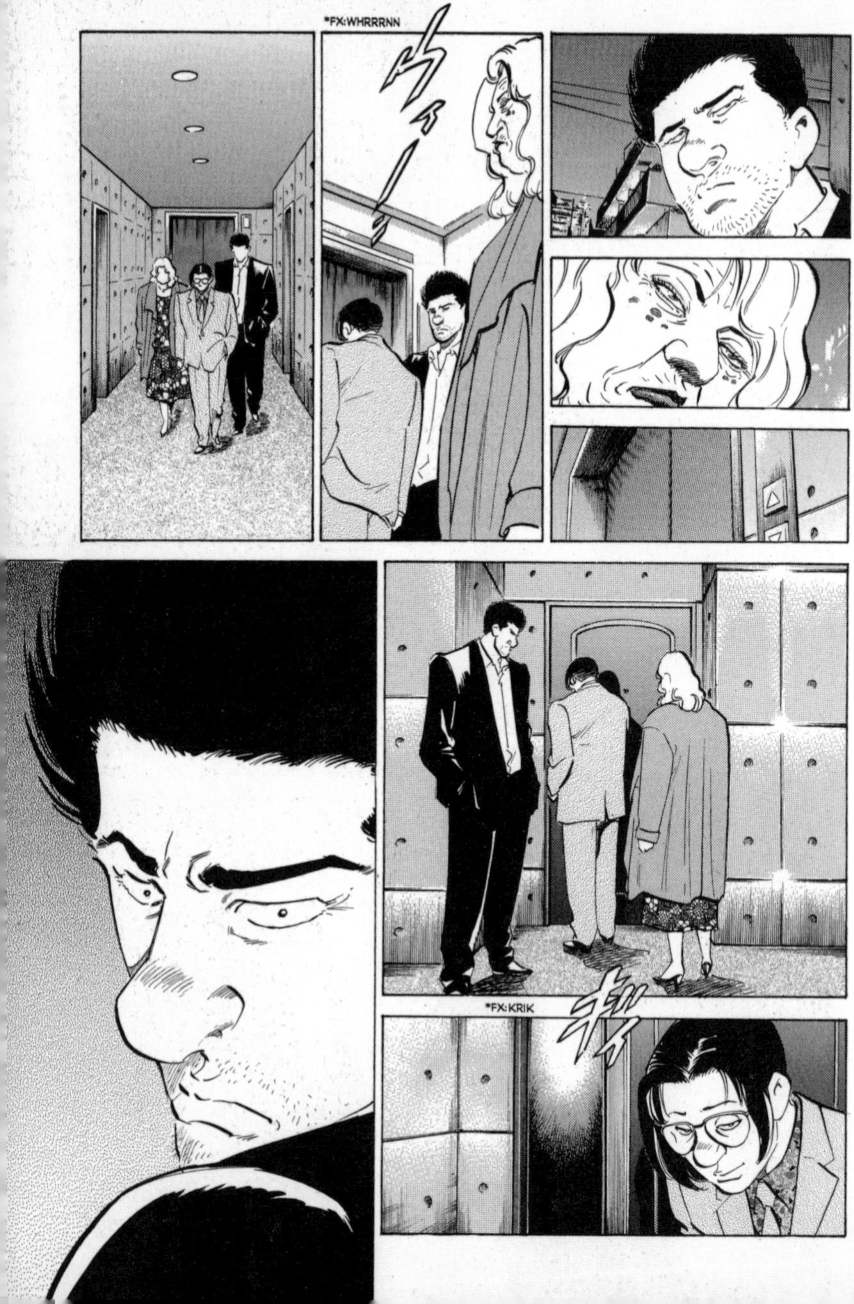
*FX:WHRRRNN
*FX:KRIK

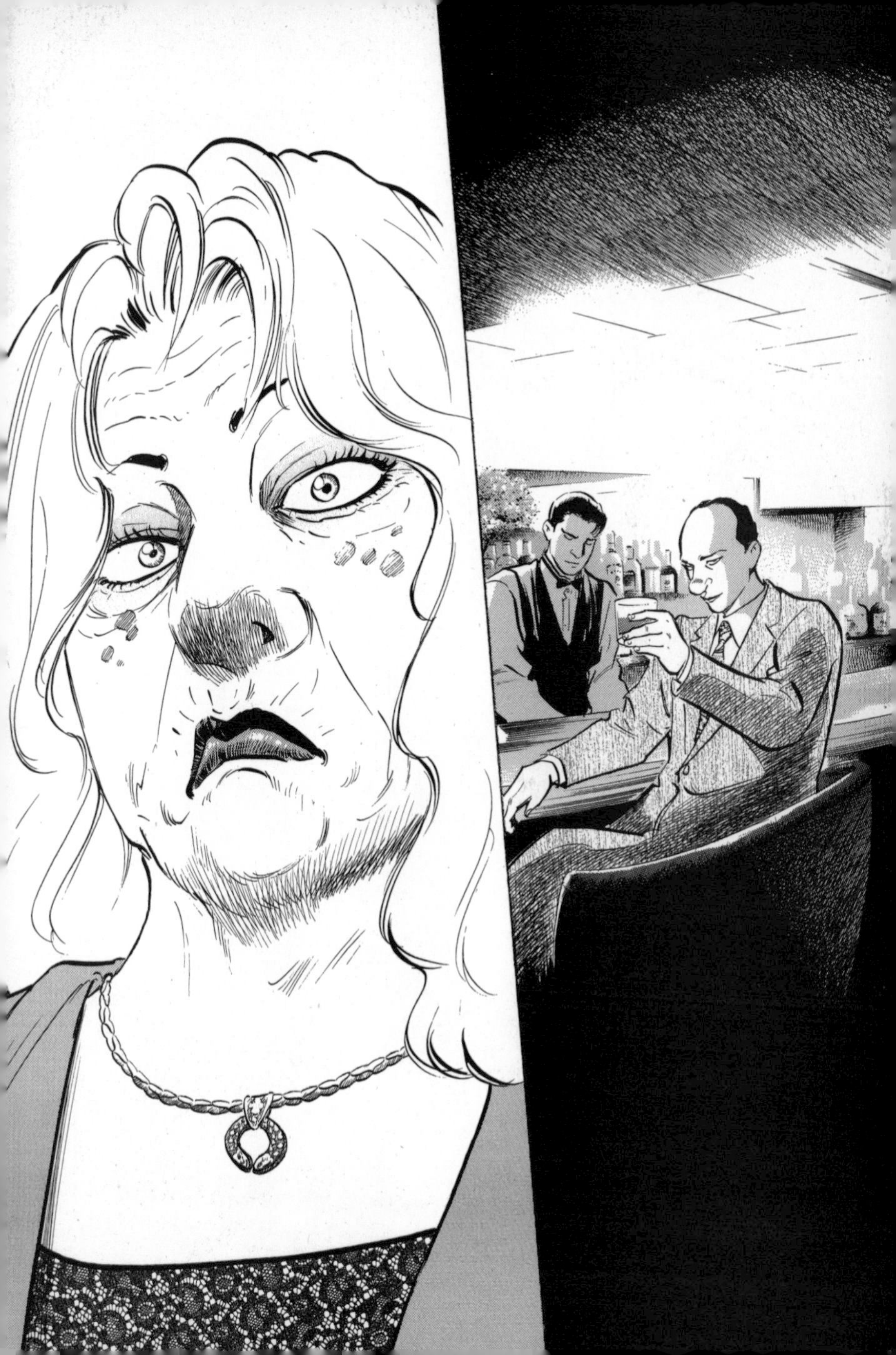

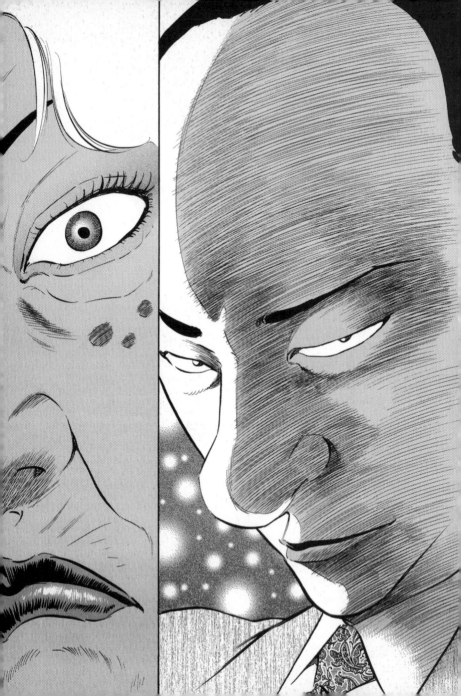

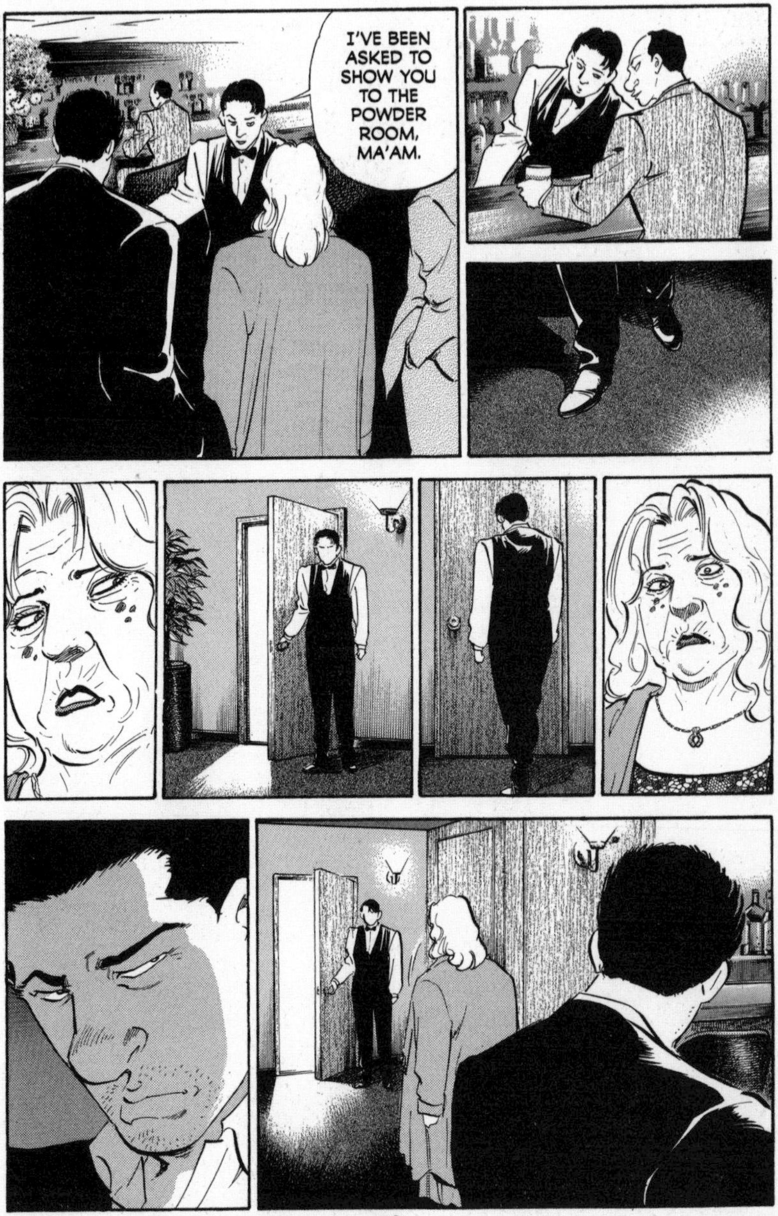
I'VE BEEN ASKED TO SHOW YOU TO THE POWDER ROOM, MA'AM.

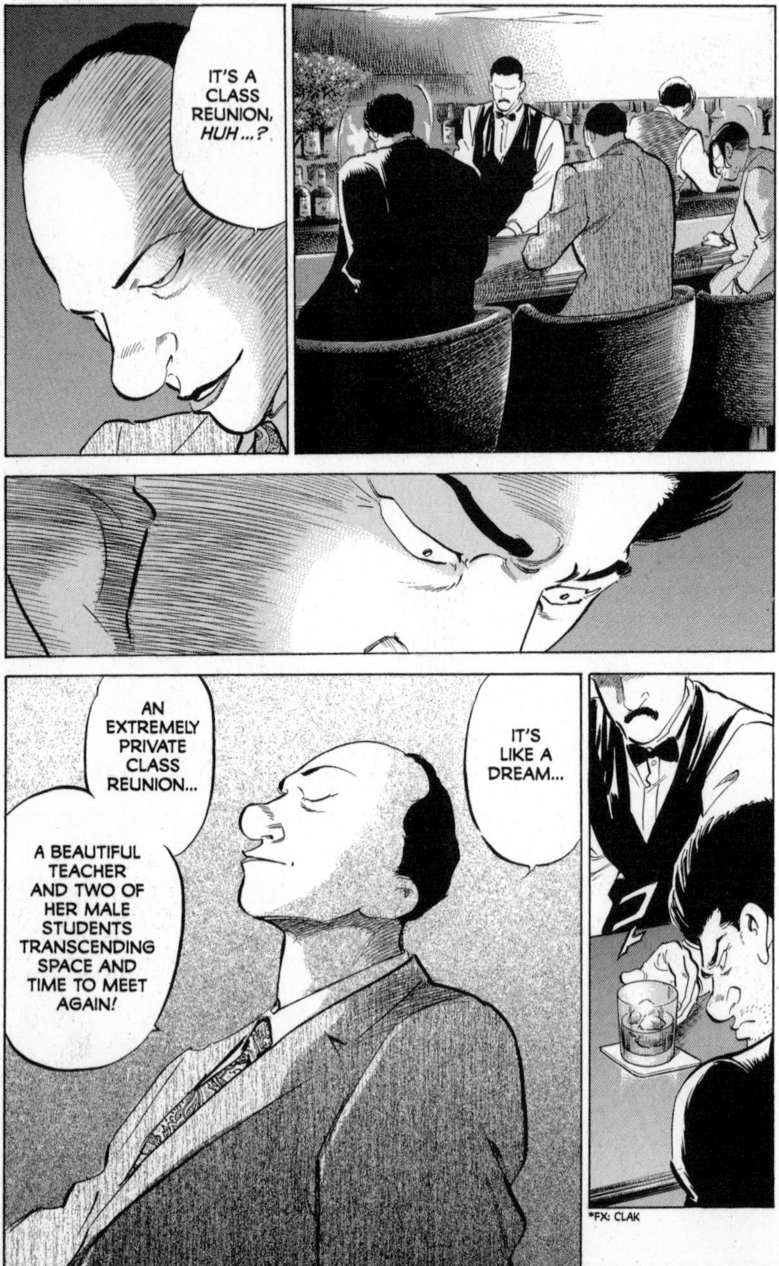
IT'S A CLASS REUNION, *HUH...?*
IT'S LIKE A DREAM...
AN EXTREMELY PRIVATE CLASS REUNION...
A BEAUTIFUL TEACHER AND TWO OF HER MALE STUDENTS TRANSCENDING SPACE AND TIME TO MEET AGAIN!

*FX: CLAK

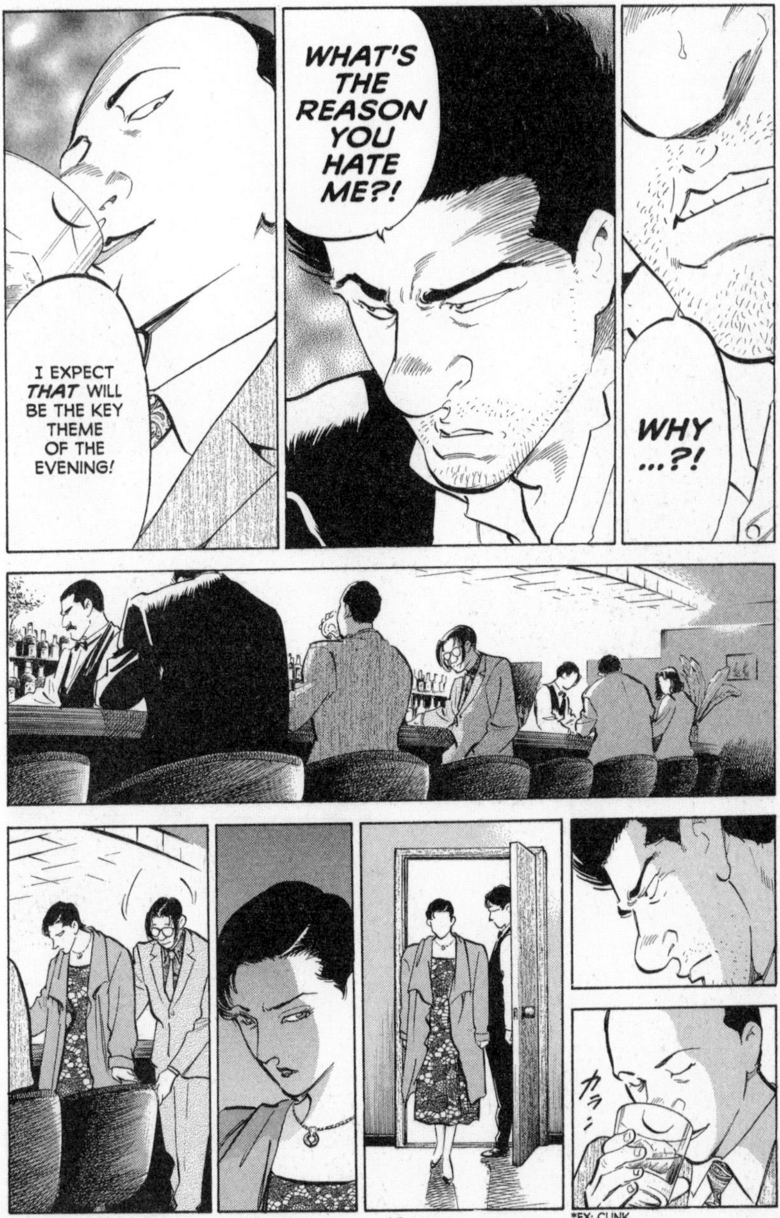
WHY ...?!
WHAT'S THE REASON YOU HATE ME?!
I EXPECT *THAT* WILL BE THE KEY THEME OF THE EVENING!
カラン

*FX: CLINK

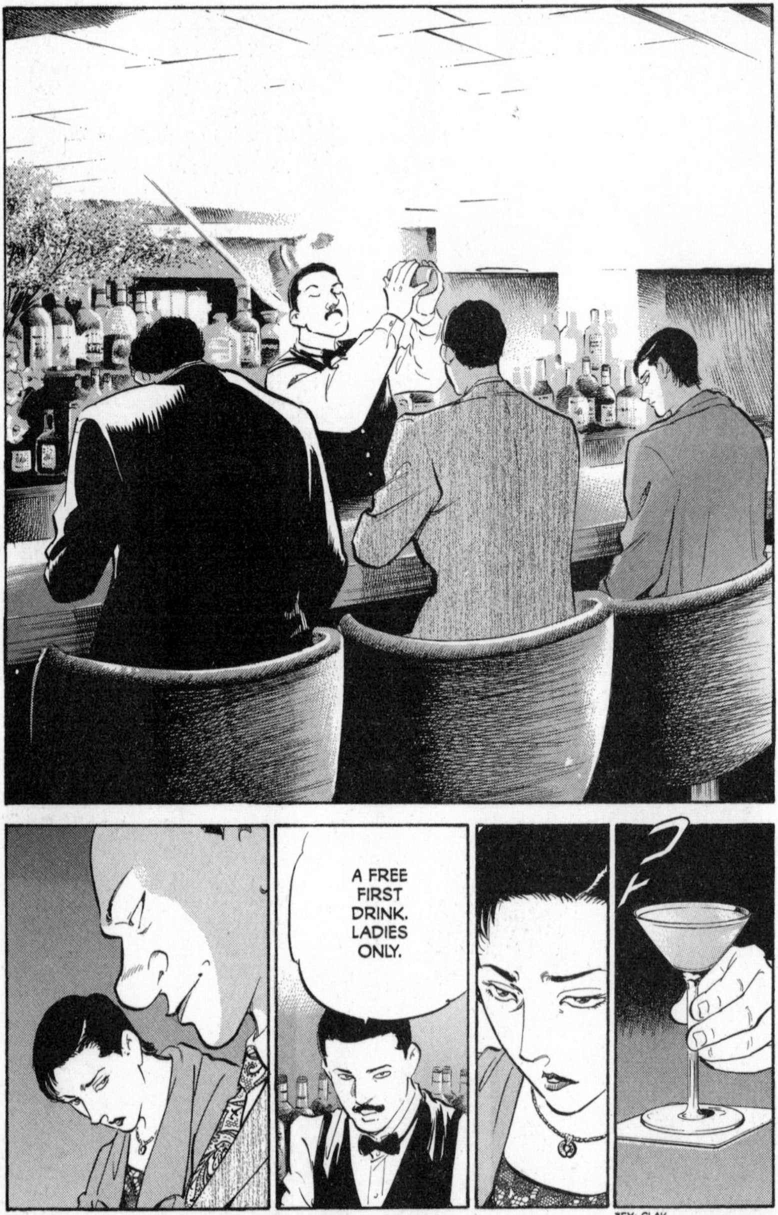
A FREE FIRST DRINK. LADIES ONLY.

*FX: CLAK

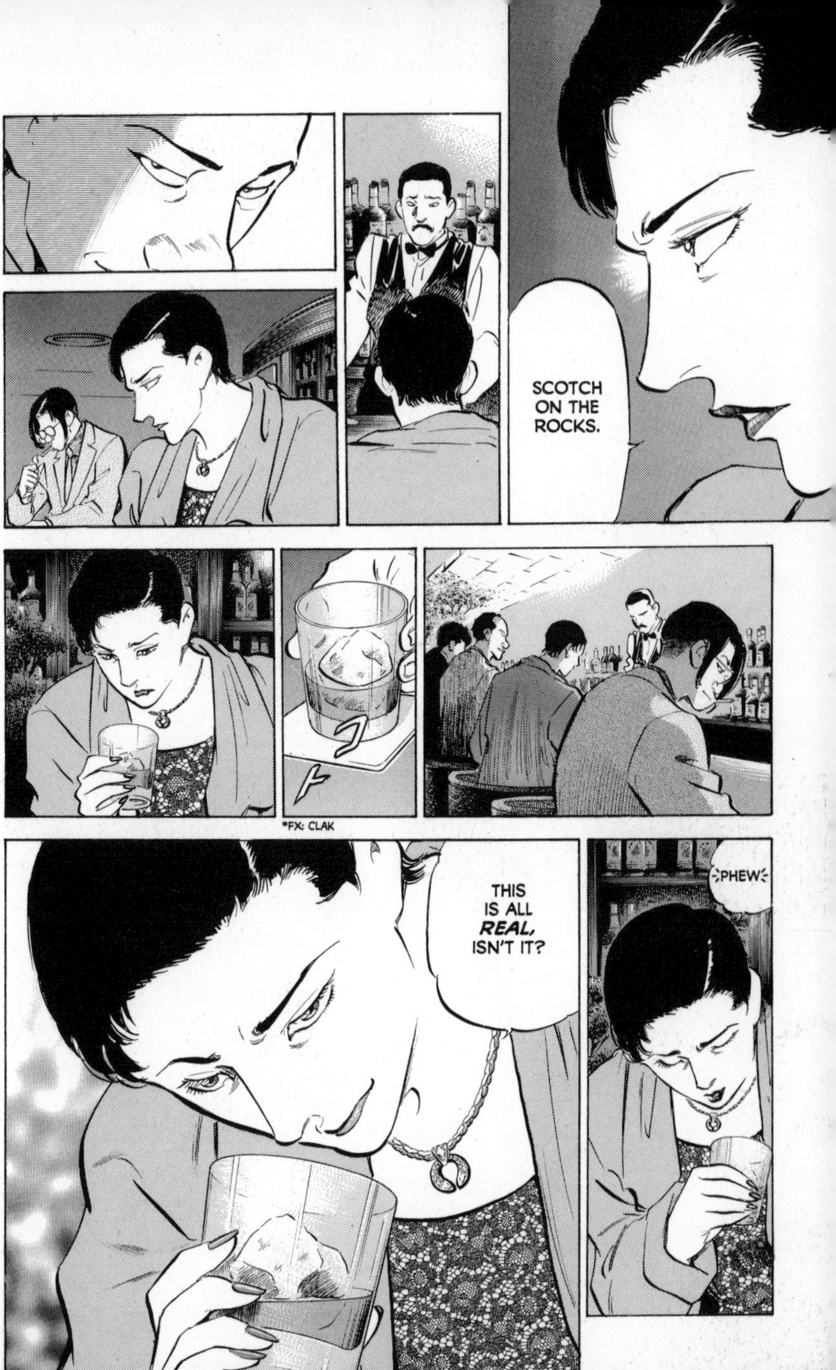
SCOTCH ON THE ROCKS.
*FX: CLAK
PHEW
THIS IS ALL *REAL*, ISN'T IT?

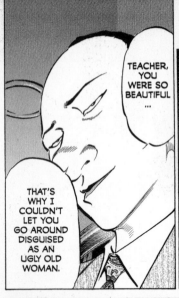

TEACHER, YOU WERE SO BEAUTIFUL...

THAT'S WHY I COULDN'T LET YOU GO AROUND DISGUISED AS AN UGLY OLD WOMAN.

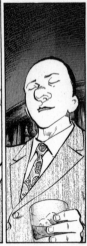

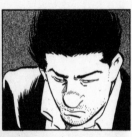

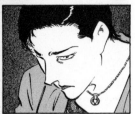

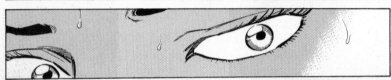

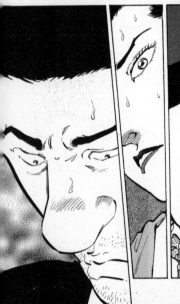

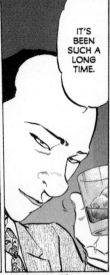

IT'S BEEN SUCH A LONG TIME.

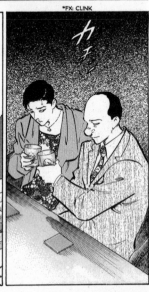

カチン

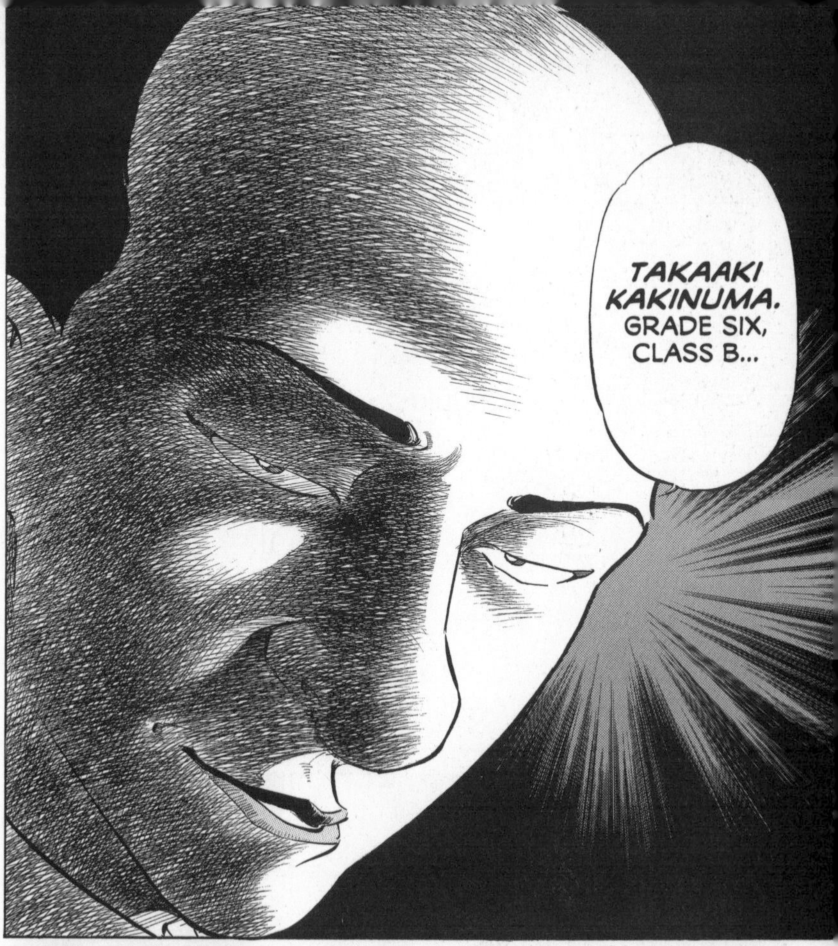
TAKAAKI KAKINUMA. GRADE SIX, CLASS B...
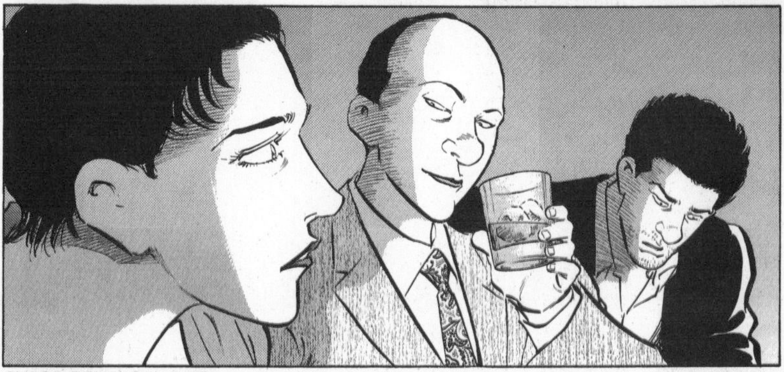

CLASS REUNION: END

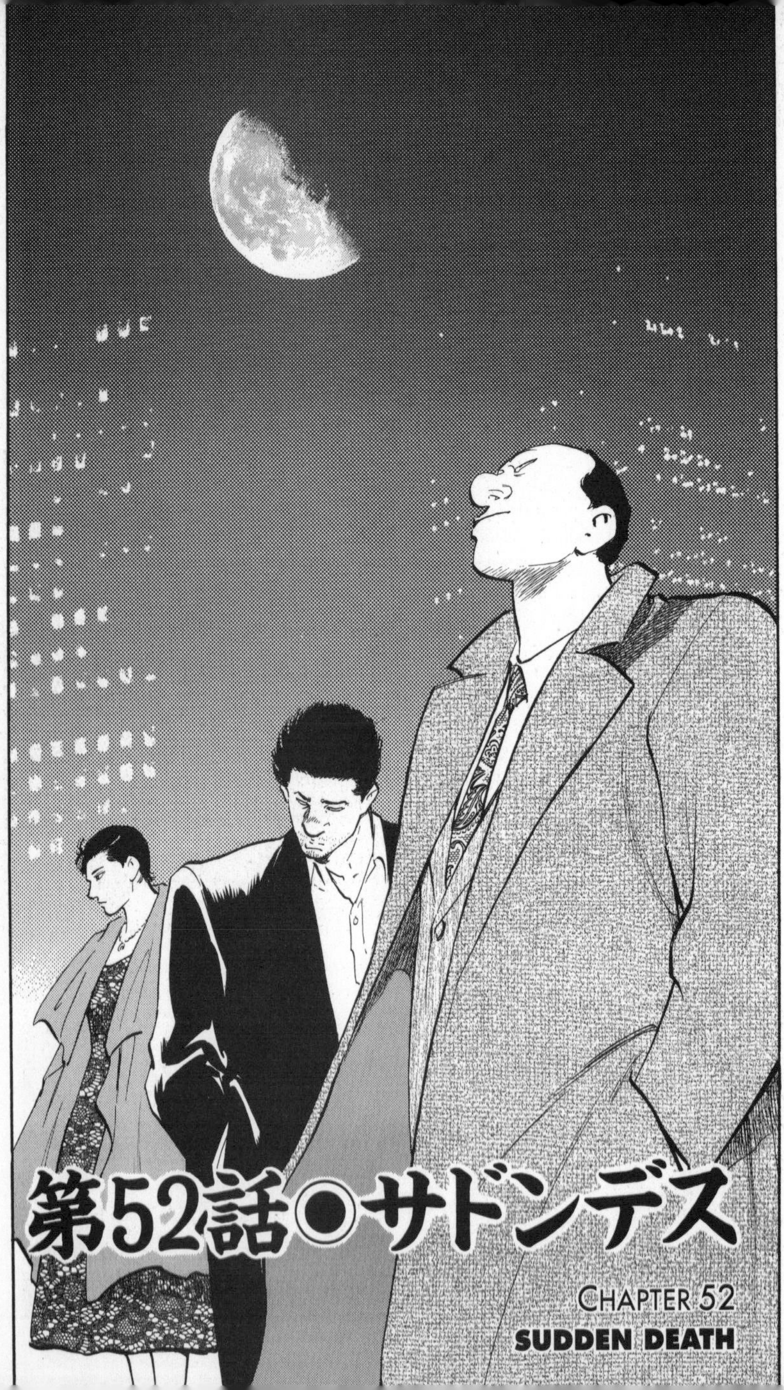
第52話○サドンデス
CHAPTER 52
SUDDEN DEATH

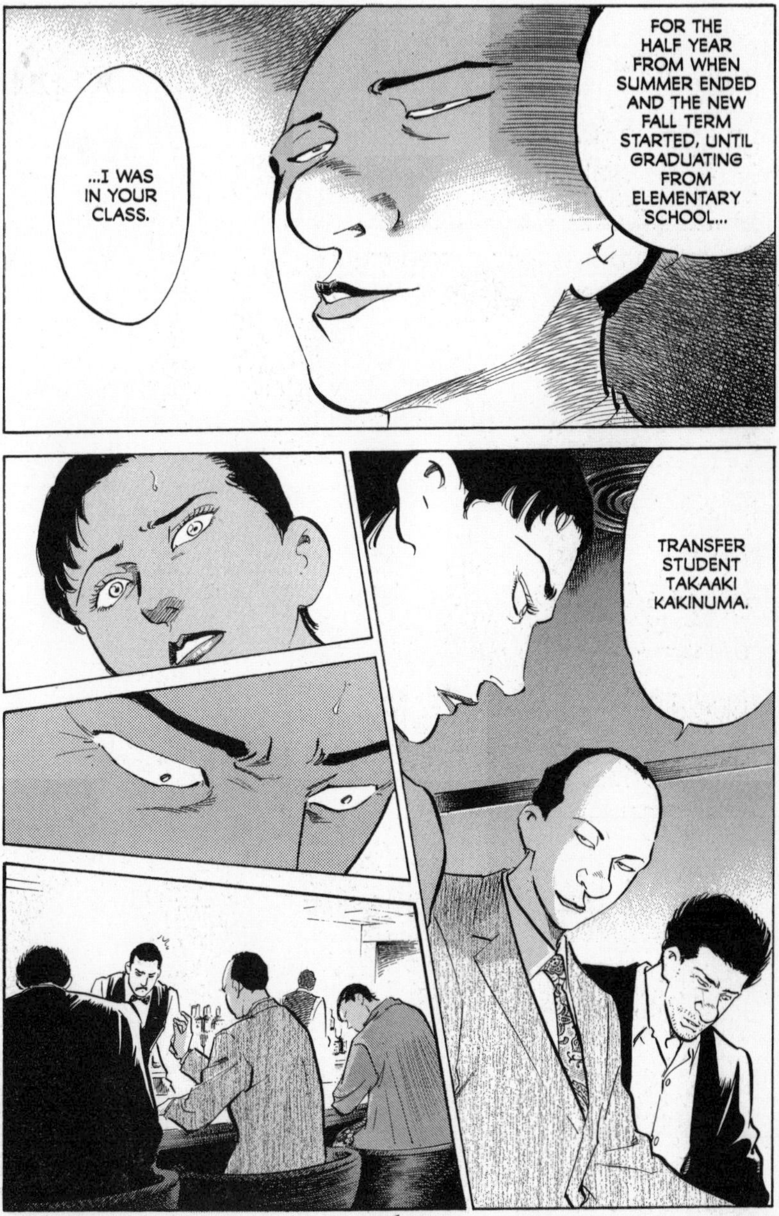
FOR THE HALF YEAR FROM WHEN SUMMER ENDED AND THE NEW FALL TERM STARTED, UNTIL GRADUATING FROM ELEMENTARY SCHOOL...
...I WAS IN YOUR CLASS.
TRANSFER STUDENT TAKAAKI KAKINUMA.

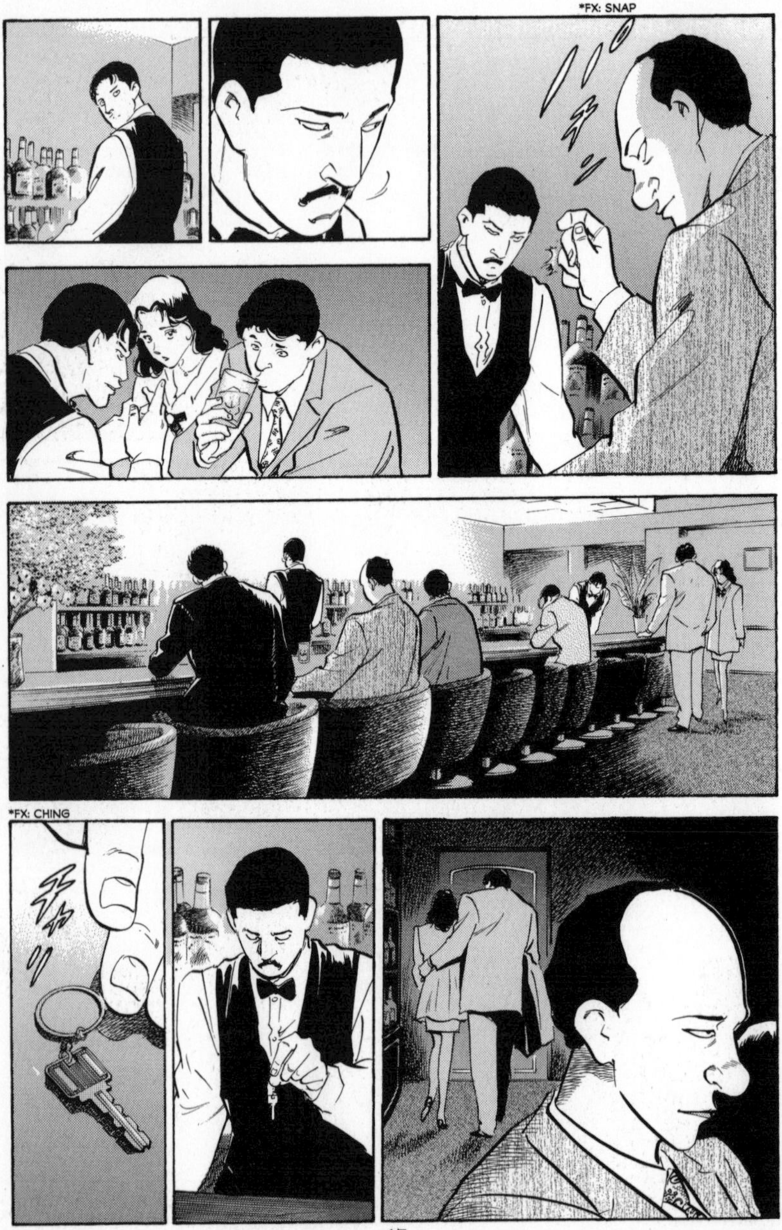
*FX: SNAP
*FX: CHING

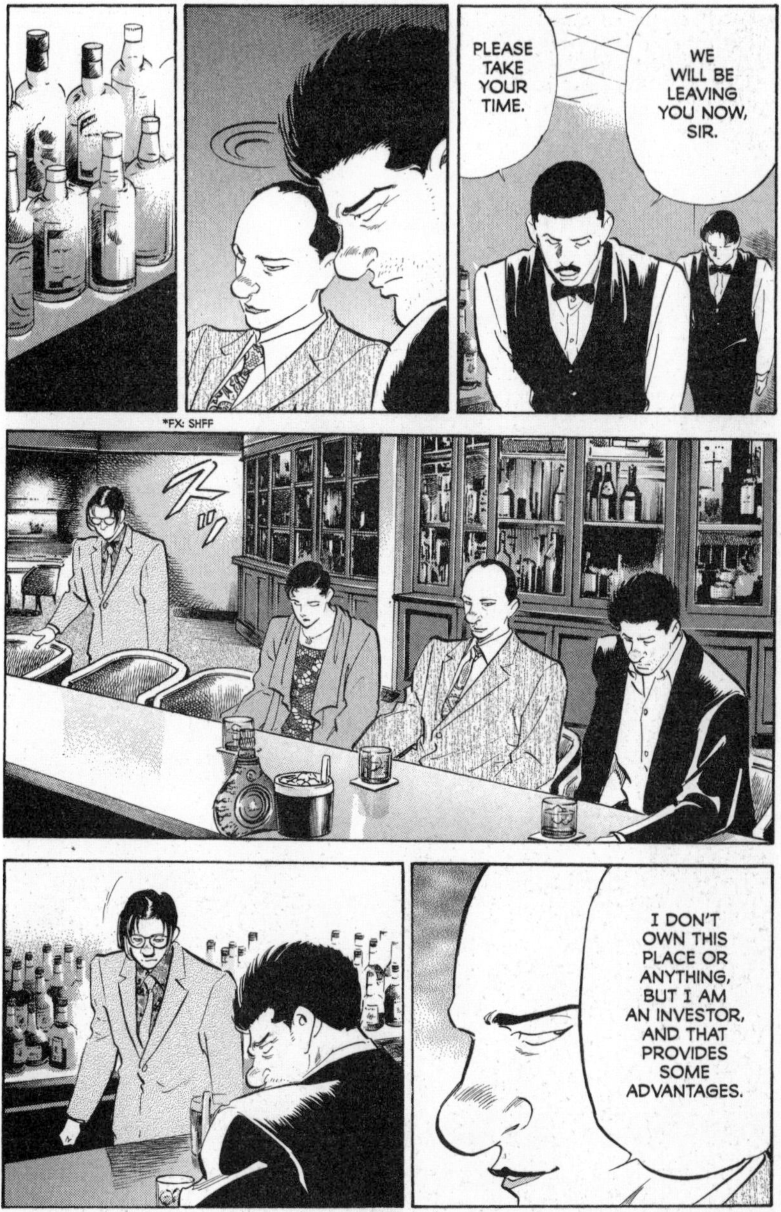
WE WILL BE LEAVING YOU NOW, SIR.
PLEASE TAKE YOUR TIME.
*FX: SHFF
I DON'T OWN THIS PLACE OR ANYTHING, BUT I AM AN INVESTOR, AND THAT PROVIDES SOME ADVANTAGES.

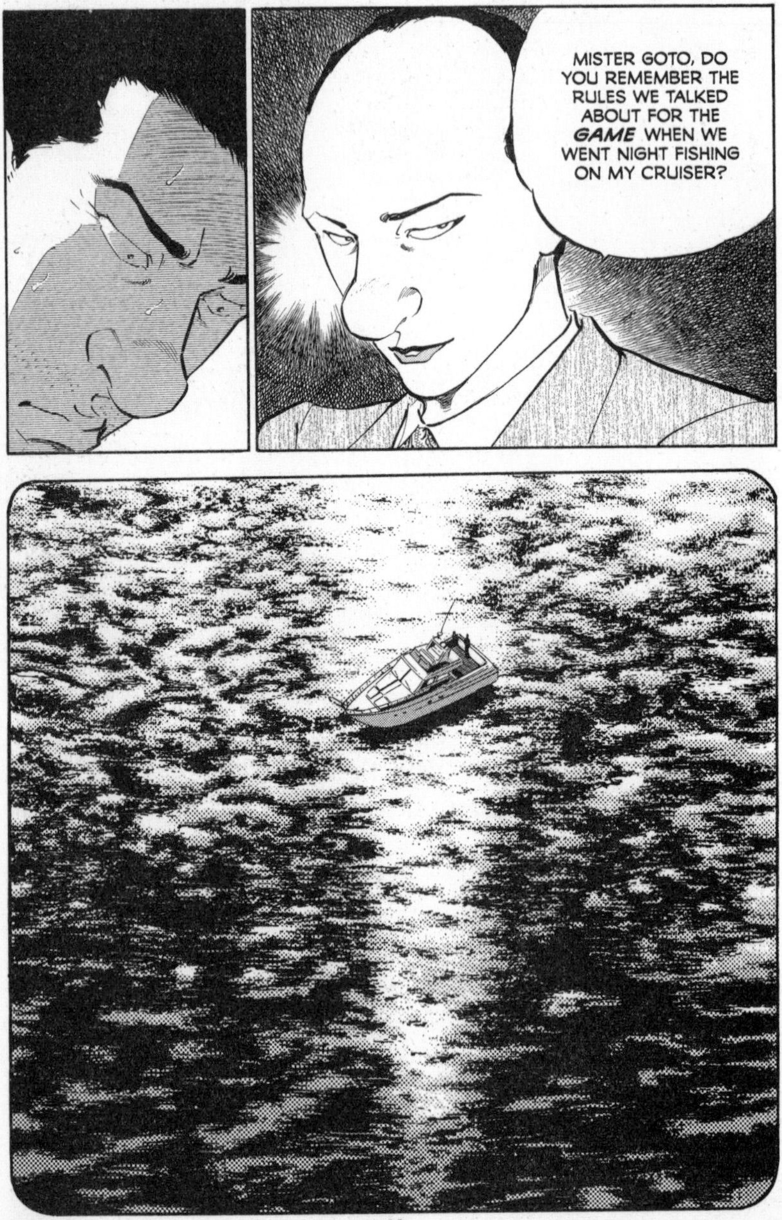
MISTER GOTO, DO YOU REMEMBER THE RULES WE TALKED ABOUT FOR THE *GAME* WHEN WE WENT NIGHT FISHING ON MY CRUISER?

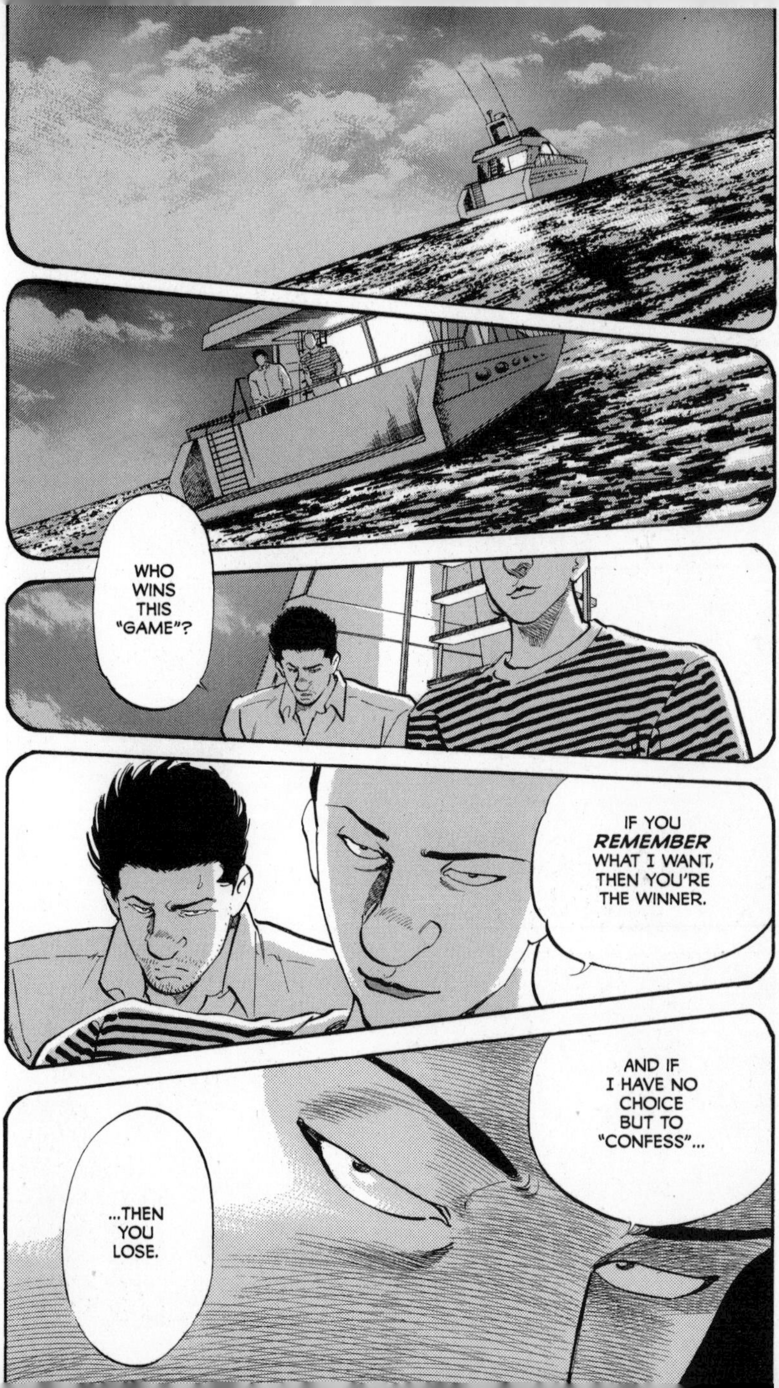
WHO WINS THIS "GAME"?
IF YOU *REMEMBER* WHAT I WANT, THEN YOU'RE THE WINNER.
AND IF I HAVE NO CHOICE BUT TO "CONFESS"...
...THEN YOU LOSE.

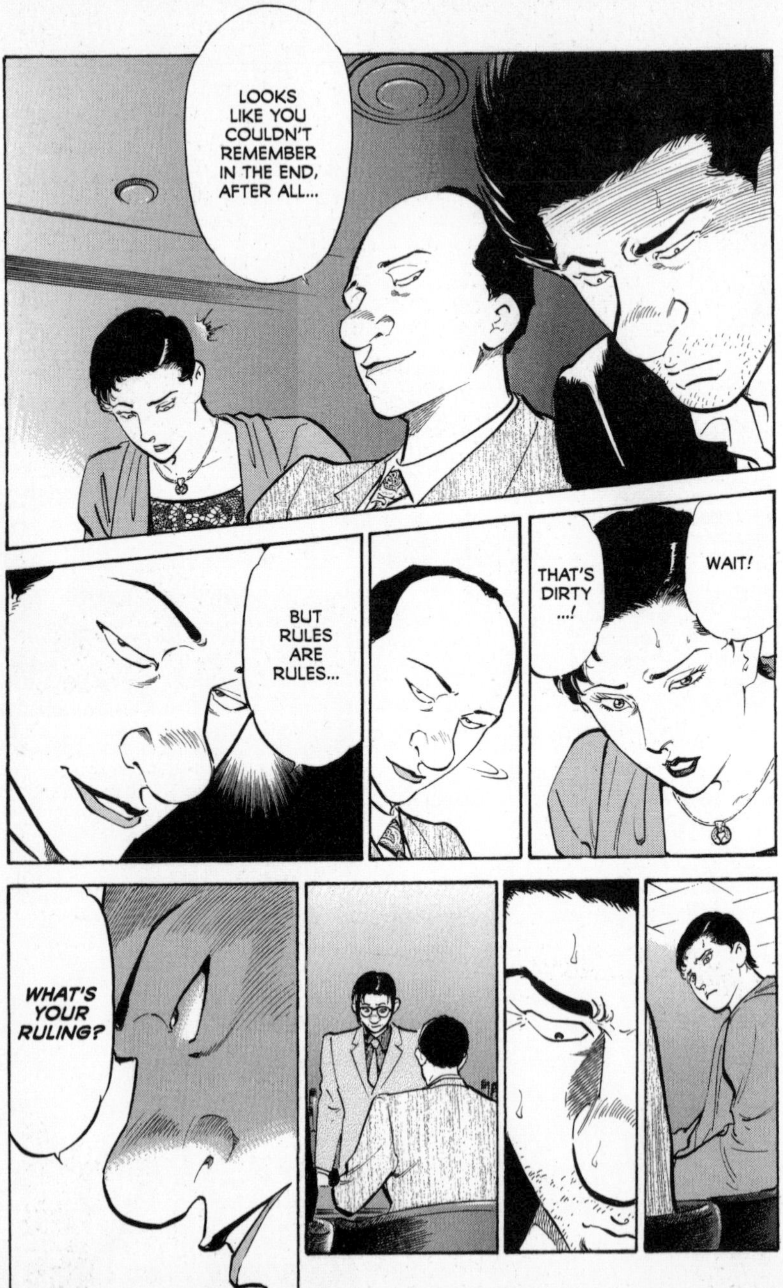
LOOKS LIKE YOU COULDN'T REMEMBER IN THE END, AFTER ALL...
WAIT!
THAT'S DIRTY ...!
BUT RULES ARE RULES...
WHAT'S YOUR RULING?

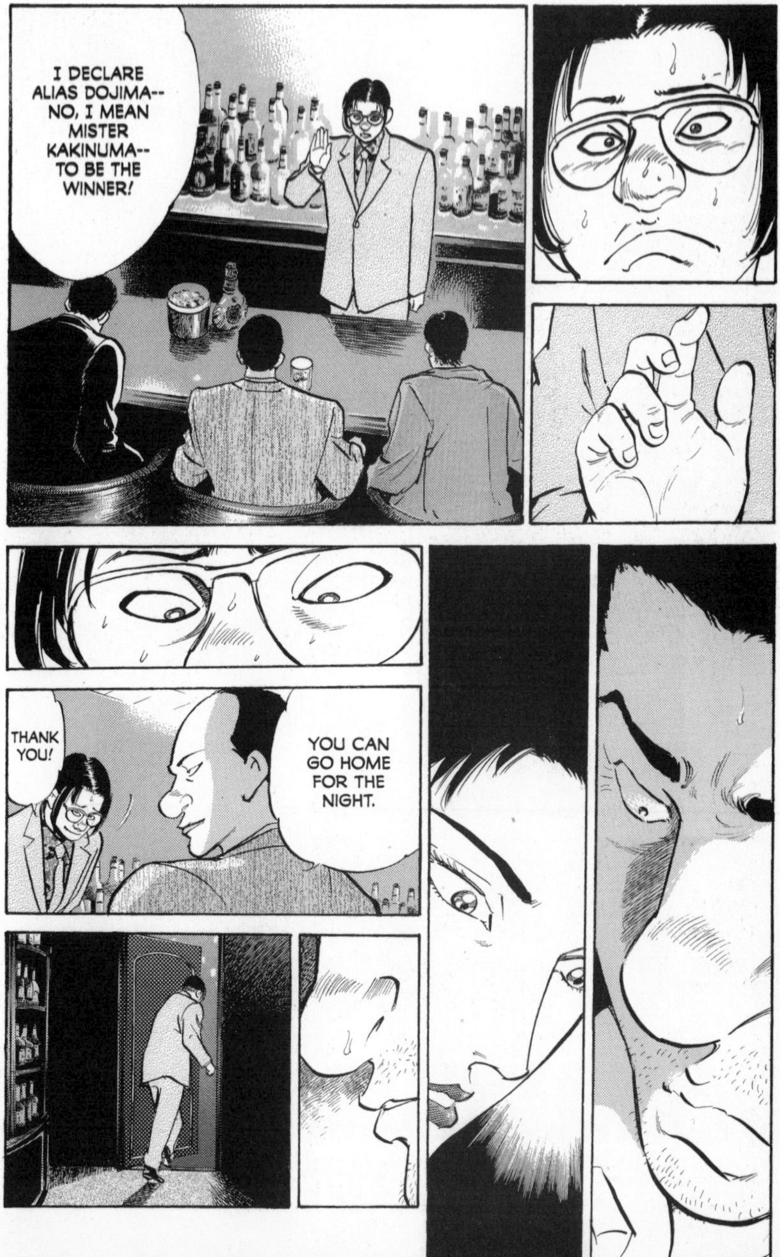
I DECLARE ALIAS DOJIMA-- NO, I MEAN MISTER KAKINUMA-- TO BE THE WINNER!
YOU CAN GO HOME FOR THE NIGHT.
THANK YOU!

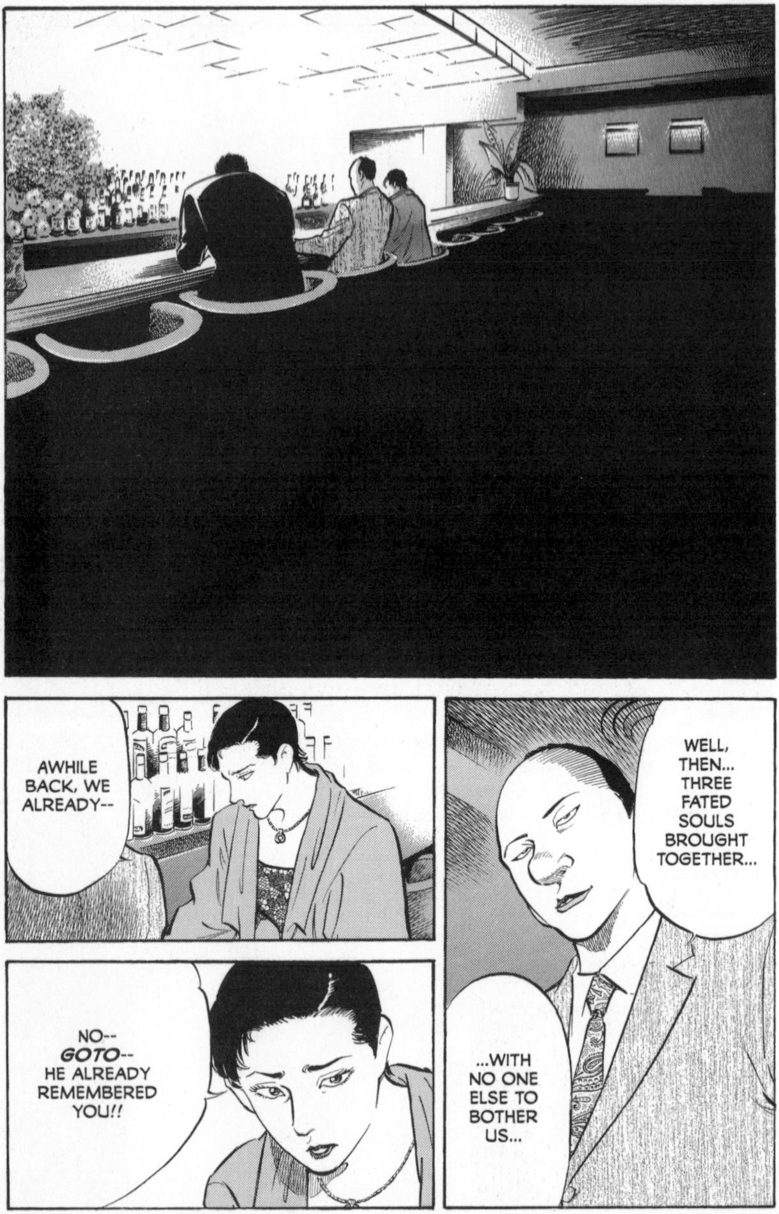
WELL, THEN... THREE FATED SOULS BROUGHT TOGETHER...
...WITH NO ONE ELSE TO BOTHER US...
AWHILE BACK, WE ALREADY--
NO-- *GOTO*-- HE ALREADY REMEMBERED YOU!!

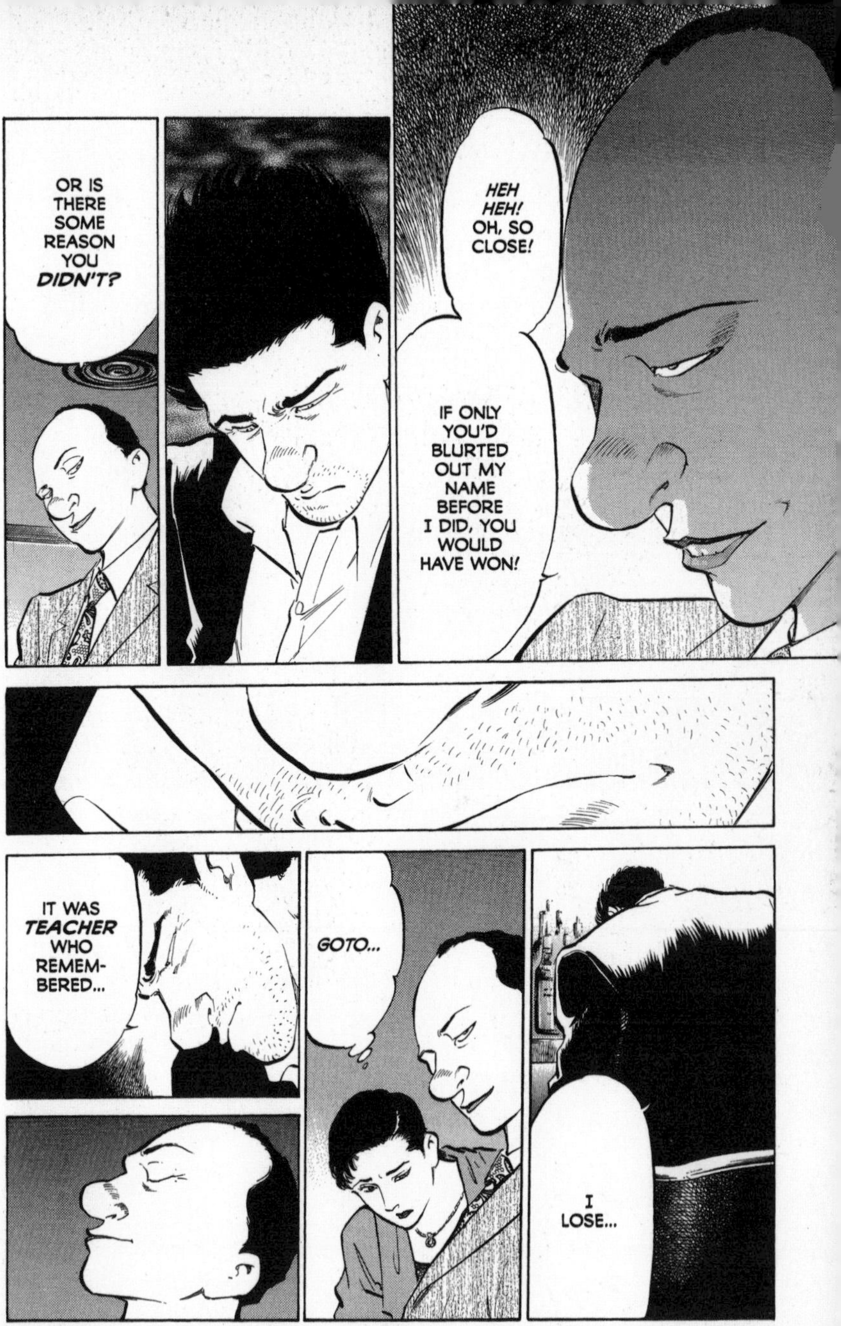
HEH HEH! OH, SO CLOSE!
IF ONLY YOU'D BLURTED OUT MY NAME BEFORE I DID, YOU WOULD HAVE WON!
OR IS THERE SOME REASON YOU *DIDN'T?*
I LOSE...
GOTO...
IT WAS *TEACHER* WHO REMEMBERED...

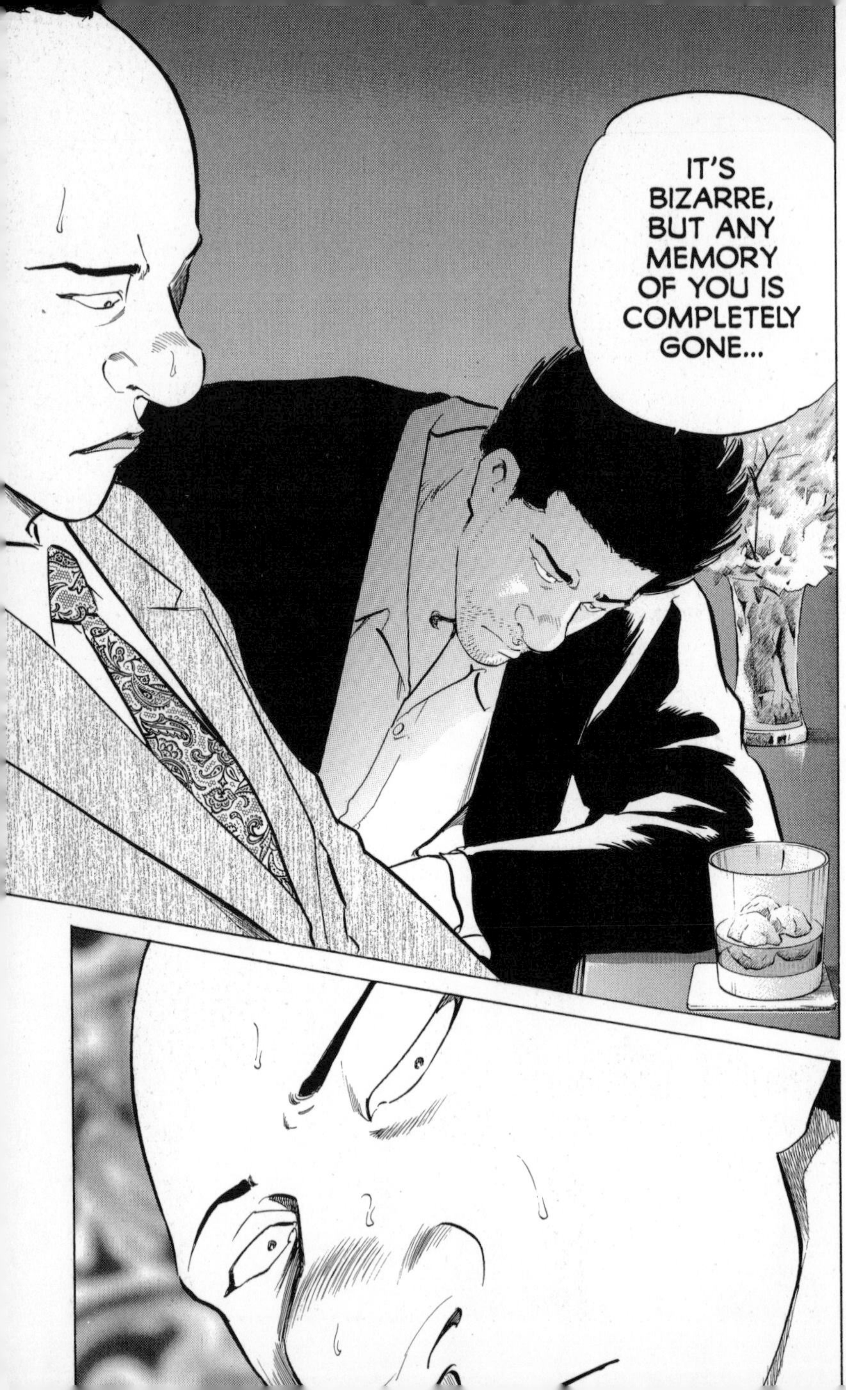
IT'S BIZARRE, BUT ANY MEMORY OF YOU IS COMPLETELY GONE...

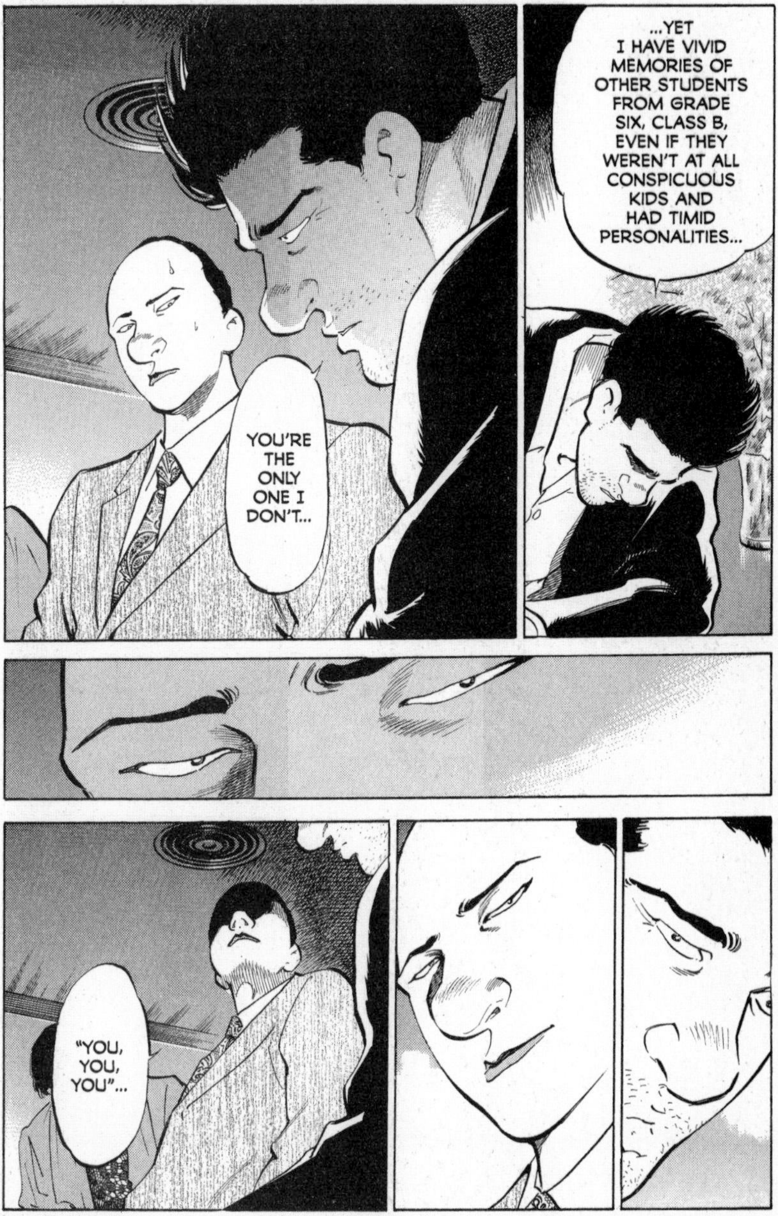
...YET I HAVE VIVID MEMORIES OF OTHER STUDENTS FROM GRADE SIX, CLASS B, EVEN IF THEY WEREN'T AT ALL CONSPICUOUS KIDS AND HAD TIMID PERSONALITIES...
YOU'RE THE ONLY ONE I DON'T...
"YOU, YOU, YOU"...

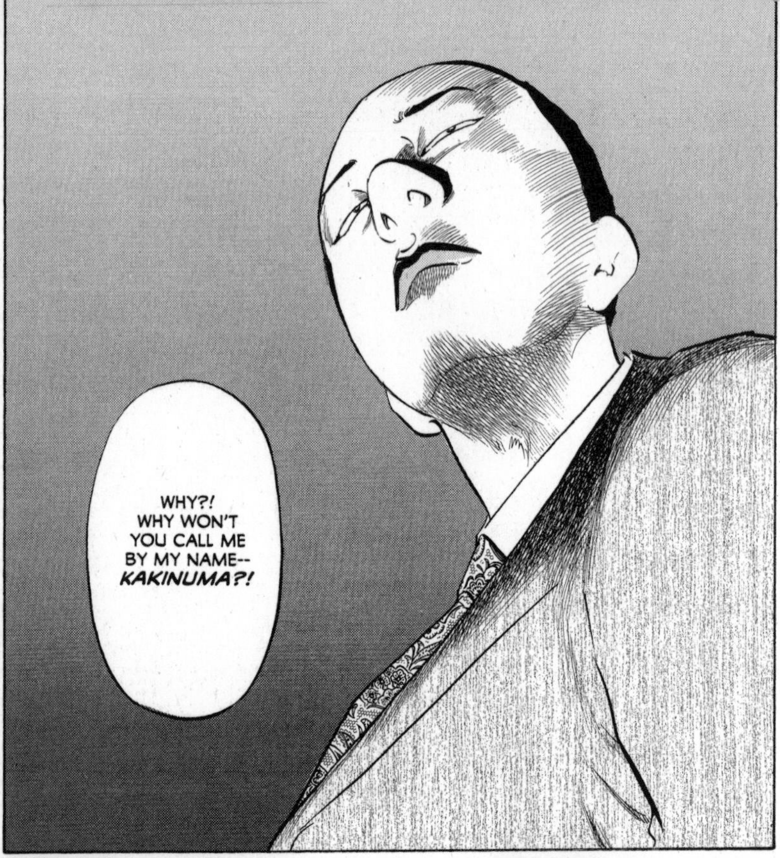
WHY?! WHY WON'T YOU CALL ME BY MY NAME-- *KAKINUMA?!*

*FX: HYUK HYUK HYUK

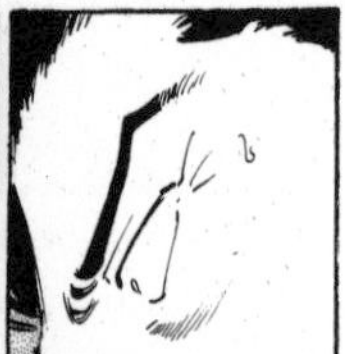

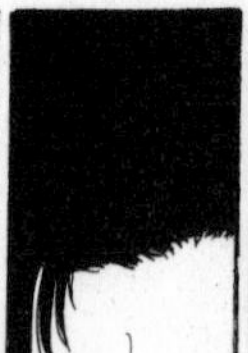

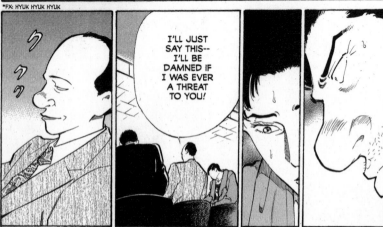

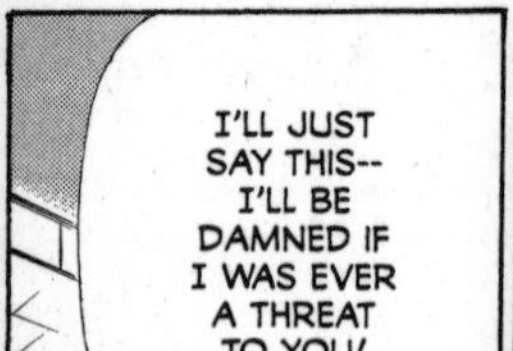
I'LL JUST SAY THIS-- I'LL BE DAMNED IF I WAS EVER A THREAT TO YOU!

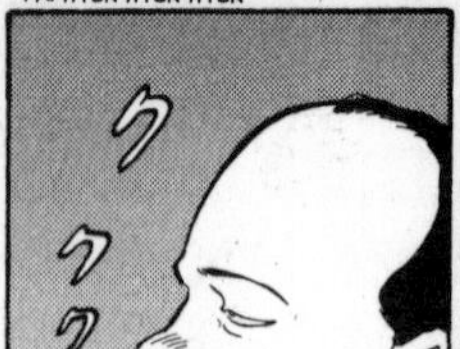
ククク

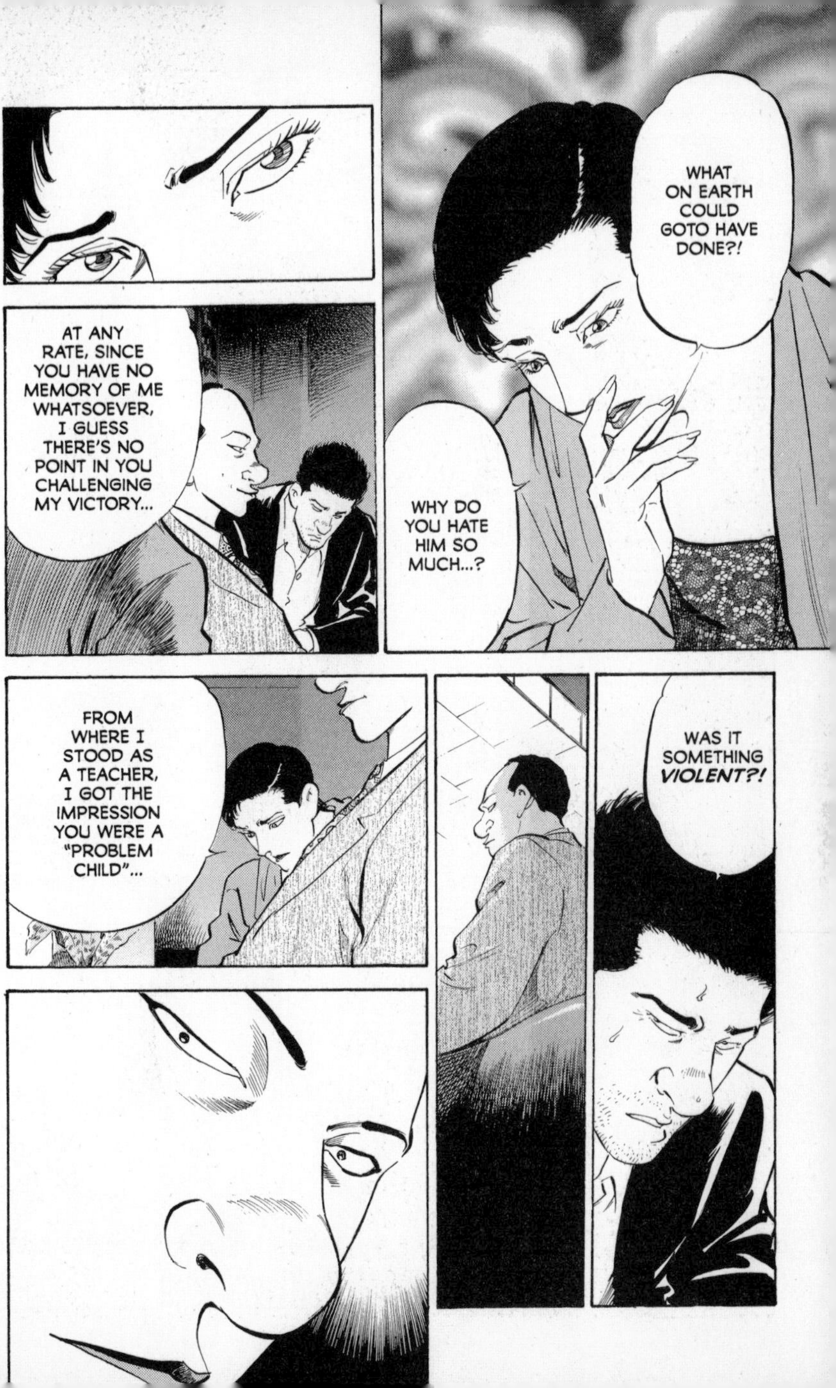
WHAT ON EARTH COULD GOTO HAVE DONE?!
WHY DO YOU HATE HIM SO MUCH...?
AT ANY RATE, SINCE YOU HAVE NO MEMORY OF ME WHATSOEVER, I GUESS THERE'S NO POINT IN YOU CHALLENGING MY VICTORY...
WAS IT SOMETHING *VIOLENT?!*
FROM WHERE I STOOD AS A TEACHER, I GOT THE IMPRESSION YOU WERE A "PROBLEM CHILD"...

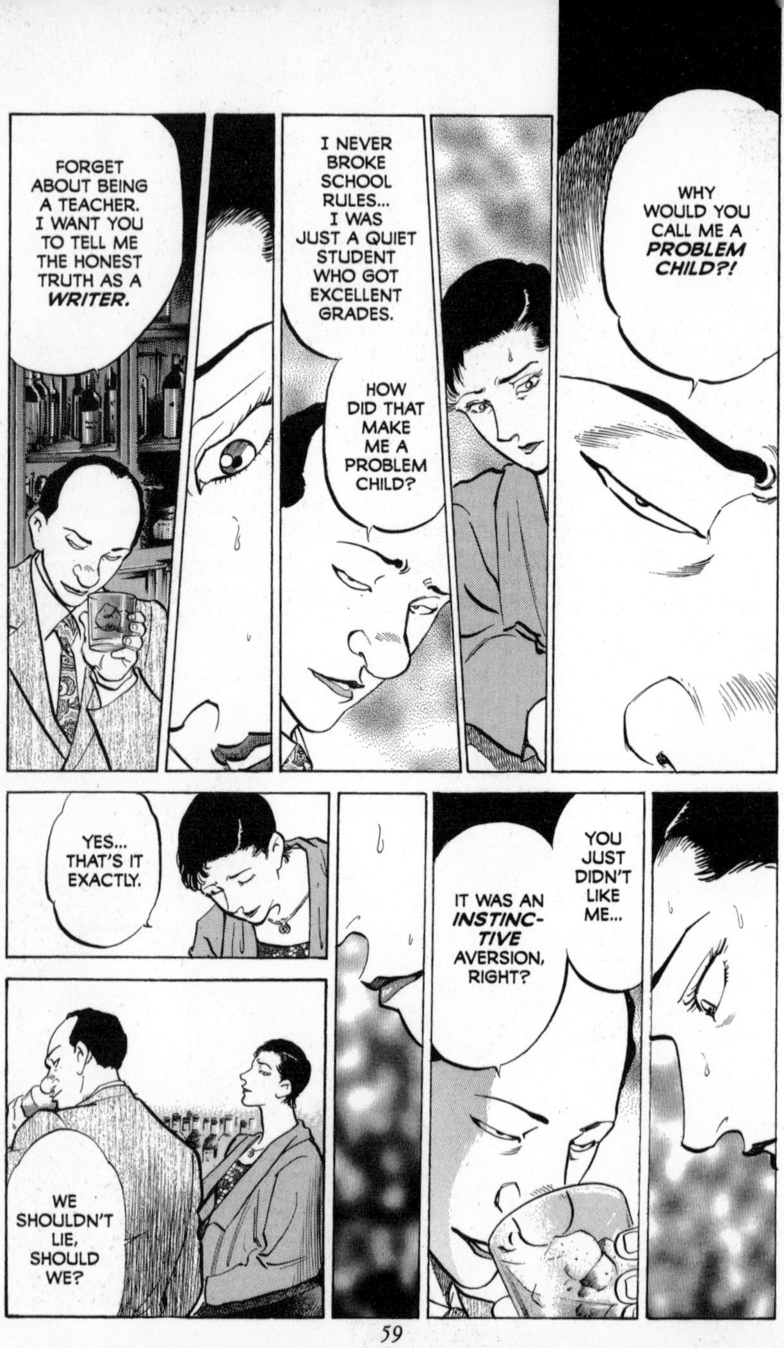
WHY WOULD YOU CALL ME A *PROBLEM CHILD?!*
I NEVER BROKE SCHOOL RULES... I WAS JUST A QUIET STUDENT WHO GOT EXCELLENT GRADES.
HOW DID THAT MAKE ME A PROBLEM CHILD?
FORGET ABOUT BEING A TEACHER. I WANT YOU TO TELL ME THE HONEST TRUTH AS A *WRITER.*
YOU JUST DIDN'T LIKE ME...
IT WAS AN *INSTINC-TIVE* AVERSION, RIGHT?
YES... THAT'S IT EXACTLY.
WE SHOULDN'T LIE, SHOULD WE?

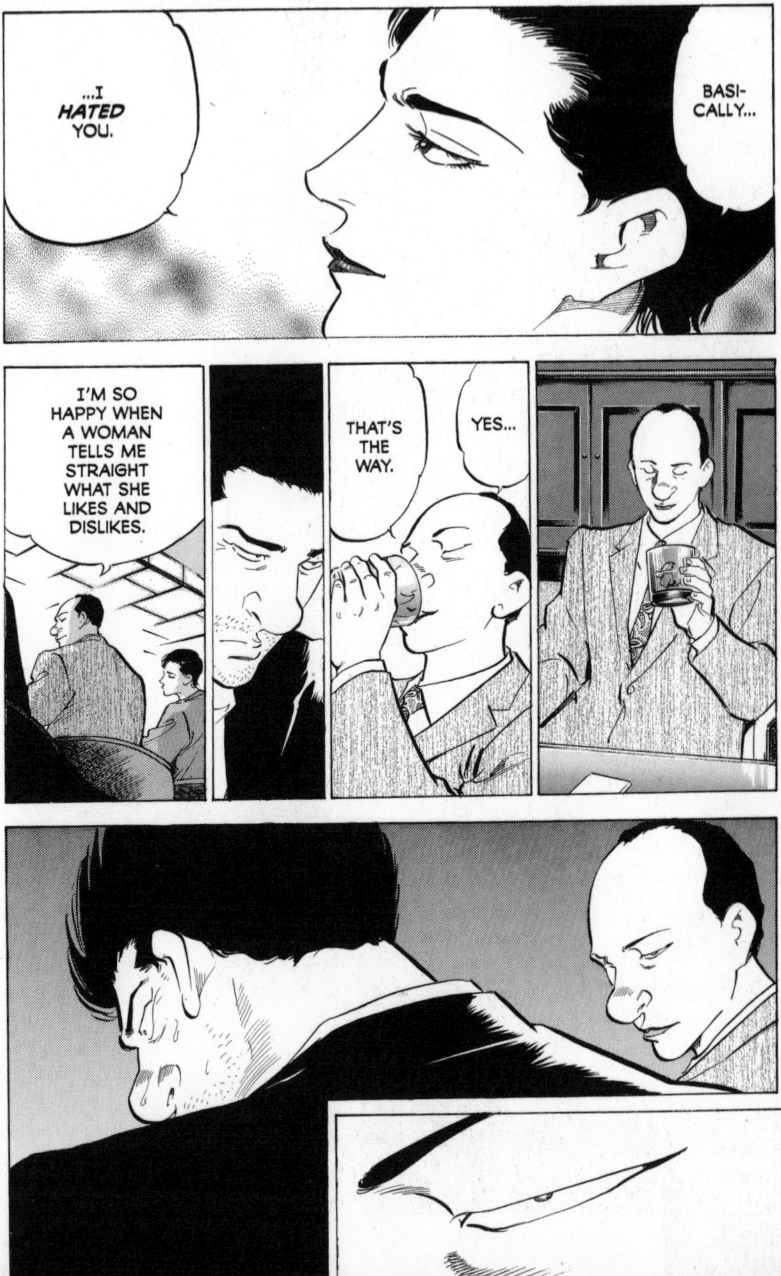
BASI-CALLY...
...I HATED YOU.
YES...
THAT'S THE WAY.
I'M SO HAPPY WHEN A WOMAN TELLS ME STRAIGHT WHAT SHE LIKES AND DISLIKES.

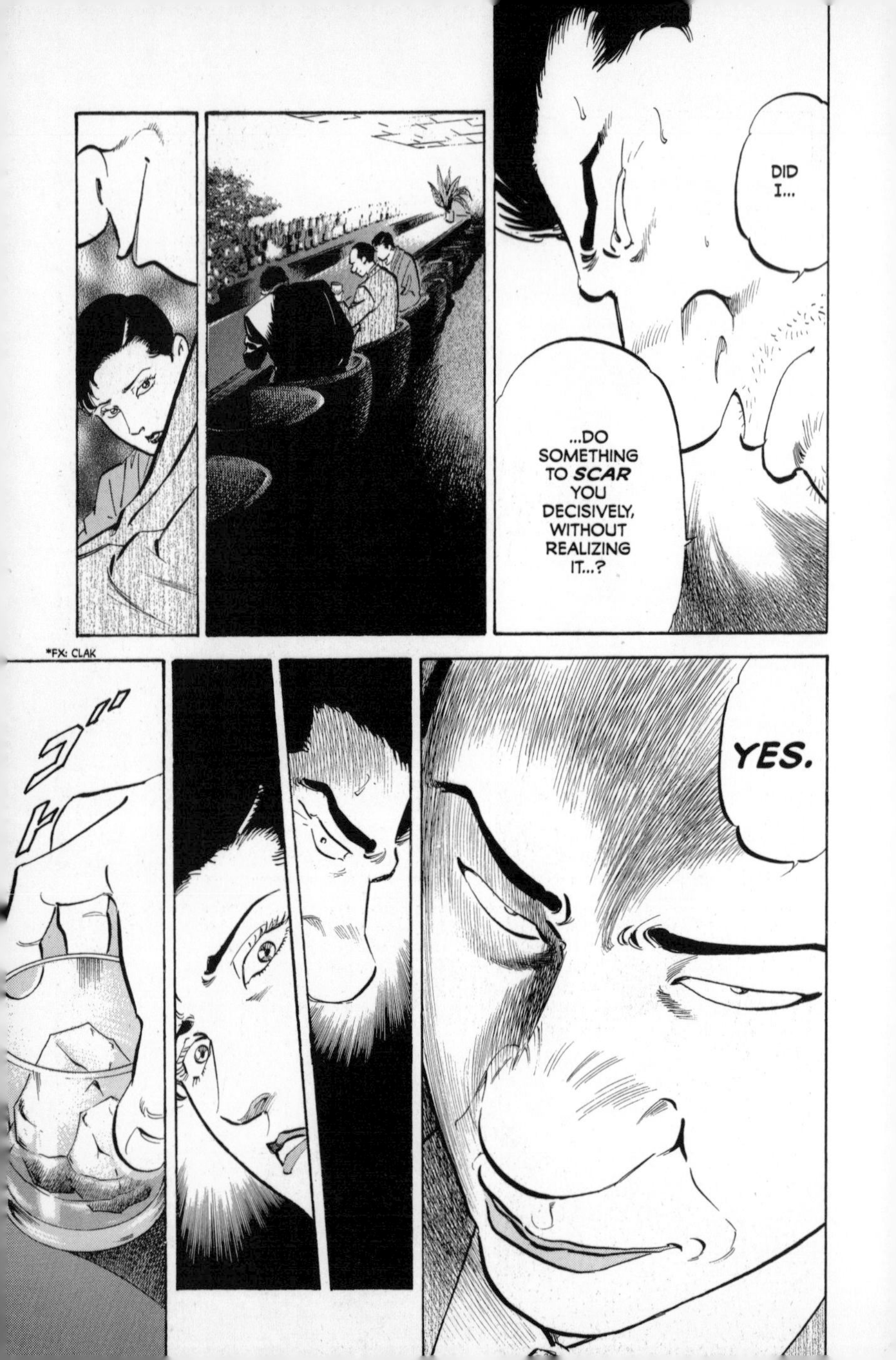
DID I...
...DO SOMETHING TO SCAR YOU DECISIVELY, WITHOUT REALIZING IT...?
*FX: CLAK
YES.

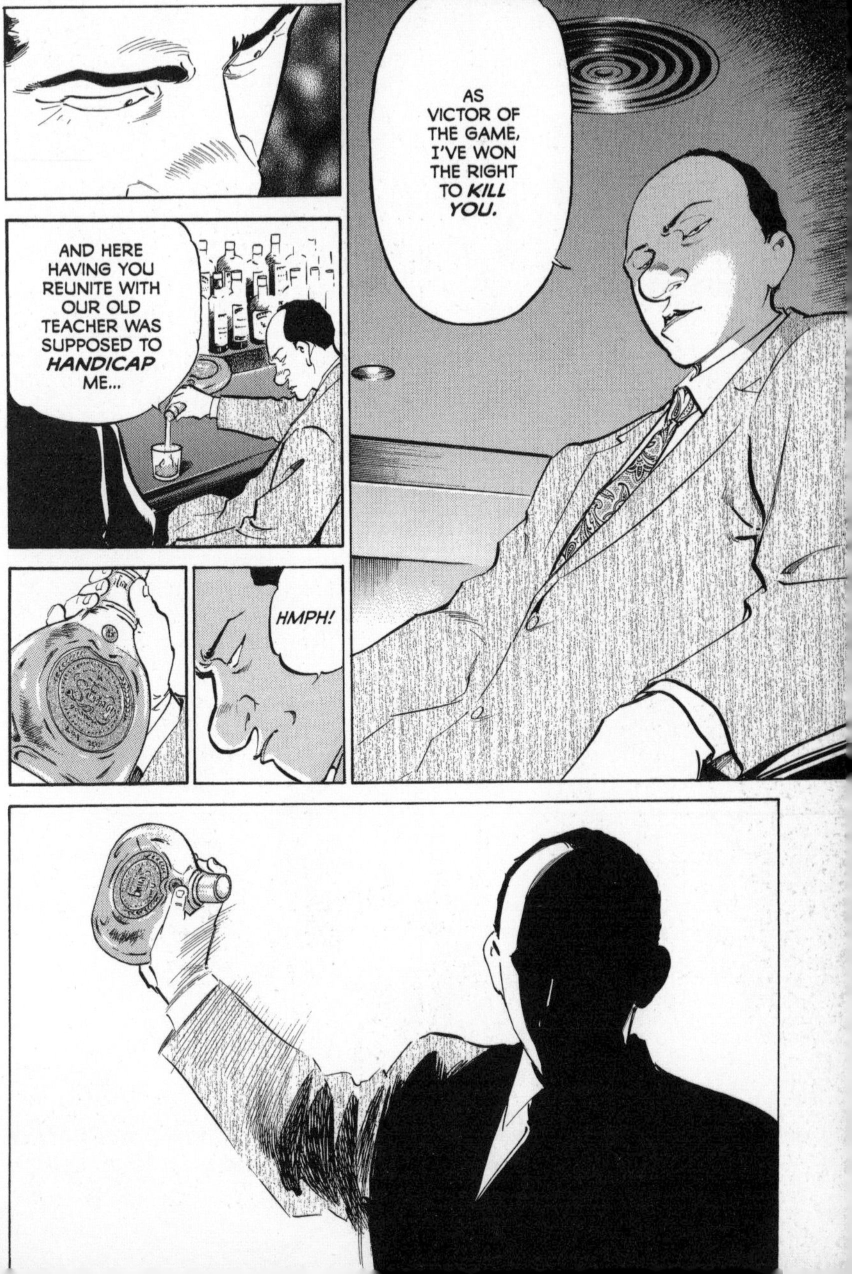
AS VICTOR OF THE GAME, I'VE WON THE RIGHT TO *KILL YOU.*
AND HERE HAVING YOU REUNITE WITH OUR OLD TEACHER WAS SUPPOSED TO *HANDICAP* ME...
HMPH!

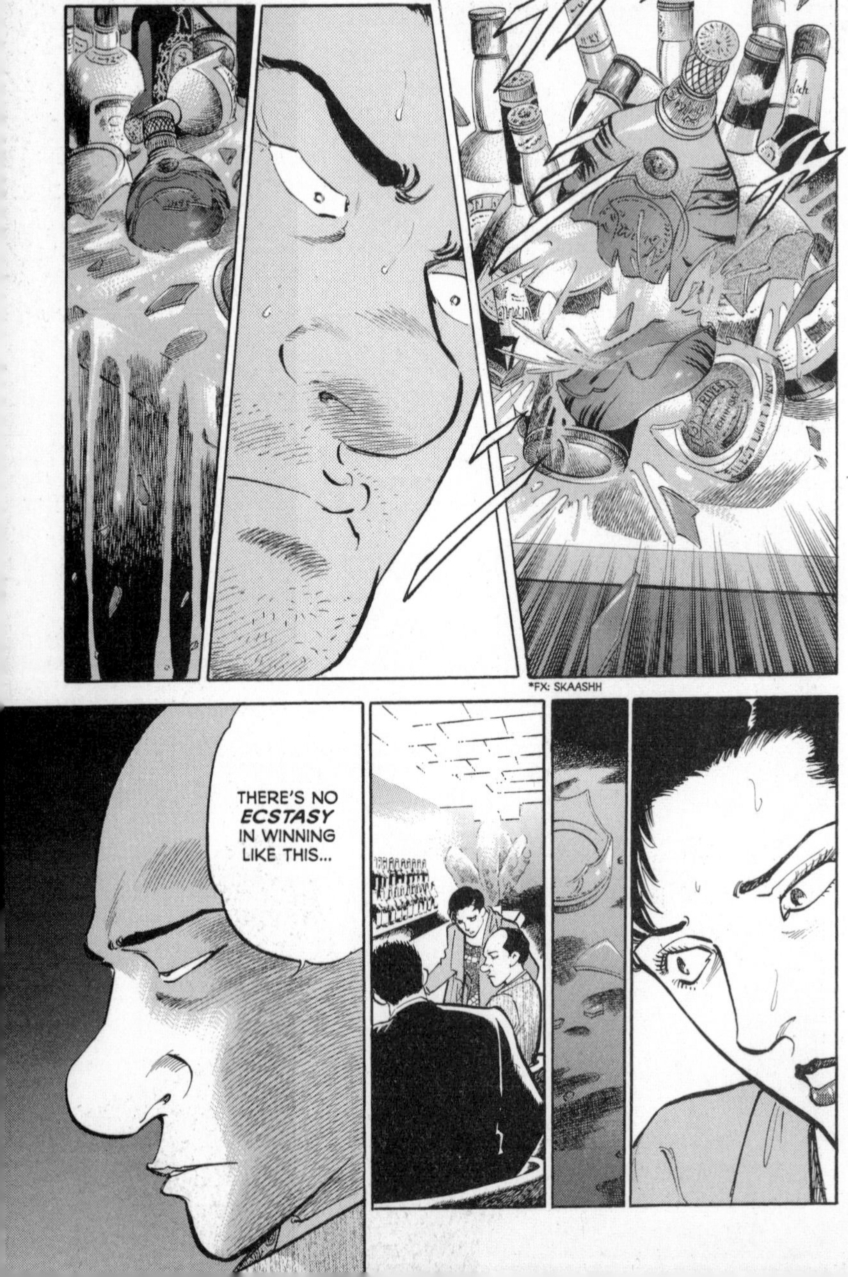
*FX: SKAASHH
THERE'S NO ECSTASY IN WINNING LIKE THIS...

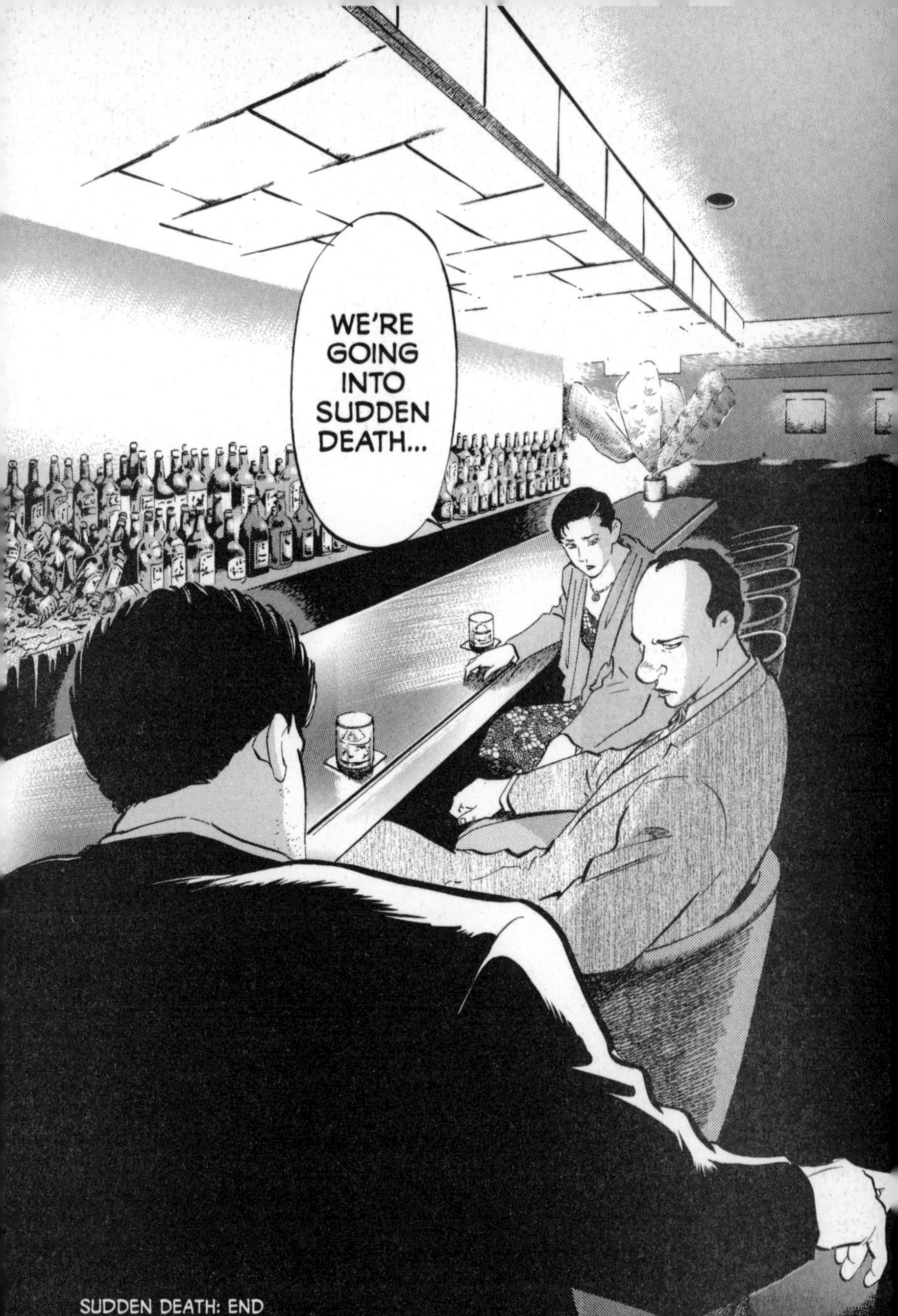
WE'RE GOING INTO SUDDEN DEATH...

SUDDEN DEATH: END

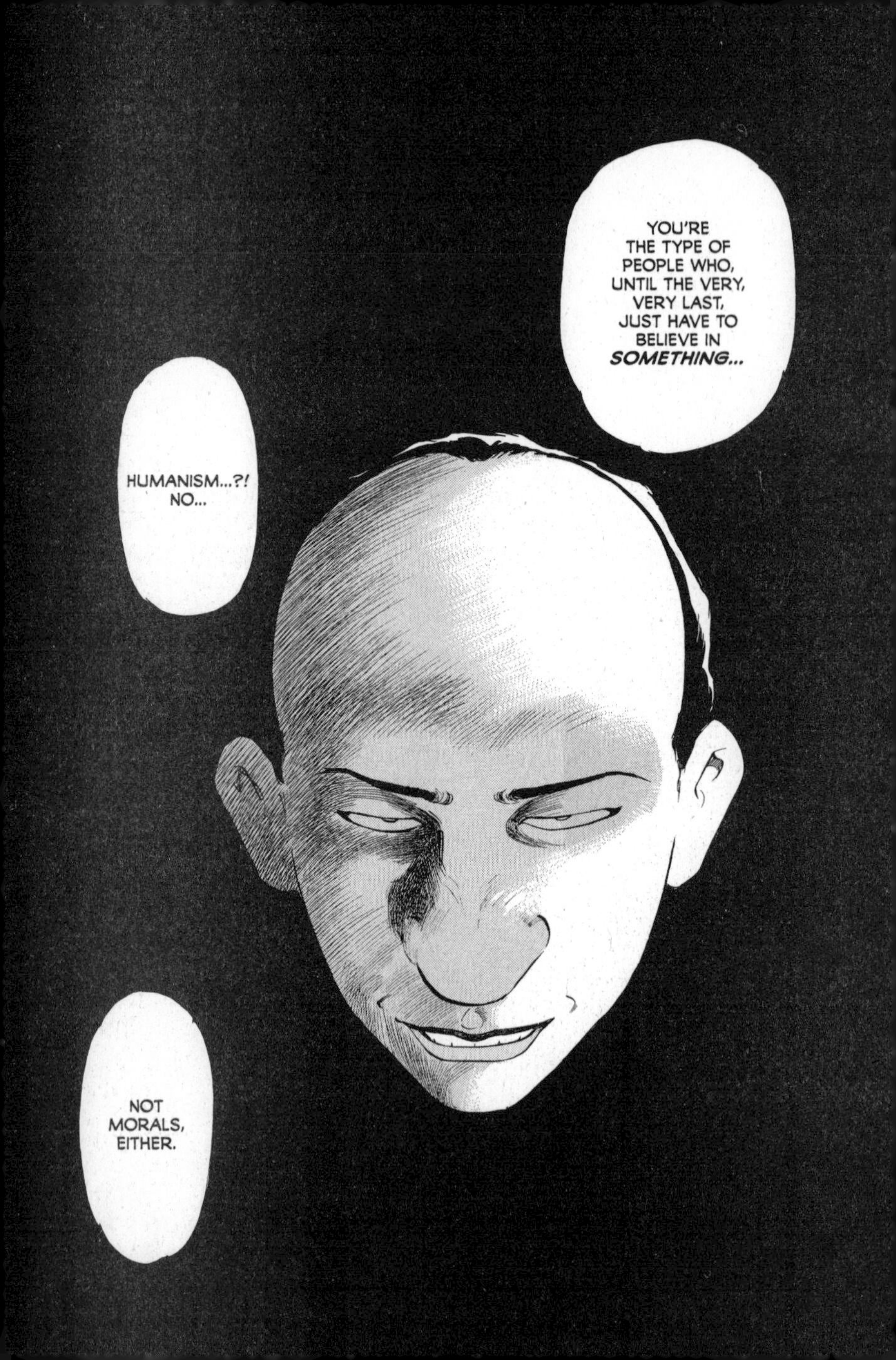
YOU'RE THE TYPE OF PEOPLE WHO, UNTIL THE VERY, VERY LAST, JUST HAVE TO BELIEVE IN *SOMETHING...*
HUMANISM...?! NO...
NOT MORALS, EITHER.

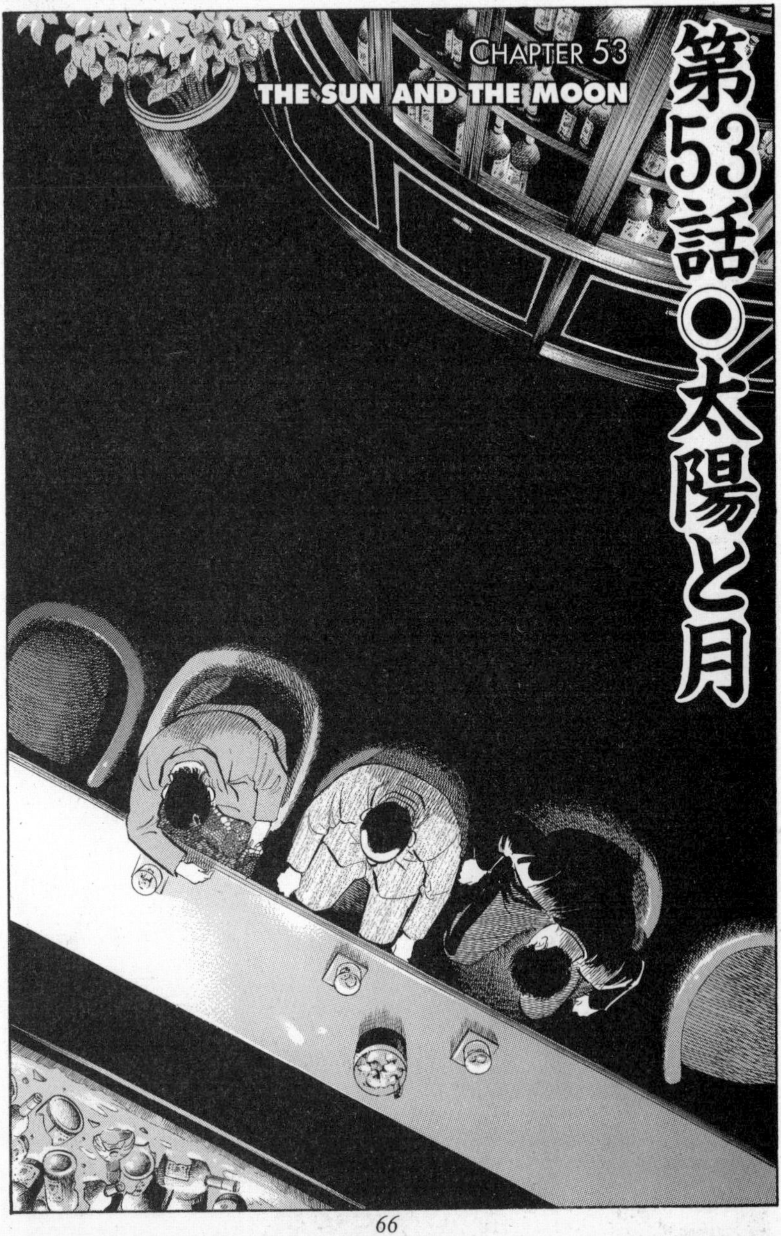

CHAPTER 53
THE SUN AND THE MOON
第53話◯太陽と月

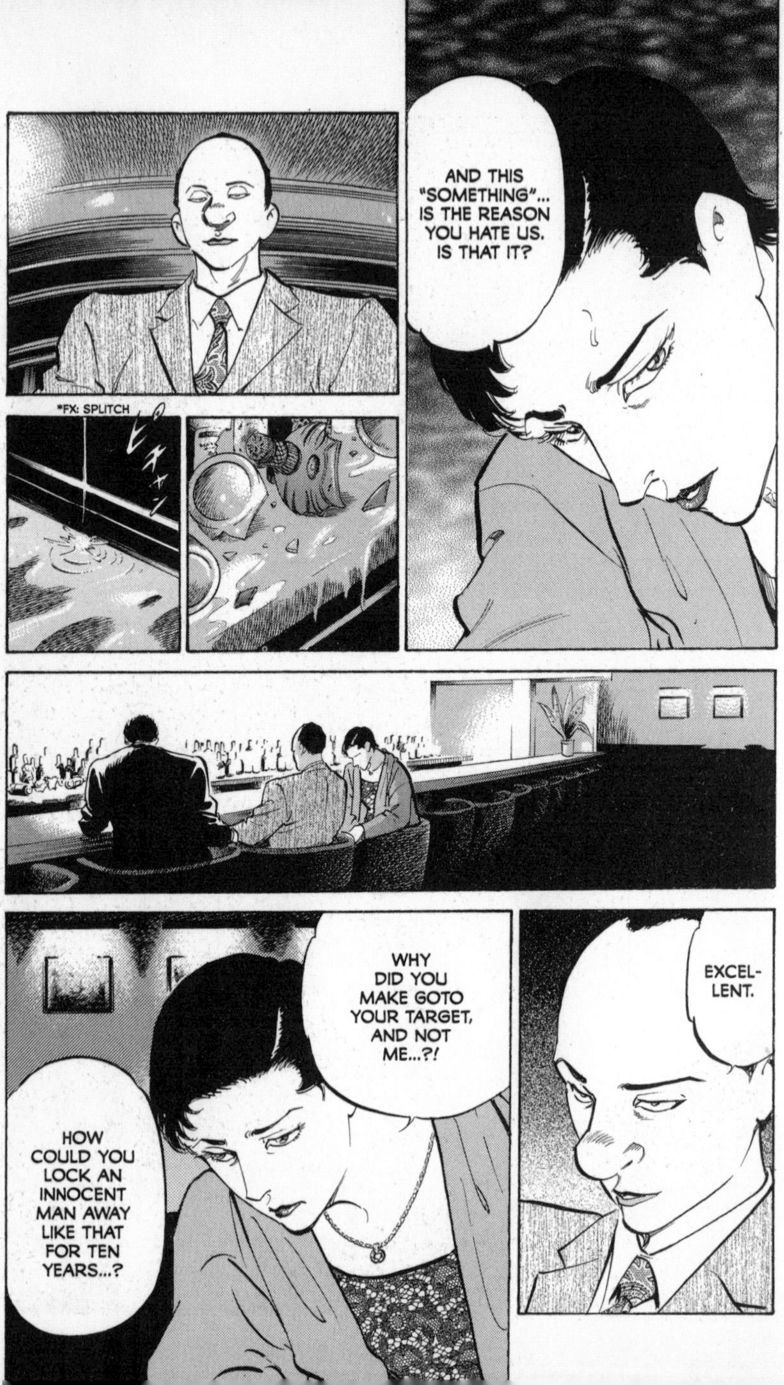
AND THIS "SOMETHING"... IS THE REASON YOU HATE US. IS THAT IT?
*FX: SPLITCH
EXCEL-LENT.
WHY DID YOU MAKE GOTO YOUR TARGET, AND NOT ME...?!
HOW COULD YOU LOCK AN INNOCENT MAN AWAY LIKE THAT FOR TEN YEARS...?

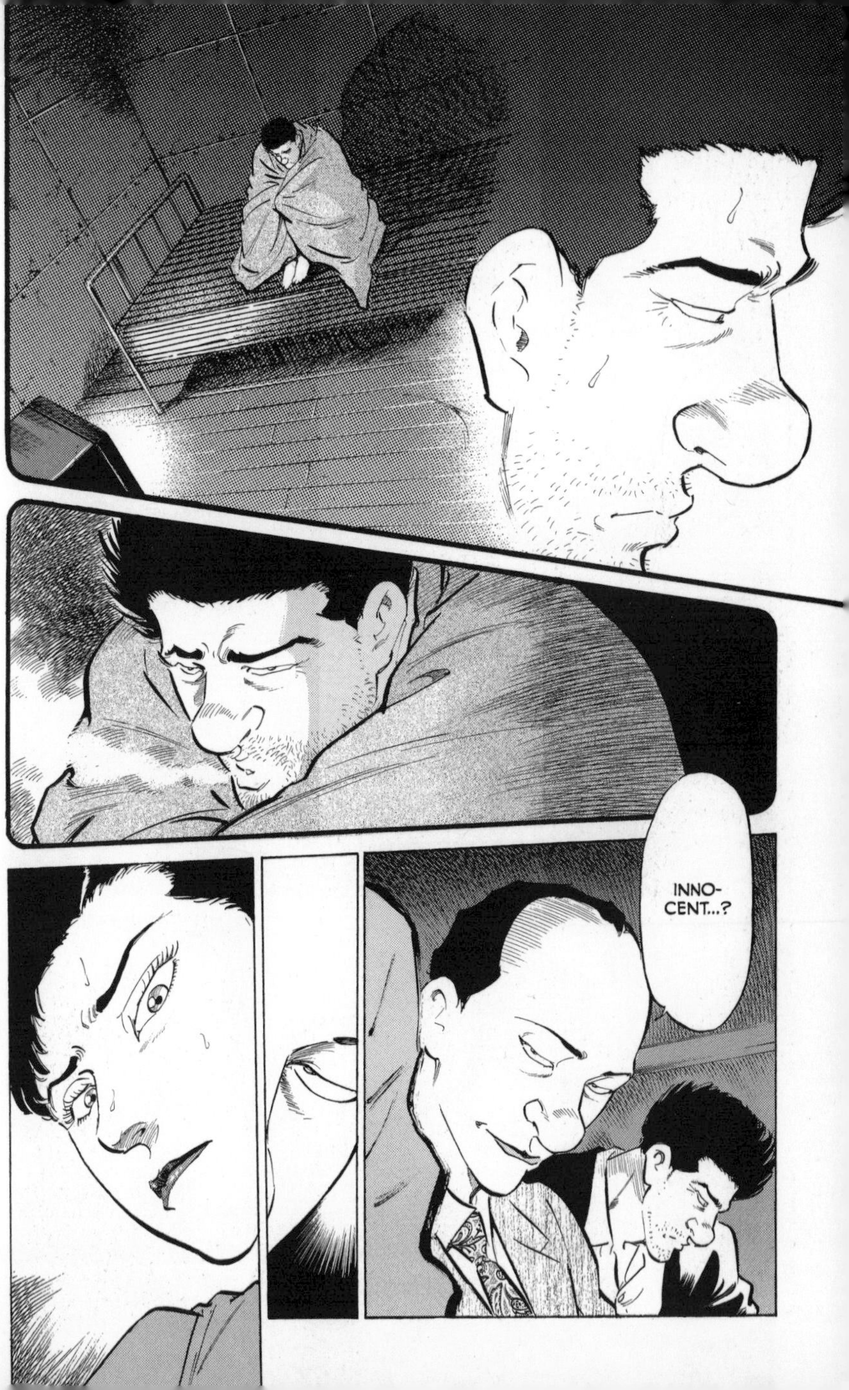
INNO-
CENT...?

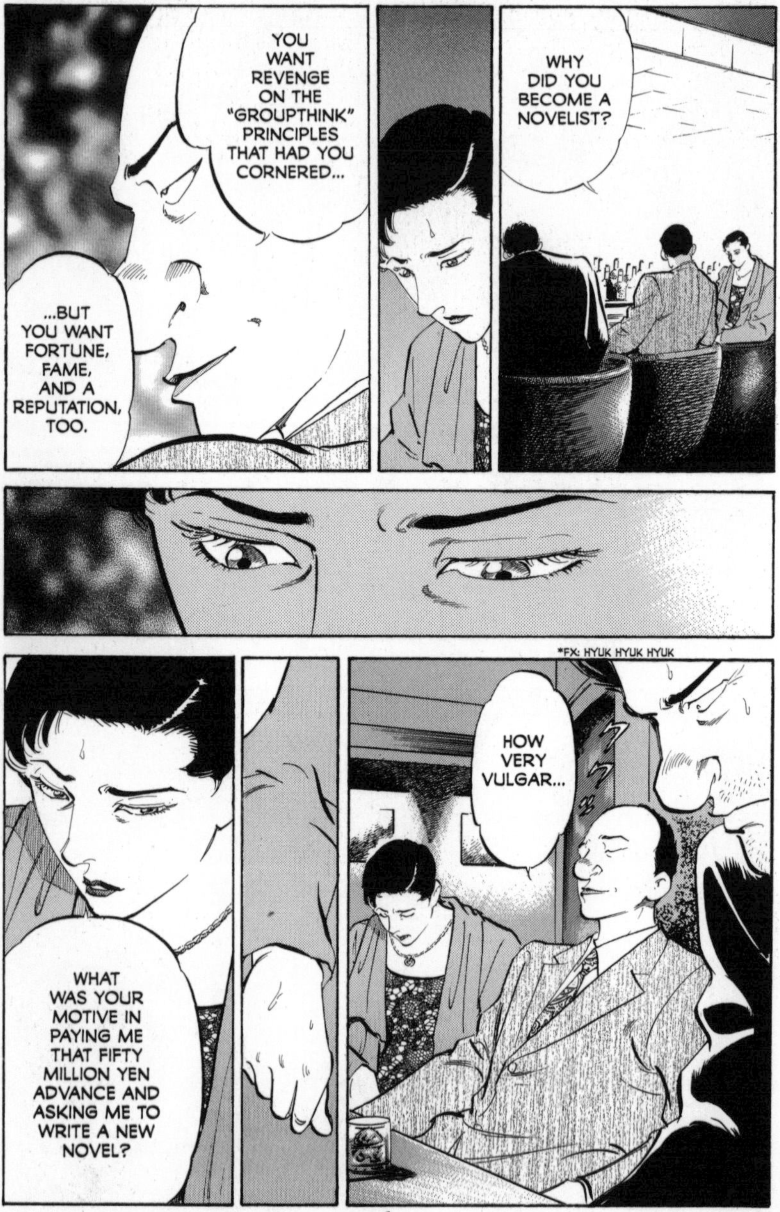
WHY DID YOU BECOME A NOVELIST?
YOU WANT REVENGE ON THE "GROUPTHINK" PRINCIPLES THAT HAD YOU CORNERED...
...BUT YOU WANT FORTUNE, FAME, AND A REPUTATION, TOO.
*FX: HYUK HYUK HYUK
HOW VERY VULGAR...
WHAT WAS YOUR MOTIVE IN PAYING ME THAT FIFTY MILLION YEN ADVANCE AND ASKING ME TO WRITE A NEW NOVEL?

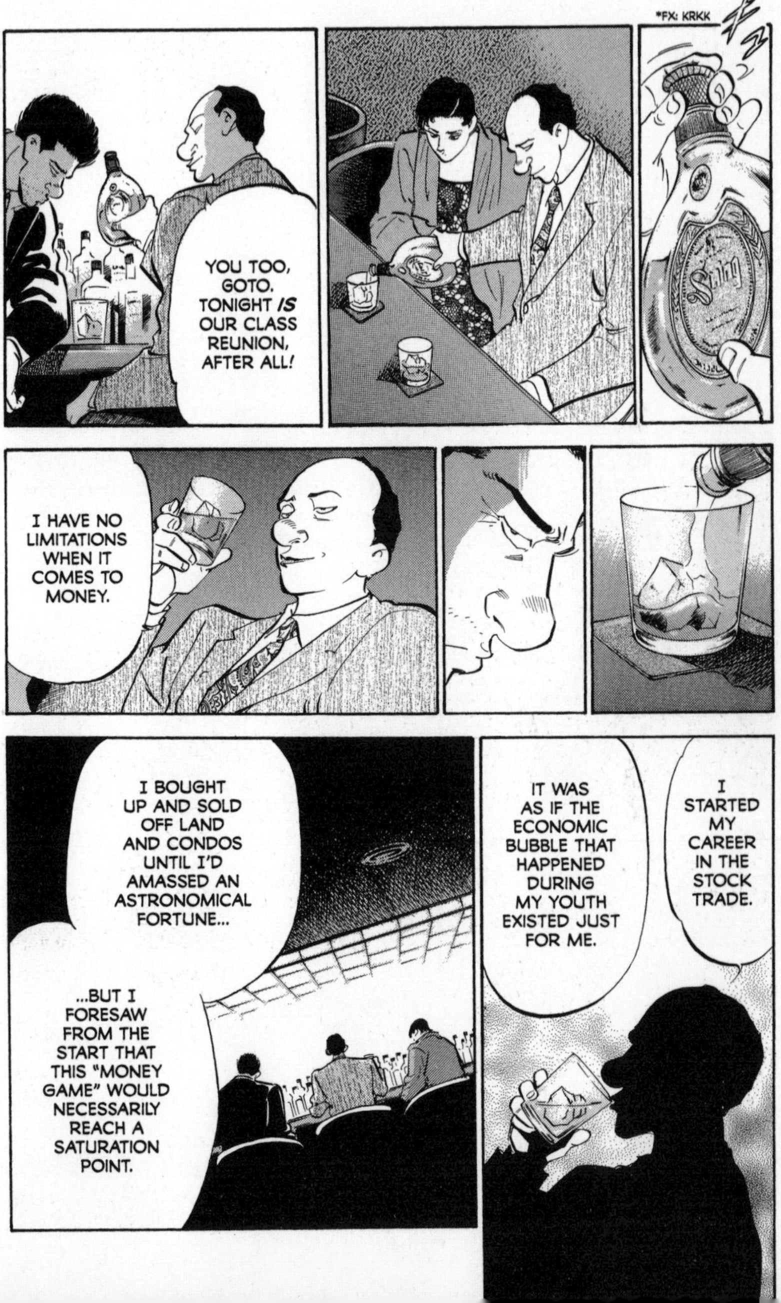
*FX: KRKK
YOU TOO, GOTO. TONIGHT *IS* OUR CLASS REUNION, AFTER ALL!
I HAVE NO LIMITATIONS WHEN IT COMES TO MONEY.
I STARTED MY CAREER IN THE STOCK TRADE.
IT WAS AS IF THE ECONOMIC BUBBLE THAT HAPPENED DURING MY YOUTH EXISTED JUST FOR ME.
I BOUGHT UP AND SOLD OFF LAND AND CONDOS UNTIL I'D AMASSED AN ASTRONOMICAL FORTUNE...
...BUT I FORESAW FROM THE START THAT THIS "MONEY GAME" WOULD NECESSARILY REACH A SATURATION POINT.

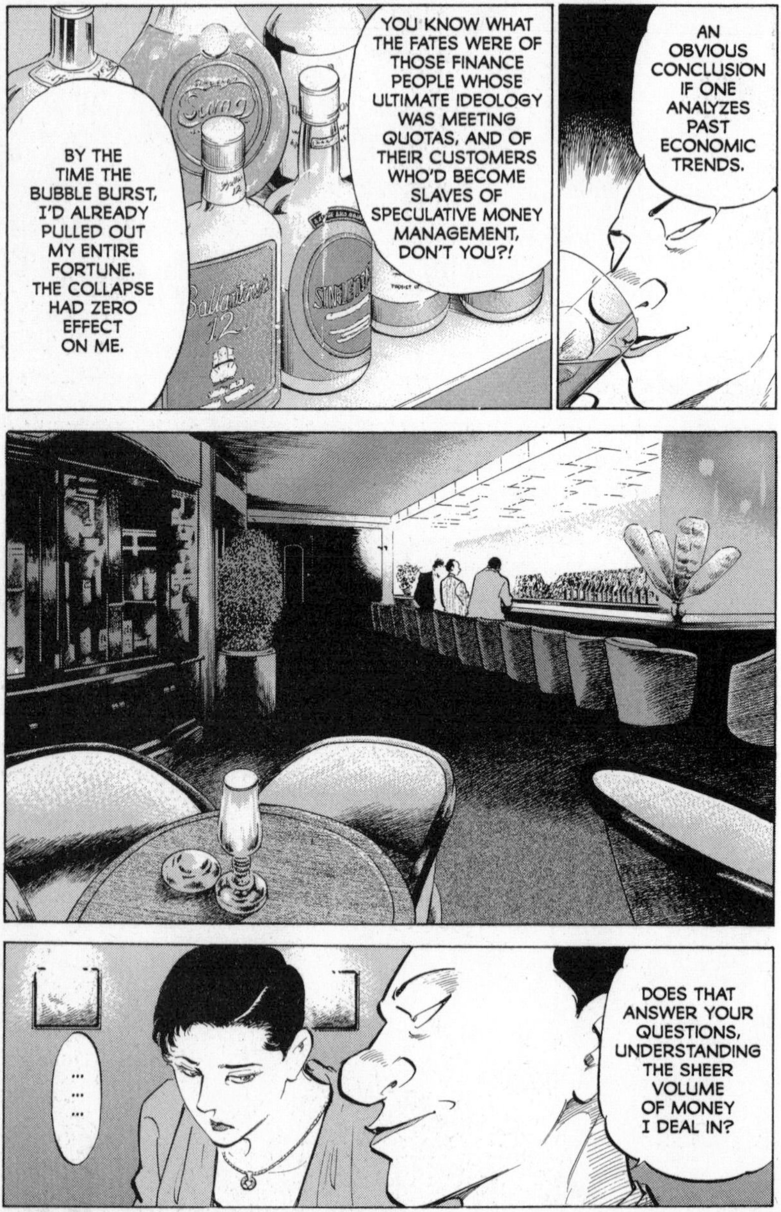
BY THE TIME THE BUBBLE BURST, I'D ALREADY PULLED OUT MY ENTIRE FORTUNE. THE COLLAPSE HAD ZERO EFFECT ON ME.
YOU KNOW WHAT THE FATES WERE OF THOSE FINANCE PEOPLE WHOSE ULTIMATE IDEOLOGY WAS MEETING QUOTAS, AND OF THEIR CUSTOMERS WHO'D BECOME SLAVES OF SPECULATIVE MONEY MANAGEMENT, DON'T YOU?!
AN OBVIOUS CONCLUSION IF ONE ANALYZES PAST ECONOMIC TRENDS.
......
DOES THAT ANSWER YOUR QUESTIONS, UNDERSTANDING THE SHEER VOLUME OF MONEY I DEAL IN?

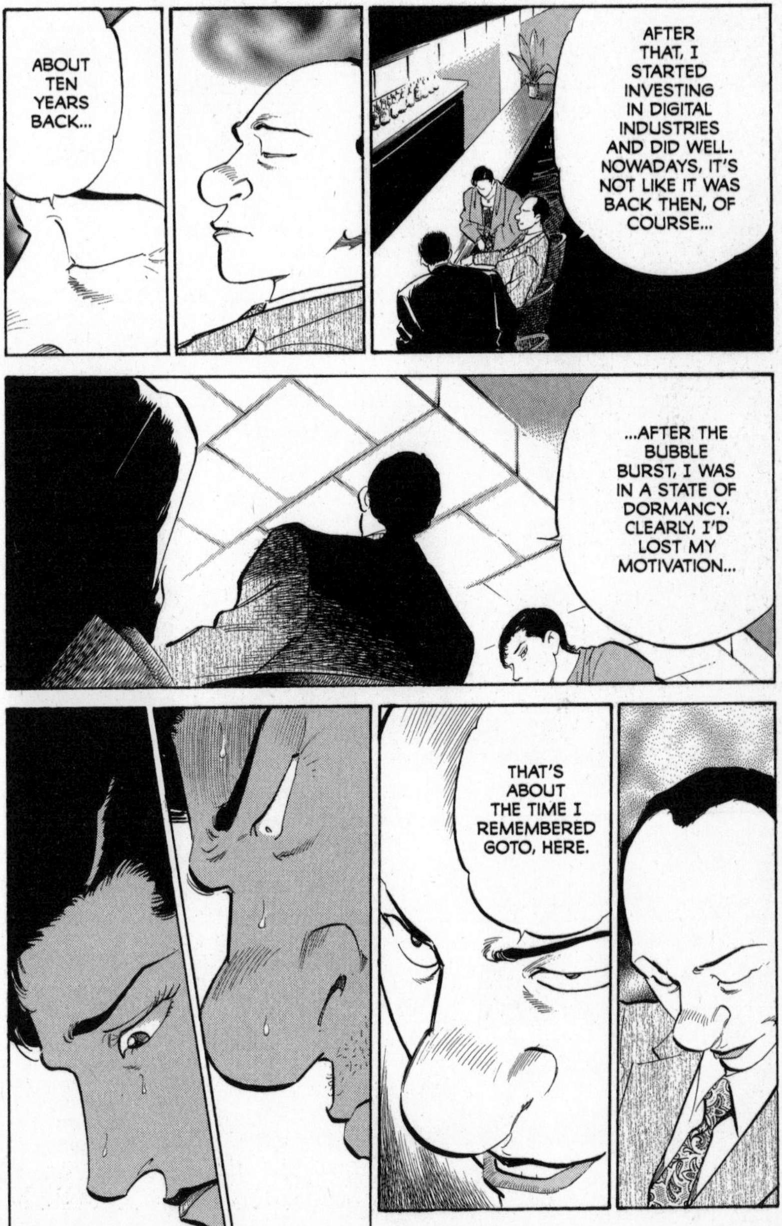
AFTER THAT, I STARTED INVESTING IN DIGITAL INDUSTRIES AND DID WELL. NOWADAYS, IT'S NOT LIKE IT WAS BACK THEN, OF COURSE...
ABOUT TEN YEARS BACK...
...AFTER THE BUBBLE BURST, I WAS IN A STATE OF DORMANCY. CLEARLY, I'D LOST MY MOTIVATION...
THAT'S ABOUT THE TIME I REMEMBERED GOTO, HERE.

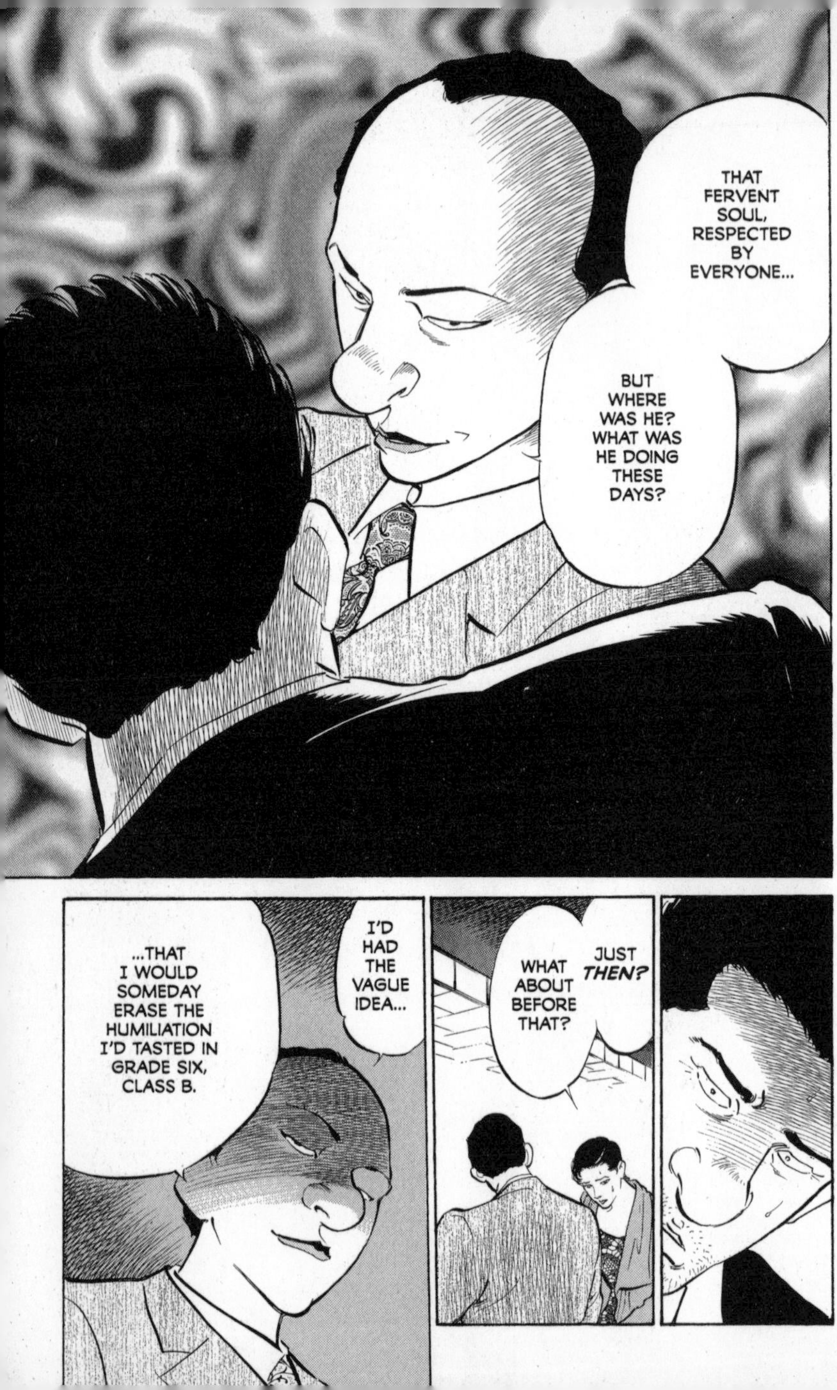
THAT FERVENT SOUL, RESPECTED BY EVERYONE...
BUT WHERE WAS HE? WHAT WAS HE DOING THESE DAYS?
JUST *THEN?*
WHAT ABOUT BEFORE THAT?
I'D HAD THE VAGUE IDEA...
...THAT I WOULD SOMEDAY ERASE THE HUMILIATION I'D TASTED IN GRADE SIX, CLASS B.

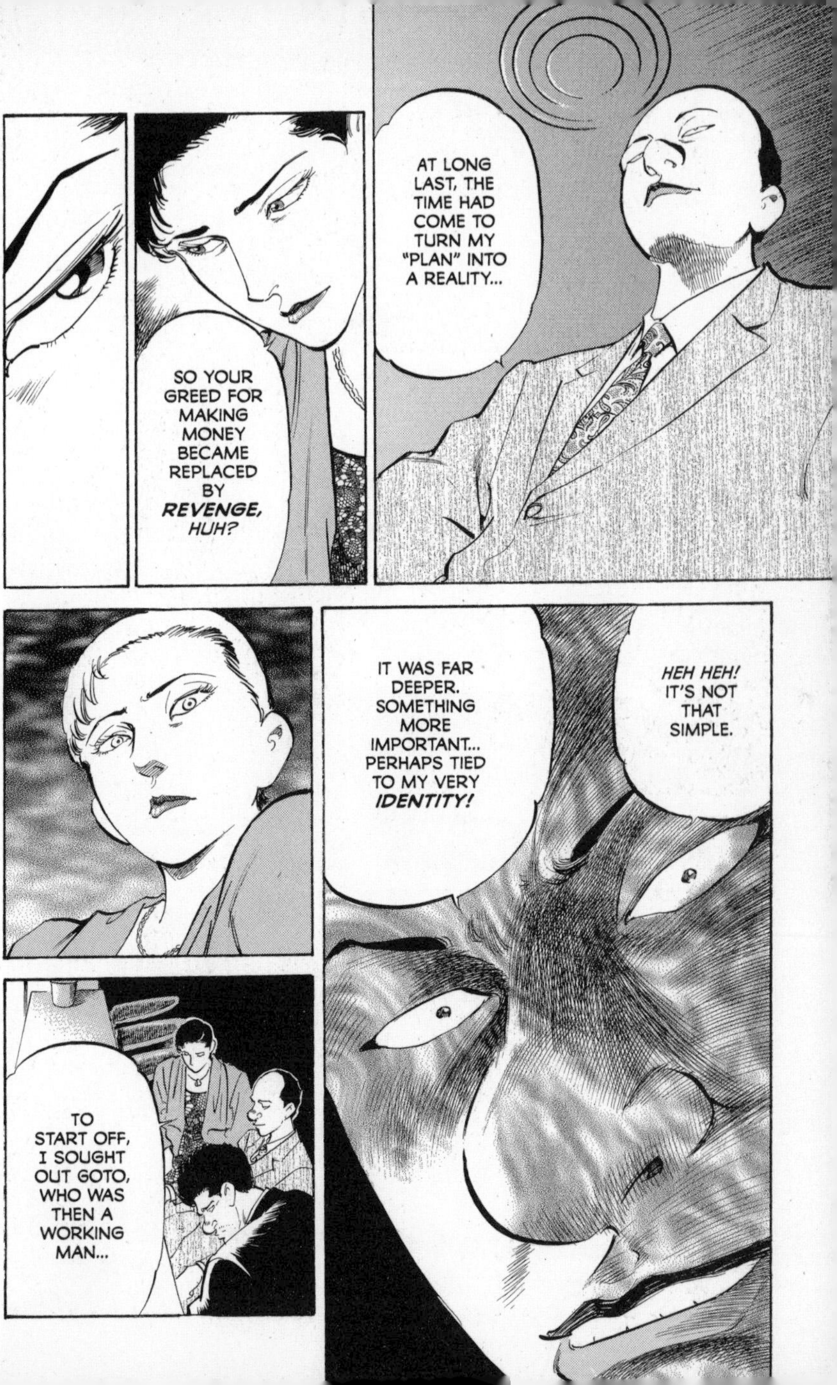
AT LONG LAST, THE TIME HAD COME TO TURN MY "PLAN" INTO A REALITY...
SO YOUR GREED FOR MAKING MONEY BECAME REPLACED BY *REVENGE,* HUH?
HEH HEH! IT'S NOT THAT SIMPLE.
IT WAS FAR DEEPER. SOMETHING MORE IMPORTANT... PERHAPS TIED TO MY VERY *IDENTITY!*
TO START OFF, I SOUGHT OUT GOTO, WHO WAS THEN A WORKING MAN...

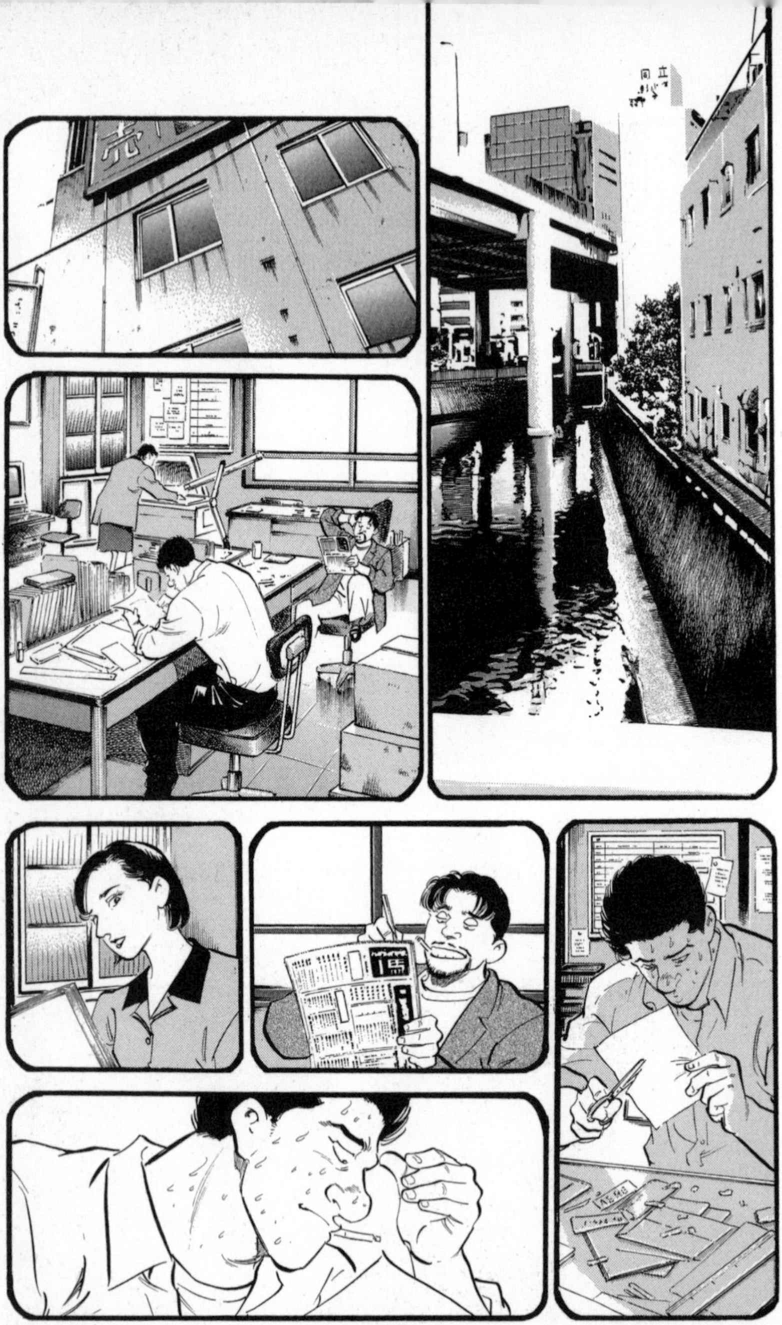

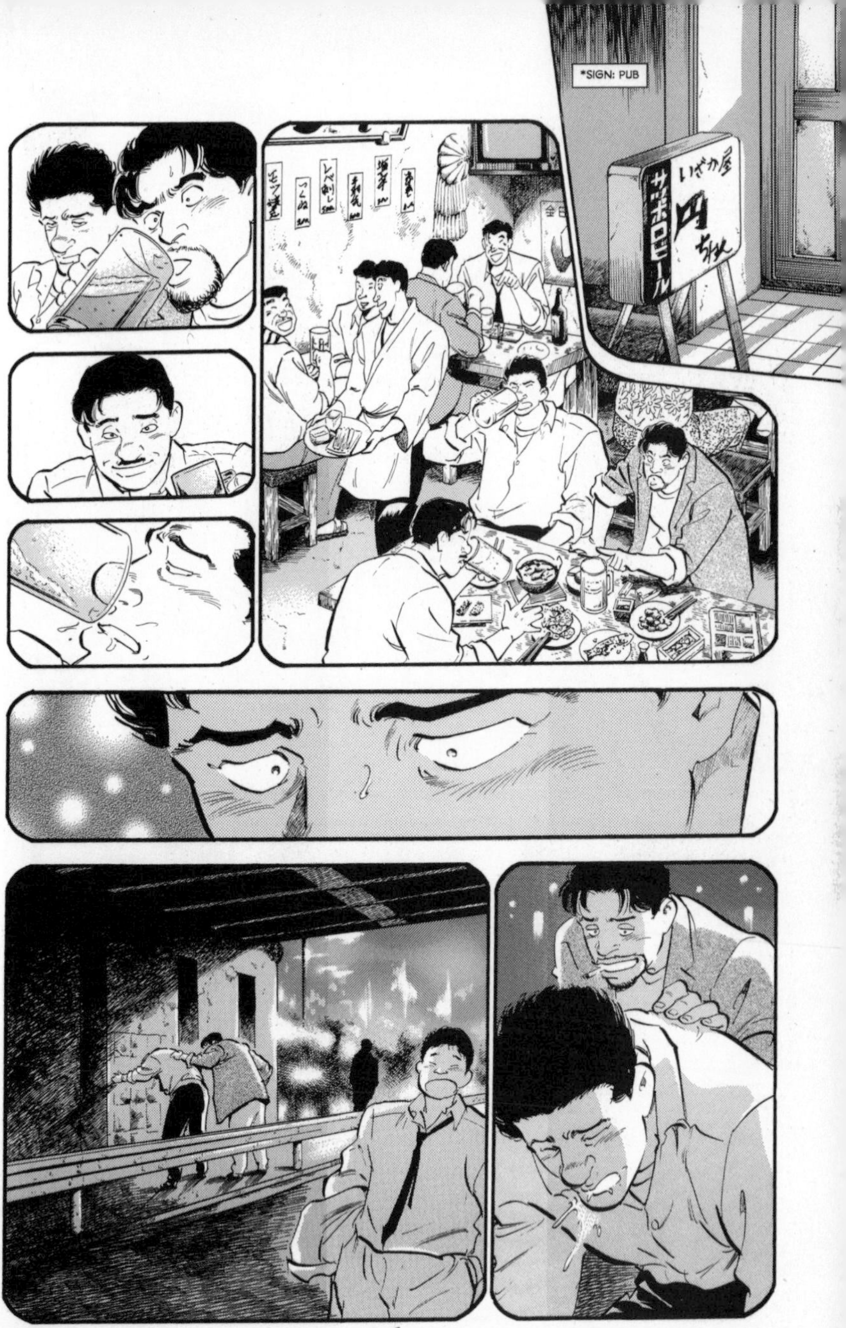
*SIGN: PUB

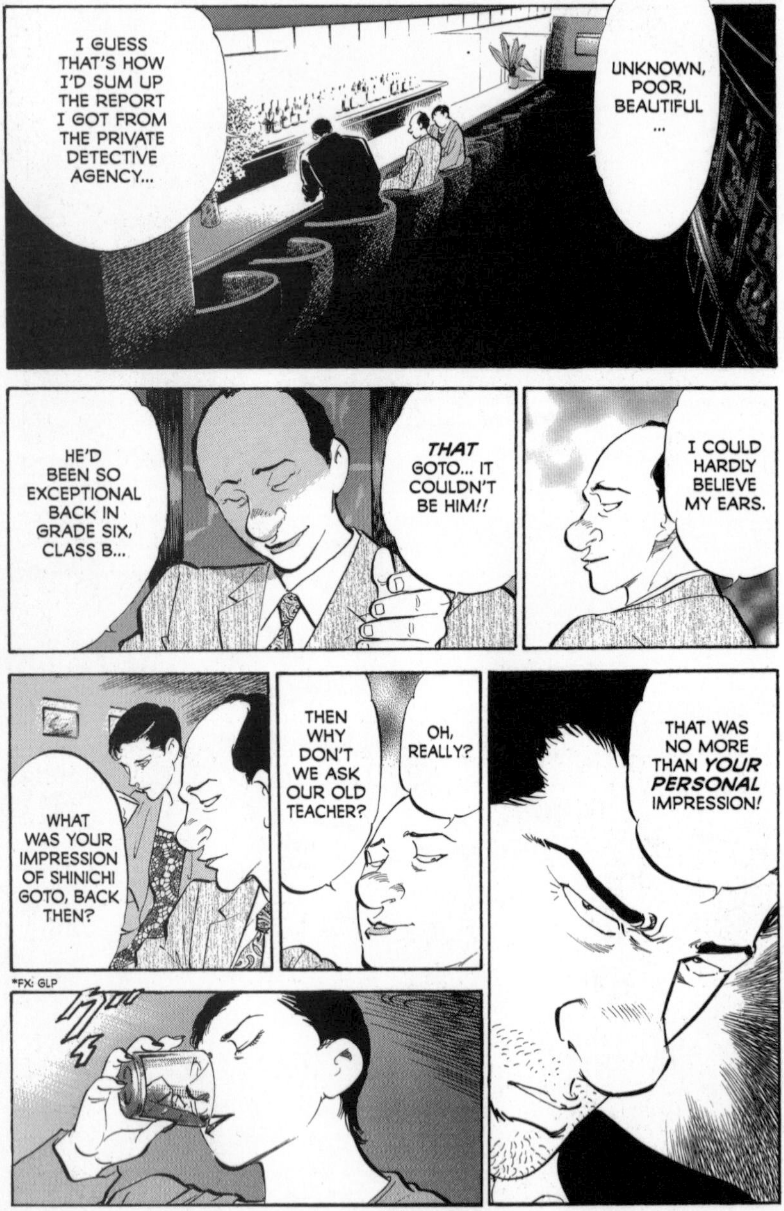
UNKNOWN, POOR, BEAUTIFUL ...
I GUESS THAT'S HOW I'D SUM UP THE REPORT I GOT FROM THE PRIVATE DETECTIVE AGENCY...
I COULD HARDLY BELIEVE MY EARS.
THAT GOTO... IT COULDN'T BE HIM!!
HE'D BEEN SO EXCEPTIONAL BACK IN GRADE SIX, CLASS B...
THAT WAS NO MORE THAN ***YOUR PERSONAL*** IMPRESSION!
OH, REALLY?
THEN WHY DON'T WE ASK OUR OLD TEACHER?
WHAT WAS YOUR IMPRESSION OF SHINICHI GOTO, BACK THEN?
*FX: GLP

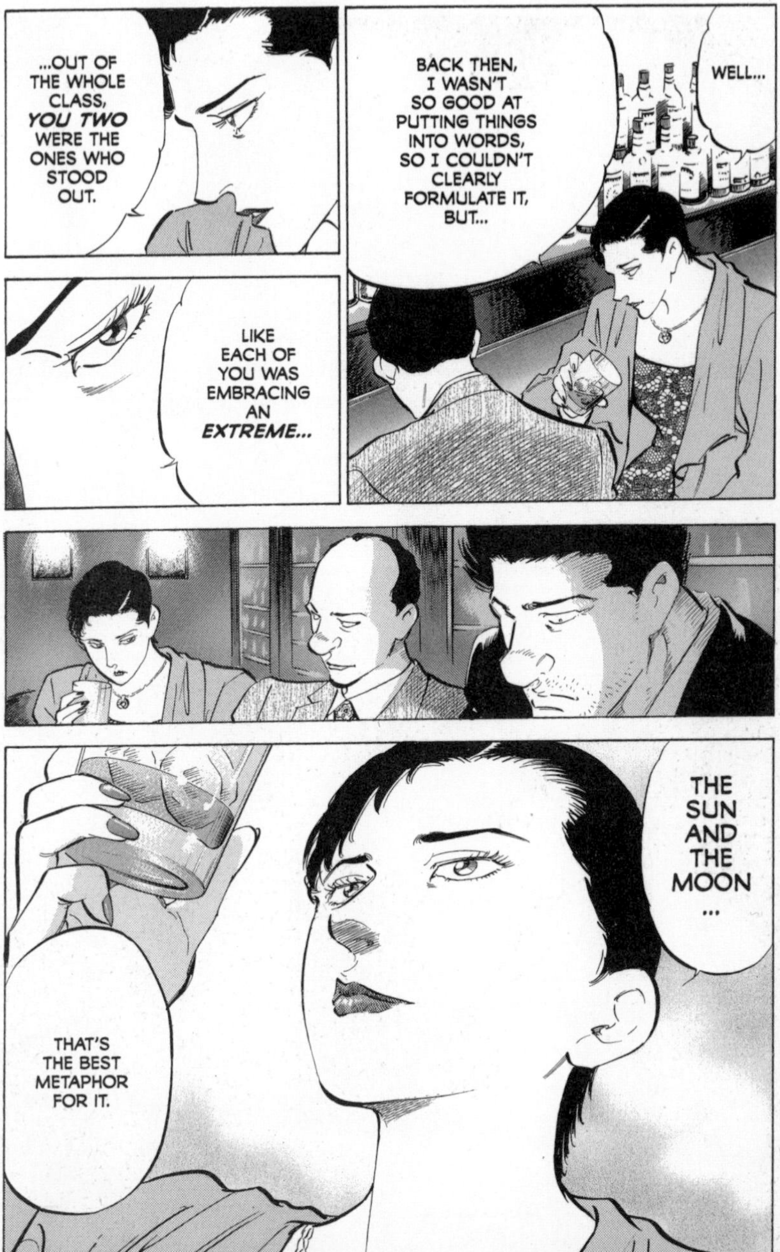
WELL...
BACK THEN, I WASN'T SO GOOD AT PUTTING THINGS INTO WORDS, SO I COULDN'T CLEARLY FORMULATE IT, BUT...
...OUT OF THE WHOLE CLASS, *YOU TWO* WERE THE ONES WHO STOOD OUT.
LIKE EACH OF YOU WAS EMBRACING AN *EXTREME...*
THE SUN AND THE MOON ...
THAT'S THE BEST METAPHOR FOR IT.

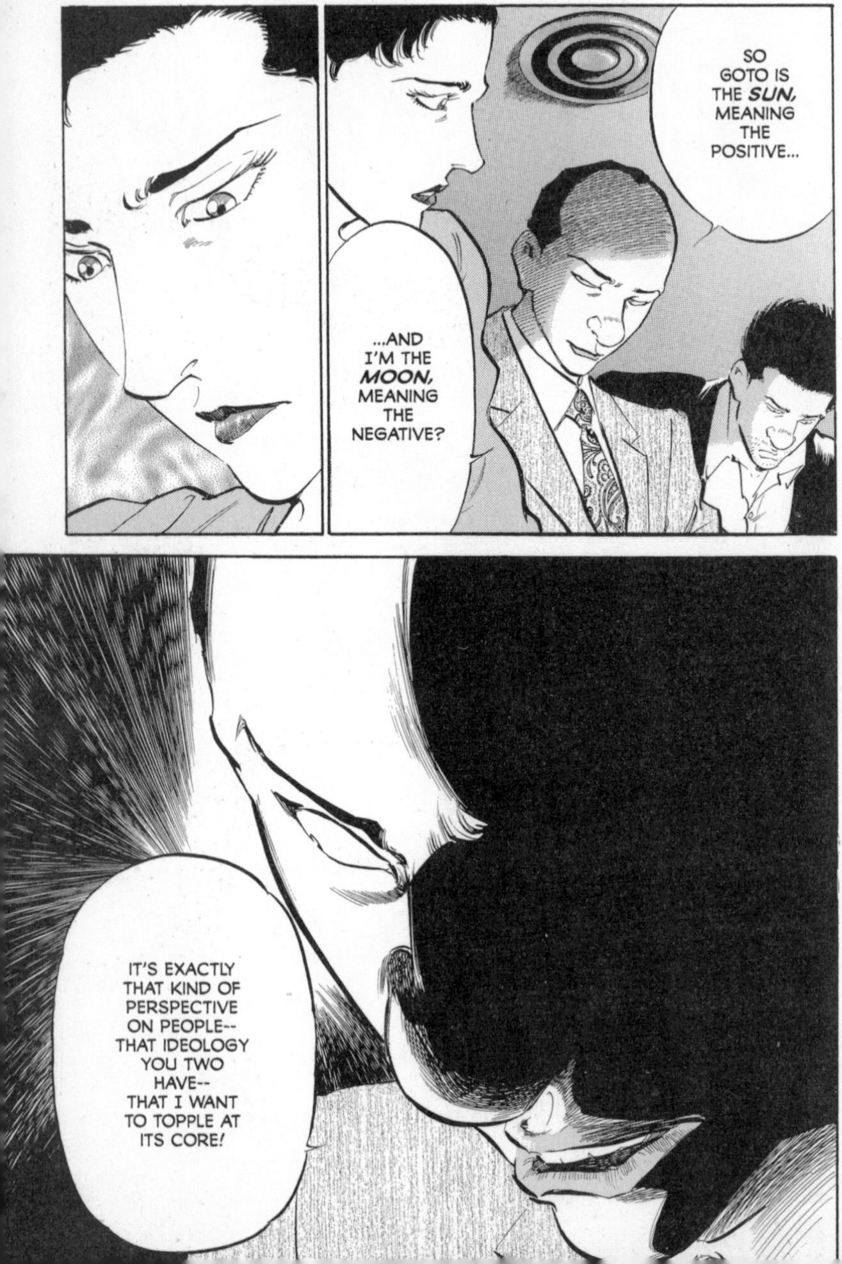
SO GOTO IS THE SUN, MEANING THE POSITIVE...
...AND I'M THE MOON, MEANING THE NEGATIVE?
IT'S EXACTLY THAT KIND OF PERSPECTIVE ON PEOPLE-- THAT IDEOLOGY YOU TWO HAVE-- THAT I WANT TO TOPPLE AT ITS CORE!

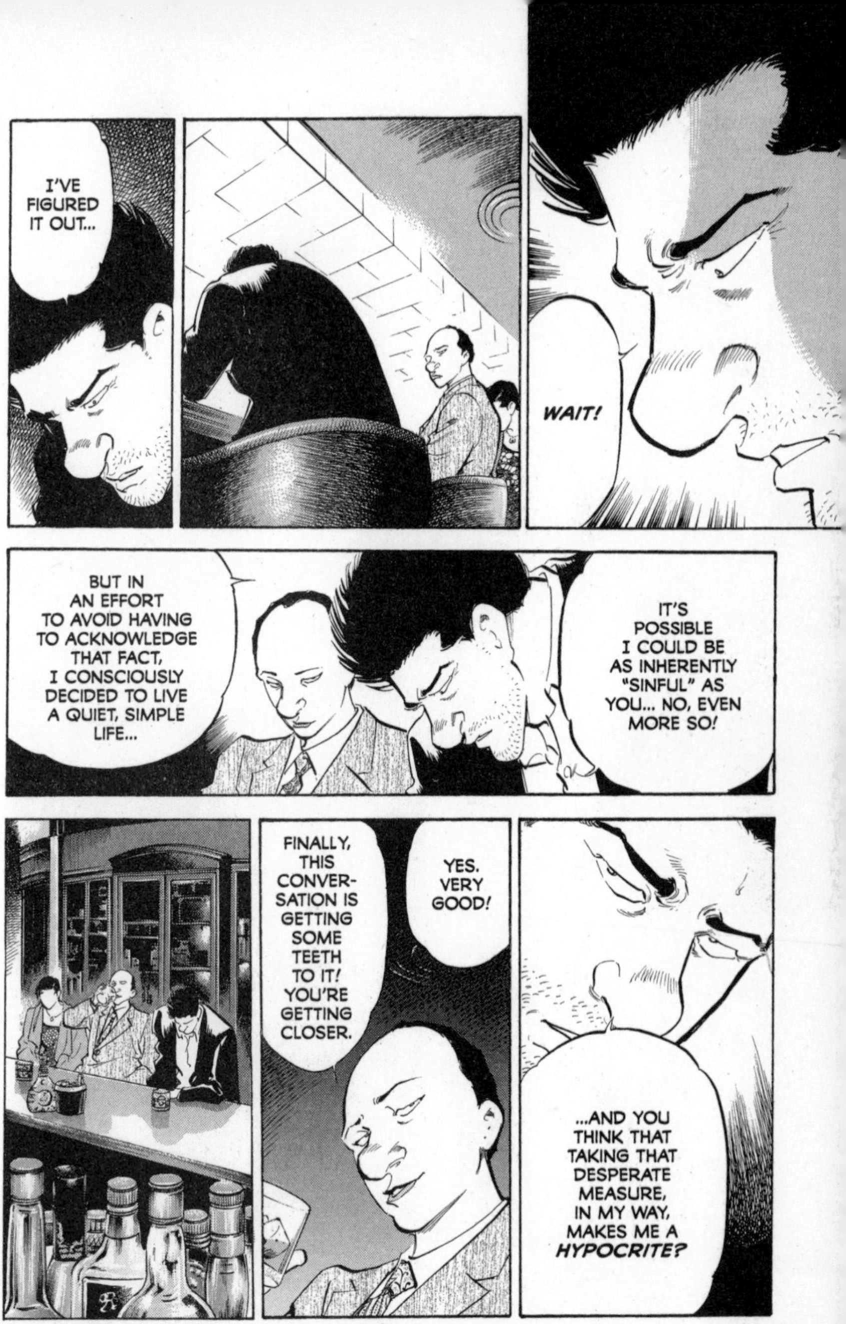
WAIT!
I'VE FIGURED IT OUT...
IT'S POSSIBLE I COULD BE AS INHERENTLY "SINFUL" AS YOU... NO, EVEN MORE SO!
BUT IN AN EFFORT TO AVOID HAVING TO ACKNOWLEDGE THAT FACT, I CONSCIOUSLY DECIDED TO LIVE A QUIET, SIMPLE LIFE...
...AND YOU THINK THAT TAKING THAT DESPERATE MEASURE, IN MY WAY, MAKES ME A ***HYPOCRITE?***
YES. VERY GOOD!
FINALLY, THIS CONVERSATION IS GETTING SOME TEETH TO IT! YOU'RE GETTING CLOSER.

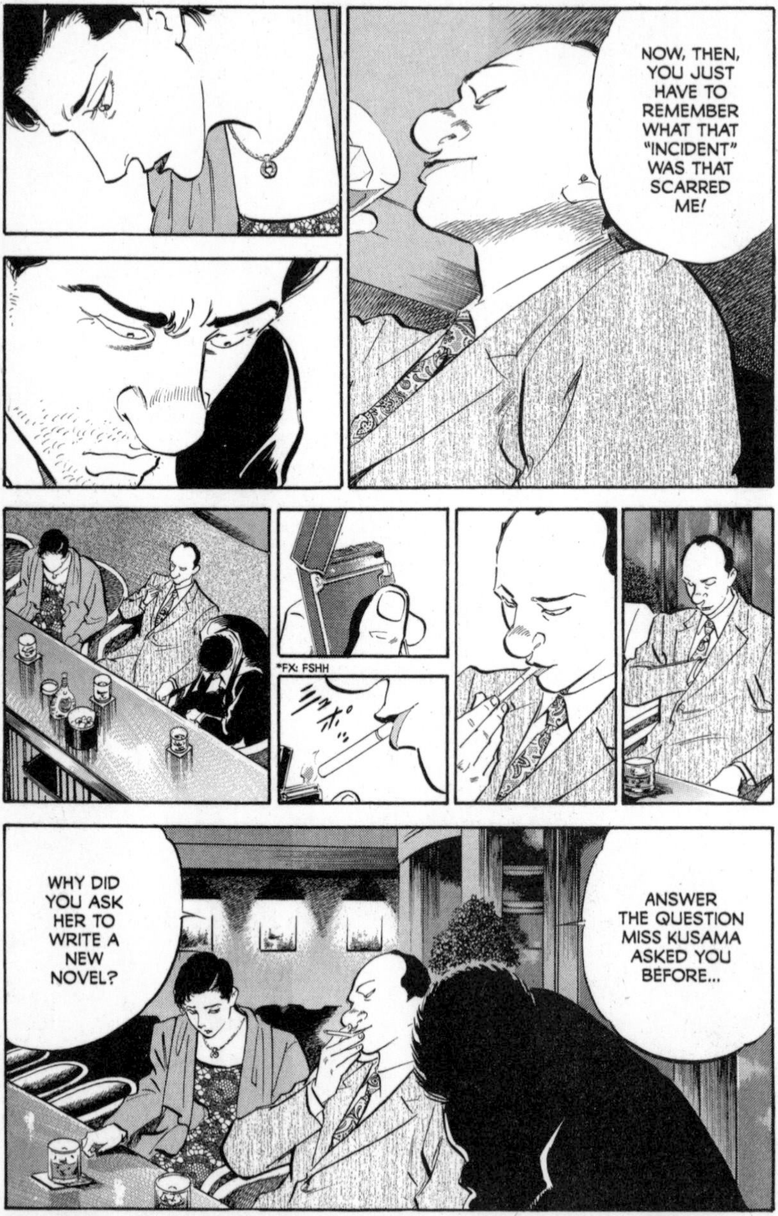
NOW, THEN, YOU JUST HAVE TO REMEMBER WHAT THAT "INCIDENT" WAS THAT SCARRED ME!
*FX: FSHH
ANSWER THE QUESTION MISS KUSAMA ASKED YOU BEFORE...
WHY DID YOU ASK HER TO WRITE A NEW NOVEL?

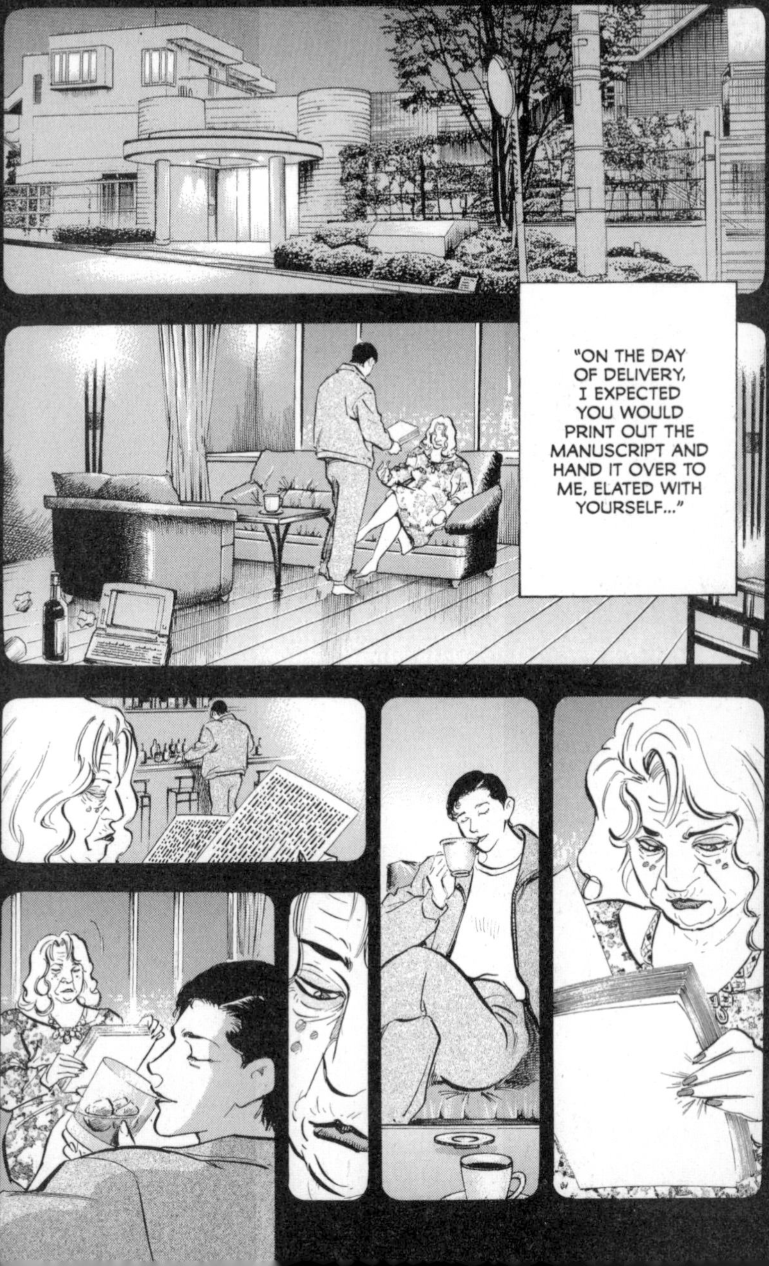
"ON THE DAY OF DELIVERY, I EXPECTED YOU WOULD PRINT OUT THE MANUSCRIPT AND HAND IT OVER TO ME, ELATED WITH YOURSELF..."

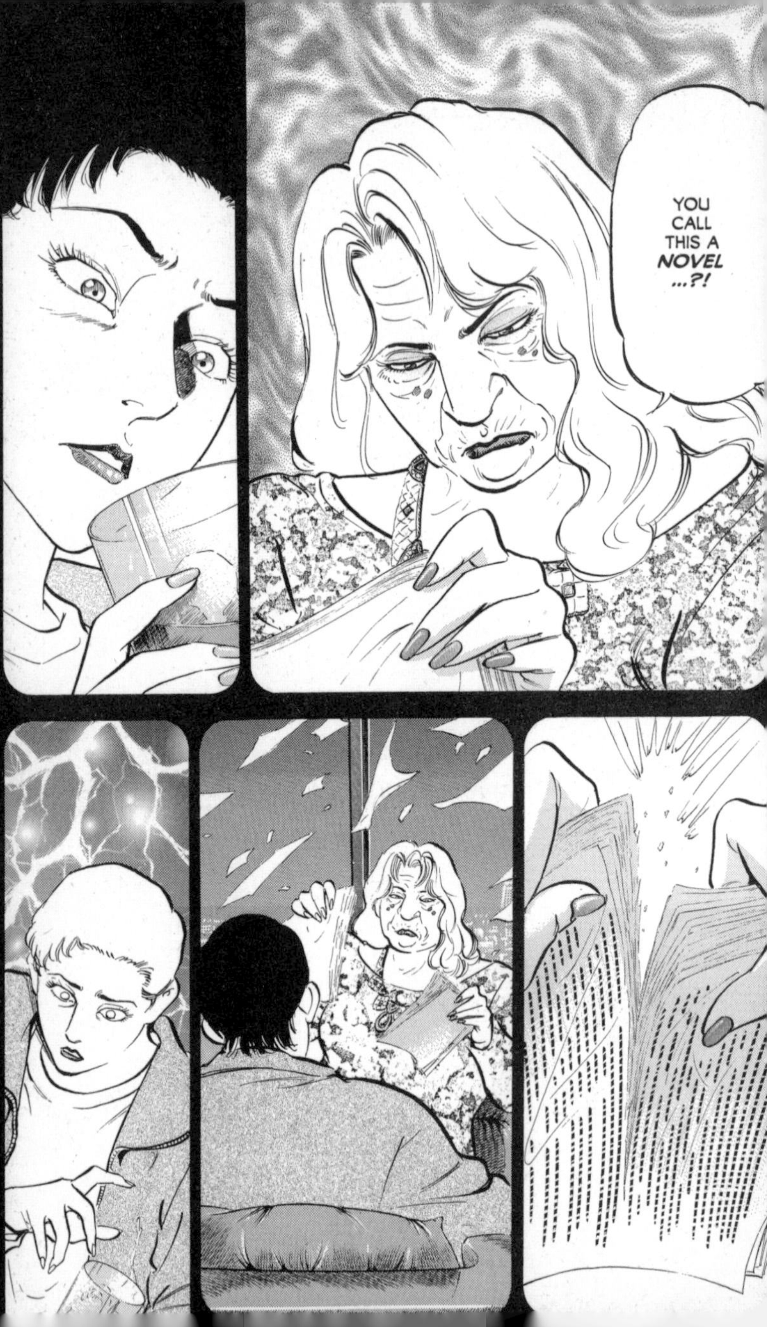
YOU CALL THIS A *NOVEL* ...?!

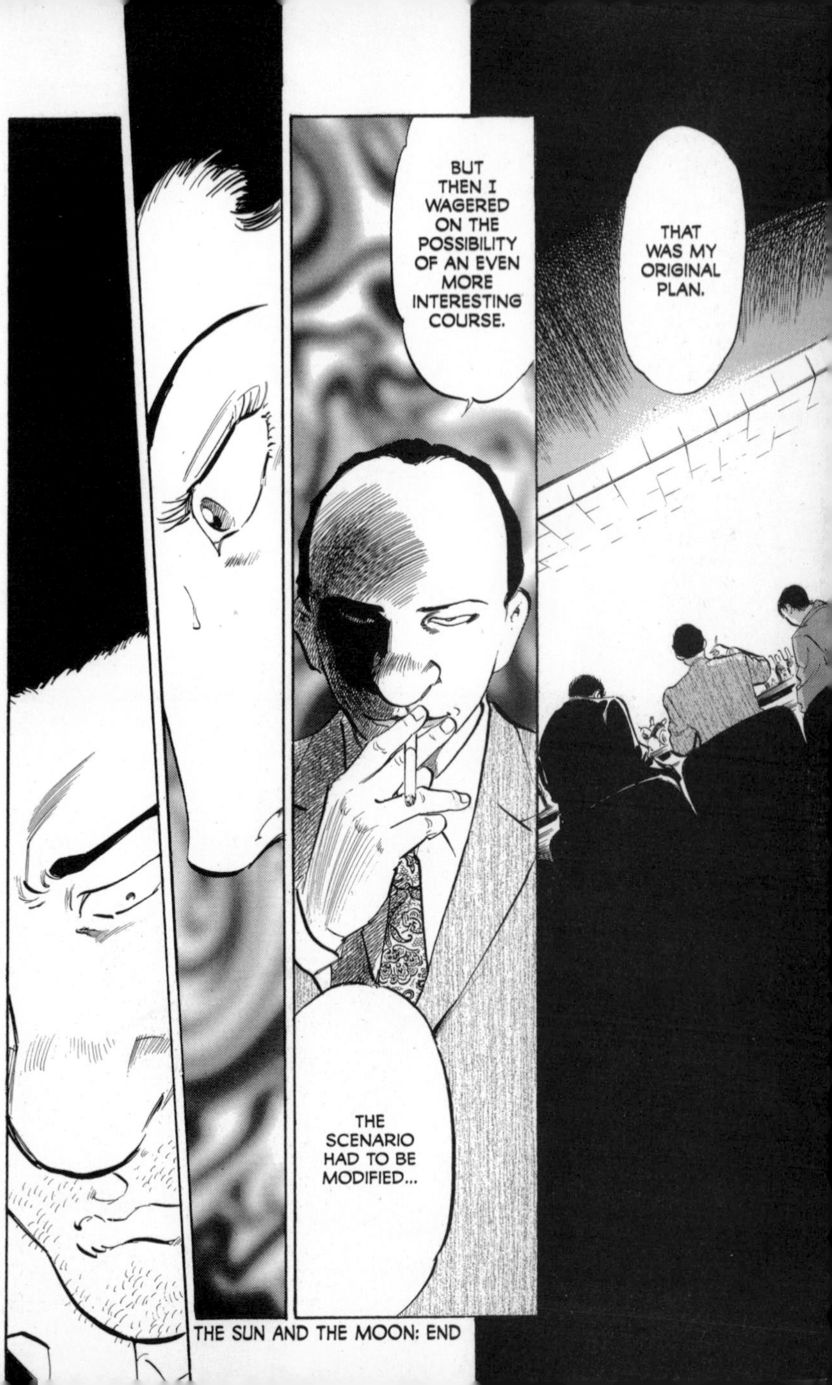
THAT WAS MY ORIGINAL PLAN.
BUT THEN I WAGERED ON THE POSSIBILITY OF AN EVEN MORE INTERESTING COURSE.
THE SCENARIO HAD TO BE MODIFIED...

THE SUN AND THE MOON: END

Chapter 54

Floating in the Canal

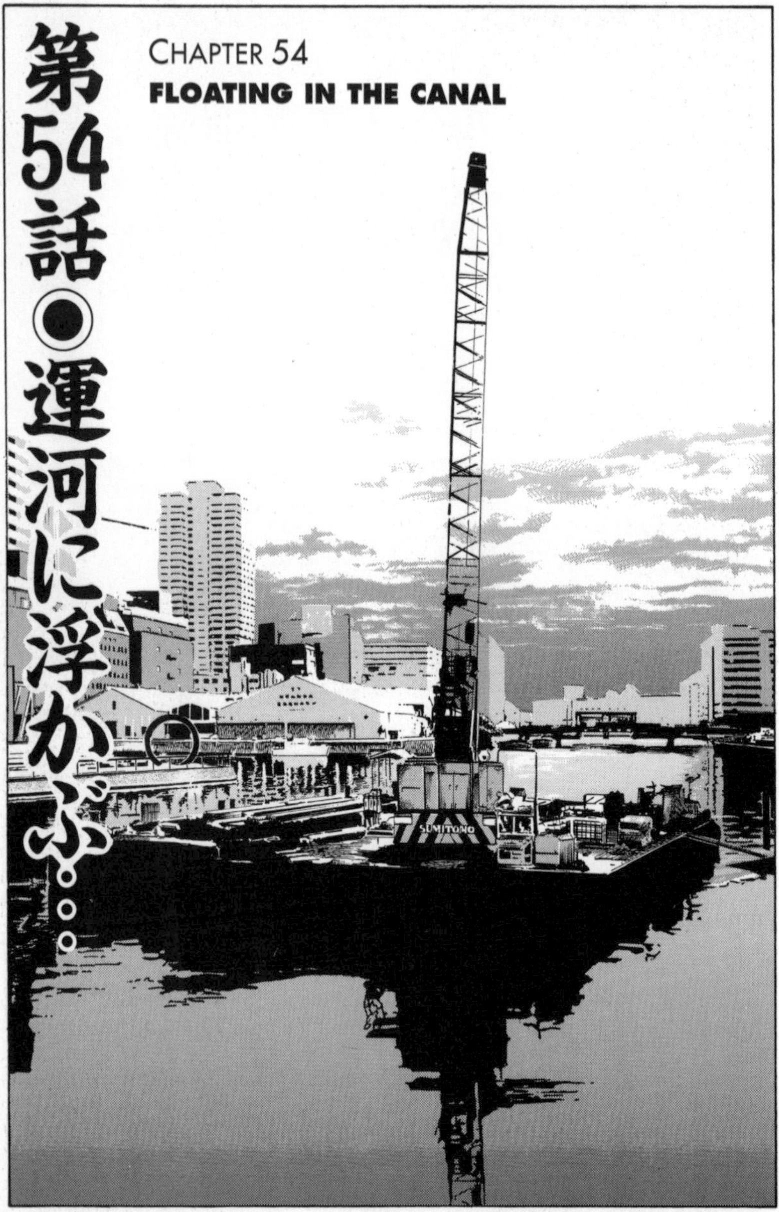
第54話◉運河に浮かぶ。。。
SUMITOMO

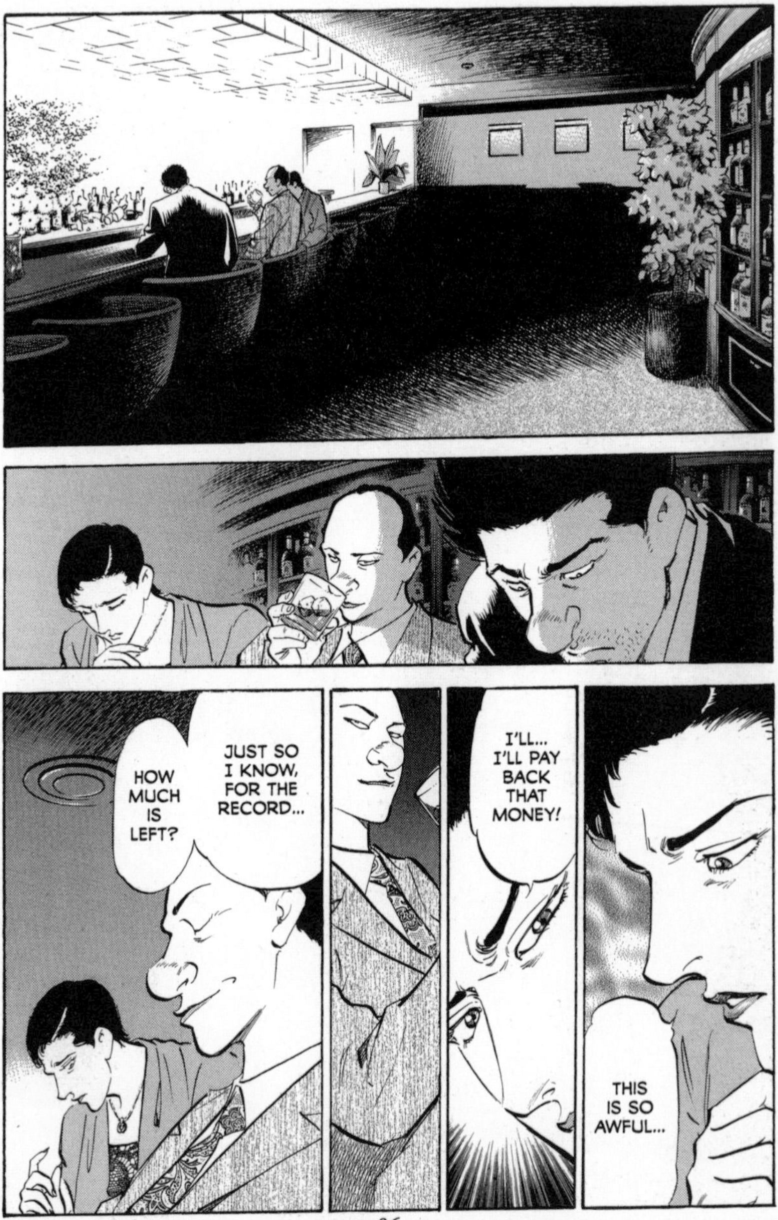
THIS IS SO AWFUL...
I'LL... I'LL PAY BACK THAT MONEY!
JUST SO I KNOW, FOR THE RECORD...
HOW MUCH IS LEFT?

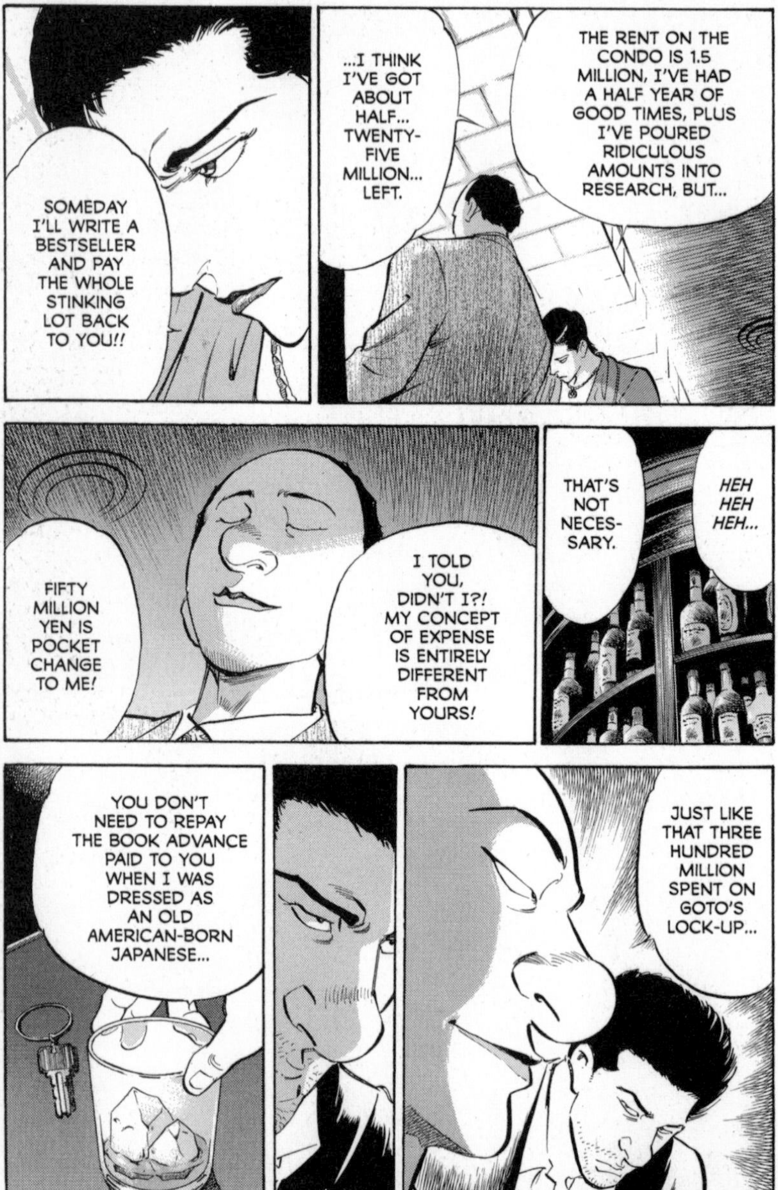
THE RENT ON THE CONDO IS 1.5 MILLION, I'VE HAD A HALF YEAR OF GOOD TIMES, PLUS I'VE POURED RIDICULOUS AMOUNTS INTO RESEARCH, BUT...
...I THINK I'VE GOT ABOUT HALF... TWENTY-FIVE MILLION... LEFT.
SOMEDAY I'LL WRITE A BESTSELLER AND PAY THE WHOLE STINKING LOT BACK TO YOU!!
HEH HEH HEH...
THAT'S NOT NECES-SARY.
I TOLD YOU, DIDN'T I?! MY CONCEPT OF EXPENSE IS ENTIRELY DIFFERENT FROM YOURS!
FIFTY MILLION YEN IS POCKET CHANGE TO ME!
JUST LIKE THAT THREE HUNDRED MILLION SPENT ON GOTO'S LOCK-UP...
YOU DON'T NEED TO REPAY THE BOOK ADVANCE PAID TO YOU WHEN I WAS DRESSED AS AN OLD AMERICAN-BORN JAPANESE...

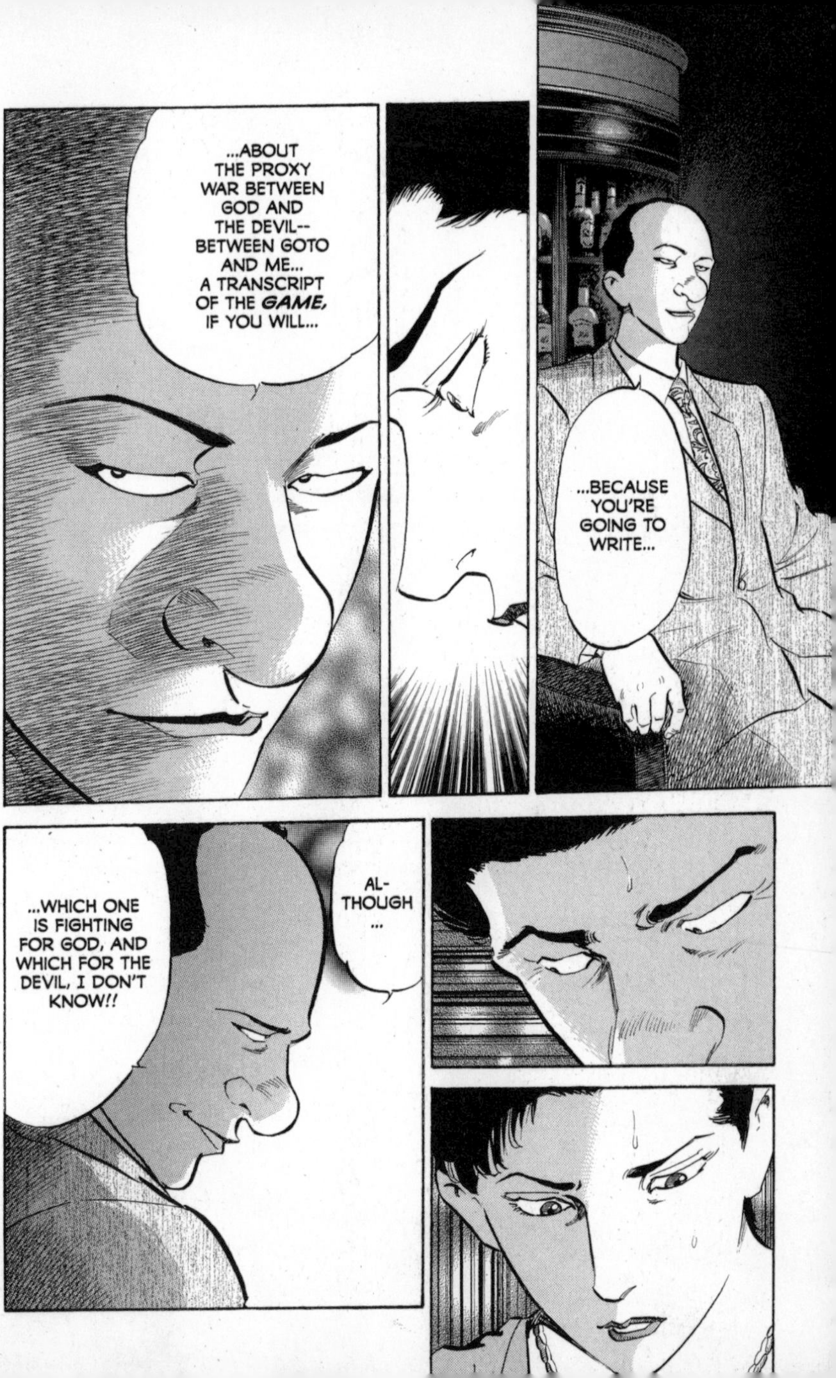
...BECAUSE YOU'RE GOING TO WRITE...
...ABOUT THE PROXY WAR BETWEEN GOD AND THE DEVIL-- BETWEEN GOTO AND ME... A TRANSCRIPT OF THE *GAME,* IF YOU WILL...
AL- THOUGH ...
...WHICH ONE IS FIGHTING FOR GOD, AND WHICH FOR THE DEVIL, I DON'T KNOW!!

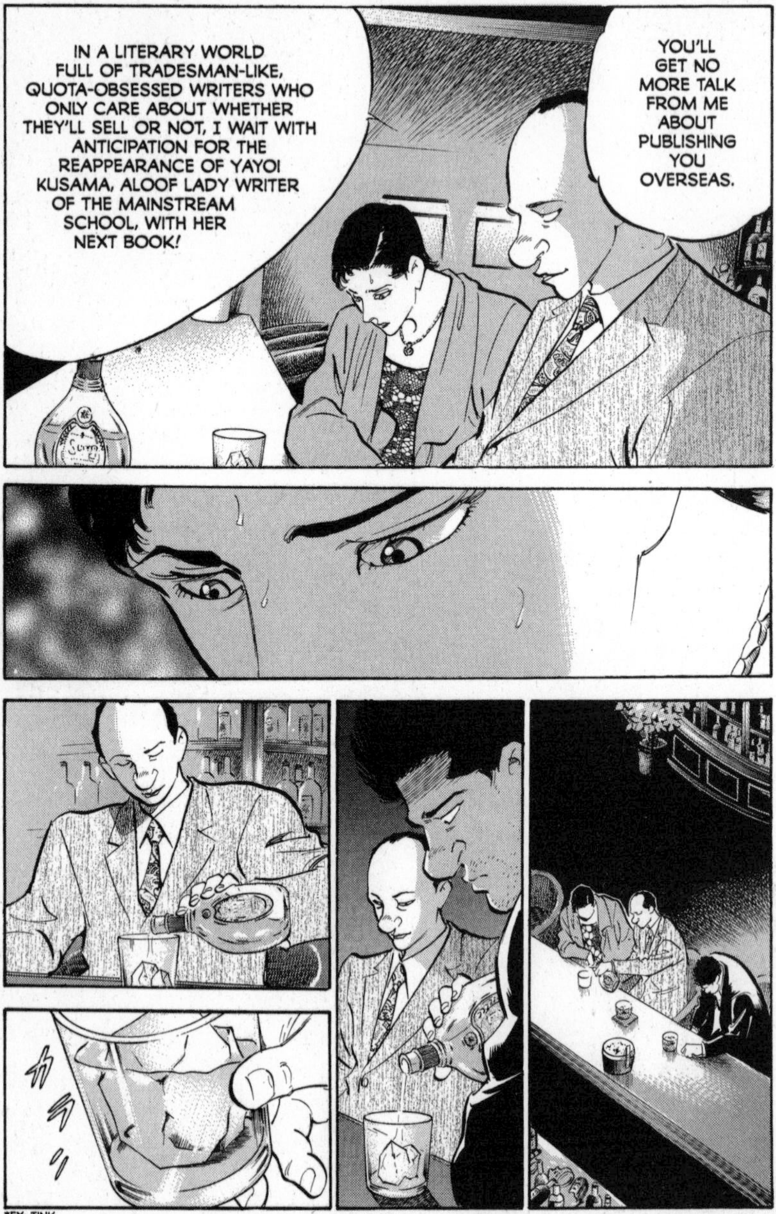
YOU'LL GET NO MORE TALK FROM ME ABOUT PUBLISHING YOU OVERSEAS.
IN A LITERARY WORLD FULL OF TRADESMAN-LIKE, QUOTA-OBSESSED WRITERS WHO ONLY CARE ABOUT WHETHER THEY'LL SELL OR NOT, I WAIT WITH ANTICIPATION FOR THE REAPPEARANCE OF YAYOI KUSAMA, ALOOF LADY WRITER OF THE MAINSTREAM SCHOOL, WITH HER NEXT BOOK!

*FX: TINK

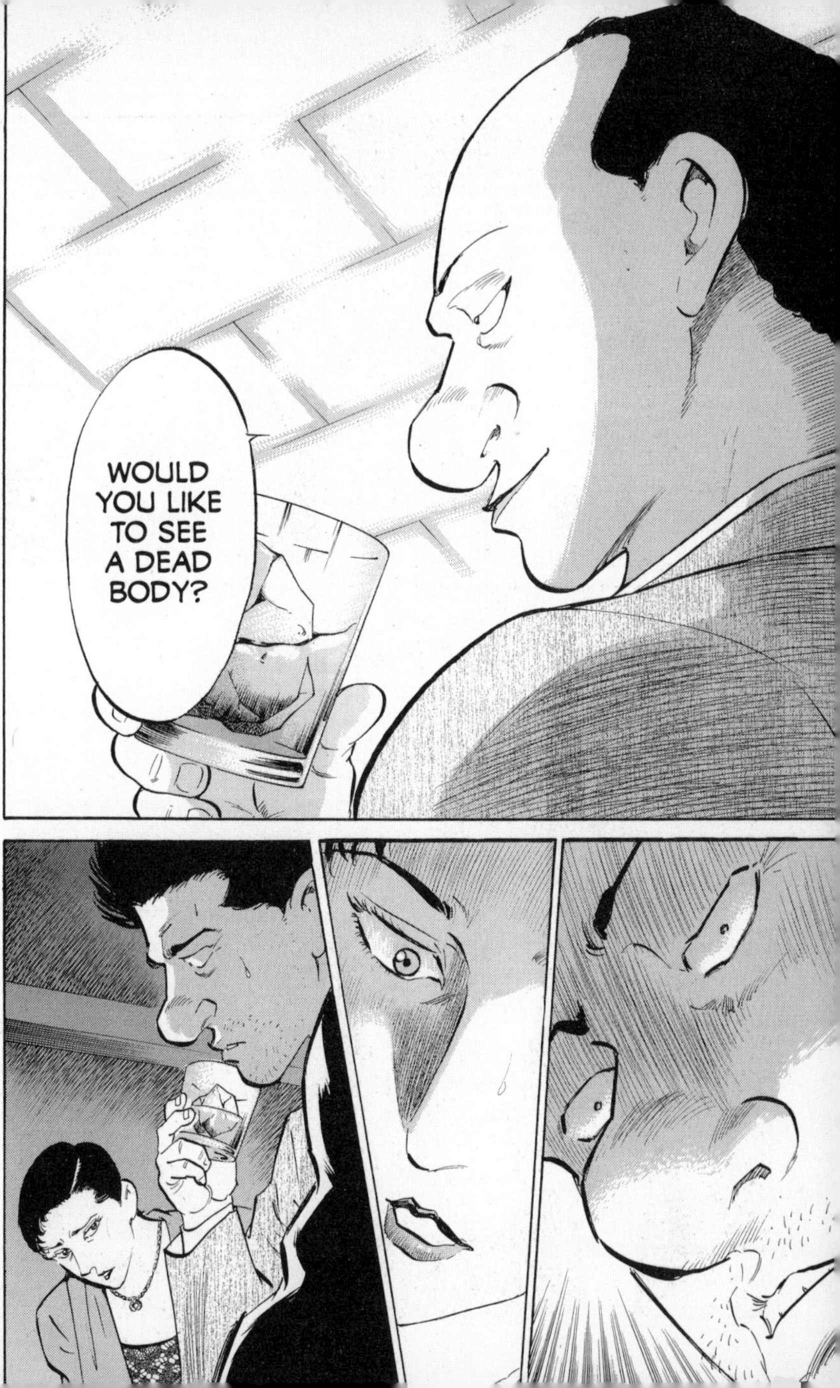
WOULD YOU LIKE TO SEE A DEAD BODY?

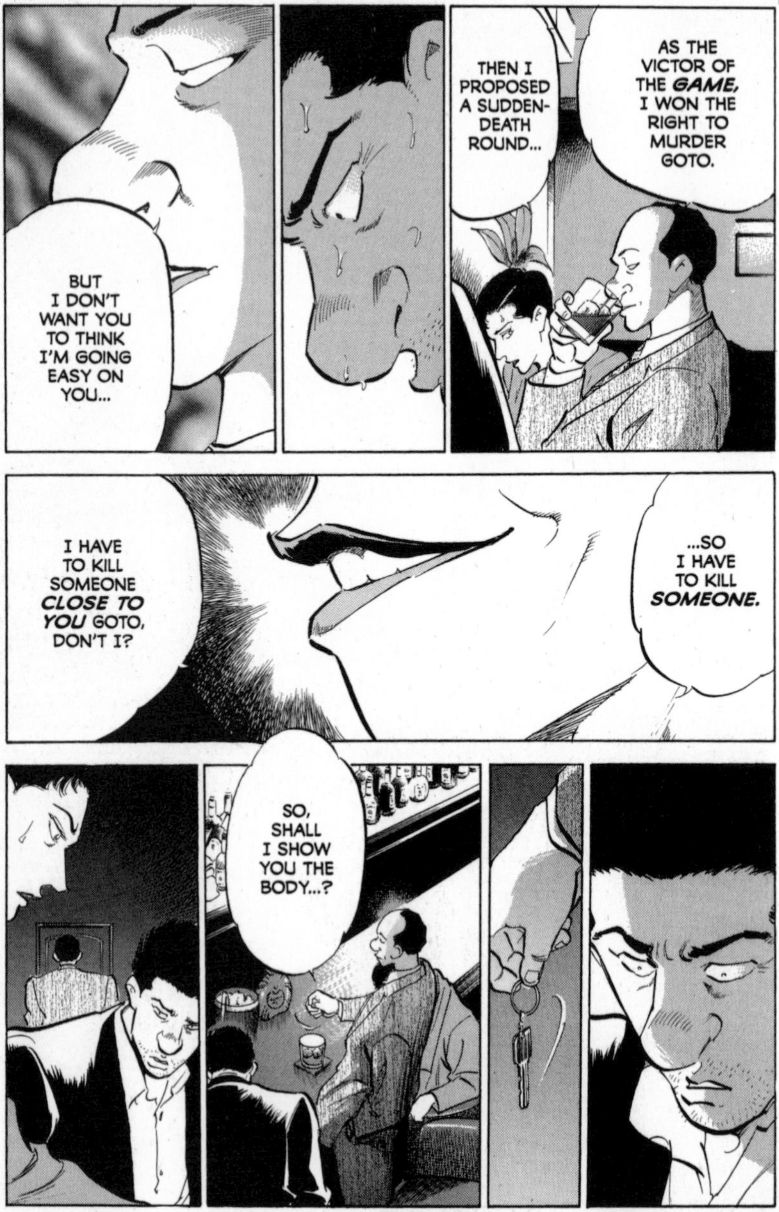
AS THE VICTOR OF THE *GAME,* I WON THE RIGHT TO MURDER GOTO.
THEN I PROPOSED A SUDDEN-DEATH ROUND...
BUT I DON'T WANT YOU TO THINK I'M GOING EASY ON YOU...
...SO I HAVE TO KILL *SOMEONE.*
I HAVE TO KILL SOMEONE *CLOSE TO YOU* GOTO, DON'T I?
SO, SHALL I SHOW YOU THE BODY...?

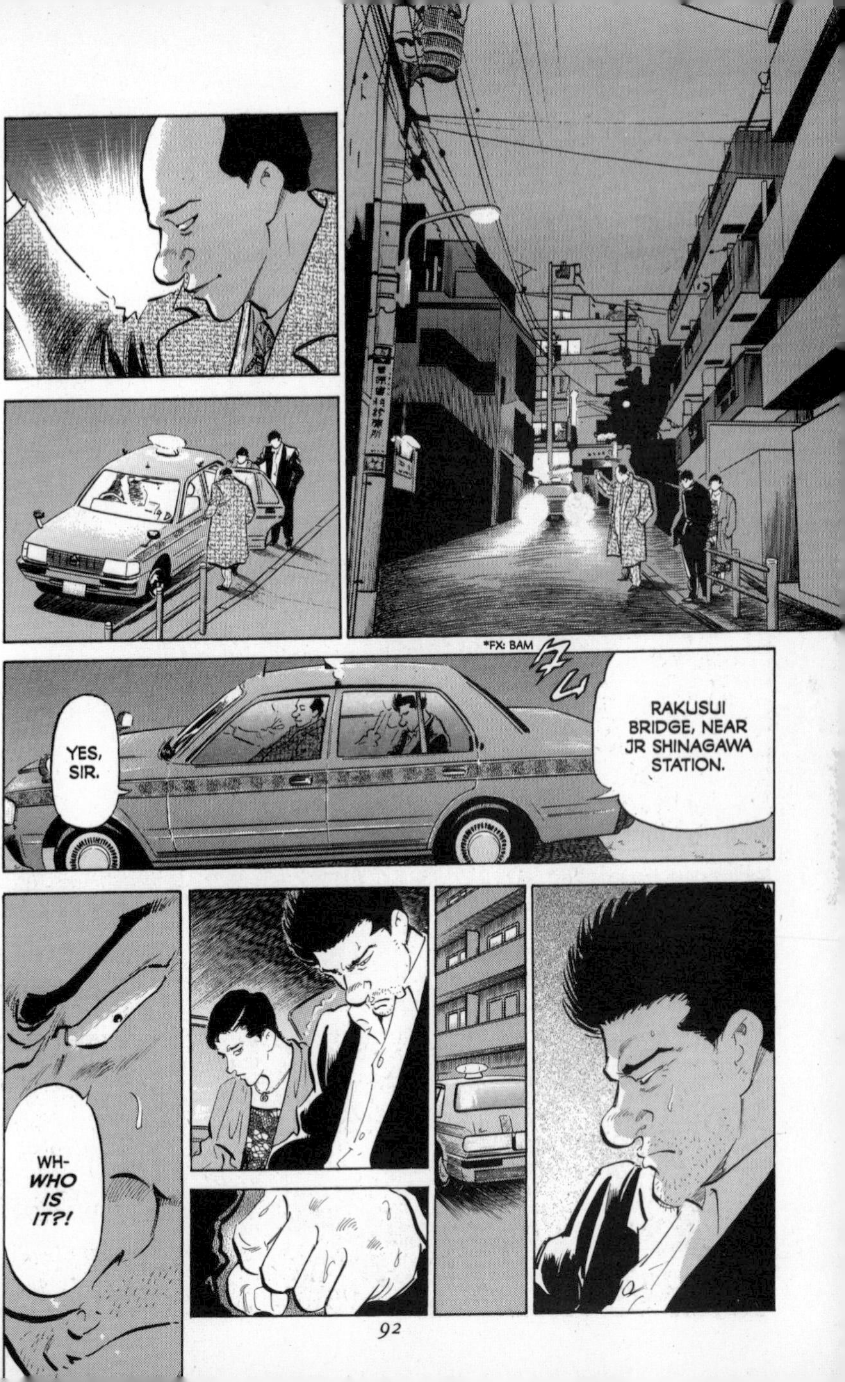
*FX: BAM
RAKUSUI BRIDGE, NEAR JR SHINAGAWA STATION.
YES, SIR.
WH- *WHO IS IT?!*

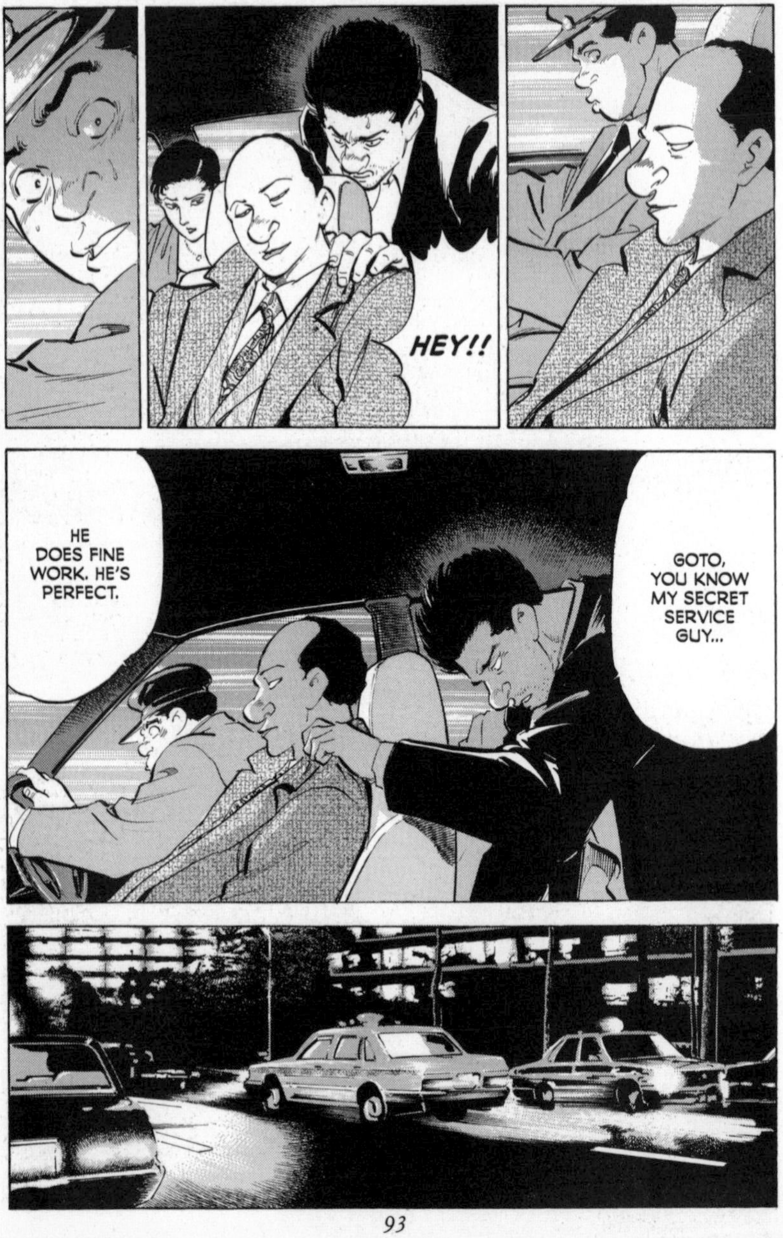
HEY!!
GOTO, YOU KNOW MY SECRET SERVICE GUY...
HE DOES FINE WORK. HE'S PERFECT.

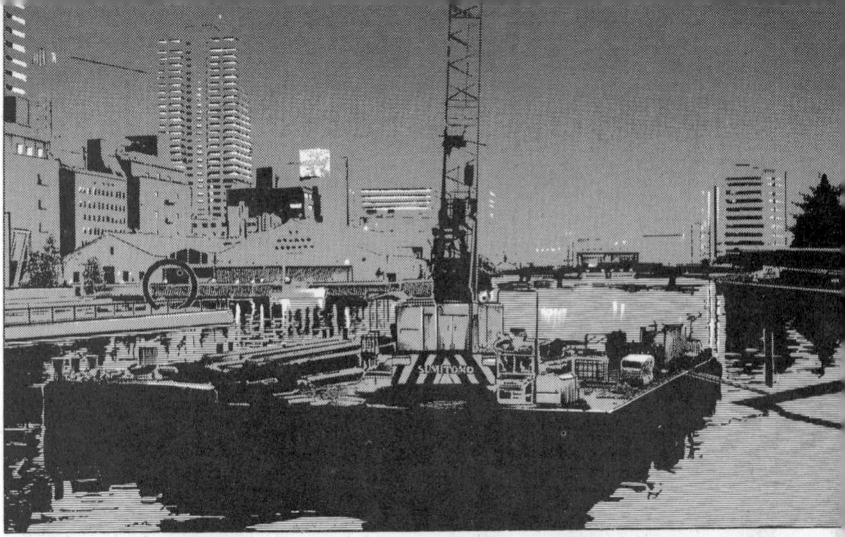
SUMITOMO
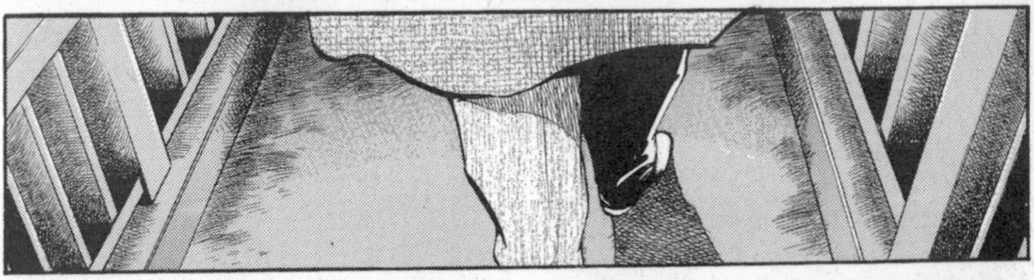
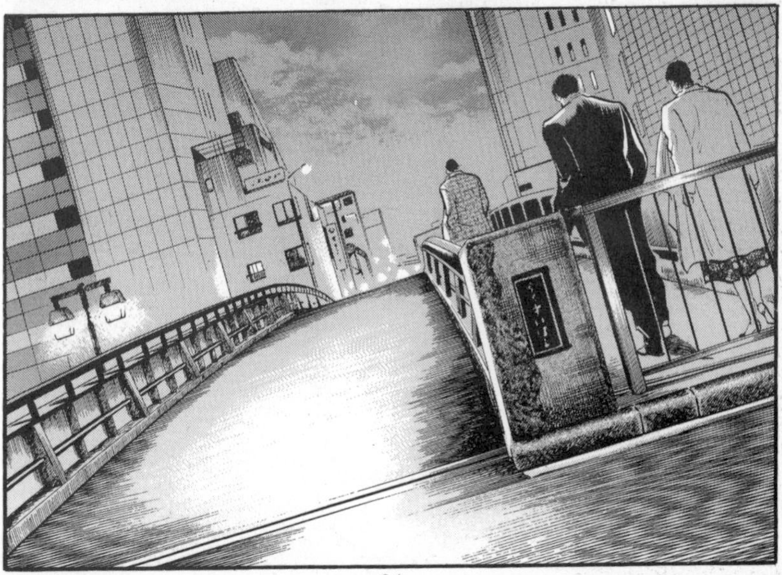

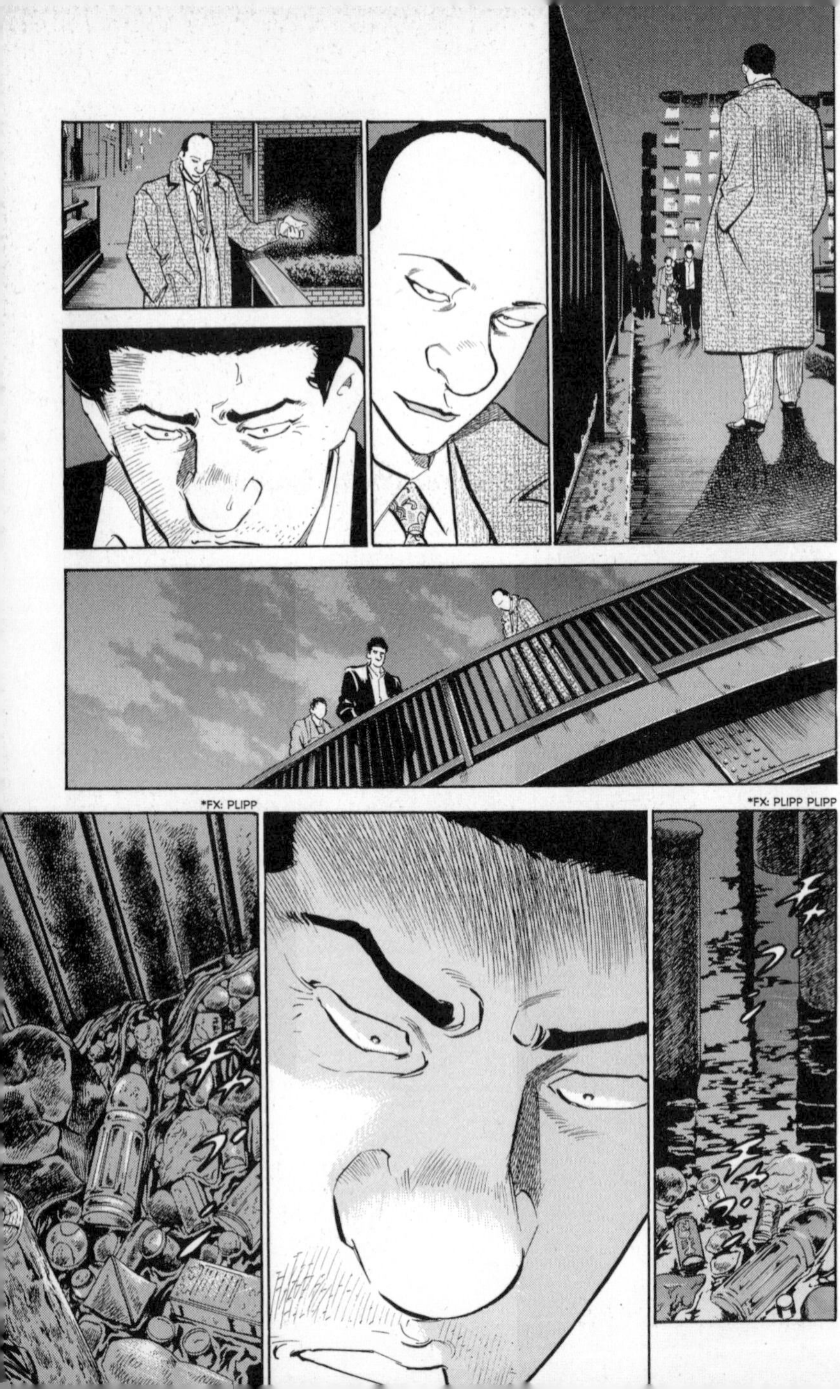
*FX: PLIPP PLIPP
*FX: PLIPP

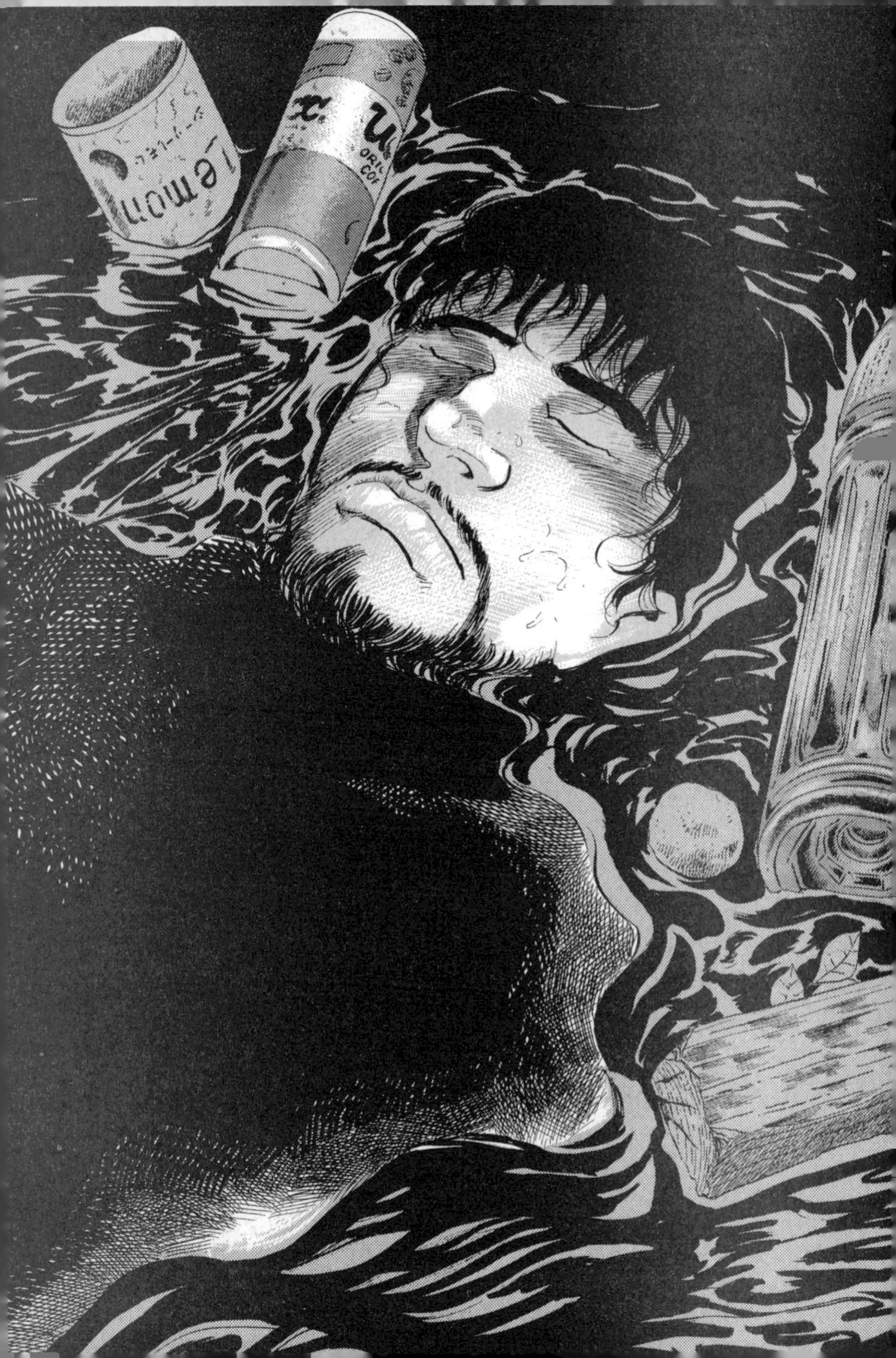
lemon

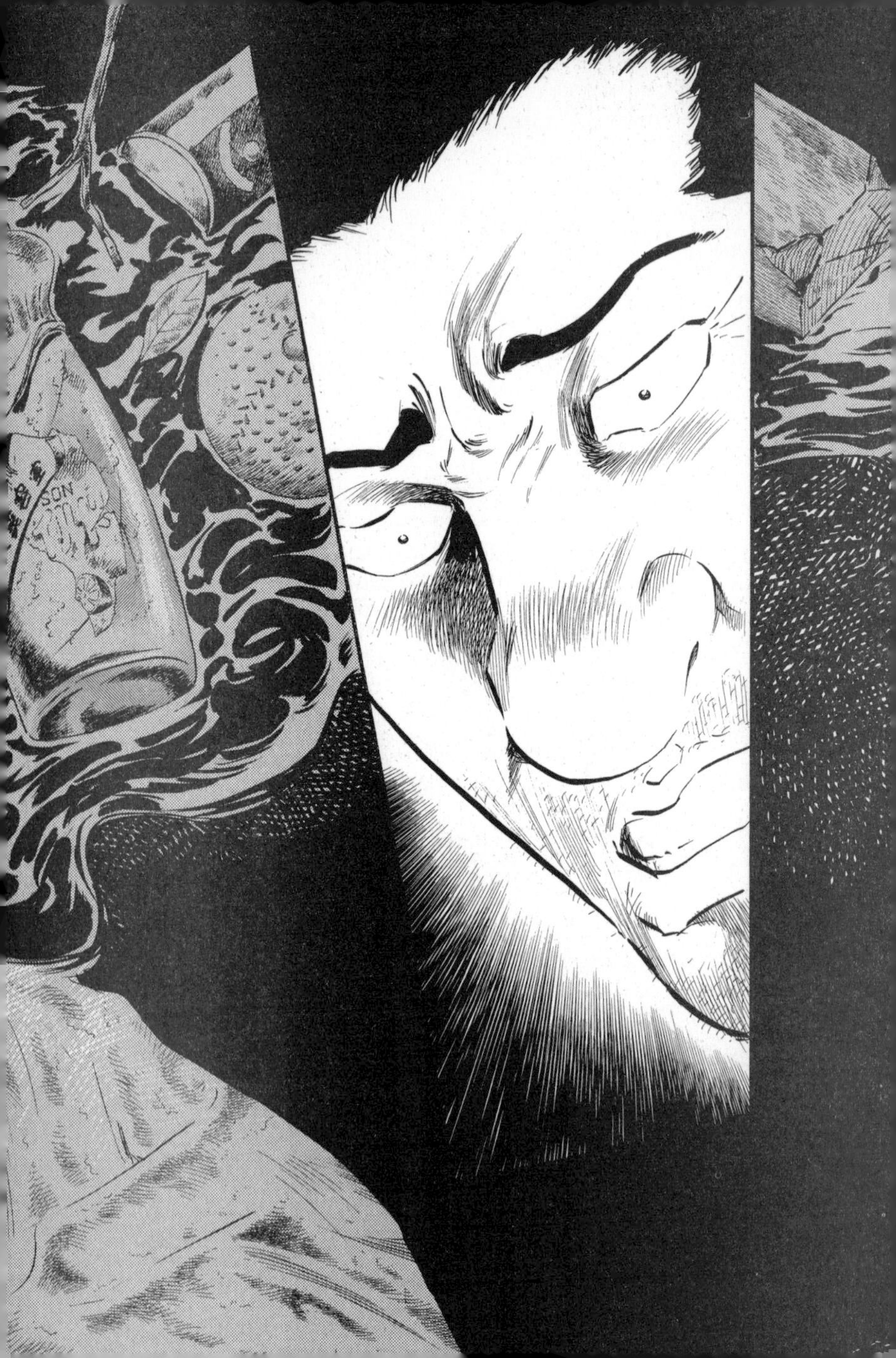

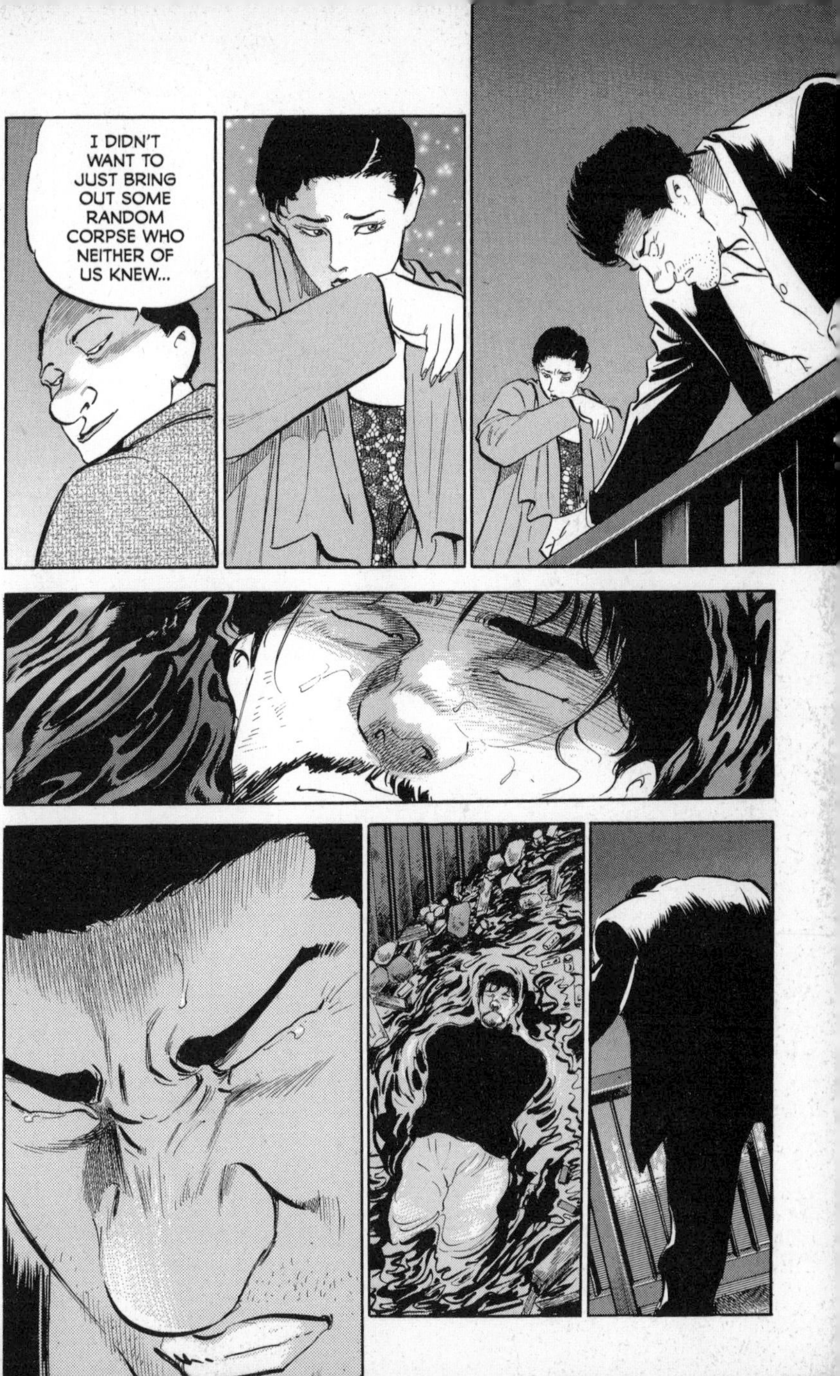
I DIDN'T WANT TO JUST BRING OUT SOME RANDOM CORPSE WHO NEITHER OF US KNEW...

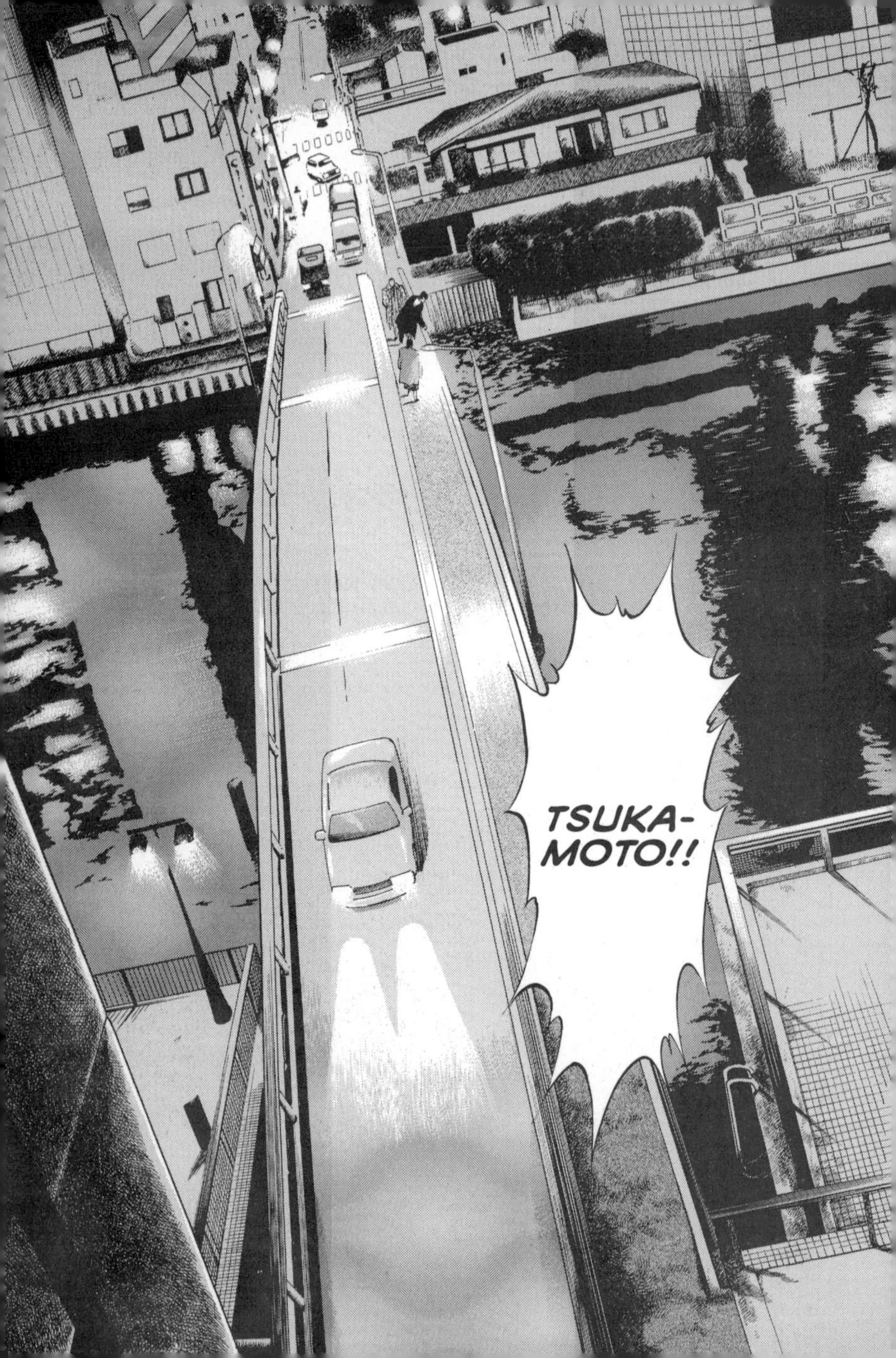
TSUKA-
MOTO!!

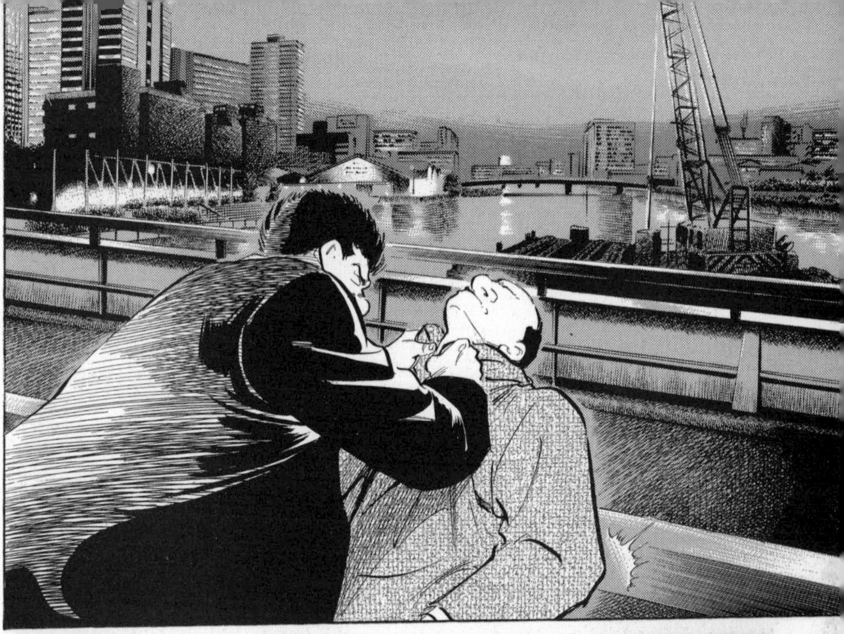
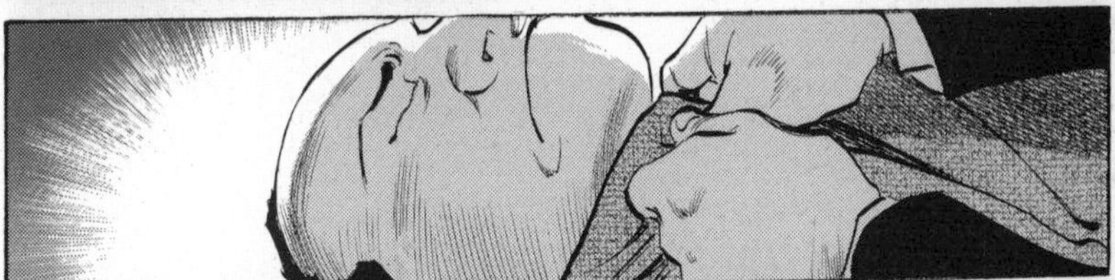
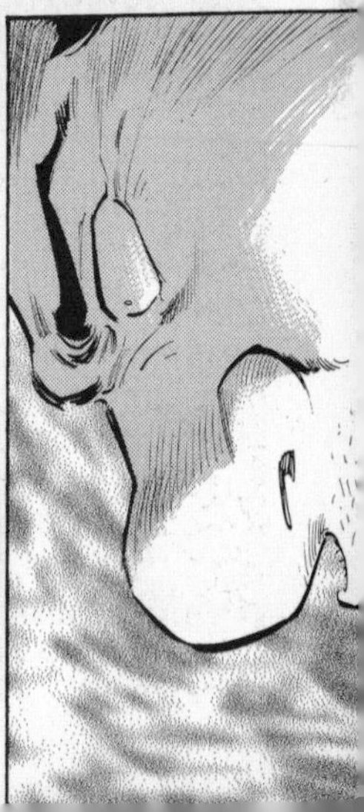
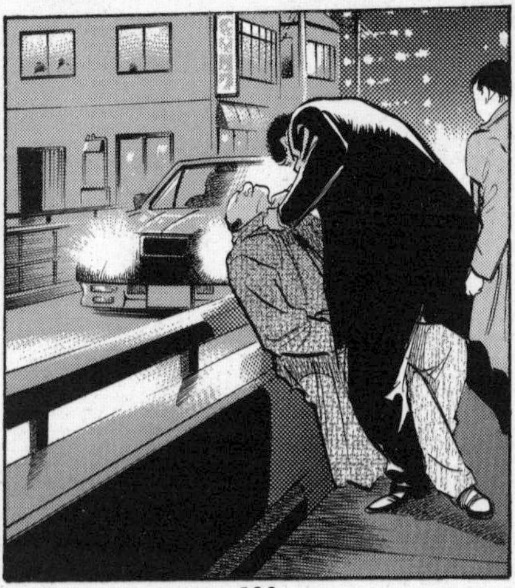
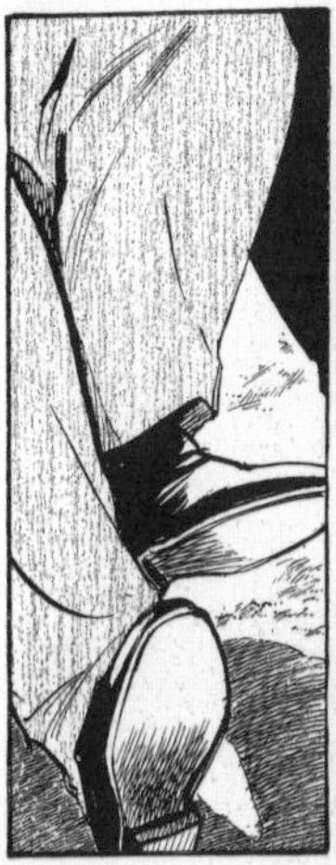

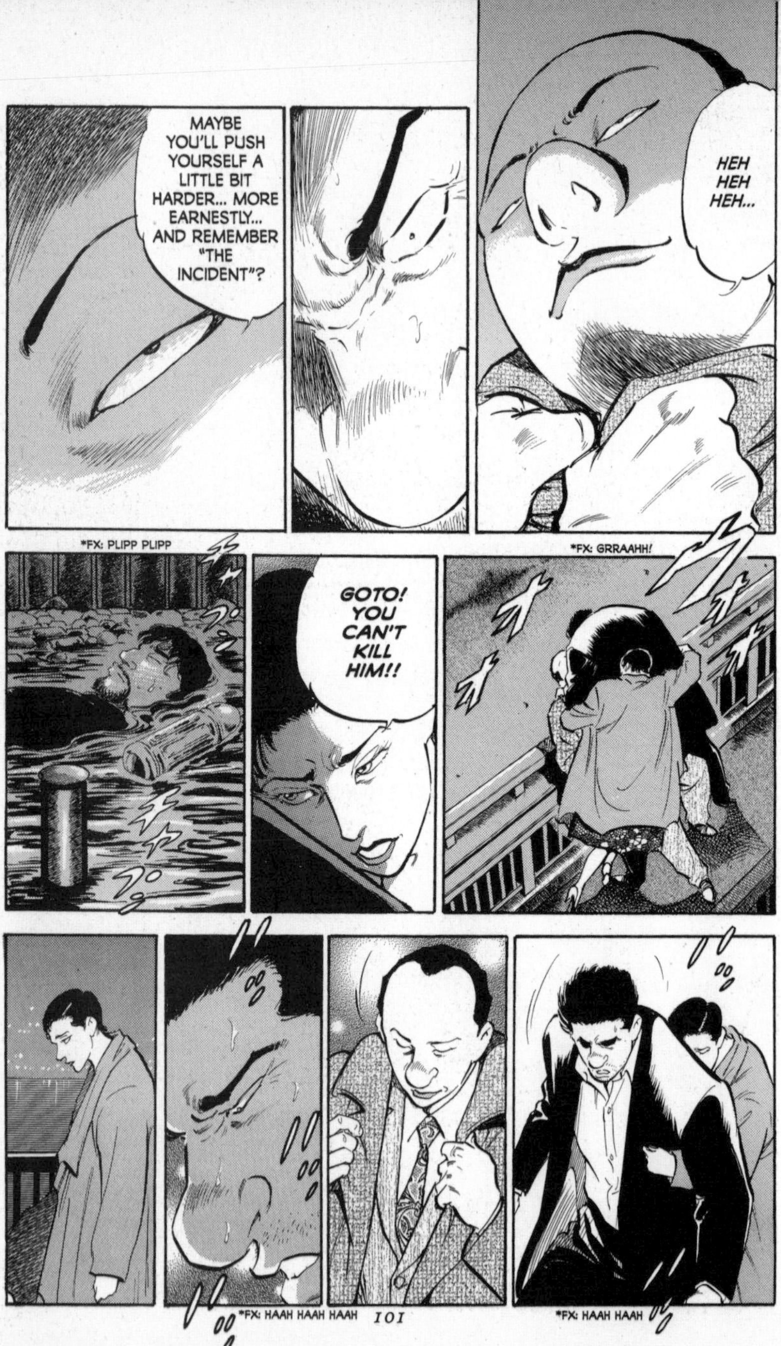
HEH HEH HEH...
MAYBE YOU'LL PUSH YOURSELF A LITTLE BIT HARDER... MORE EARNESTLY... AND REMEMBER "THE INCIDENT"?
*FX: GRRAAHH!
GOTO! YOU CAN'T KILL HIM!!
*FX: PLIPP PLIPP
*FX: HAAH HAAH
*FX: HAAH HAAH HAAH

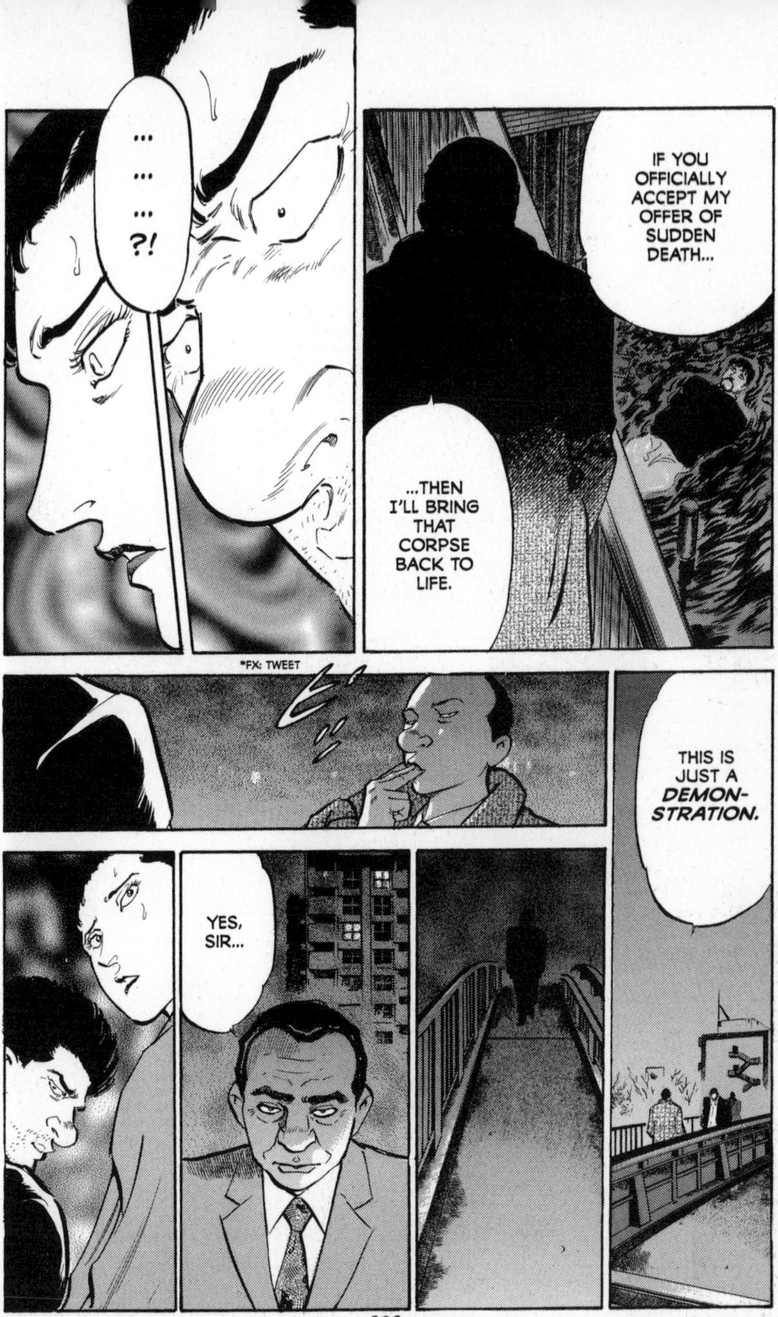
IF YOU OFFICIALLY ACCEPT MY OFFER OF SUDDEN DEATH...
...THEN I'LL BRING THAT CORPSE BACK TO LIFE.
... ... ?!
THIS IS JUST A *DEMON-STRATION.*
*FX: TWEET
YES, SIR...

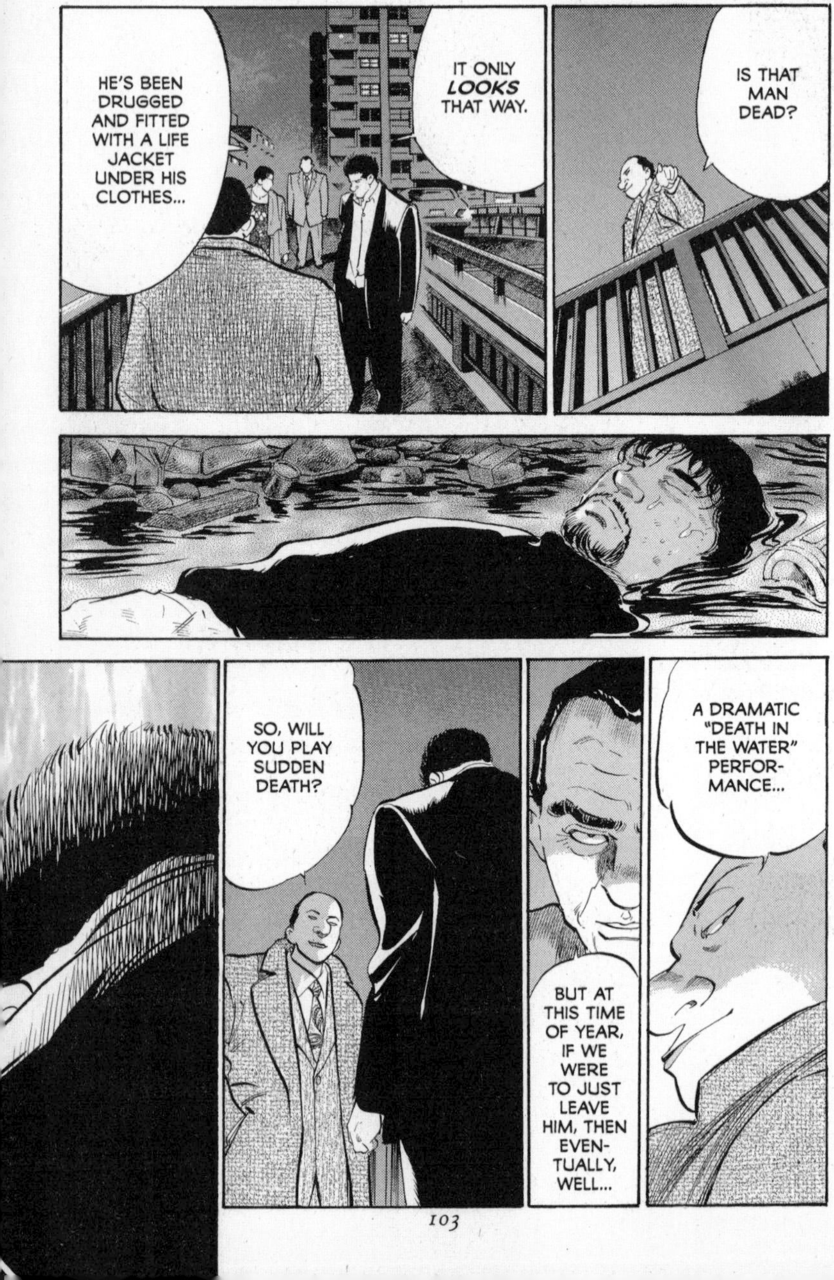
IS THAT MAN DEAD?
IT ONLY *LOOKS* THAT WAY.
HE'S BEEN DRUGGED AND FITTED WITH A LIFE JACKET UNDER HIS CLOTHES...
A DRAMATIC "DEATH IN THE WATER" PERFORMANCE...
BUT AT THIS TIME OF YEAR, IF WE WERE TO JUST LEAVE HIM, THEN EVENTUALLY, WELL...
SO, WILL YOU PLAY SUDDEN DEATH?

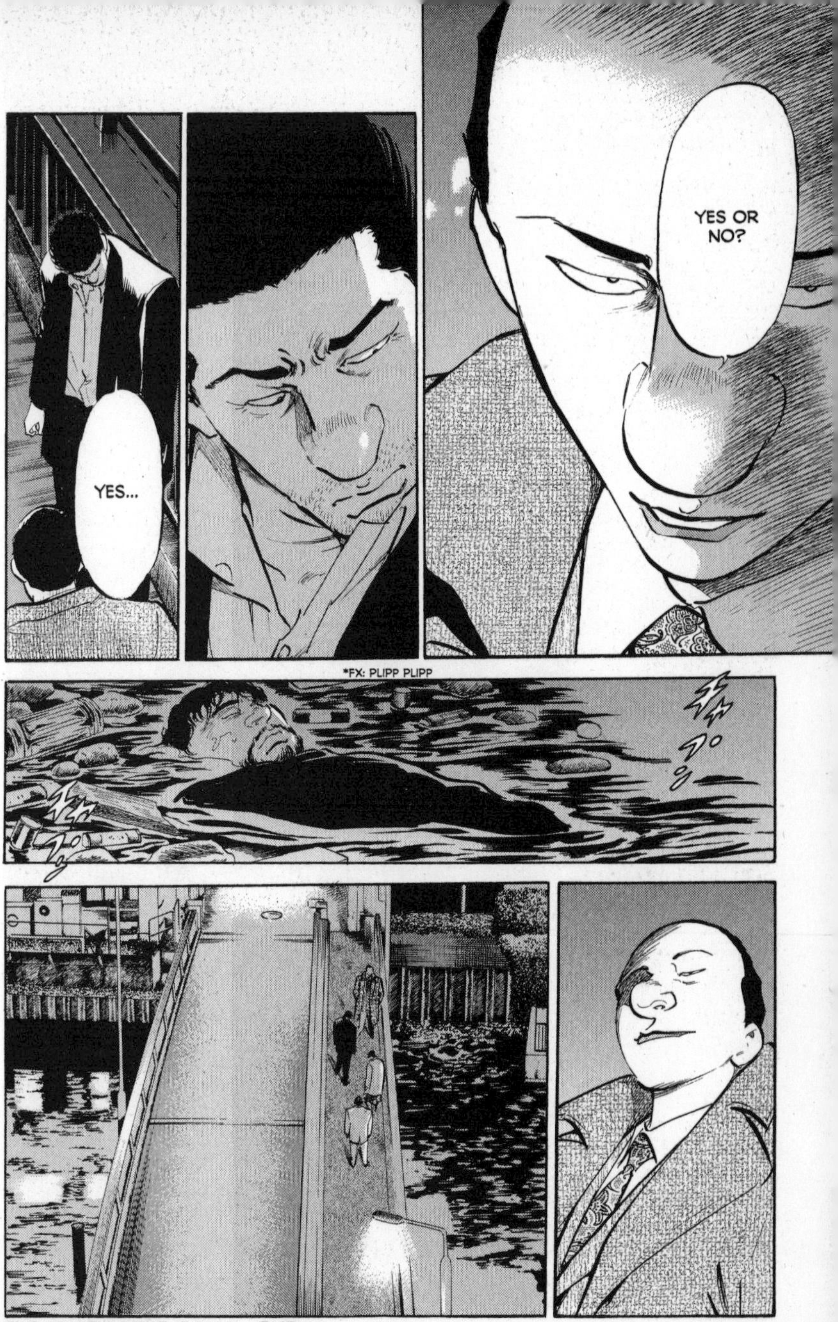
YES OR NO?
YES...
*FX: PLIPP PLIPP

FLOATING IN THE CANAL: END

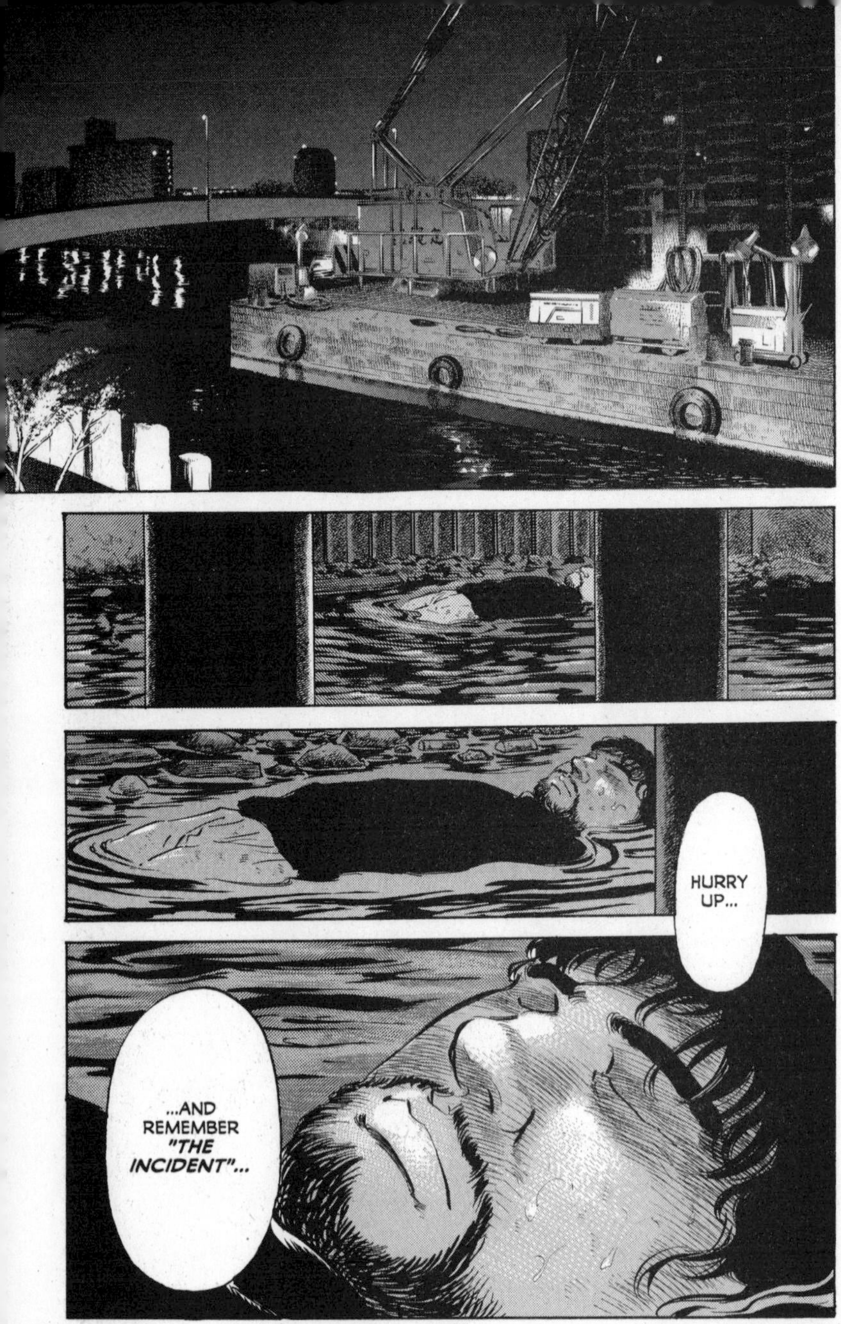
HURRY UP...
...AND REMEMBER "THE INCIDENT"...

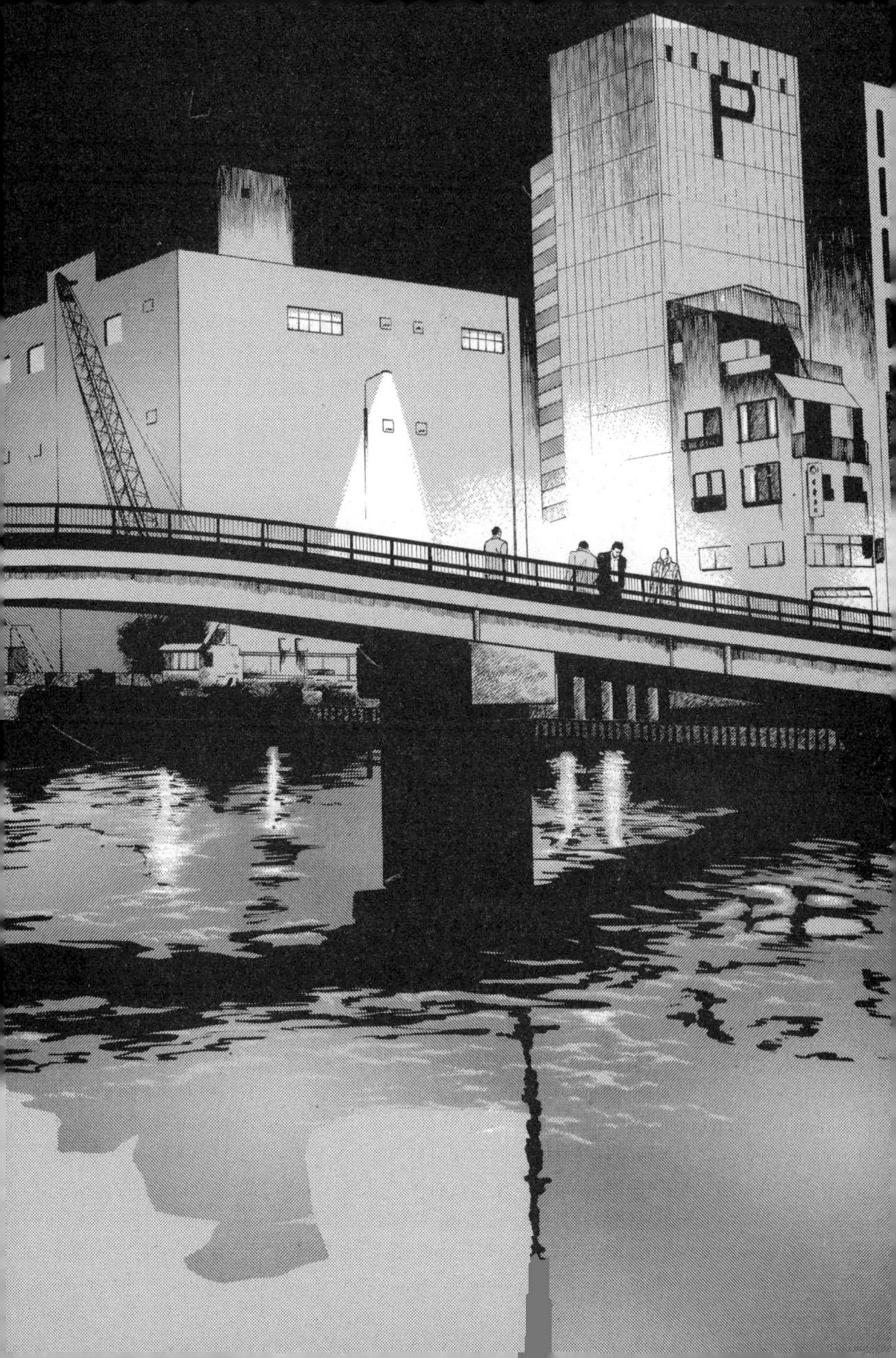
P

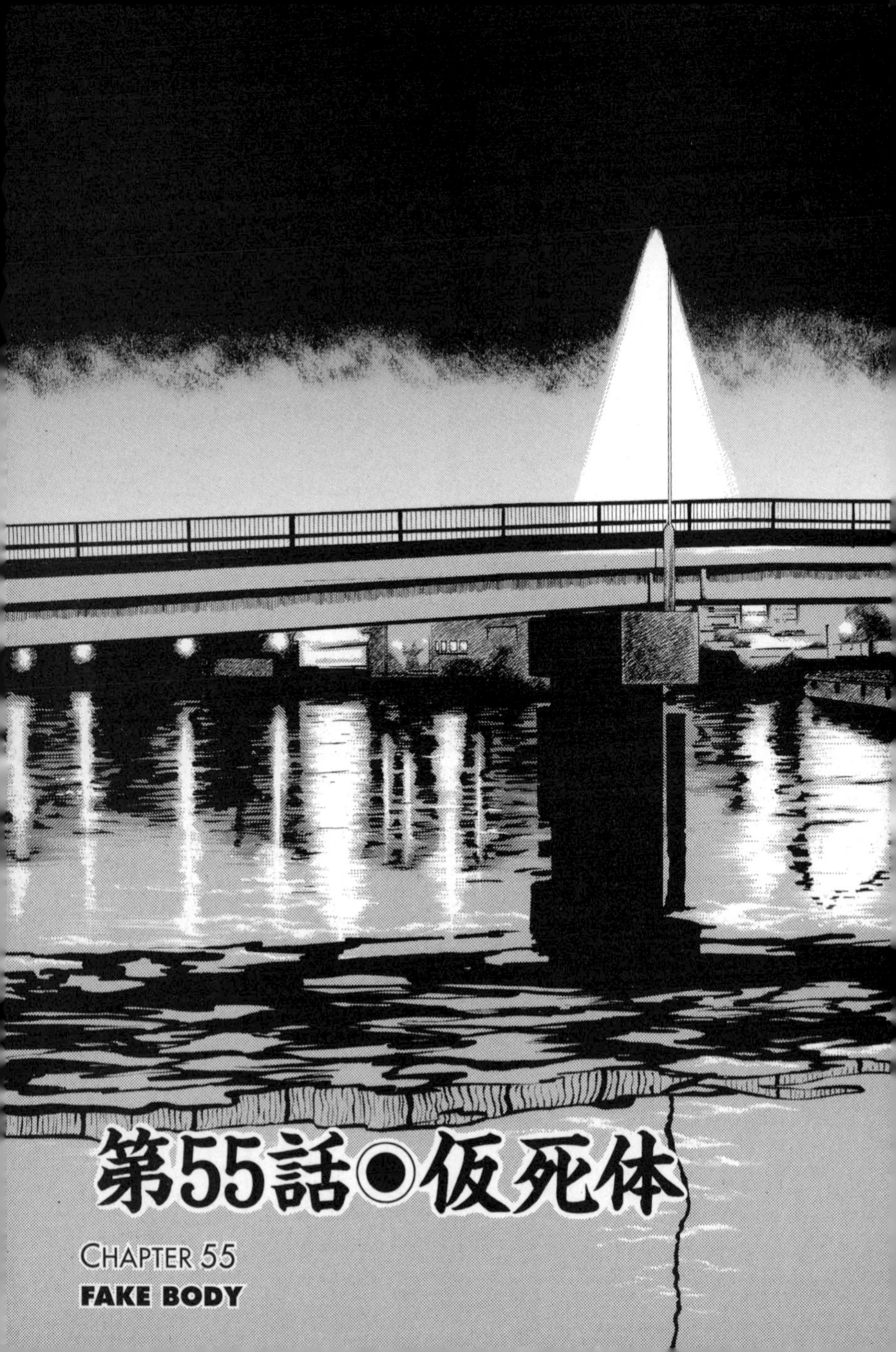

第55話◎仮死体

CHAPTER 55
FAKE BODY

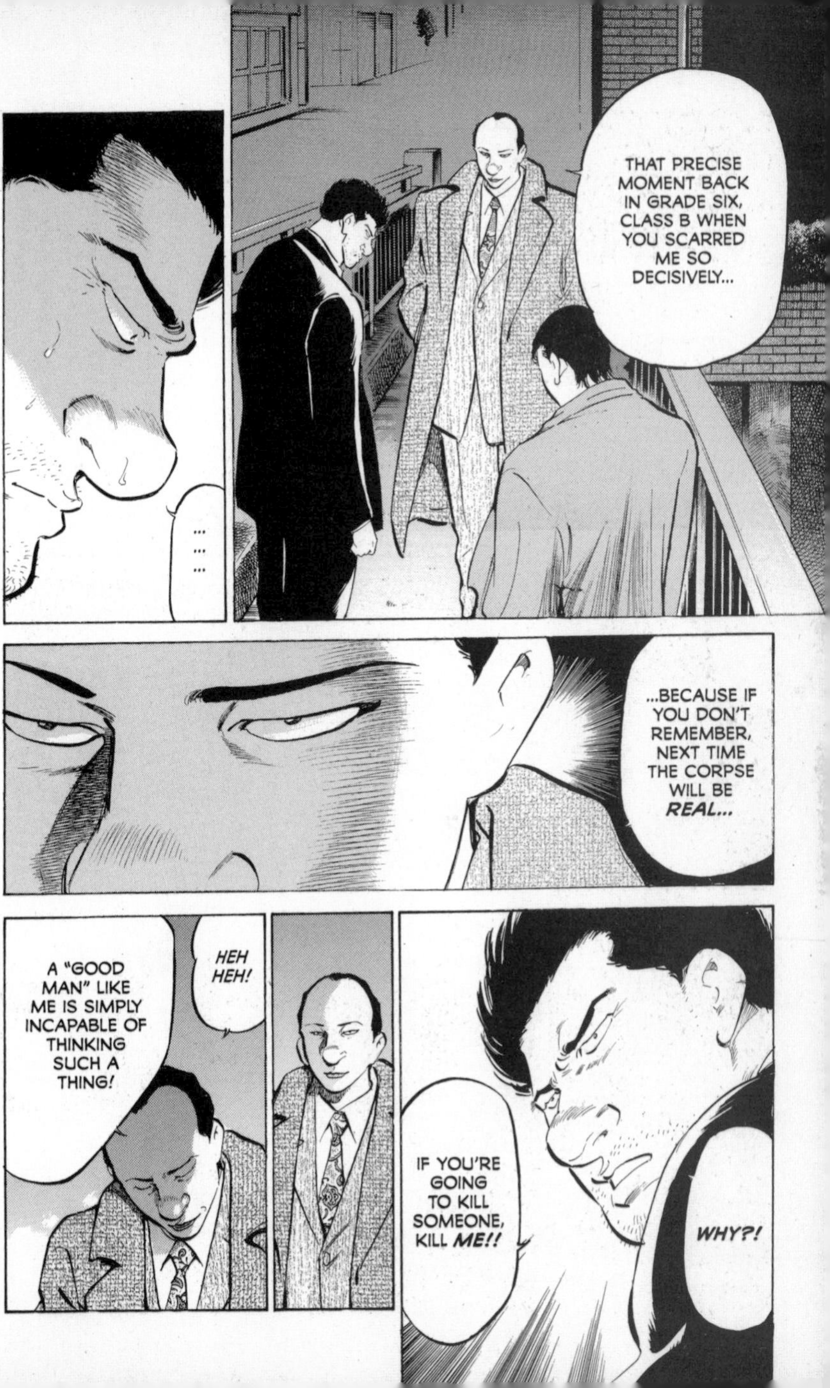
THAT PRECISE MOMENT BACK IN GRADE SIX, CLASS B WHEN YOU SCARRED ME SO DECISIVELY...
......
...BECAUSE IF YOU DON'T REMEMBER, NEXT TIME THE CORPSE WILL BE *REAL...*
IF YOU'RE GOING TO KILL SOMEONE, KILL *ME!!*
WHY?!
HEH HEH!
A "GOOD MAN" LIKE ME IS SIMPLY INCAPABLE OF THINKING SUCH A THING!

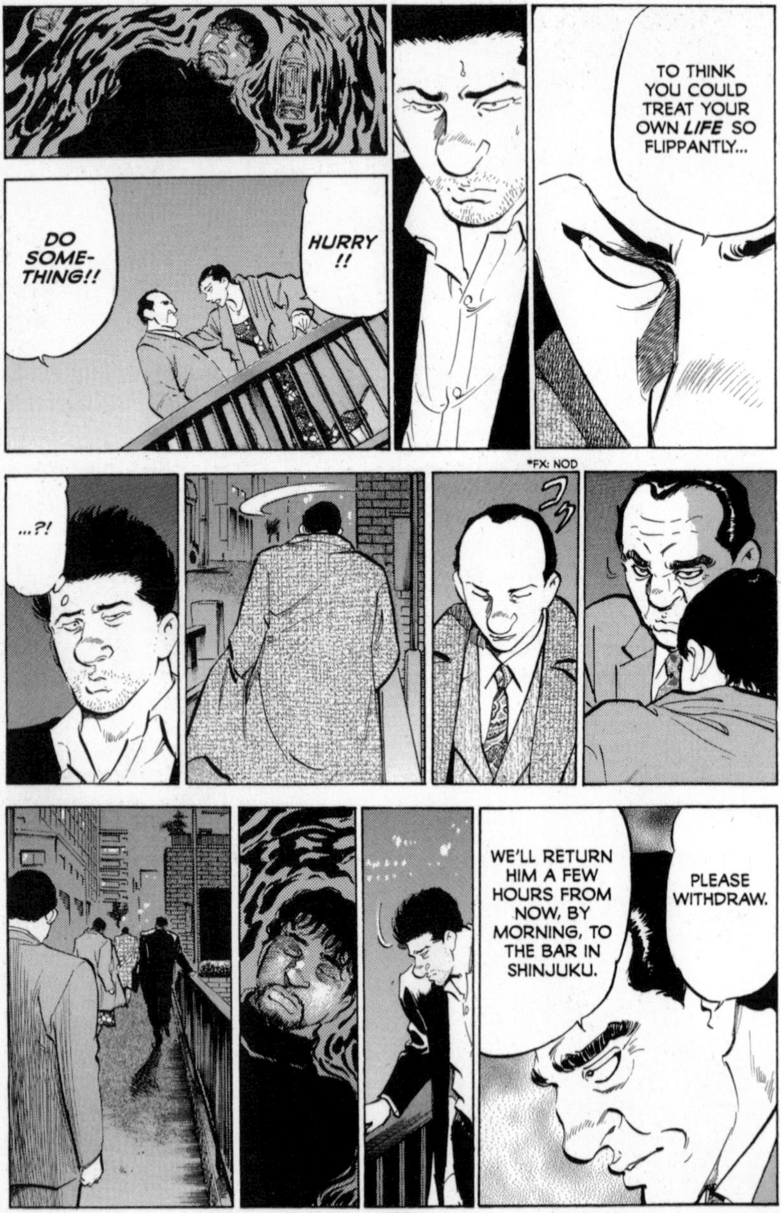
TO THINK YOU COULD TREAT YOUR OWN *LIFE* SO FLIPPANTLY...
HURRY !!
DO SOME-THING!!
*FX: NOD
...?!
PLEASE WITHDRAW.
WE'LL RETURN HIM A FEW HOURS FROM NOW, BY MORNING, TO THE BAR IN SHINJUKU.

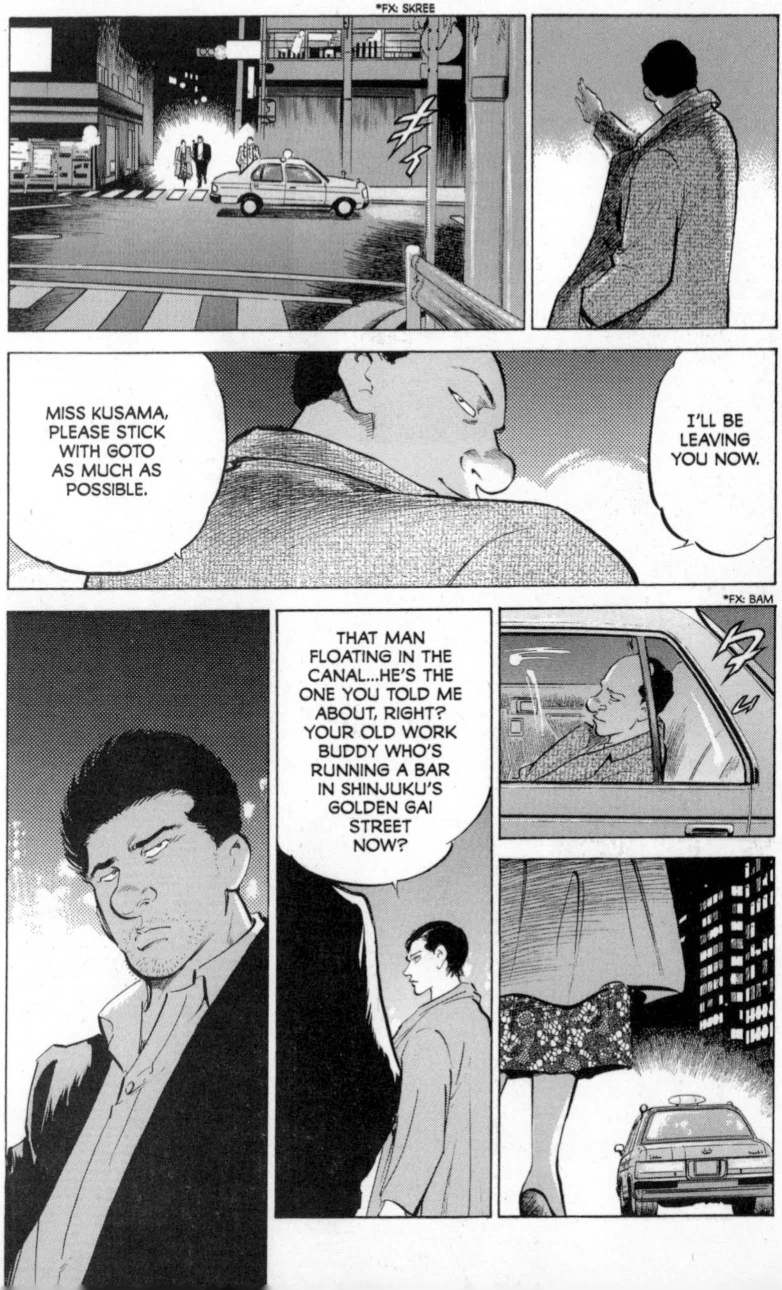
*FX: SKREE
I'LL BE LEAVING YOU NOW.
MISS KUSAMA, PLEASE STICK WITH GOTO AS MUCH AS POSSIBLE.
*FX: BAM
THAT MAN FLOATING IN THE CANAL...HE'S THE ONE YOU TOLD ME ABOUT, RIGHT? YOUR OLD WORK BUDDY WHO'S RUNNING A BAR IN SHINJUKU'S GOLDEN GAI STREET NOW?

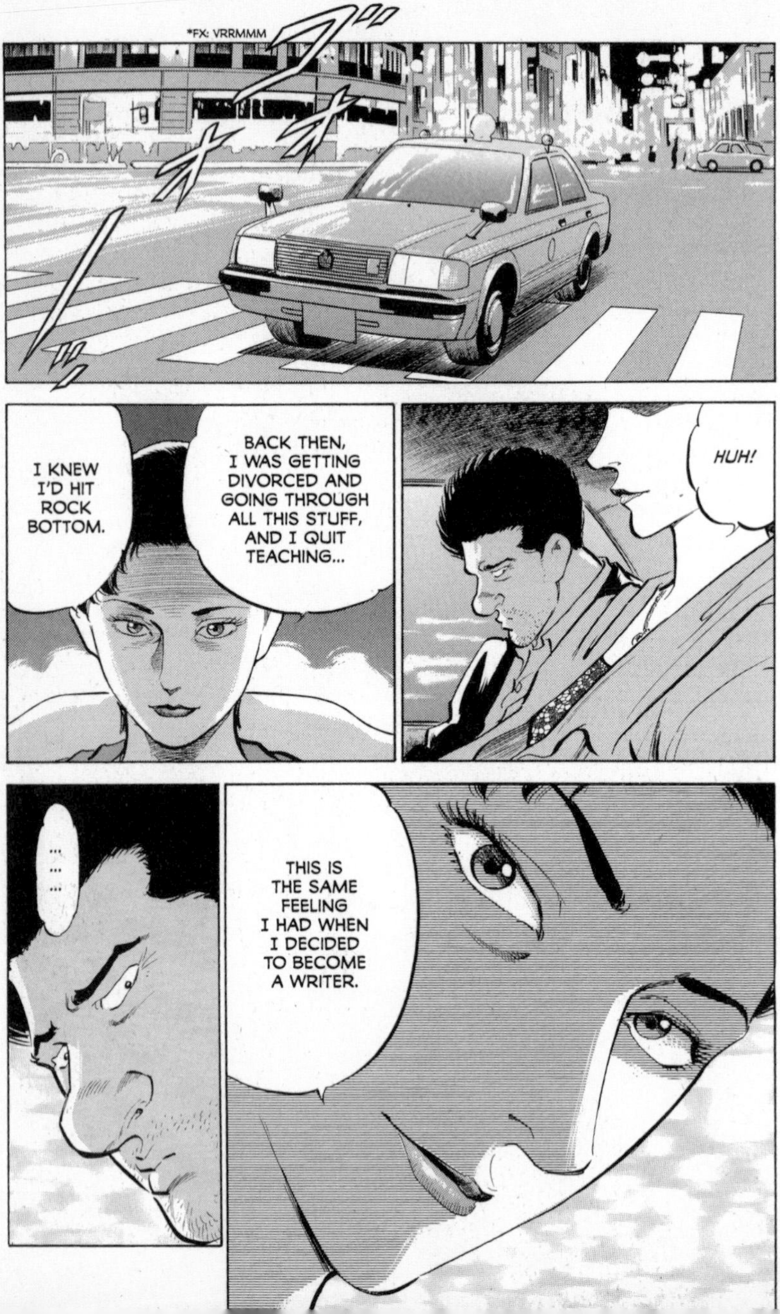
*FX: VRRMMM
HUH!
BACK THEN, I WAS GETTING DIVORCED AND GOING THROUGH ALL THIS STUFF, AND I QUIT TEACHING...
I KNEW I'D HIT ROCK BOTTOM.
THIS IS THE SAME FEELING I HAD WHEN I DECIDED TO BECOME A WRITER.
......

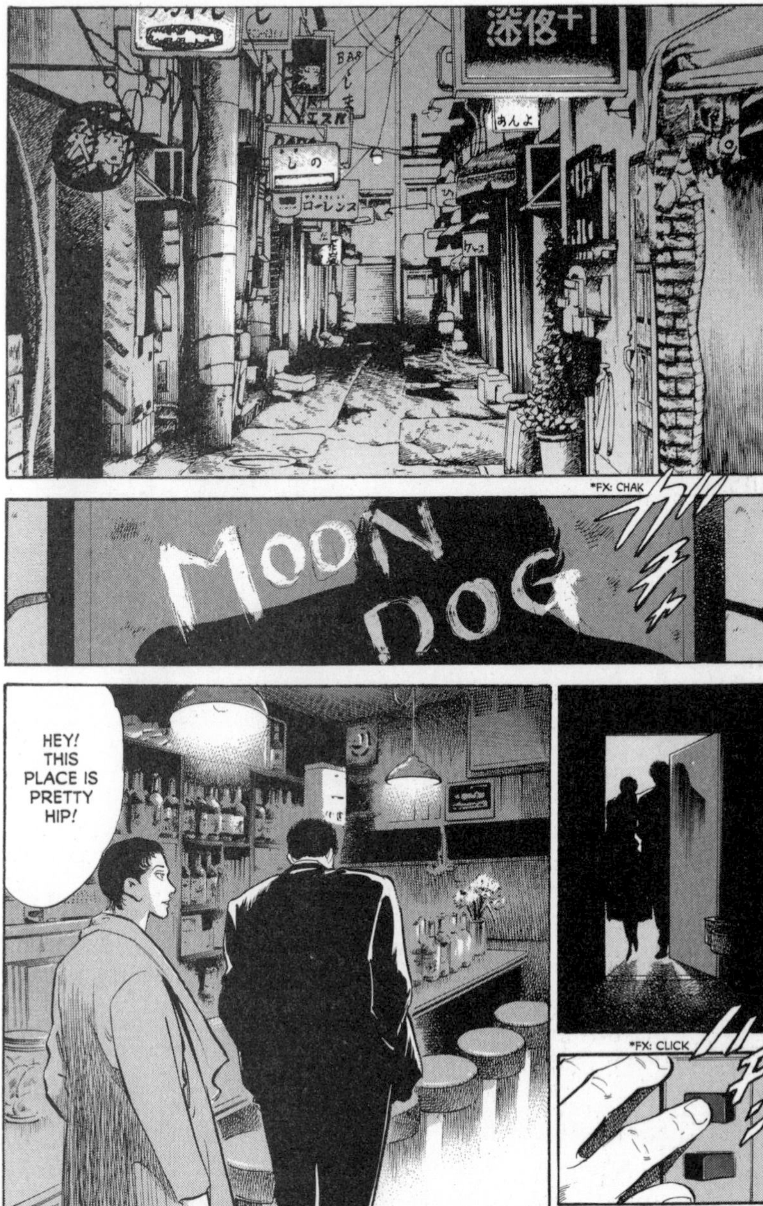
*FX: CHAK
MOON DOG
*FX: CLICK
HEY! THIS PLACE IS PRETTY HIP!

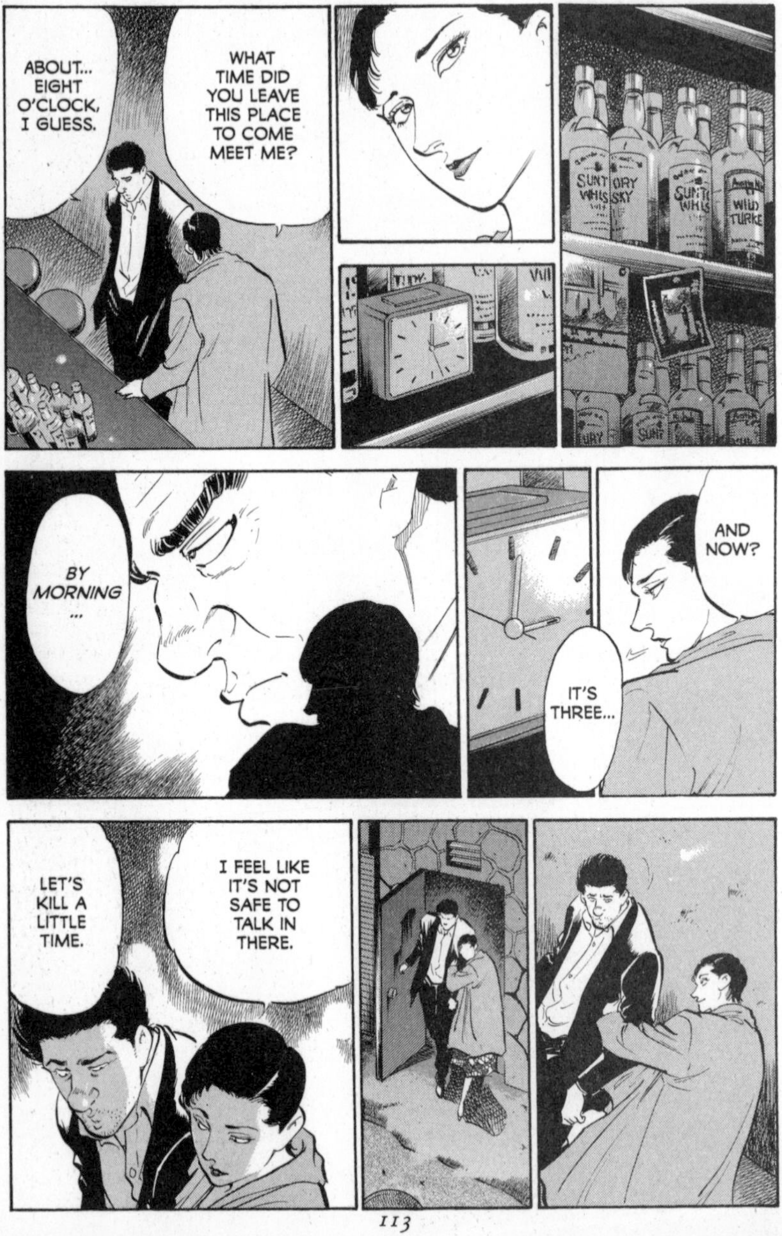
WHAT TIME DID YOU LEAVE THIS PLACE TO COME MEET ME?
ABOUT... EIGHT O'CLOCK, I GUESS.
AND NOW?
IT'S THREE...
BY MORNING ...
I FEEL LIKE IT'S NOT SAFE TO TALK IN THERE.
LET'S KILL A LITTLE TIME.

*SIGN: KARAOKE, 28 ROOMS, 5TH FLOOR

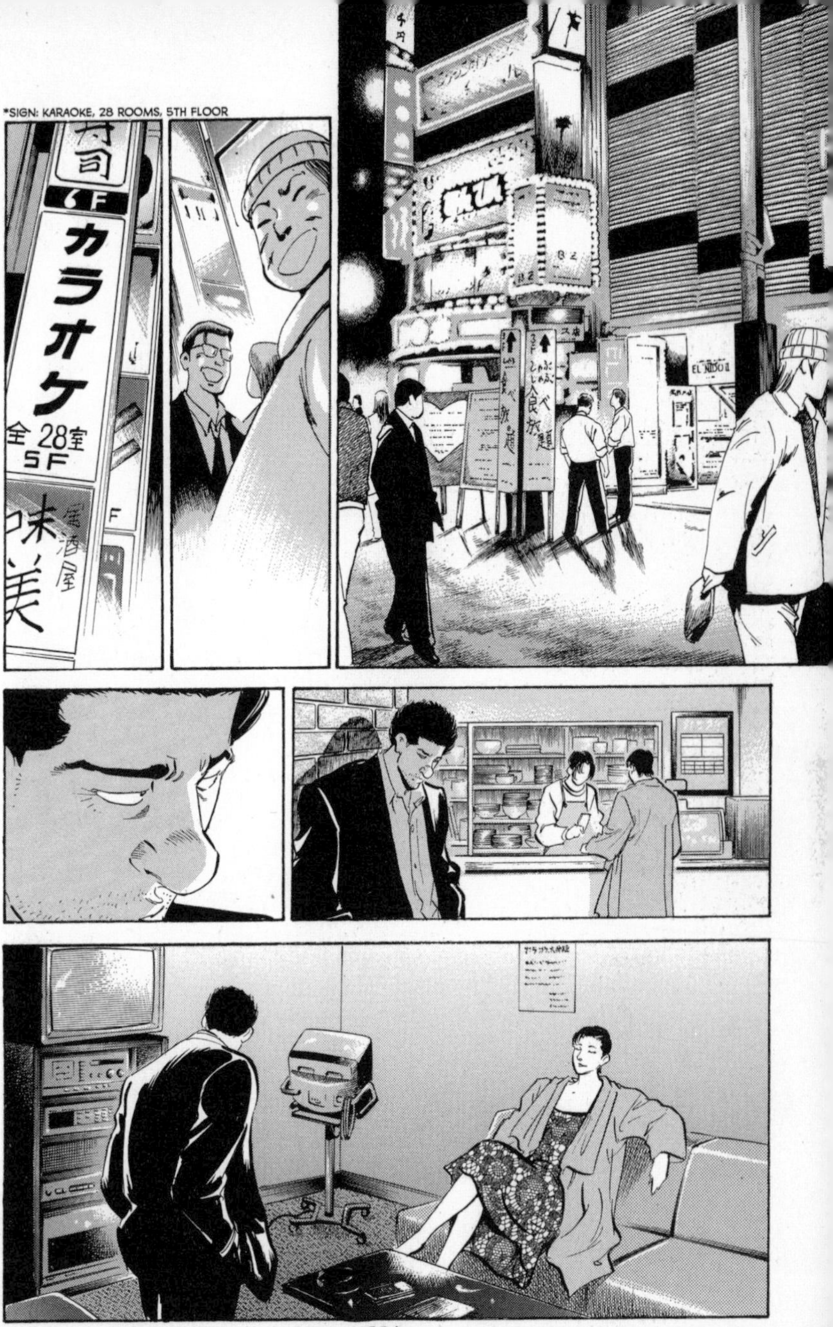
6F
カラオケ
全28室
5F
居酒屋
EL NIDO II

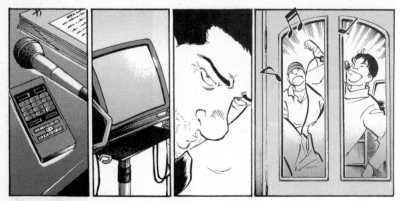

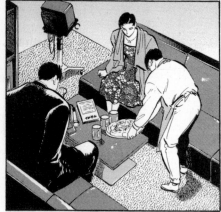

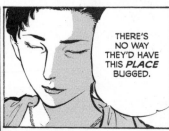

THERE'S NO WAY THEY'D HAVE THIS *PLACE* BUGGED.

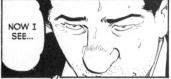

NOW I SEE...

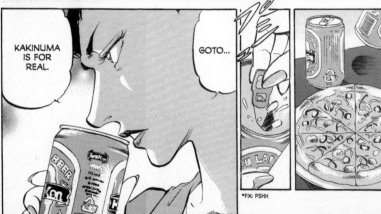

KAKINUMA IS FOR REAL.

GOTO...

*FX: PSHH

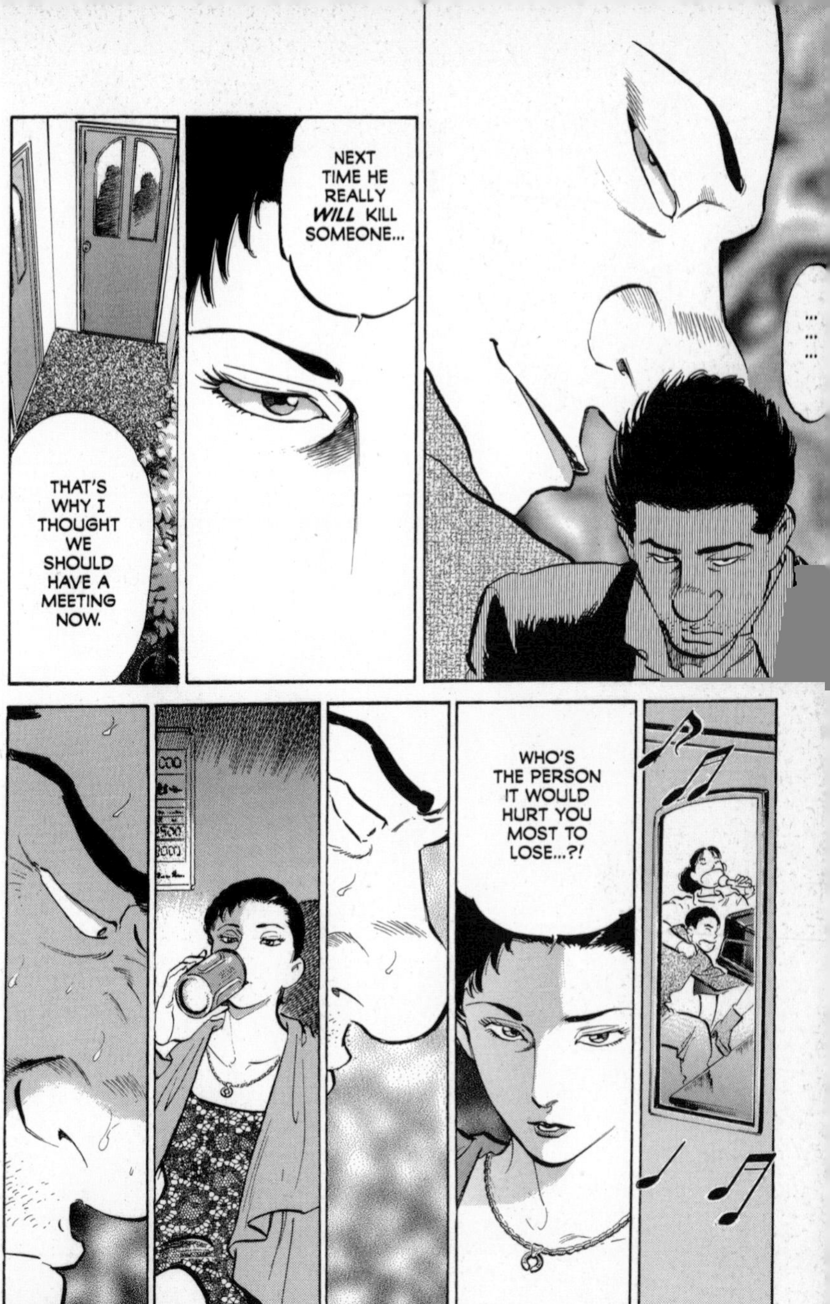

... ...
NEXT TIME HE REALLY *WILL* KILL SOMEONE...
THAT'S WHY I THOUGHT WE SHOULD HAVE A MEETING NOW.
WHO'S THE PERSON IT WOULD HURT YOU MOST TO LOSE...?!

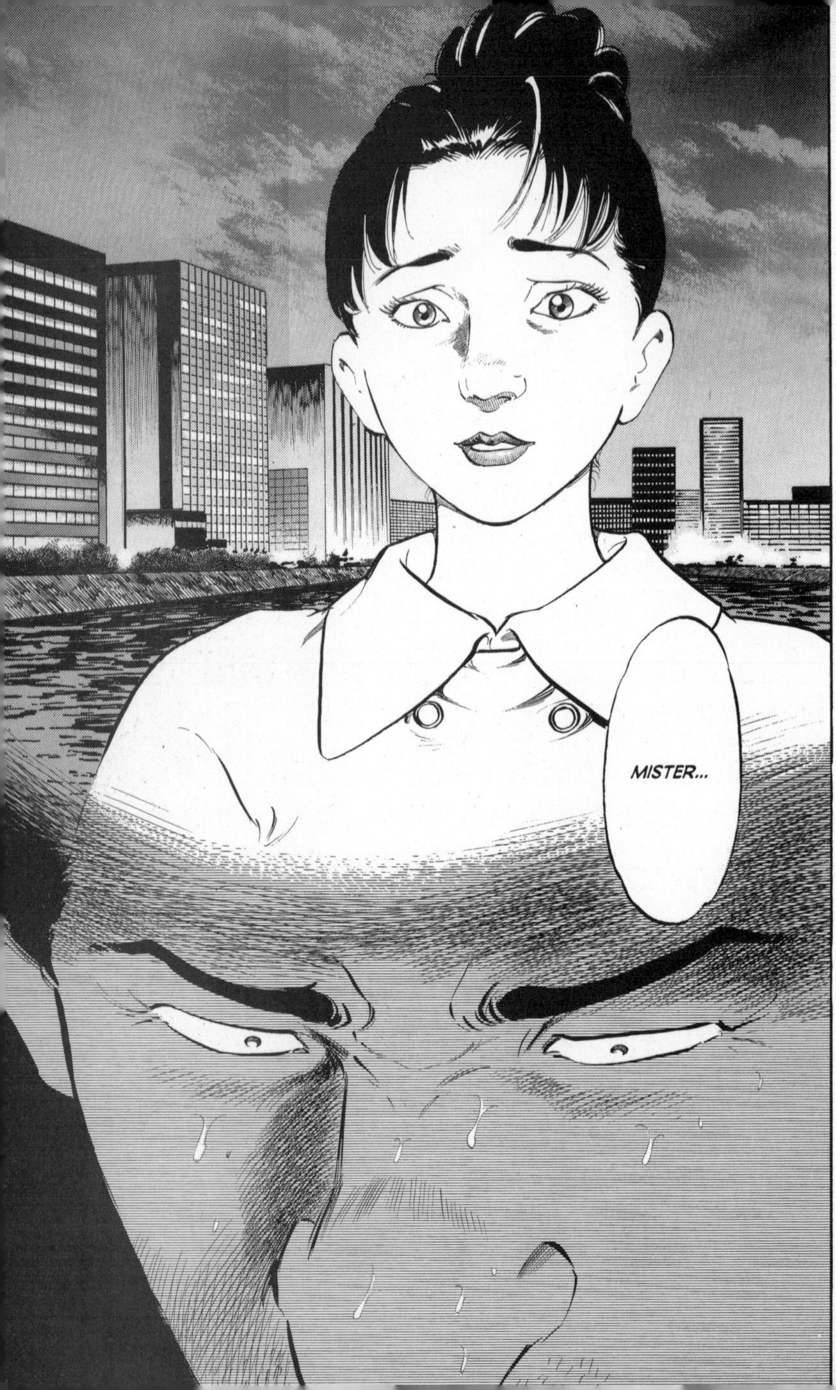
MISTER...

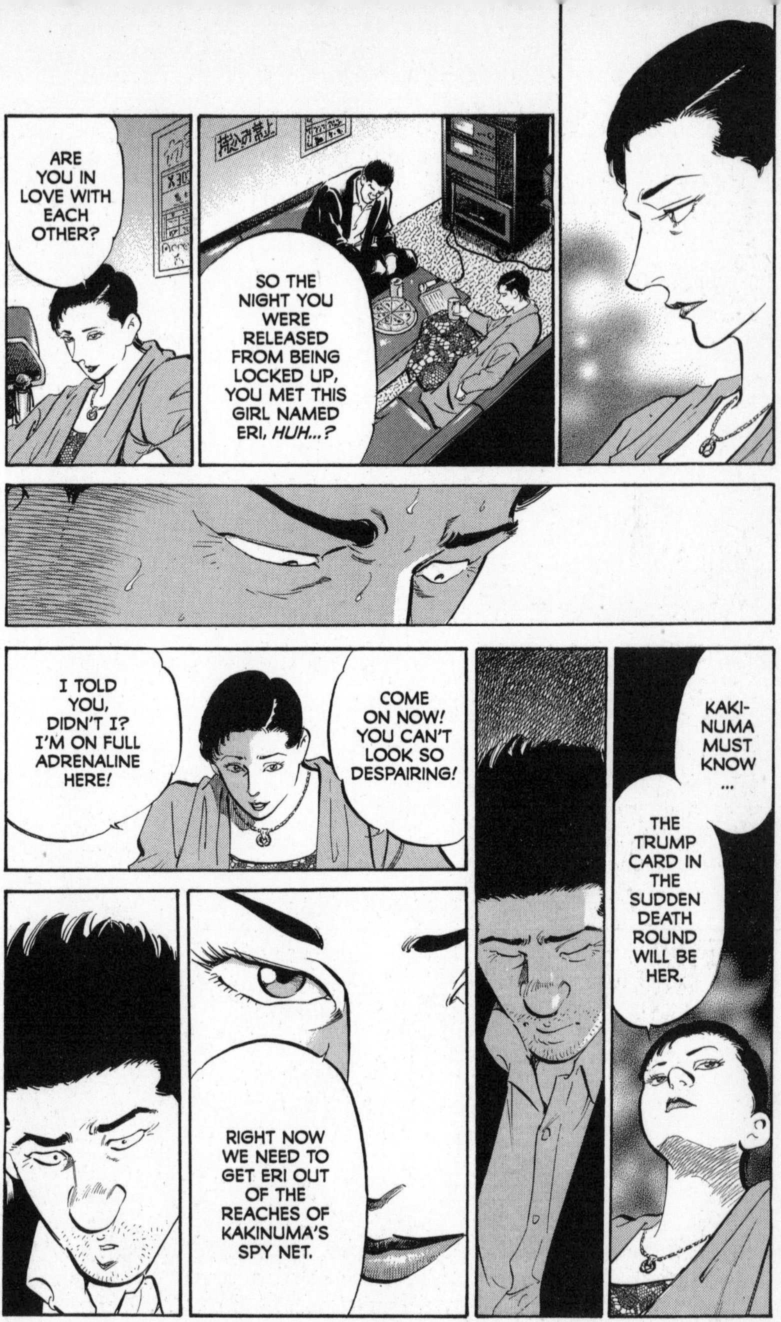
SO THE NIGHT YOU WERE RELEASED FROM BEING LOCKED UP, YOU MET THIS GIRL NAMED ERI, *HUH...?*
ARE YOU IN LOVE WITH EACH OTHER?
KAKI-NUMA MUST KNOW ...
THE TRUMP CARD IN THE SUDDEN DEATH ROUND WILL BE HER.
COME ON NOW! YOU CAN'T LOOK SO DESPAIRING!
I TOLD YOU, DIDN'T I? I'M ON FULL ADRENALINE HERE!
RIGHT NOW WE NEED TO GET ERI OUT OF THE REACHES OF KAKINUMA'S SPY NET.

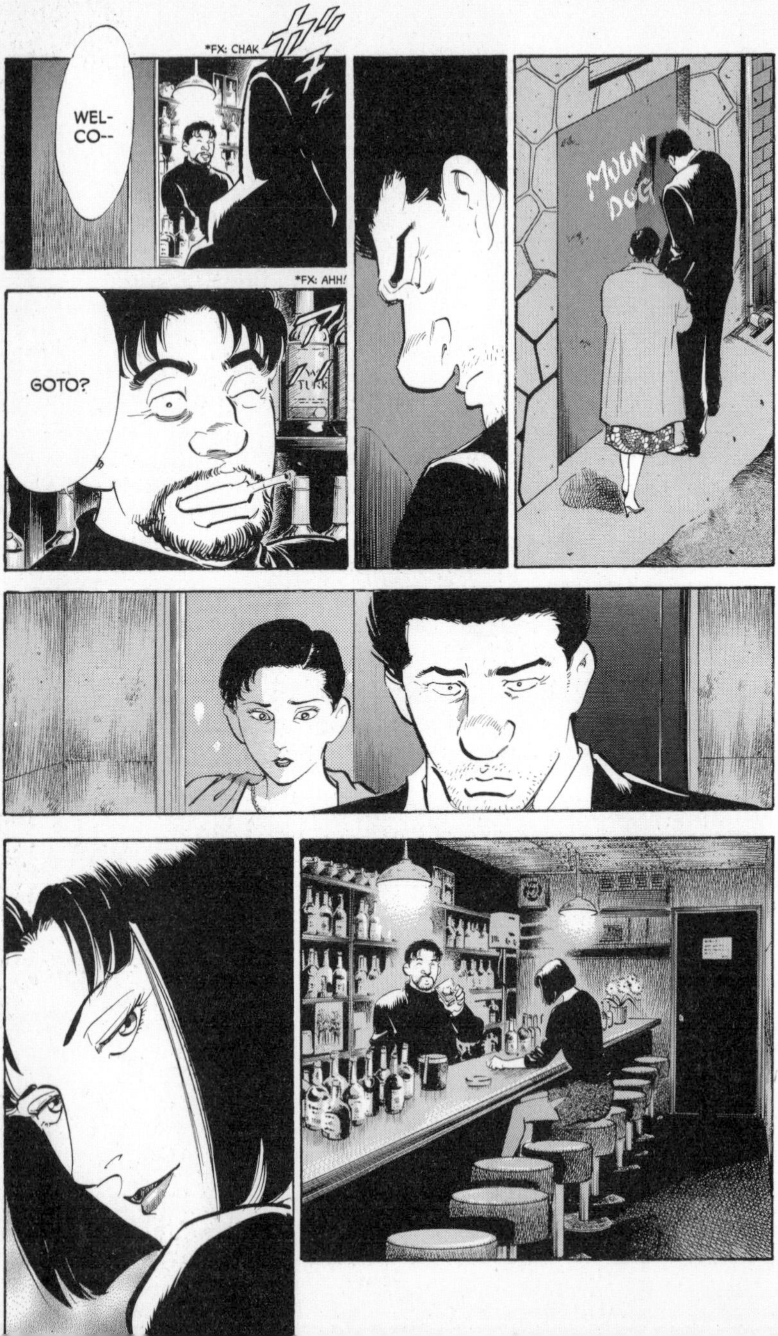
MOON DOG
WEL-
CO--
*FX: CHAK
GOTO?
*FX: AHH!

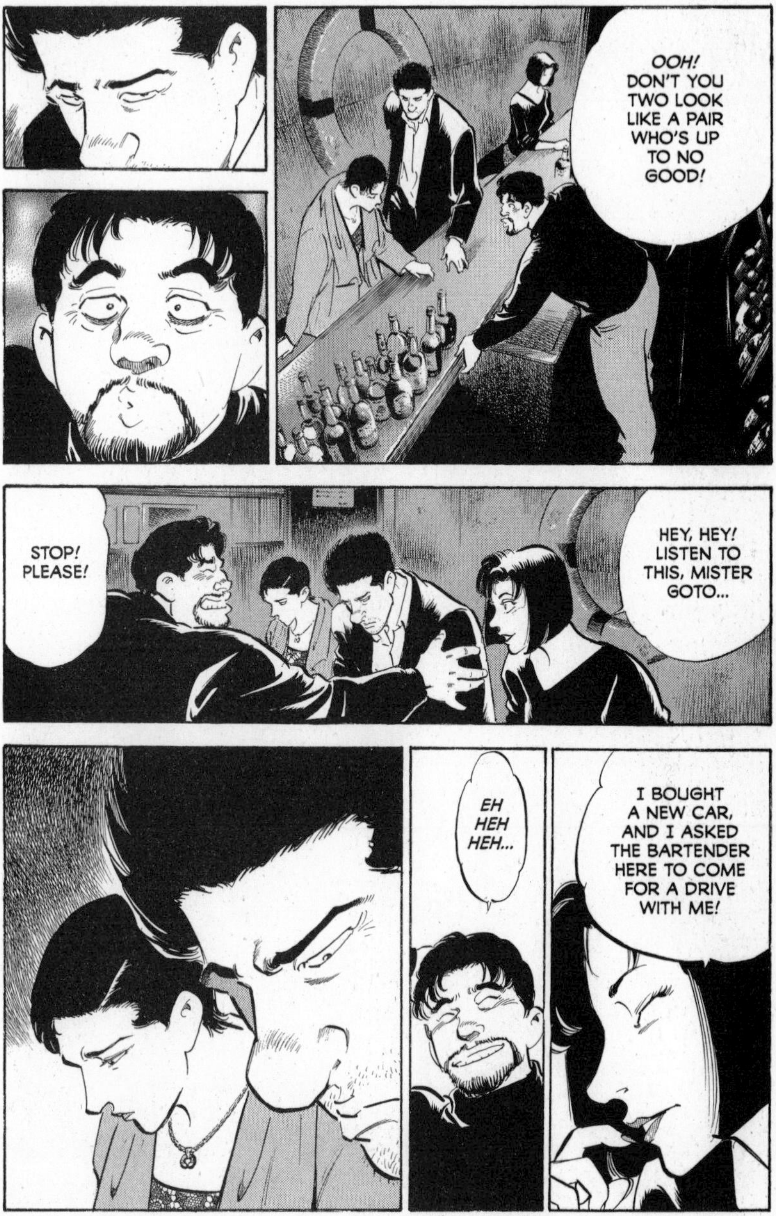
OOH! DON'T YOU TWO LOOK LIKE A PAIR WHO'S UP TO NO GOOD!
HEY, HEY! LISTEN TO THIS, MISTER GOTO...
STOP! PLEASE!
I BOUGHT A NEW CAR, AND I ASKED THE BARTENDER HERE TO COME FOR A DRIVE WITH ME!
EH HEH HEH...

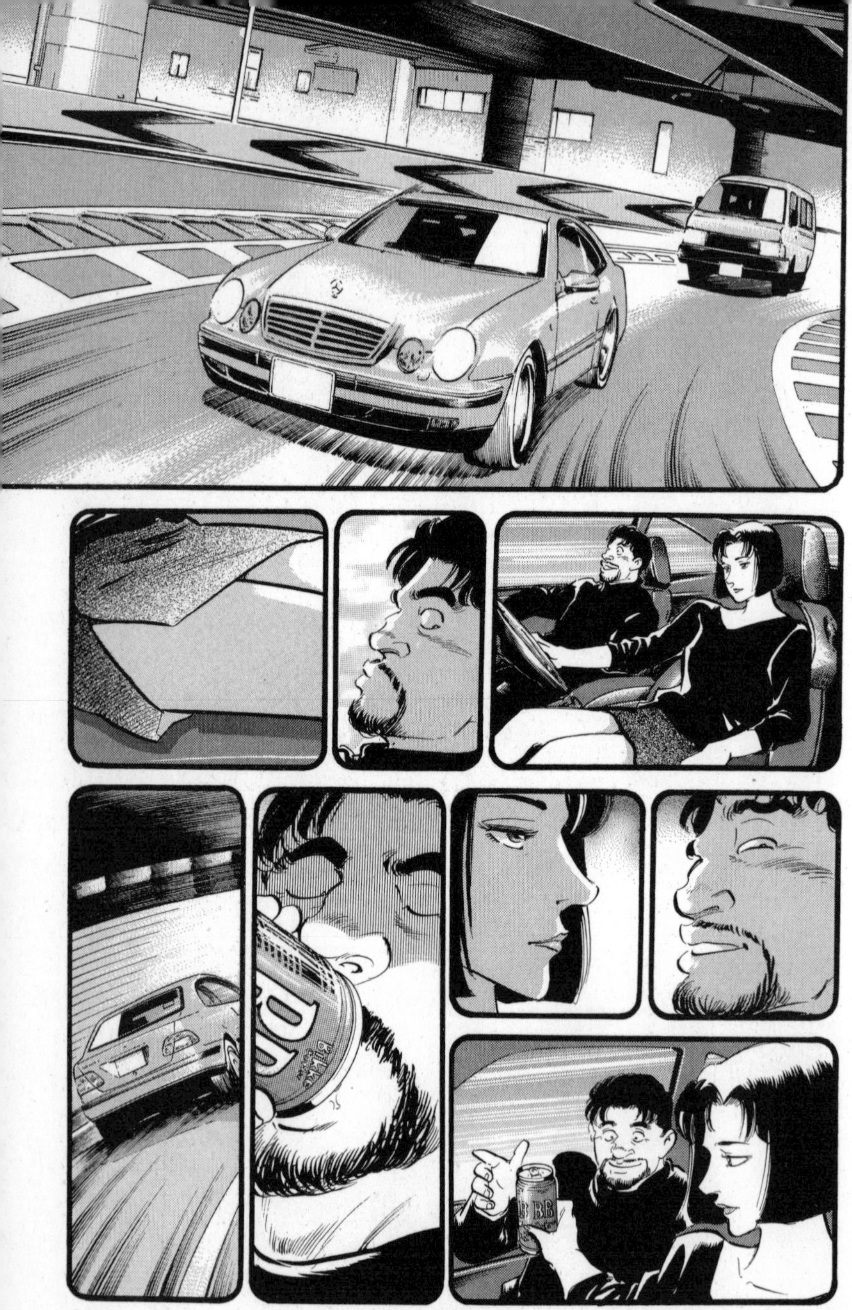

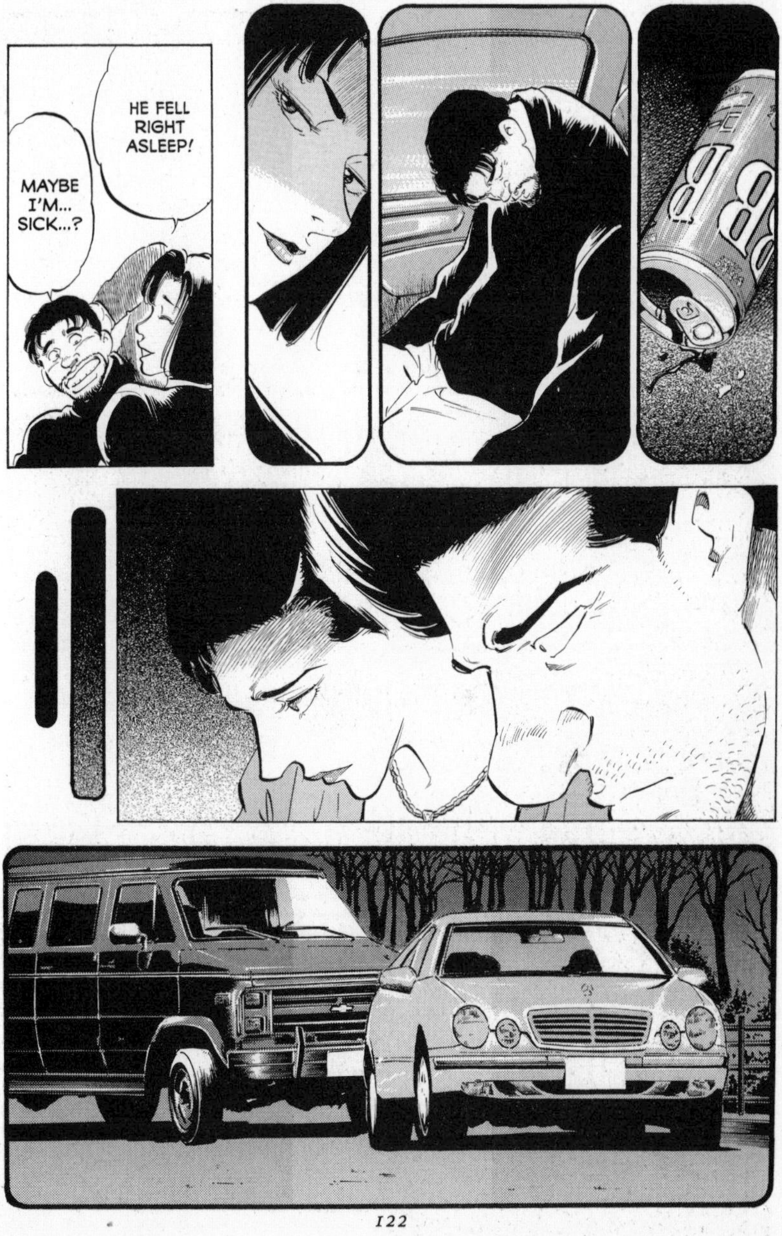
HE FELL RIGHT ASLEEP!
MAYBE I'M... SICK...?

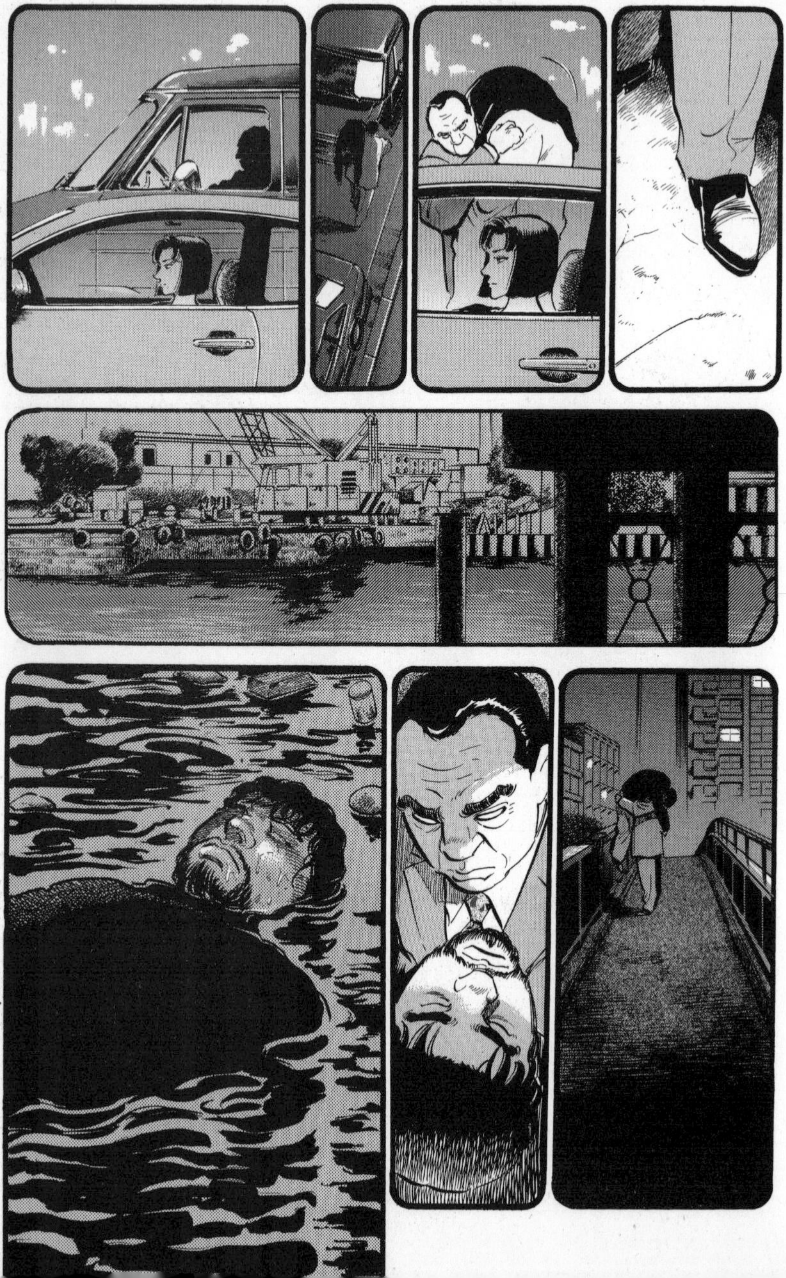

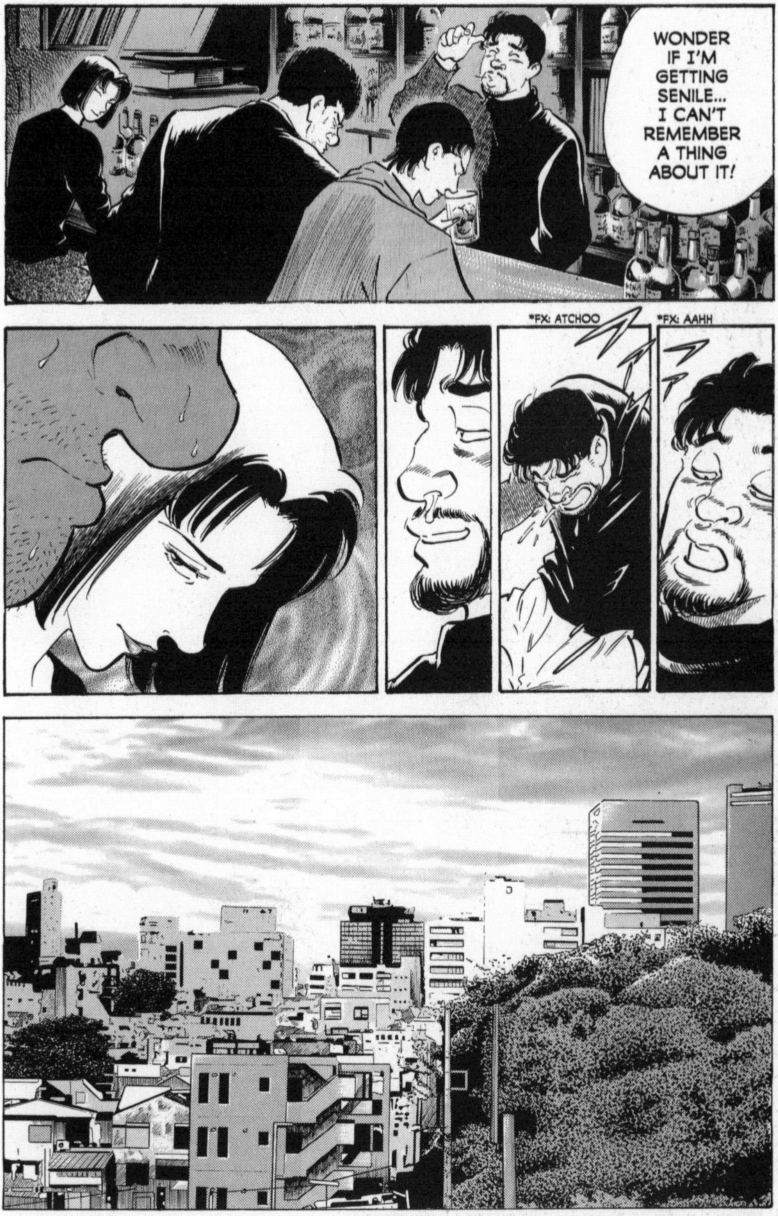
WONDER IF I'M GETTING SENILE... I CAN'T REMEMBER A THING ABOUT IT!
*FX: AAHH
*FX: ATCHOO

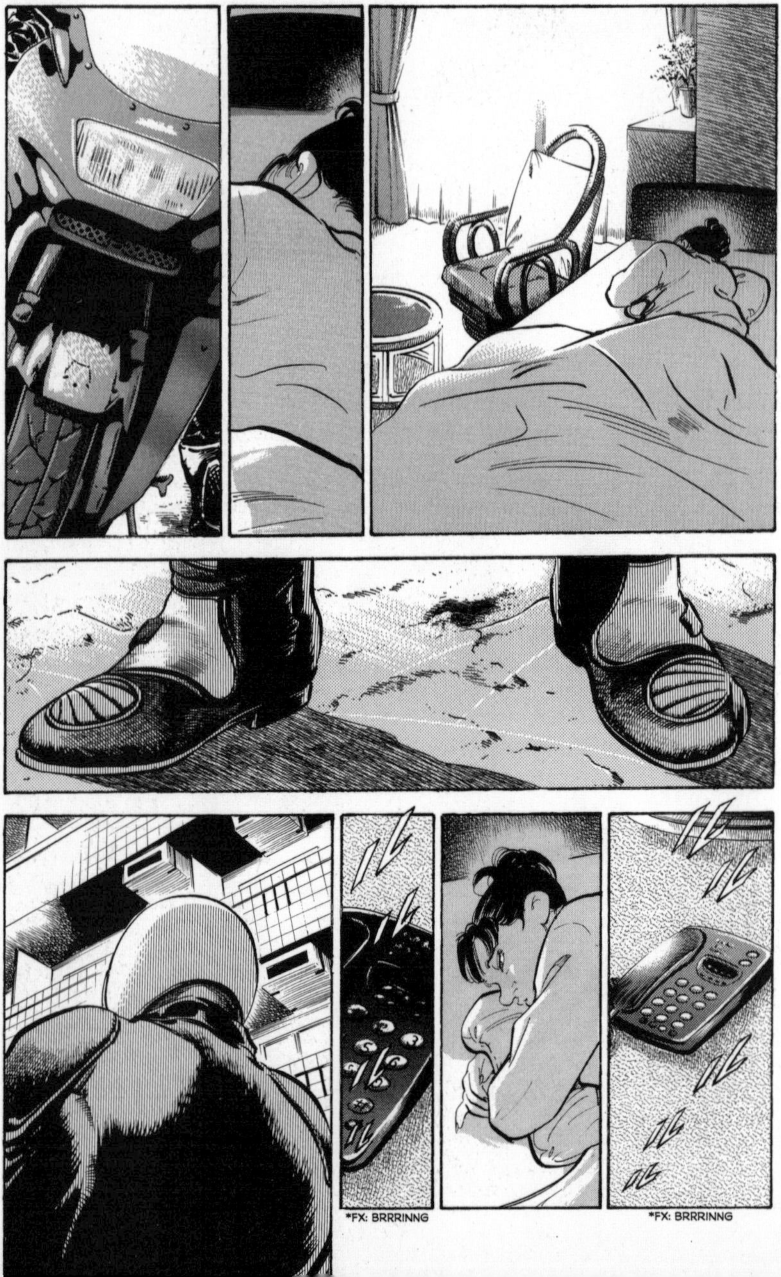
*FX: BRRRINNG
*FX: BRRRINNG

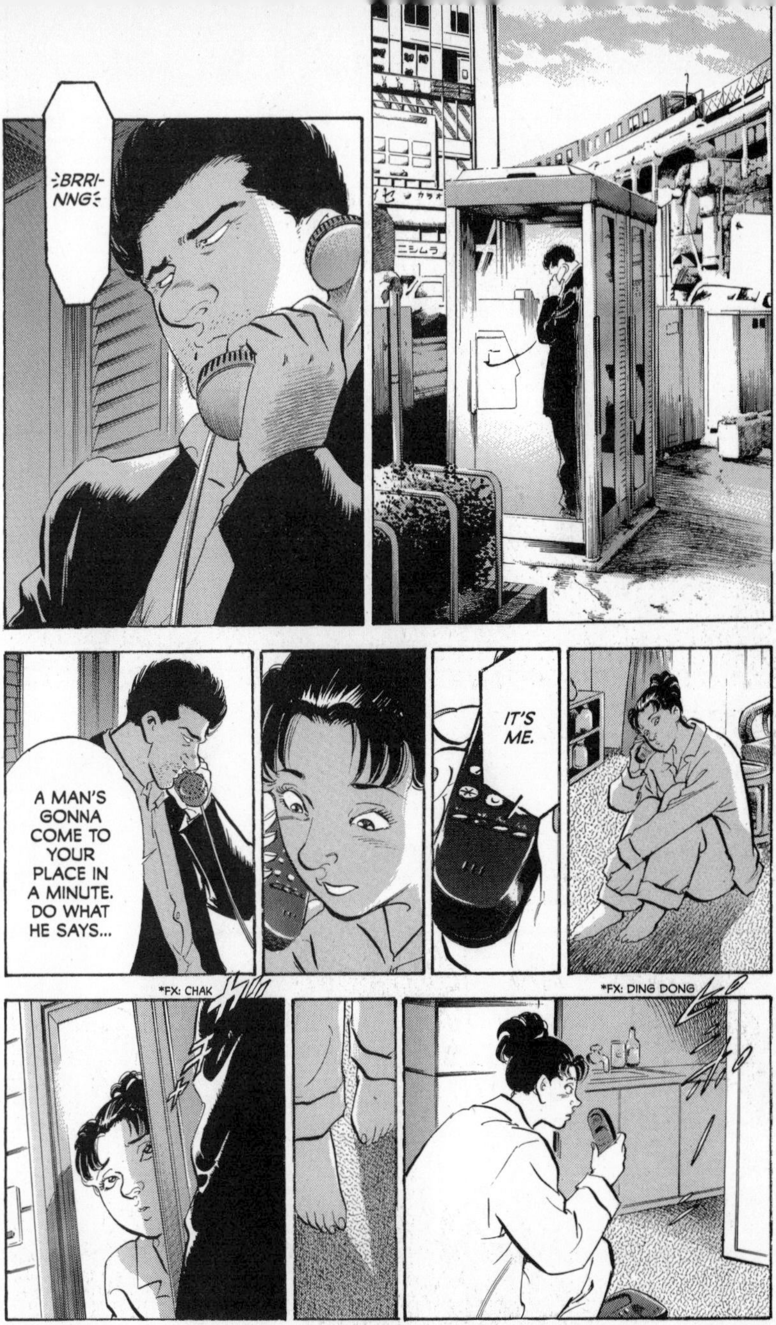
ニシムラ
BRRI-NNG
IT'S ME.
A MAN'S GONNA COME TO YOUR PLACE IN A MINUTE. DO WHAT HE SAYS...
*FX: DING DONG
*FX: CHAK

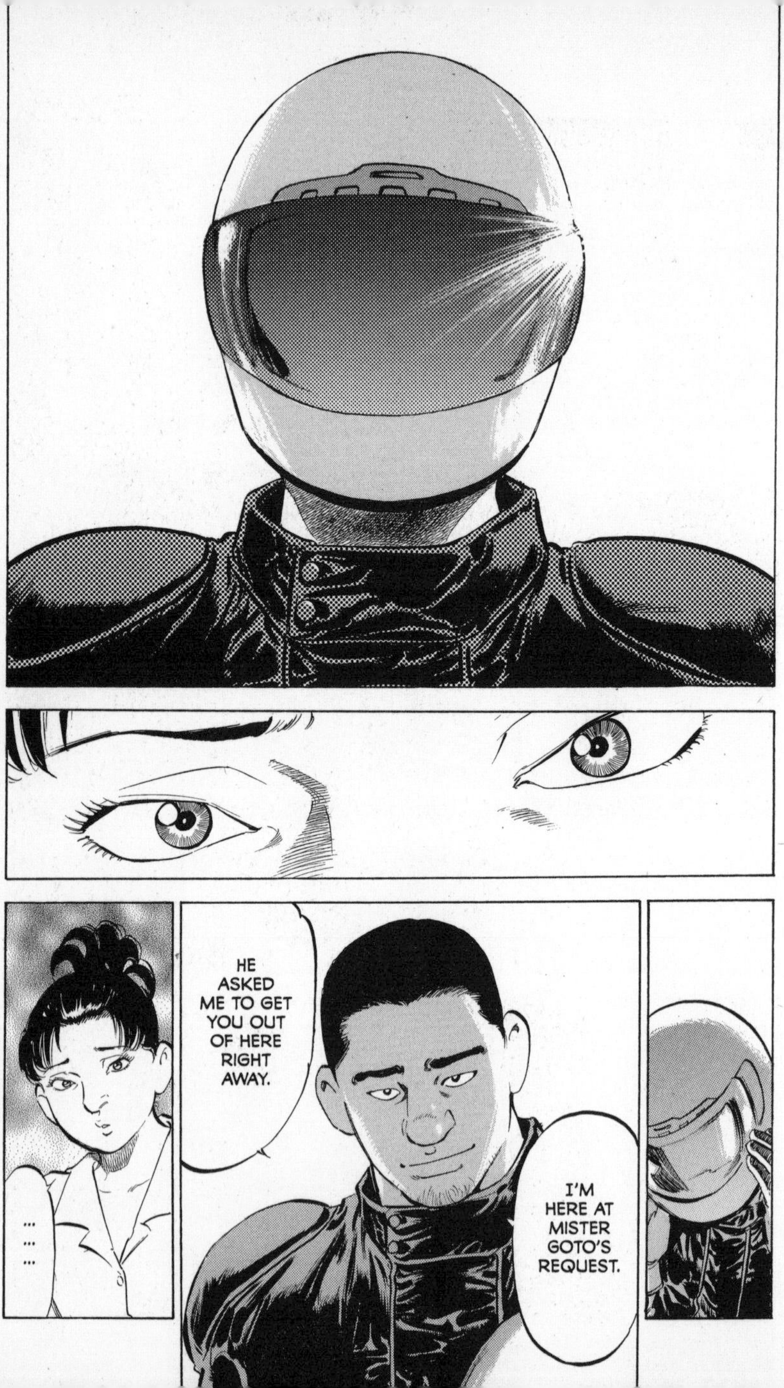
I'M HERE AT MISTER GOTO'S REQUEST.
HE ASKED ME TO GET YOU OUT OF HERE RIGHT AWAY.
...
...
...

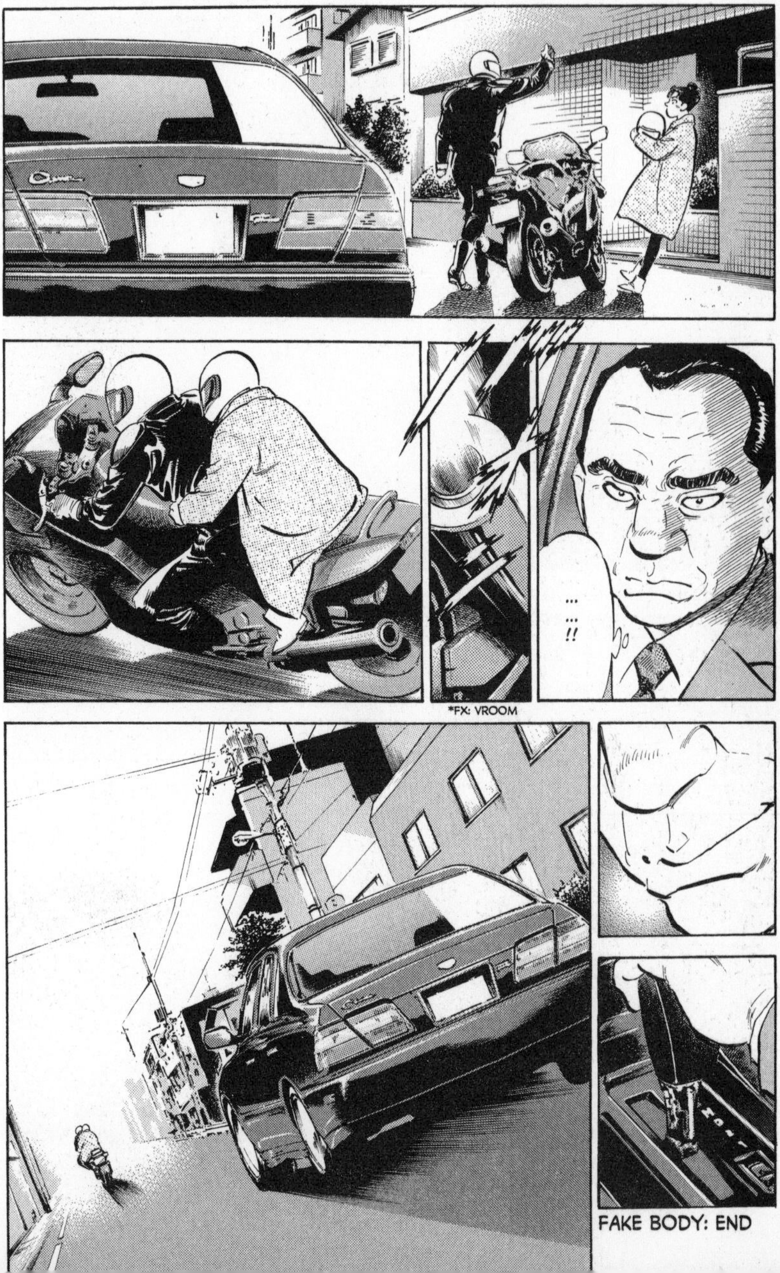
......!!
*FX: VROOM

FAKE BODY: END

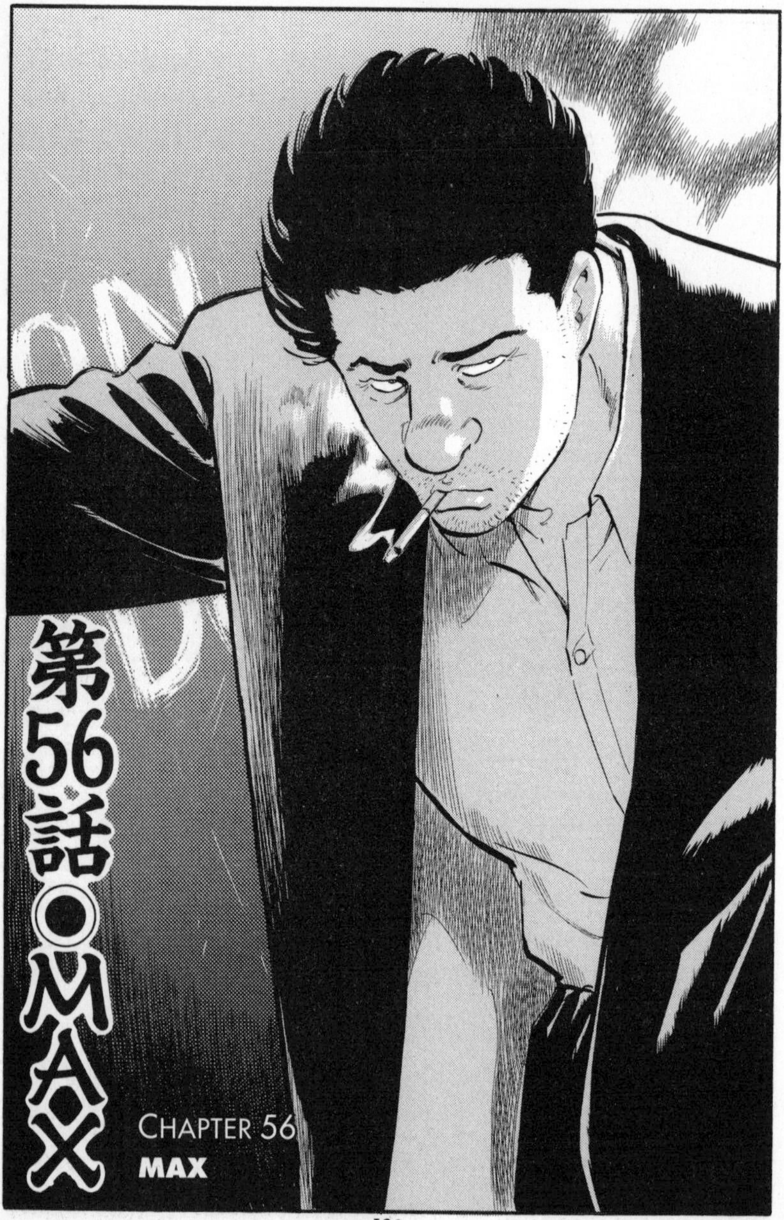
第56話○MAX
CHAPTER 56
MAX

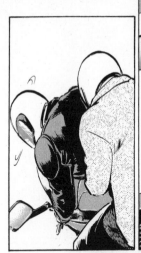

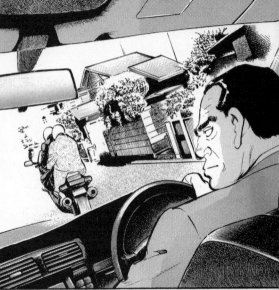

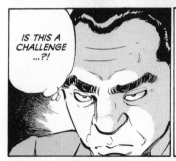

IS THIS A CHALLENGE ...?!

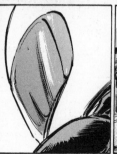

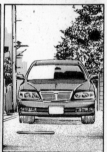

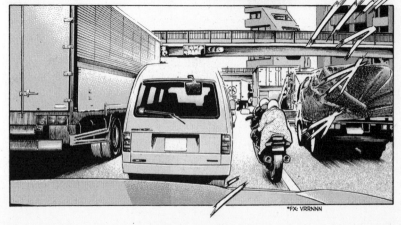

*FX: VRRNNN

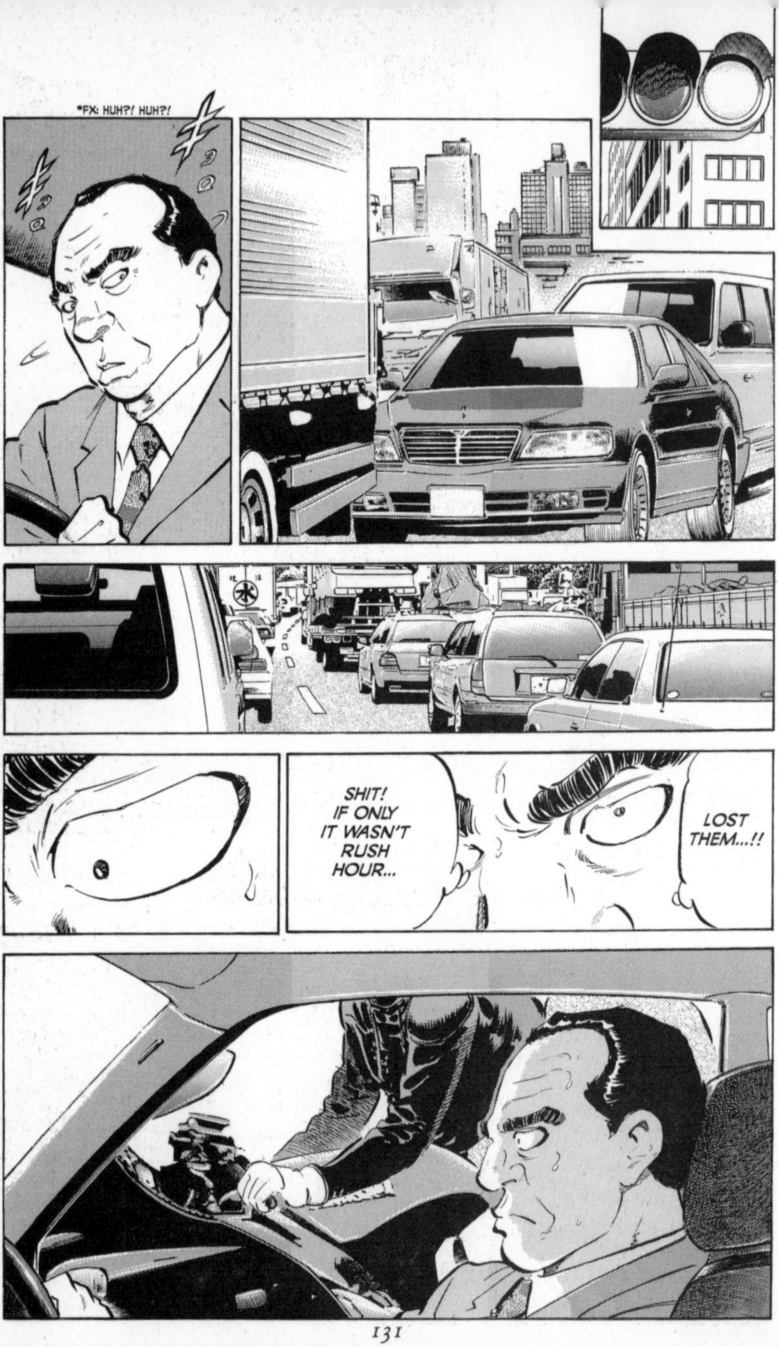
*FX: HUH?! HUH?!
SHIT! IF ONLY IT WASN'T RUSH HOUR...
LOST THEM...!!

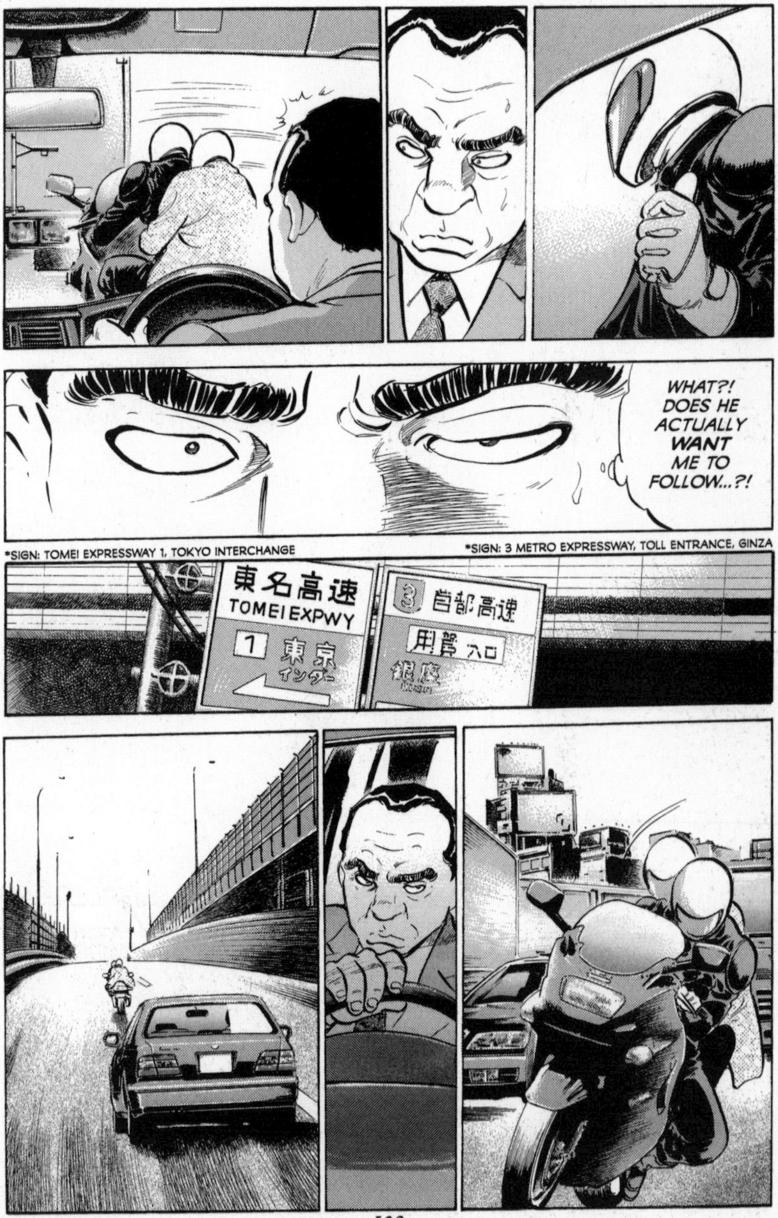
WHAT?! DOES HE ACTUALLY WANT ME TO FOLLOW...?!
*SIGN: 3 METRO EXPRESSWAY, TOLL ENTRANCE, GINZA
*SIGN: TOMEI EXPRESSWAY 1, TOKYO INTERCHANGE
東名高速
TOMEI EXPWY
1 東京 インター

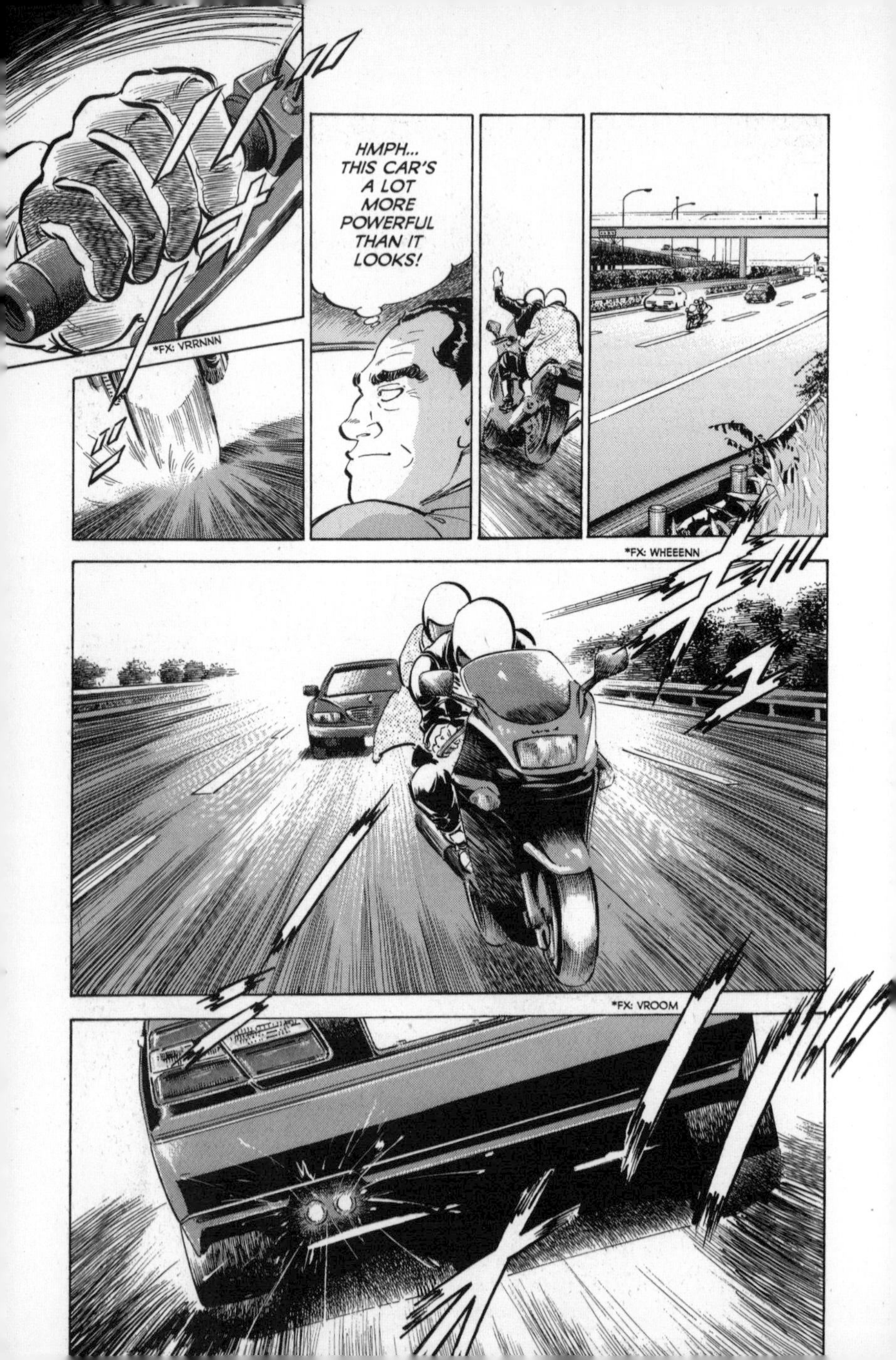
HMPH... THIS CAR'S A LOT MORE POWERFUL THAN IT LOOKS!
*FX: VRRNNN
*FX: WHEEENN
*FX: VROOM

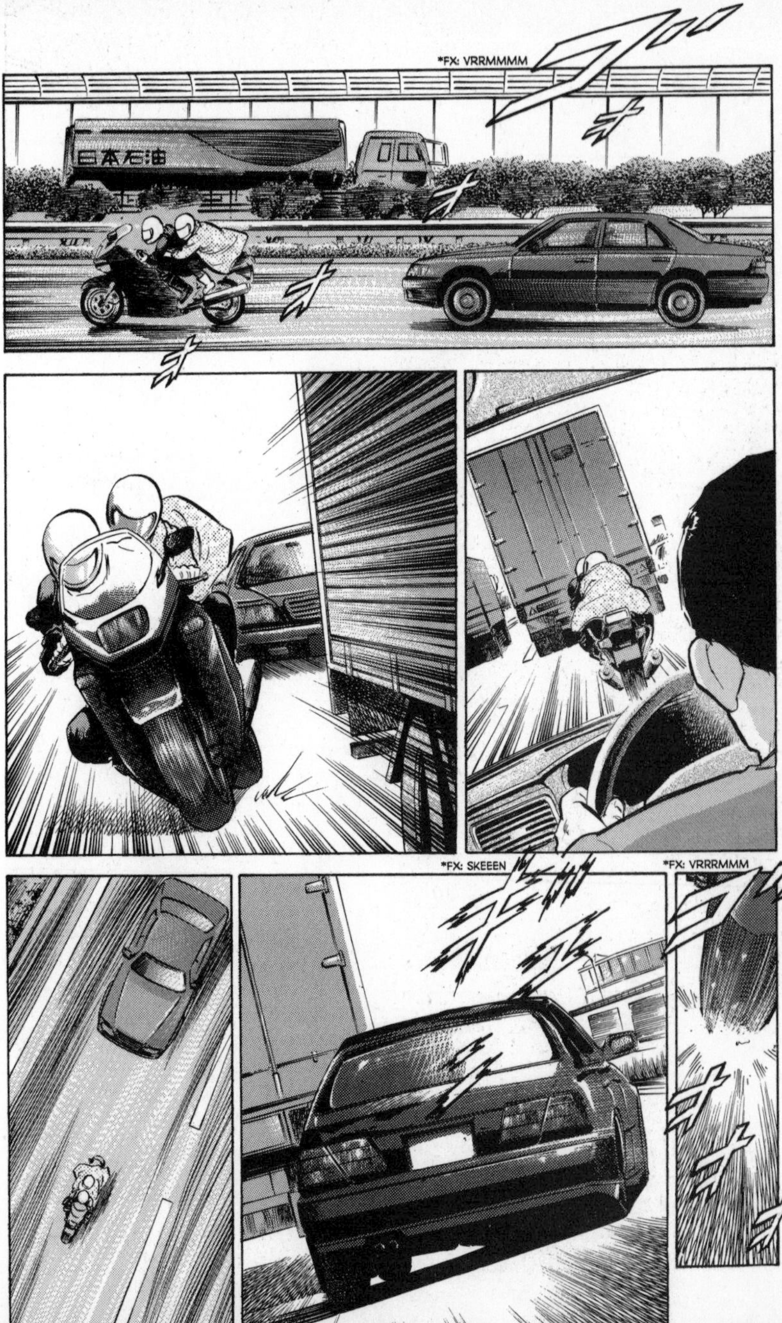
*FX: VRRMMMM
日本石油
*FX: VRRRMMM
*FX: SKEEEN

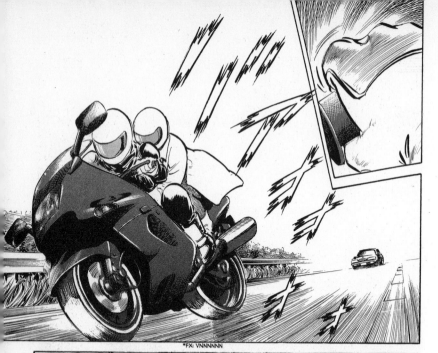

*FX: VNNNNNN

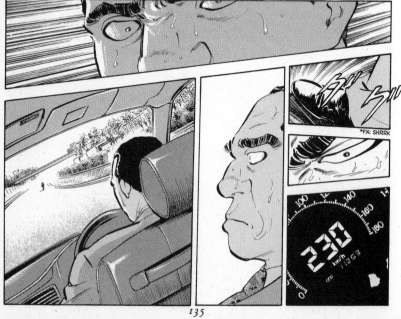

*FX: SHRRK

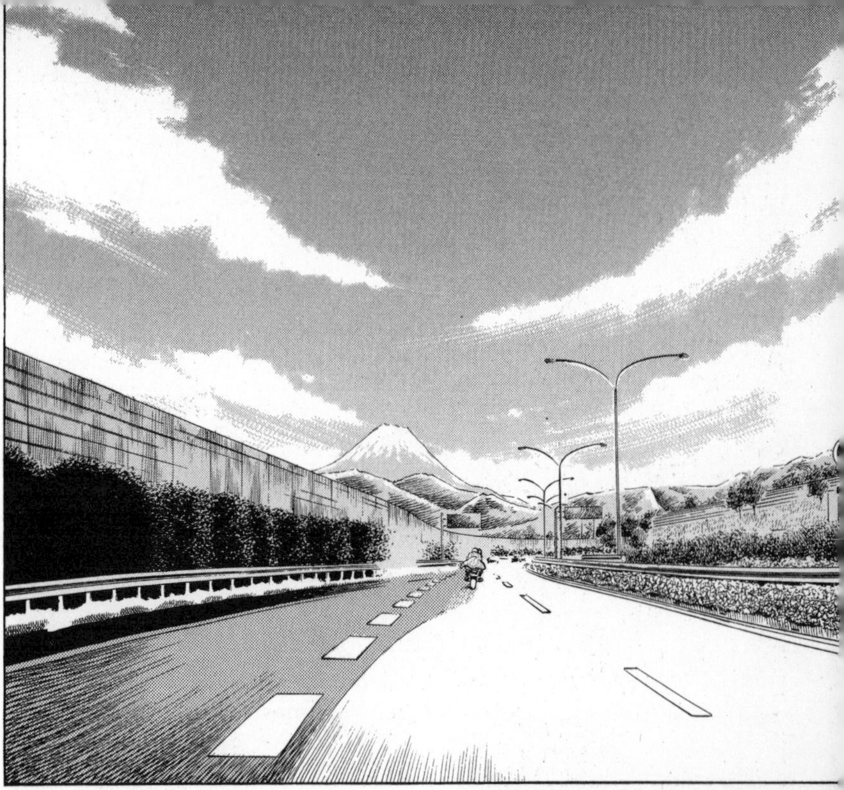

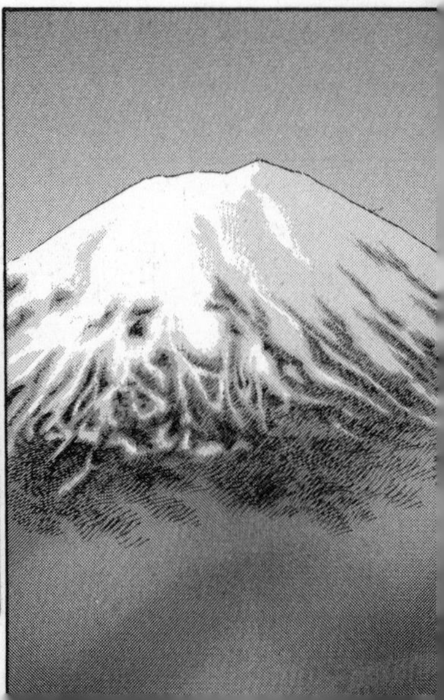

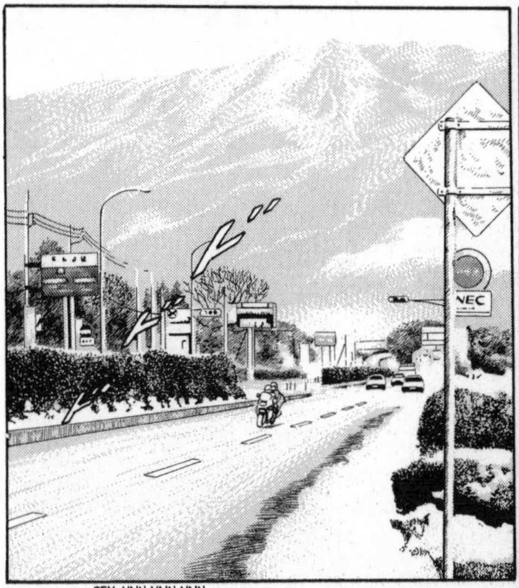
NEC

*FX: VNN VNN VNN

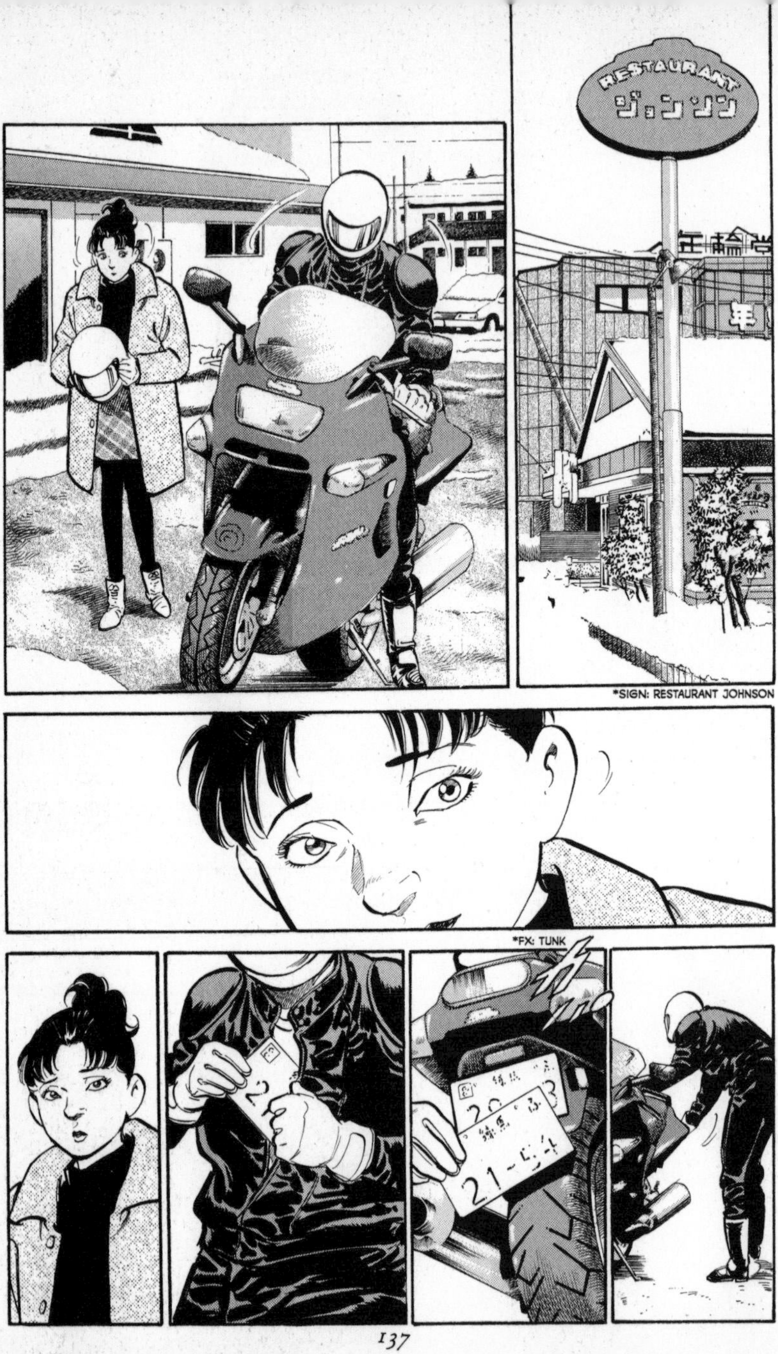
RESTAURANT
ジョンソン
*SIGN: RESTAURANT JOHNSON
*FX: TUNK

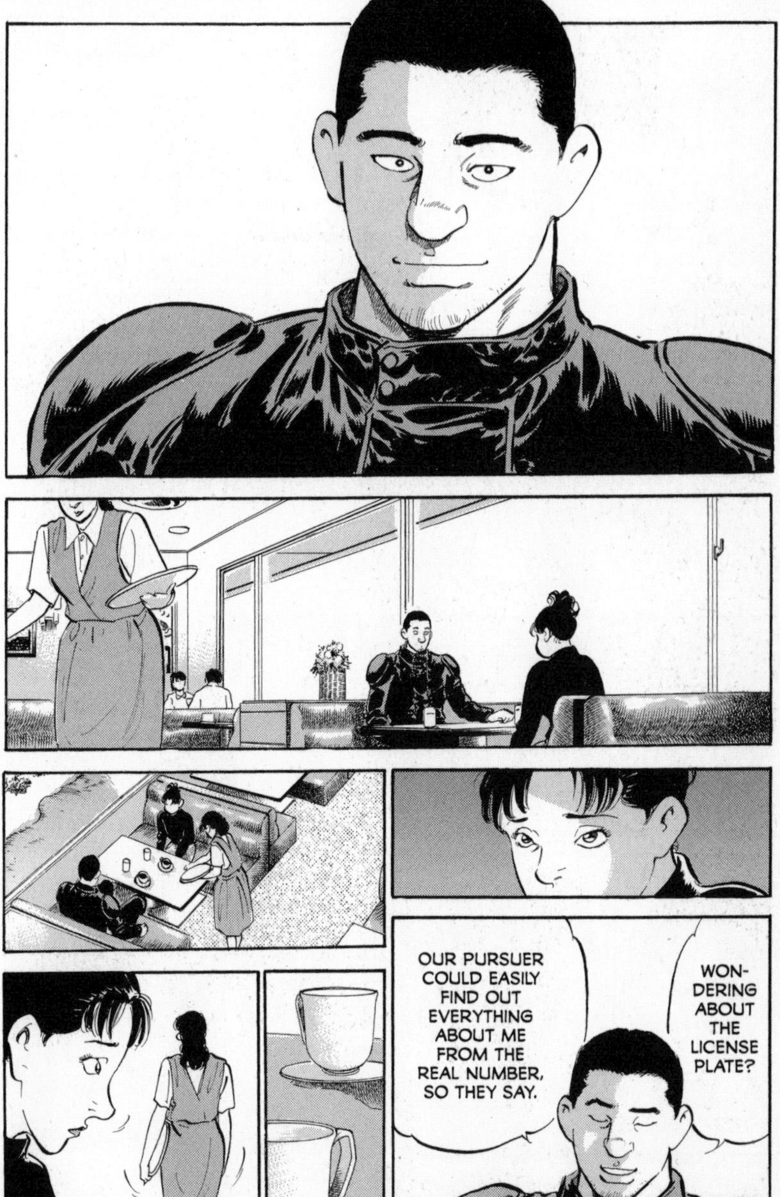
WON-DERING ABOUT THE LICENSE PLATE?
OUR PURSUER COULD EASILY FIND OUT EVERYTHING ABOUT ME FROM THE REAL NUMBER, SO THEY SAY.

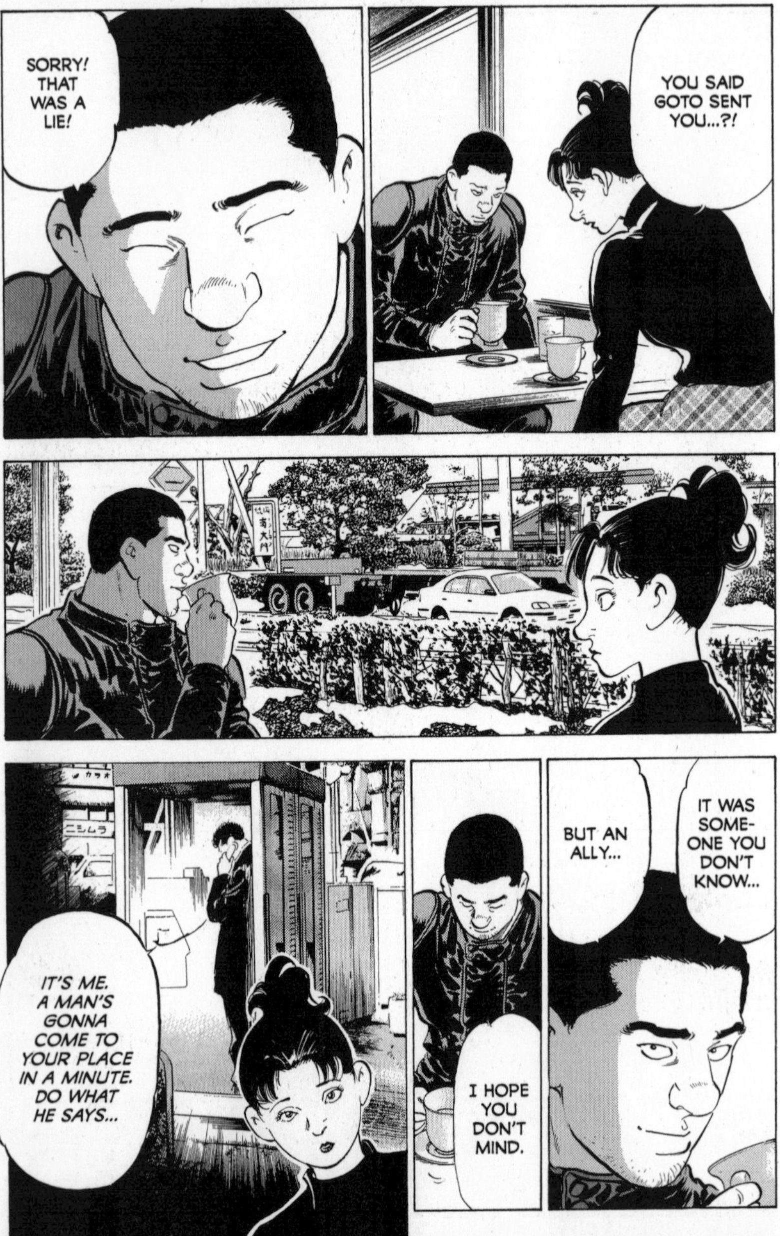
YOU SAID GOTO SENT YOU...?!
SORRY! THAT WAS A LIE!
IT WAS SOME-ONE YOU DON'T KNOW...
BUT AN ALLY...
I HOPE YOU DON'T MIND.
IT'S ME. A MAN'S GONNA COME TO YOUR PLACE IN A MINUTE. DO WHAT HE SAYS...

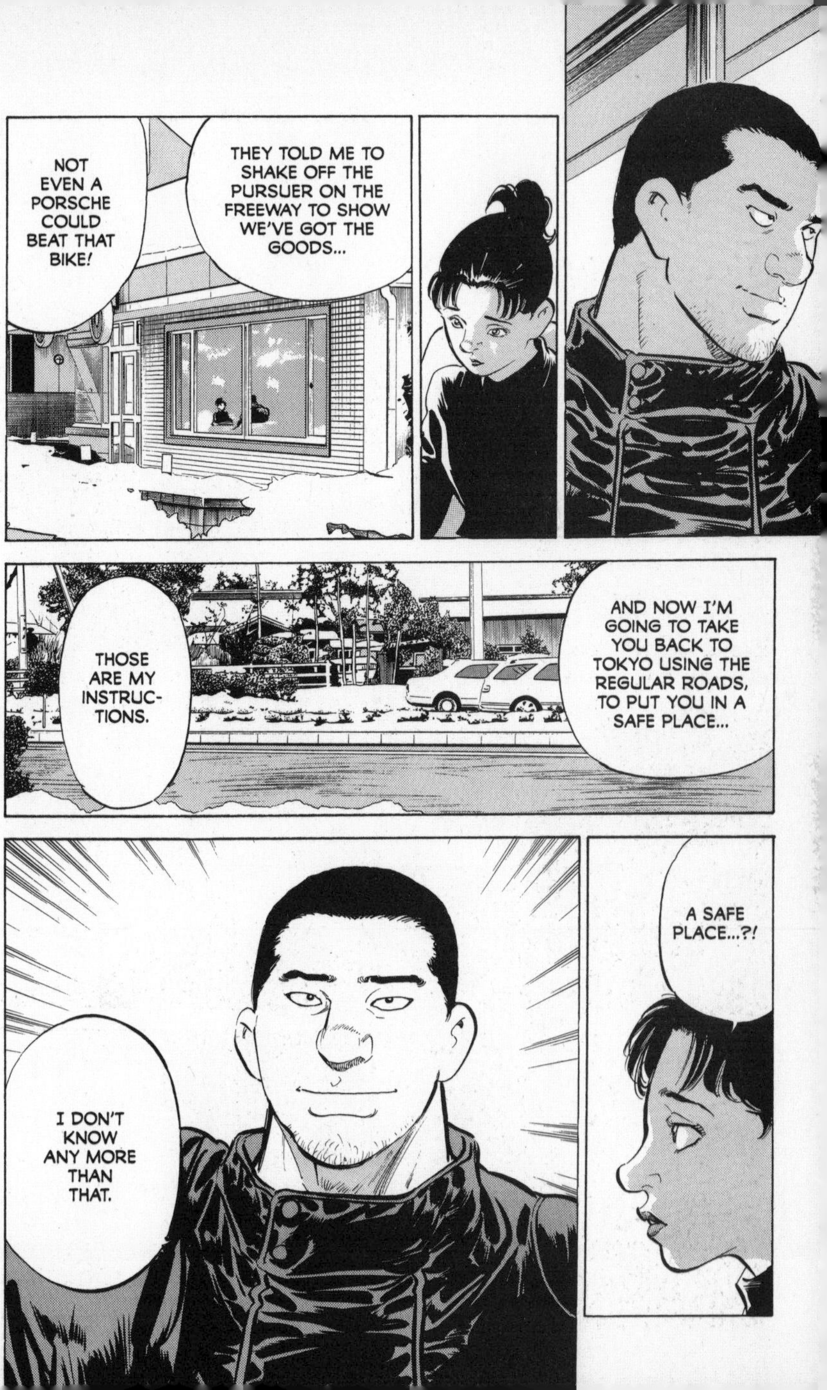
THEY TOLD ME TO SHAKE OFF THE PURSUER ON THE FREEWAY TO SHOW WE'VE GOT THE GOODS...
NOT EVEN A PORSCHE COULD BEAT THAT BIKE!
AND NOW I'M GOING TO TAKE YOU BACK TO TOKYO USING THE REGULAR ROADS, TO PUT YOU IN A SAFE PLACE...
THOSE ARE MY INSTRUC-TIONS.
A SAFE PLACE...?!
I DON'T KNOW ANY MORE THAN THAT.

*FX: VNNN

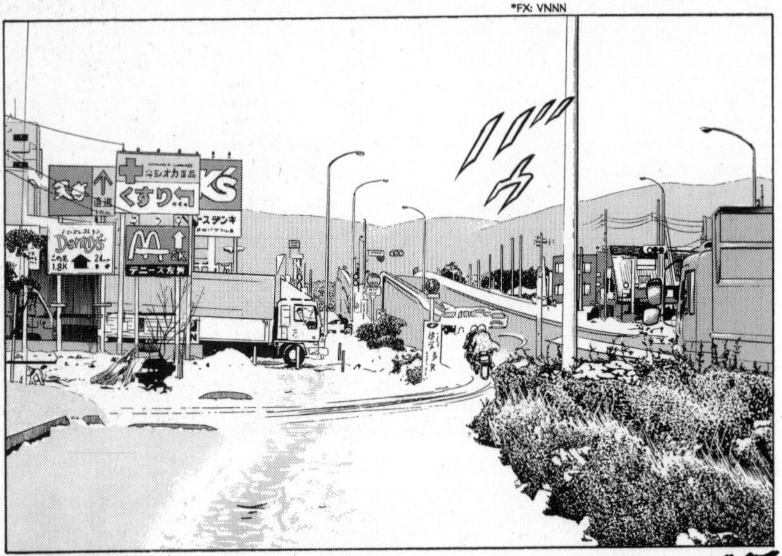

くすり
K'S
Denny's

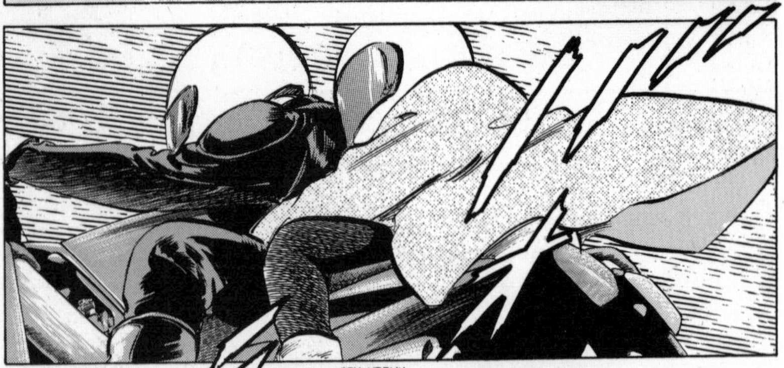

*FX: VRRNN

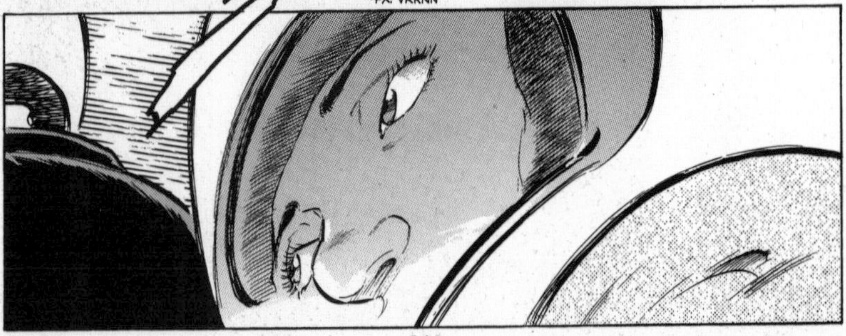

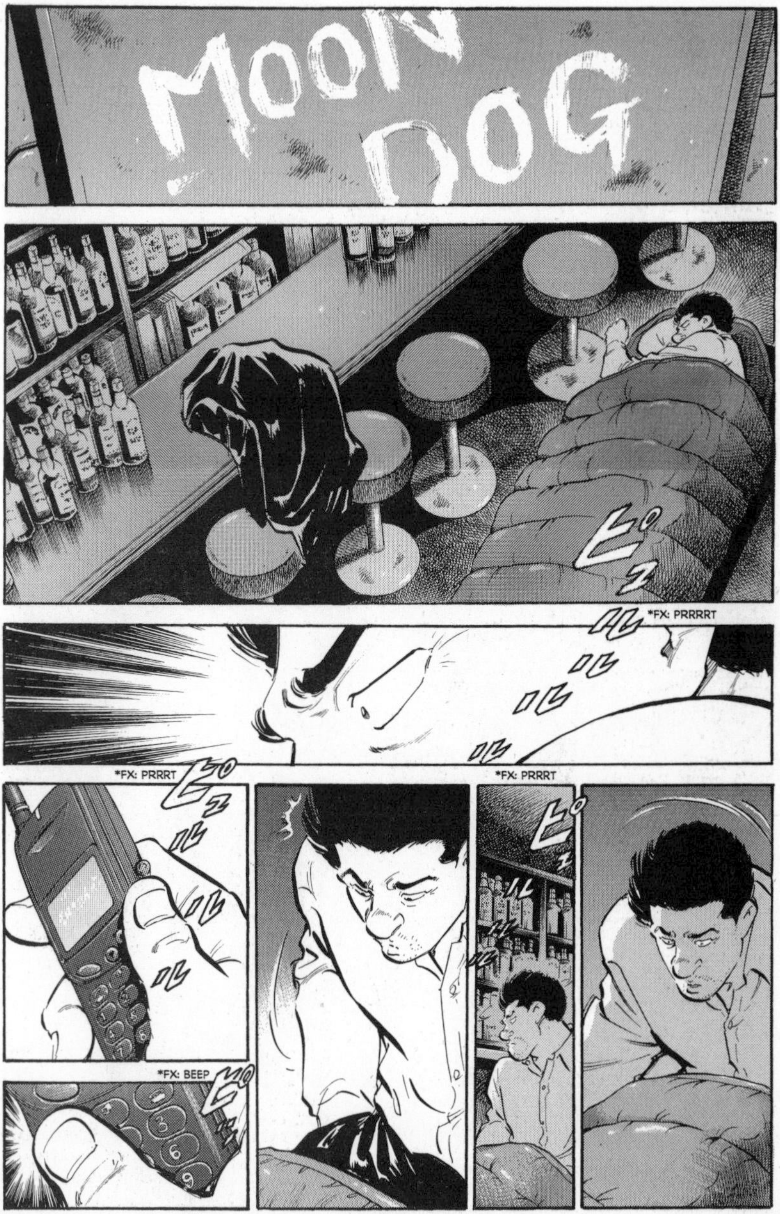
MOON DOG
*FX: PRRRRT
*FX: PRRRT
*FX: PRRRT
*FX: BEEP

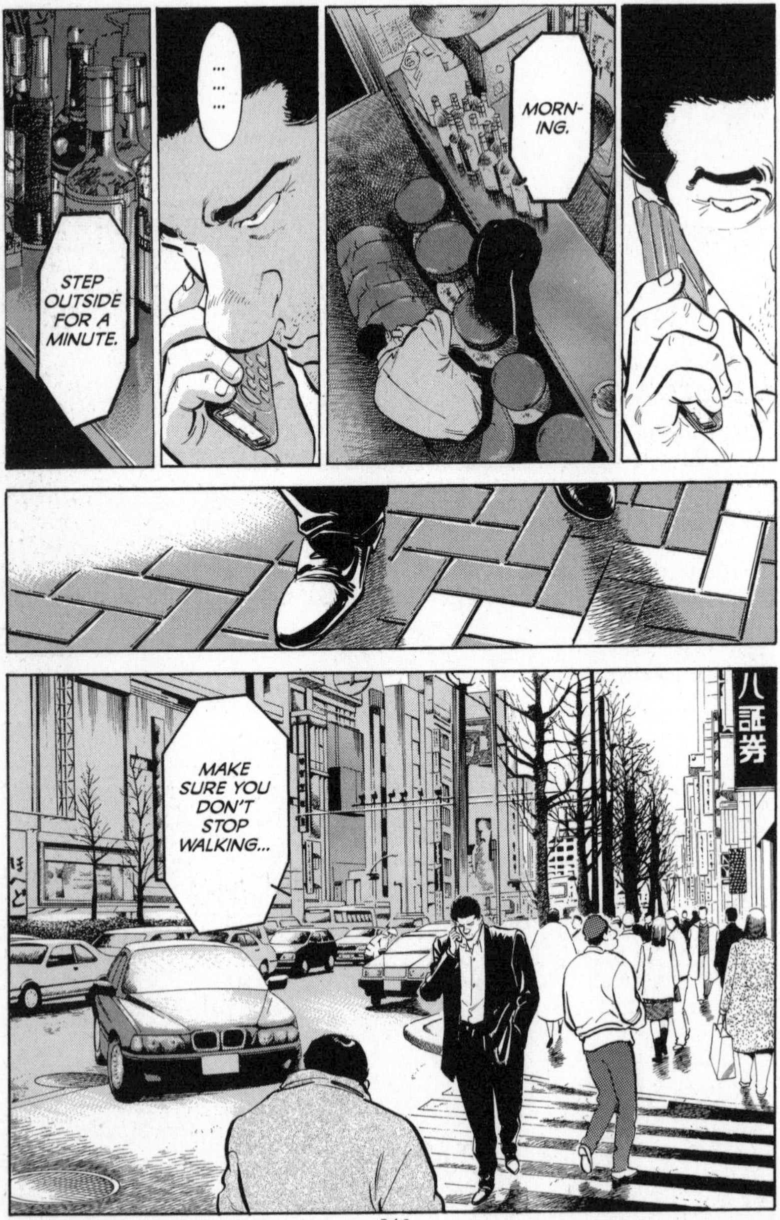
MORN-
ING.
...
...
...
STEP OUTSIDE FOR A MINUTE.
八証券
MAKE SURE YOU DON'T STOP WALKING...

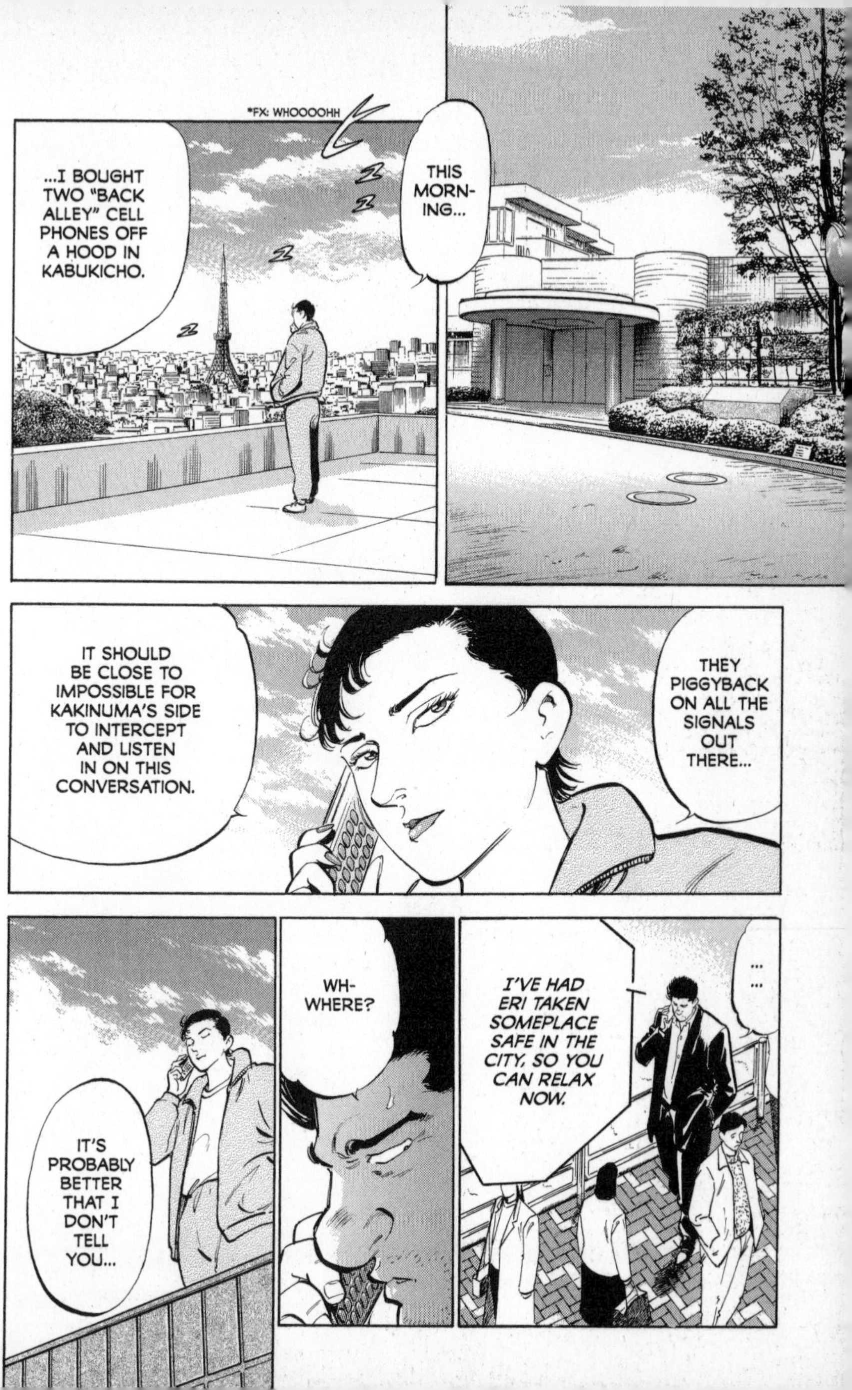
THIS MORNING...
*FX: WHOOOOHH
...I BOUGHT TWO "BACK ALLEY" CELL PHONES OFF A HOOD IN KABUKICHO.
THEY PIGGYBACK ON ALL THE SIGNALS OUT THERE...
IT SHOULD BE CLOSE TO IMPOSSIBLE FOR KAKINUMA'S SIDE TO INTERCEPT AND LISTEN IN ON THIS CONVERSATION.
......
I'VE HAD ERI TAKEN SOMEPLACE SAFE IN THE CITY, SO YOU CAN RELAX NOW.
WH-WHERE?
IT'S PROBABLY BETTER THAT I DON'T TELL YOU...

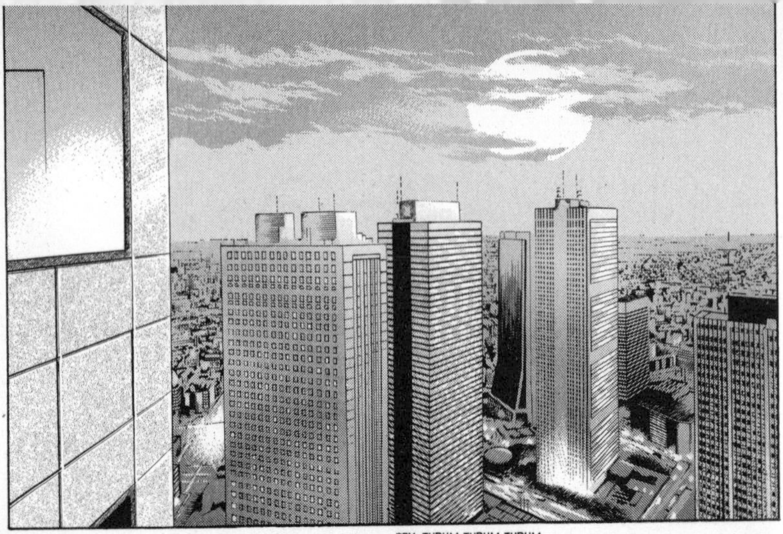

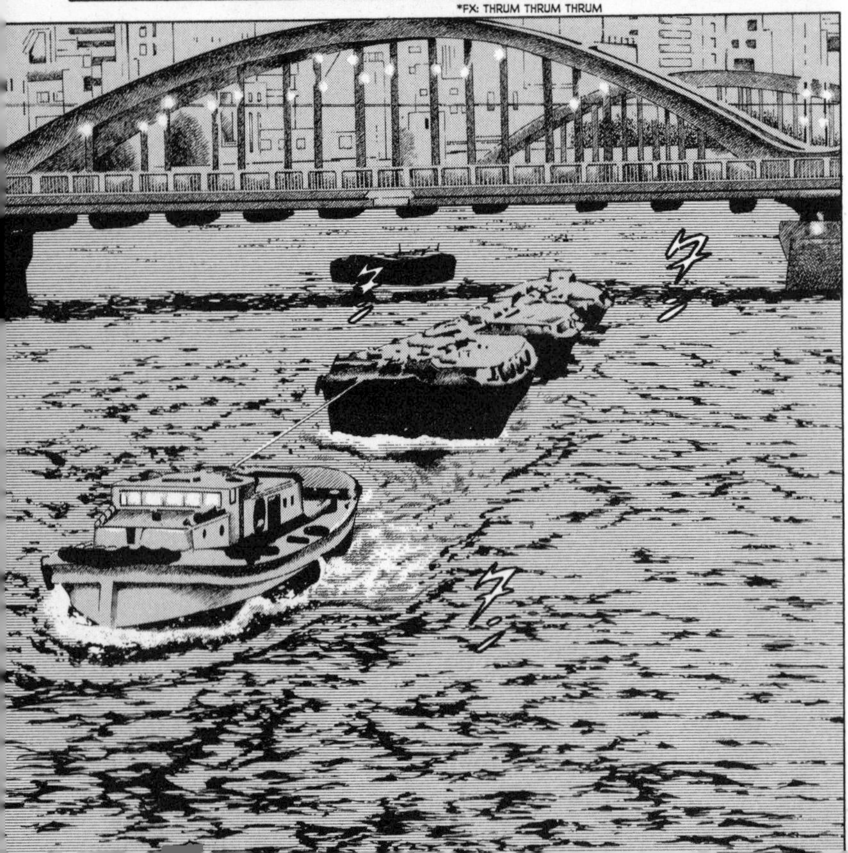
*FX: THRUM THRUM THRUM

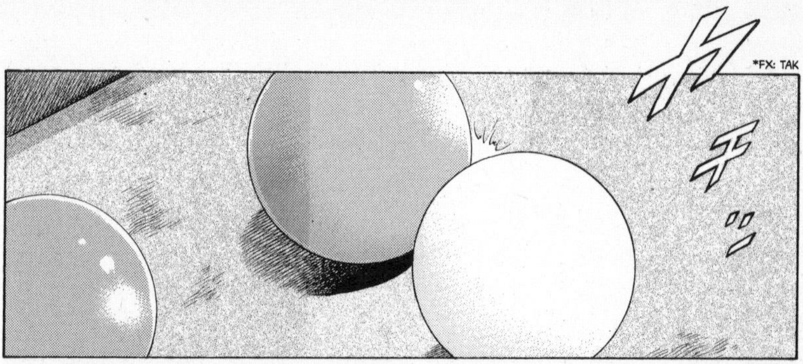
カチッ
*FX: TAK
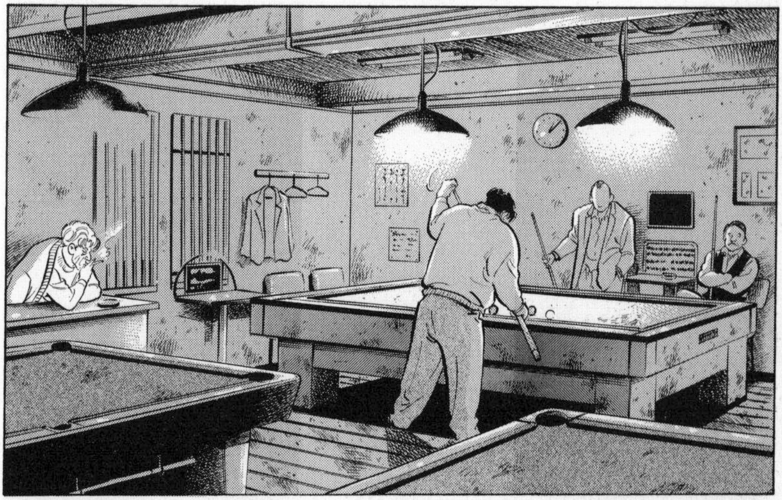
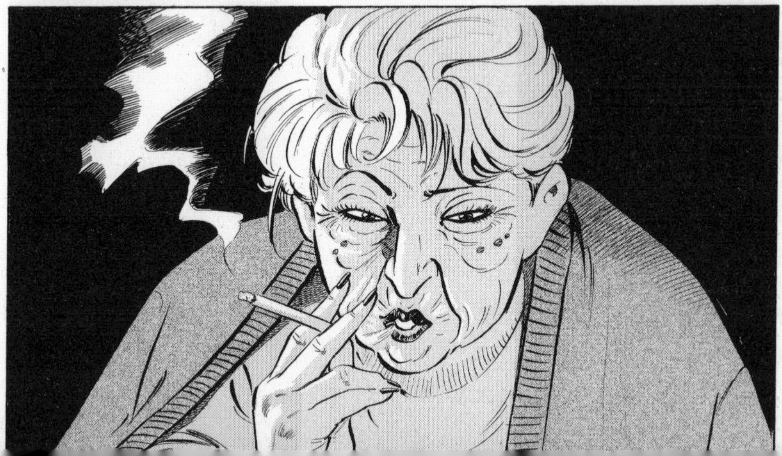

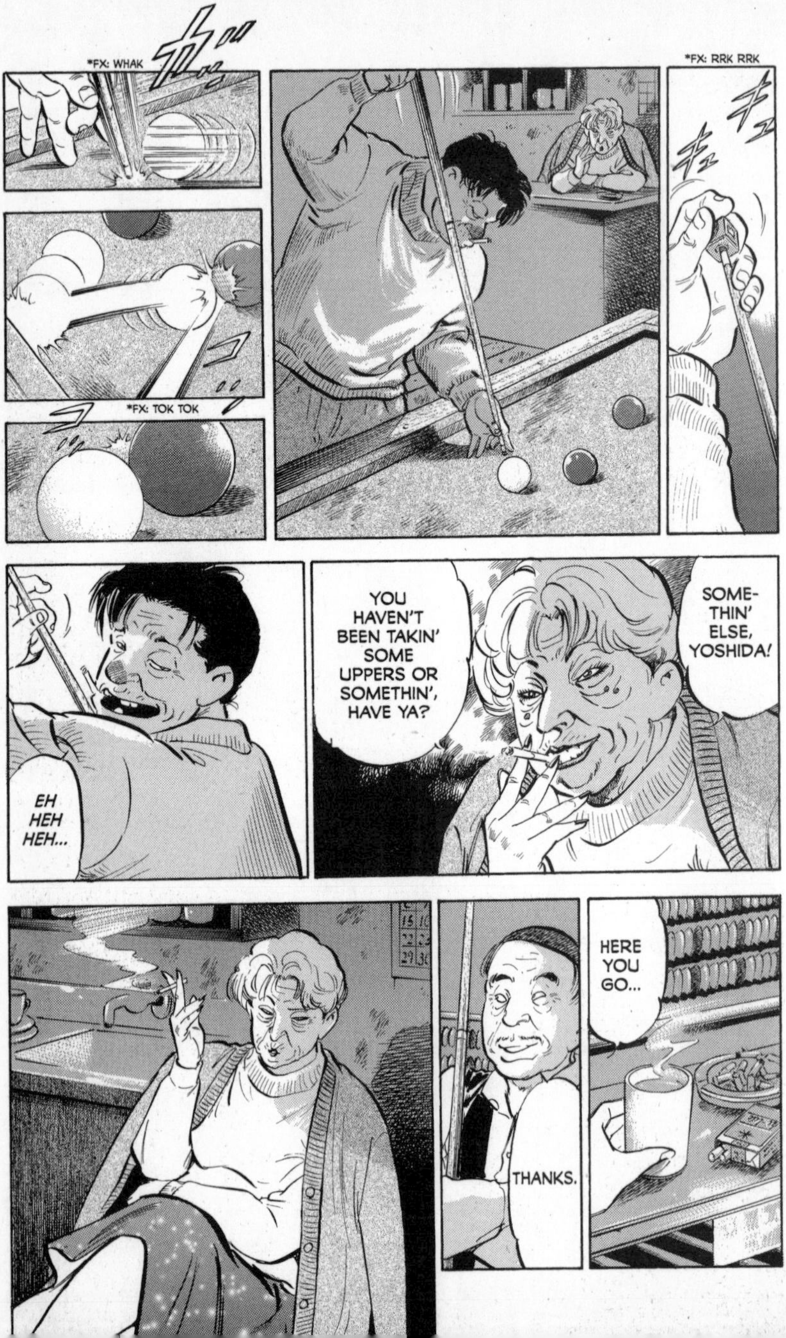
*FX: RRK RRK
*FX: WHAK
*FX: TOK TOK
SOME-THIN' ELSE, YOSHIDA!
YOU HAVEN'T BEEN TAKIN' SOME UPPERS OR SOMETHIN', HAVE YA?
EH HEH HEH...
HERE YOU GO...
THANKS.

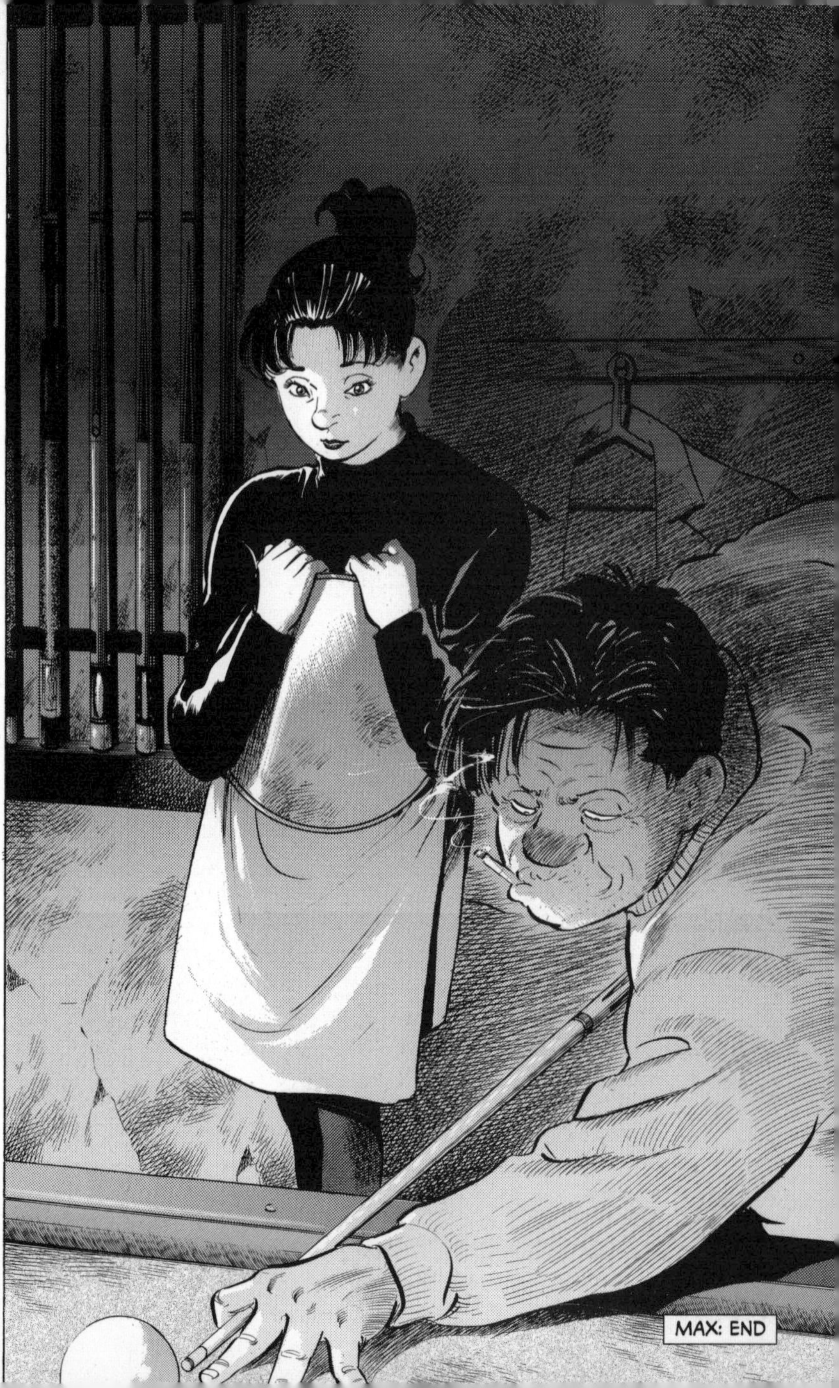
MAX: END

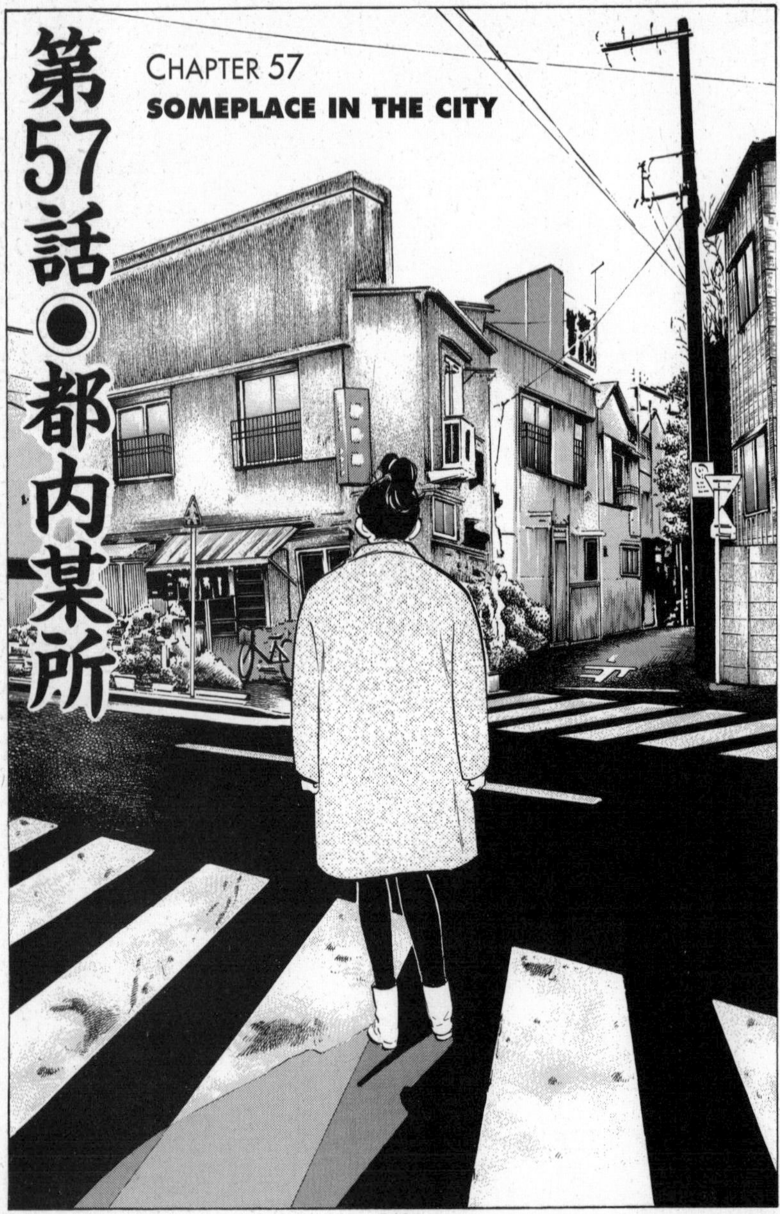
第57話◉都内某所
CHAPTER 57
SOMEPLACE IN THE CITY

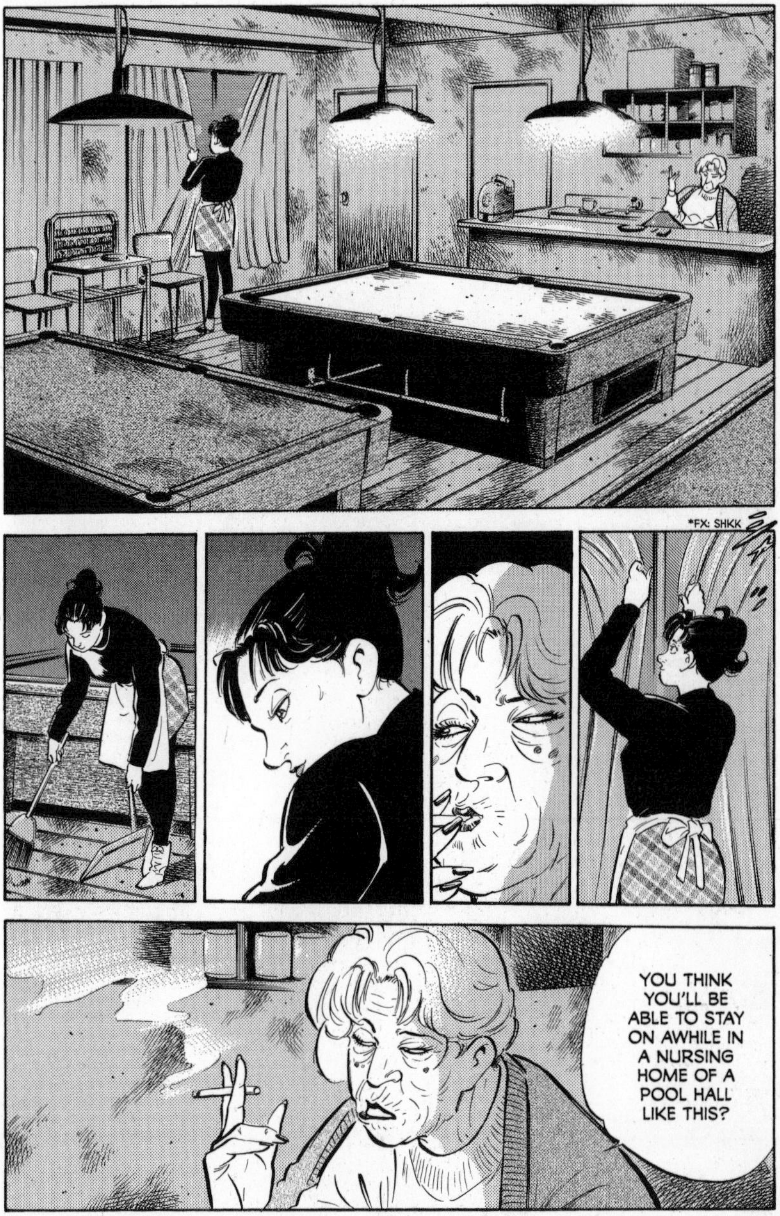
*FX: SHKK
YOU THINK YOU'LL BE ABLE TO STAY ON AWHILE IN A NURSING HOME OF A POOL HALL LIKE THIS?

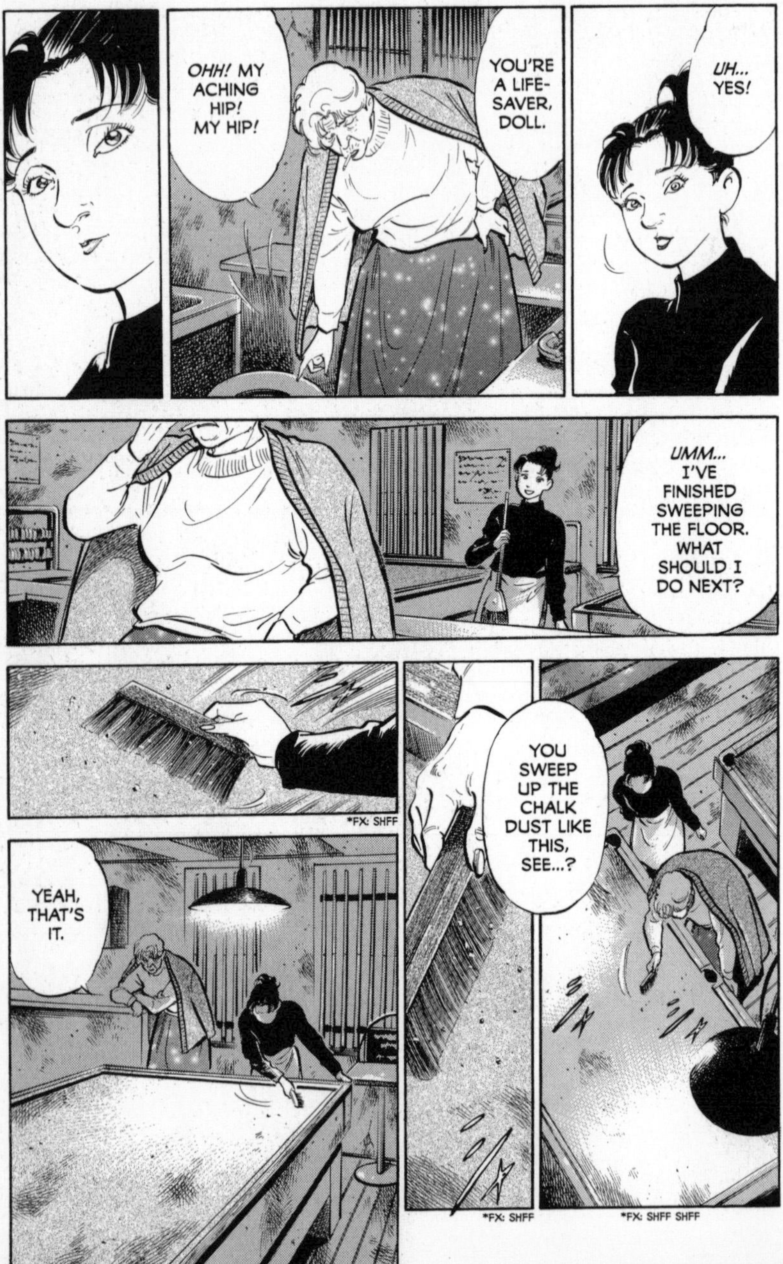
UH... YES!
YOU'RE A LIFE-SAVER, DOLL.
OHH! MY ACHING HIP! MY HIP!
UMM... I'VE FINISHED SWEEPING THE FLOOR. WHAT SHOULD I DO NEXT?
*FX: SHFF SHFF
YOU SWEEP UP THE CHALK DUST LIKE THIS, SEE...?
*FX: SHFF
*FX: SHFF
YEAH, THAT'S IT.

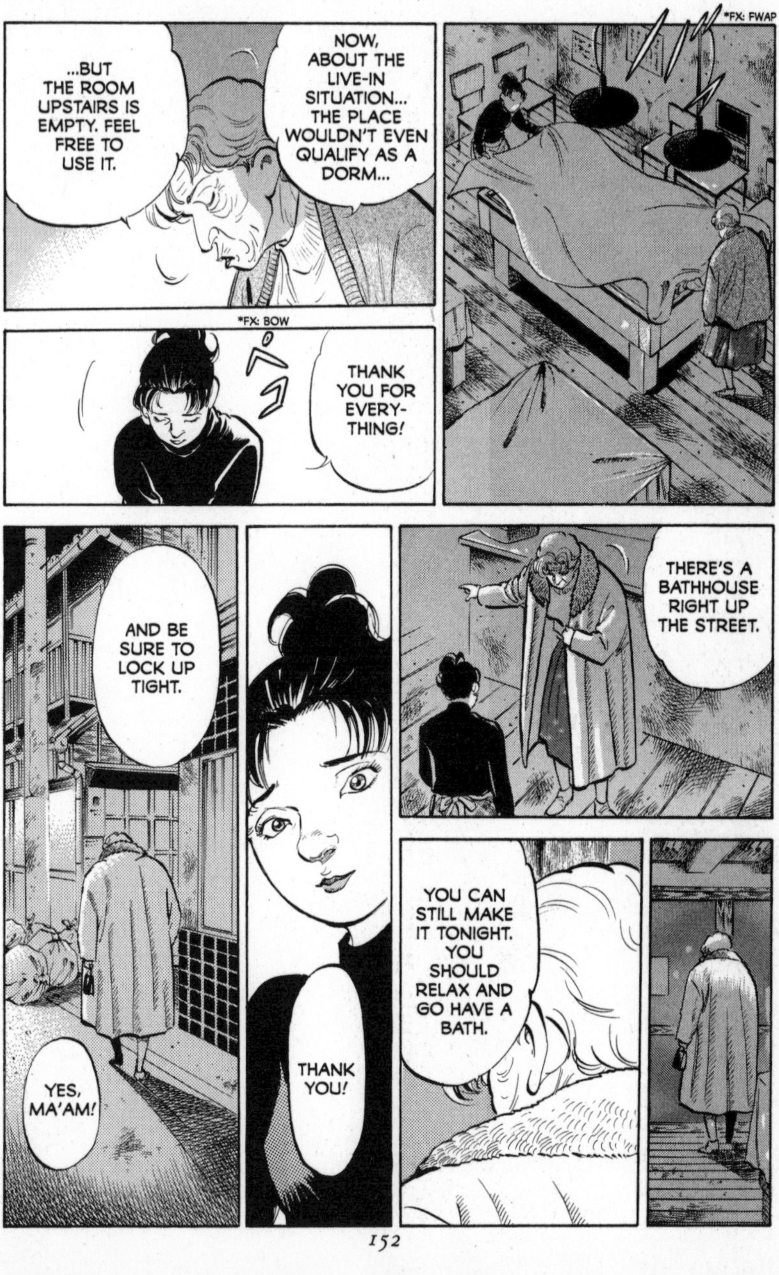
*FX: FWAP
NOW, ABOUT THE LIVE-IN SITUATION... THE PLACE WOULDN'T EVEN QUALIFY AS A DORM...
...BUT THE ROOM UPSTAIRS IS EMPTY. FEEL FREE TO USE IT.
*FX: BOW
THANK YOU FOR EVERY-THING!
THERE'S A BATHHOUSE RIGHT UP THE STREET.
YOU CAN STILL MAKE IT TONIGHT. YOU SHOULD RELAX AND GO HAVE A BATH.
THANK YOU!
AND BE SURE TO LOCK UP TIGHT.
YES, MA'AM!

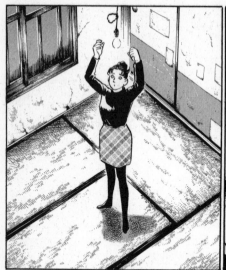

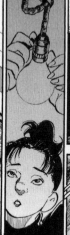

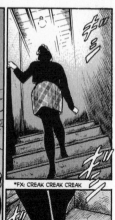

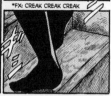

*FX: CREAK CREAK CREAK

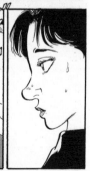

*FX: CLAK CLAK

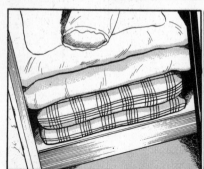

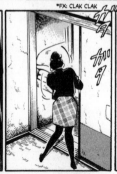

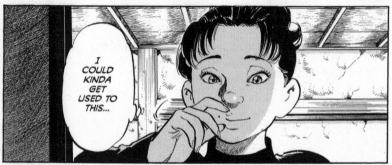

I COULD KINDA GET USED TO THIS...

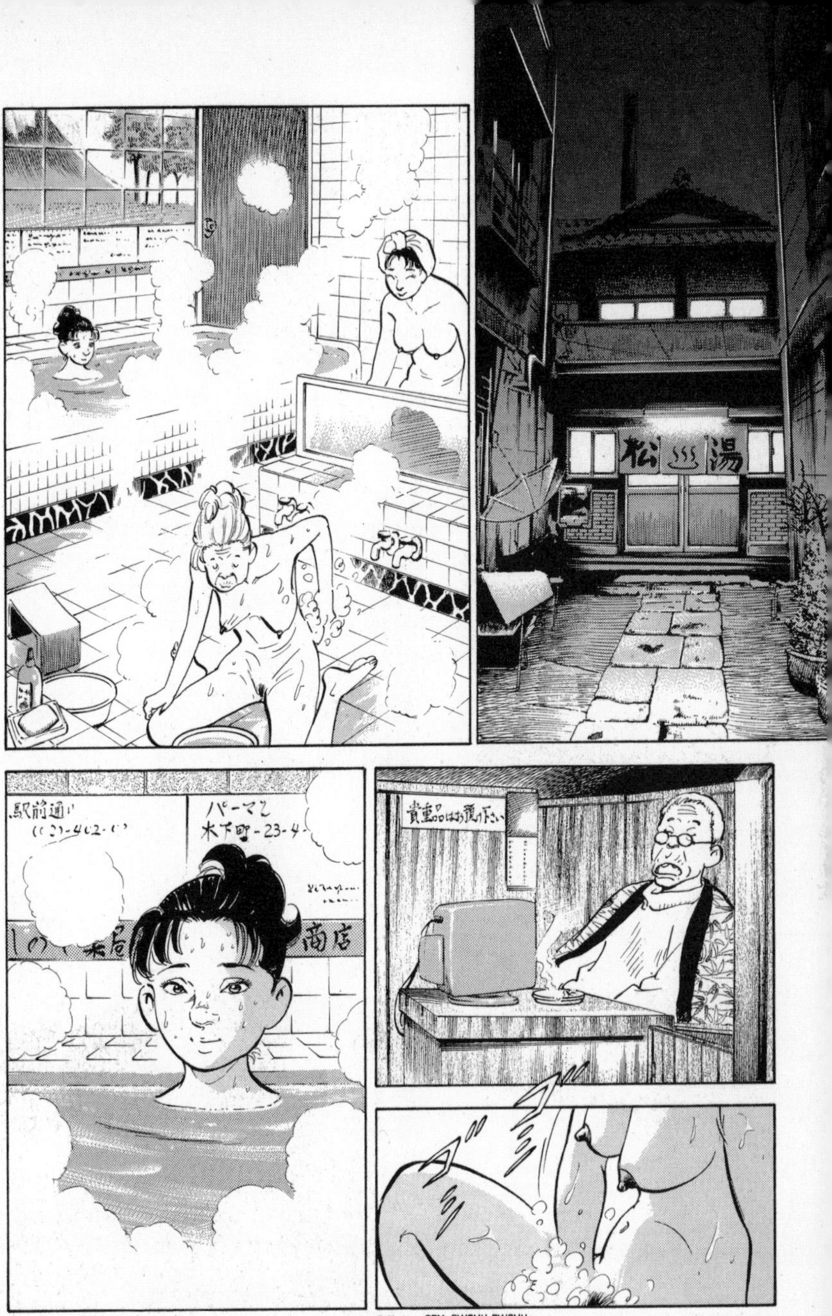
松湯
貴重品はお預け下さい
駅前通り
パーマ
木下町-23-4
商店

*FX: FWSHH FWSHH

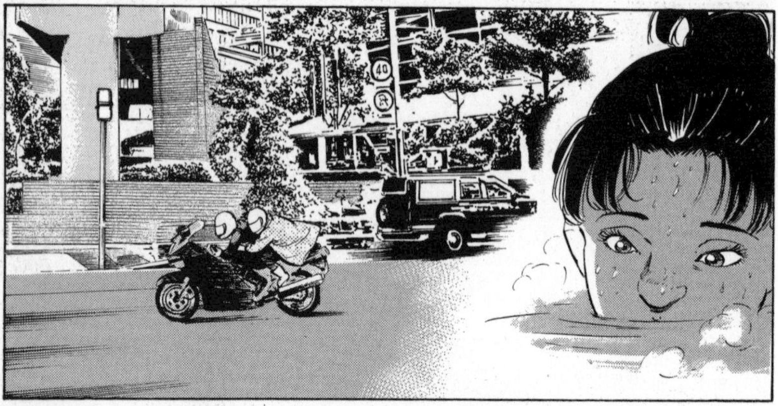

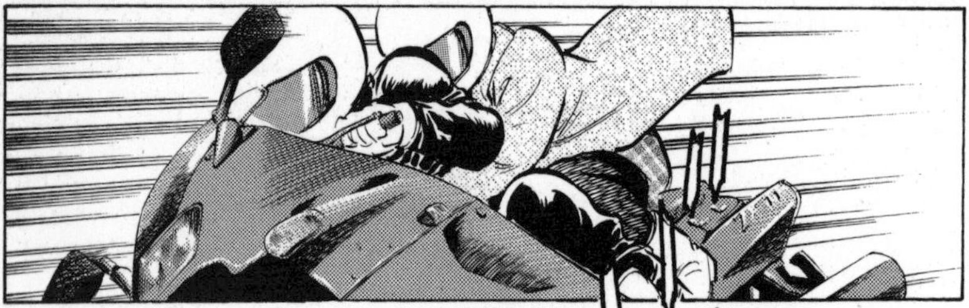

*FX: VROOOMM

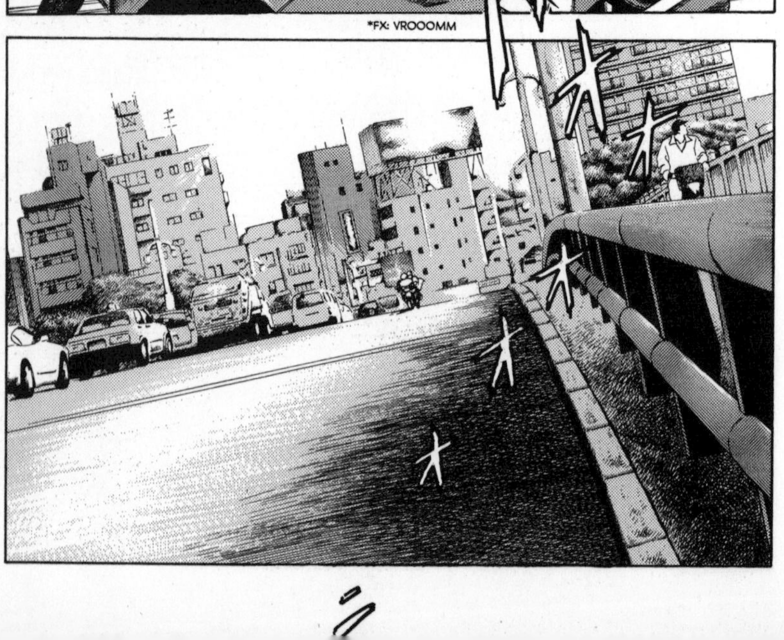

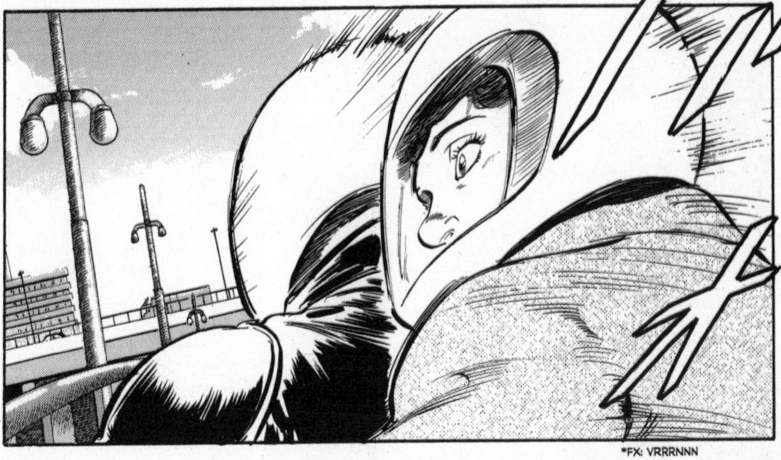

*FX: VRRRNNN

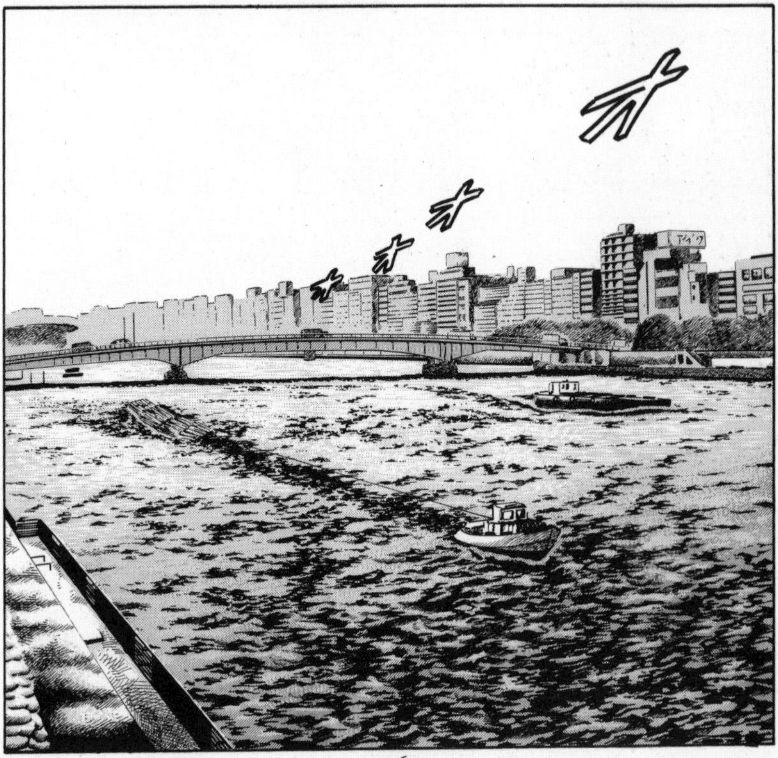

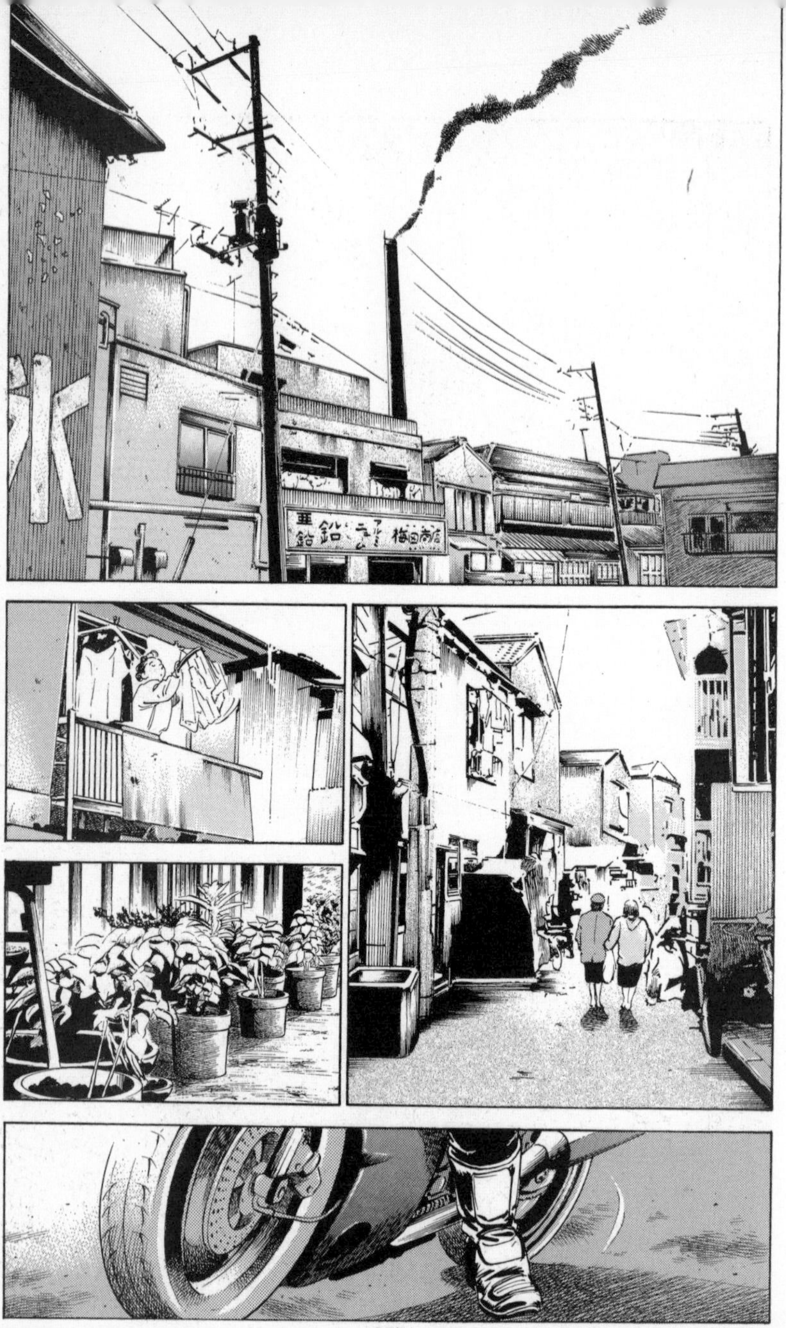
亜鉛 鉛 アルミニウム 梅田商店

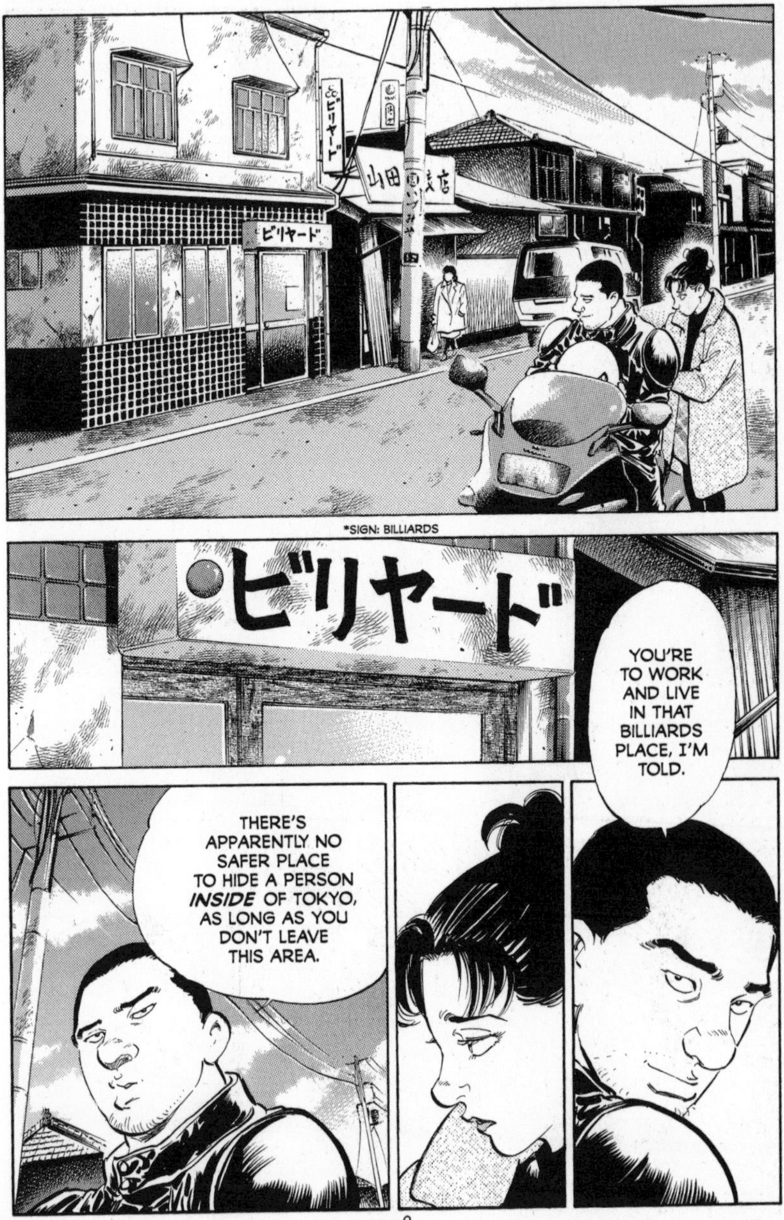
ビリヤード
ビリヤード
*SIGN: BILLIARDS
ビリヤード
YOU'RE TO WORK AND LIVE IN THAT BILLIARDS PLACE, I'M TOLD.
THERE'S APPARENTLY NO SAFER PLACE TO HIDE A PERSON *INSIDE* OF TOKYO, AS LONG AS YOU DON'T LEAVE THIS AREA.

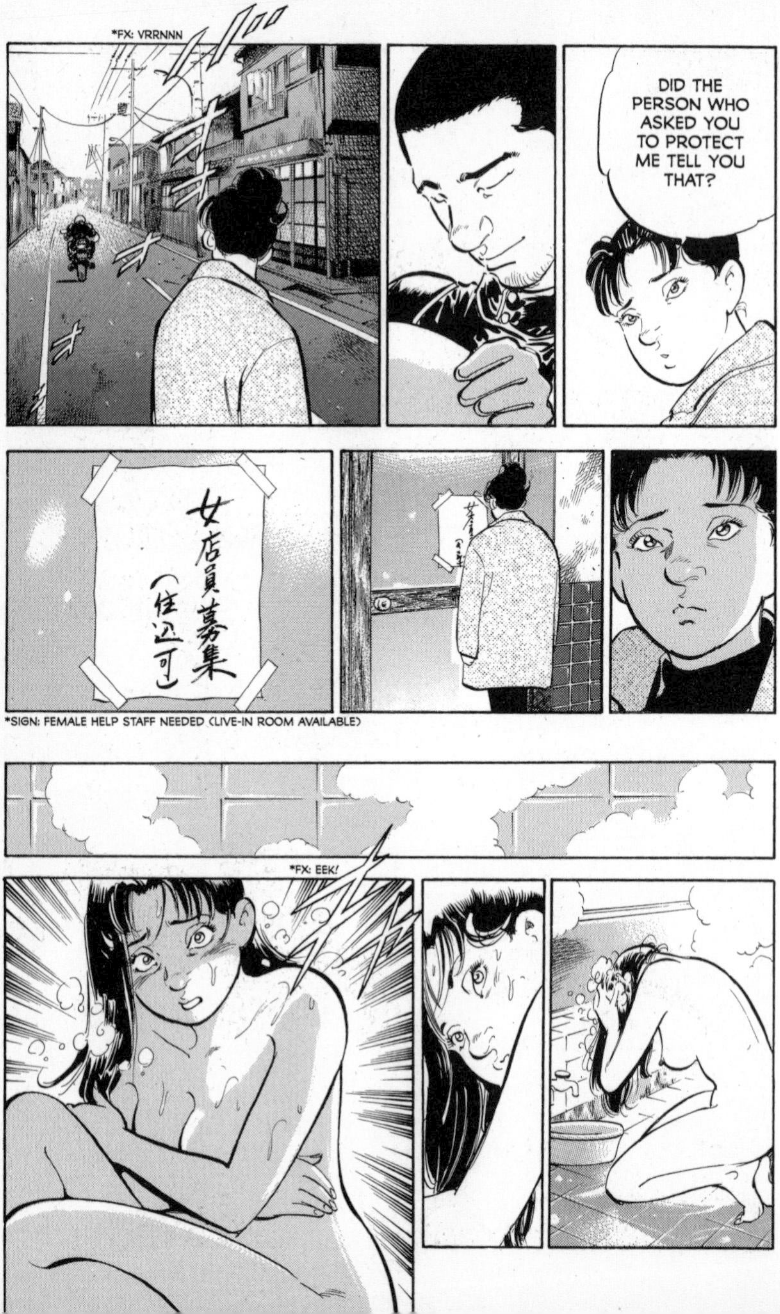
DID THE PERSON WHO ASKED YOU TO PROTECT ME TELL YOU THAT?
*FX: VRRNNN
女店員募集（住込可）
*SIGN: FEMALE HELP STAFF NEEDED (LIVE-IN ROOM AVAILABLE)
*FX: EEK!

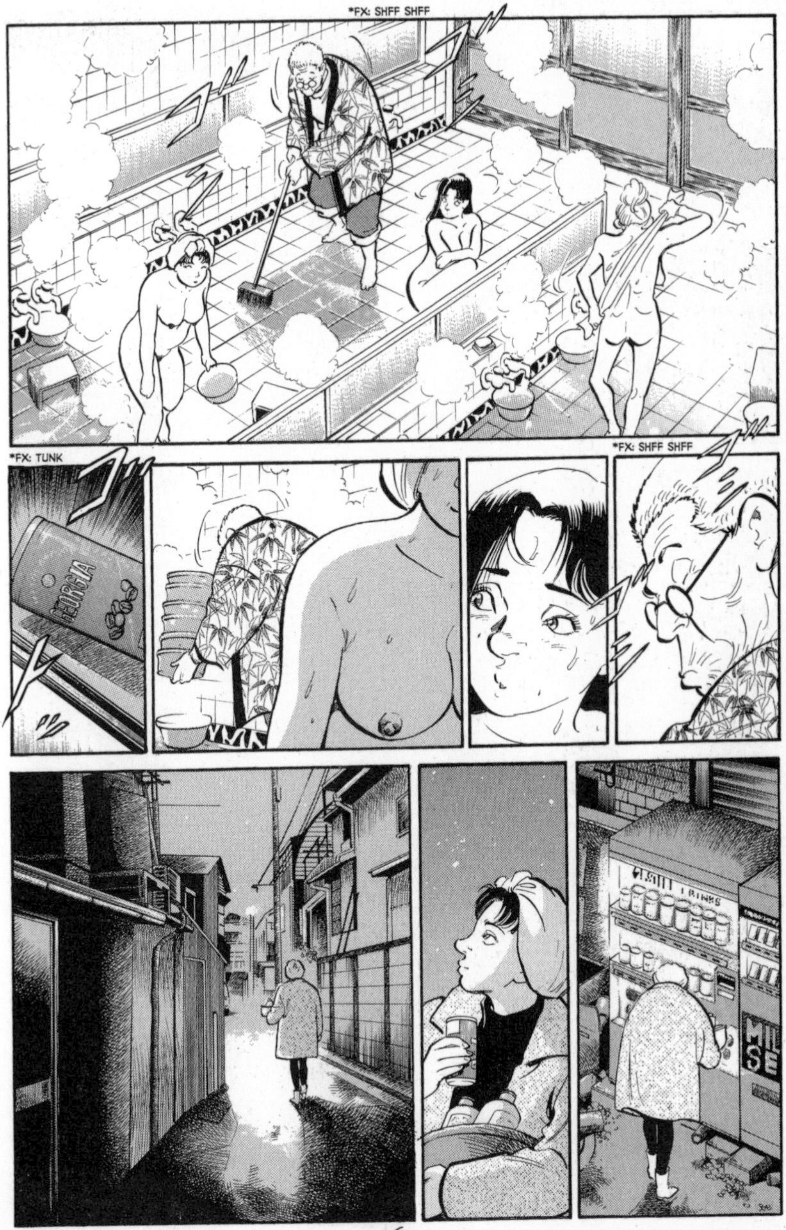
*FX: SHFF SHFF
*FX: SHFF SHFF
GEORGIA
*FX: TUNK

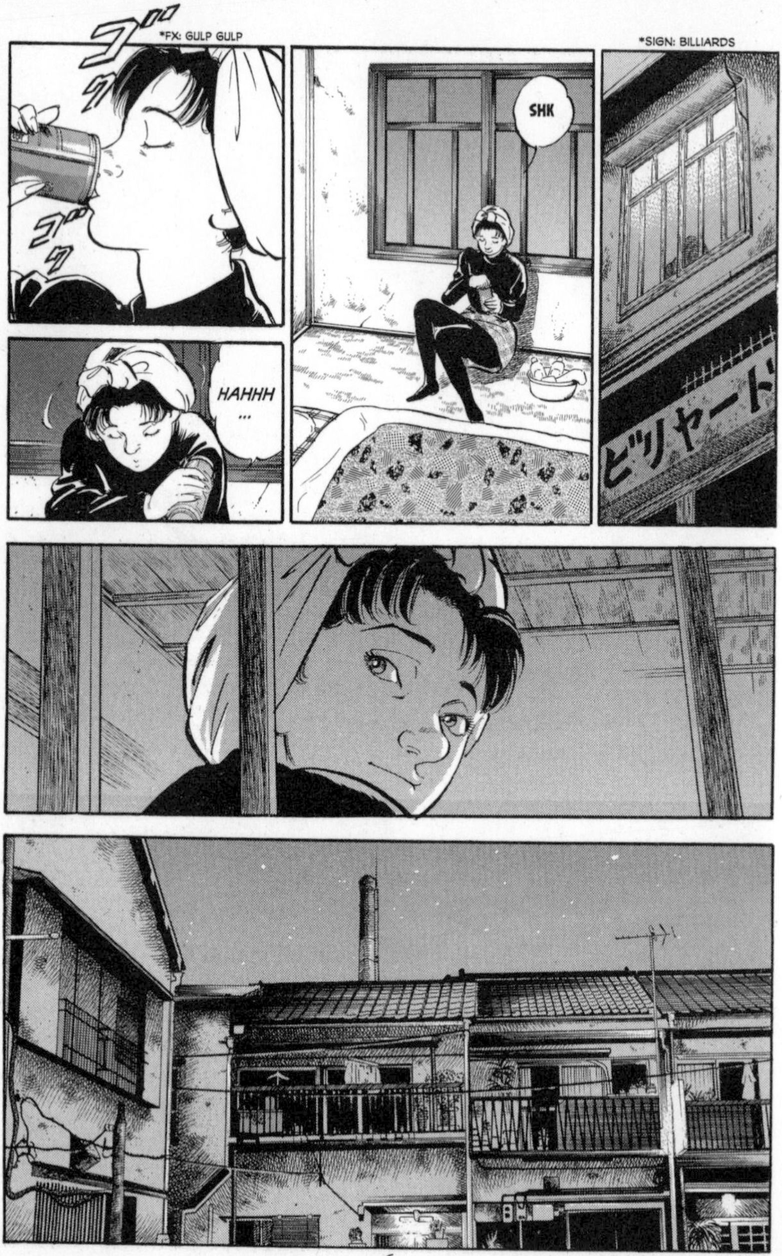
*SIGN: BILLIARDS
ビリヤード
SHK
*FX: GULP GULP
HAHHH ...

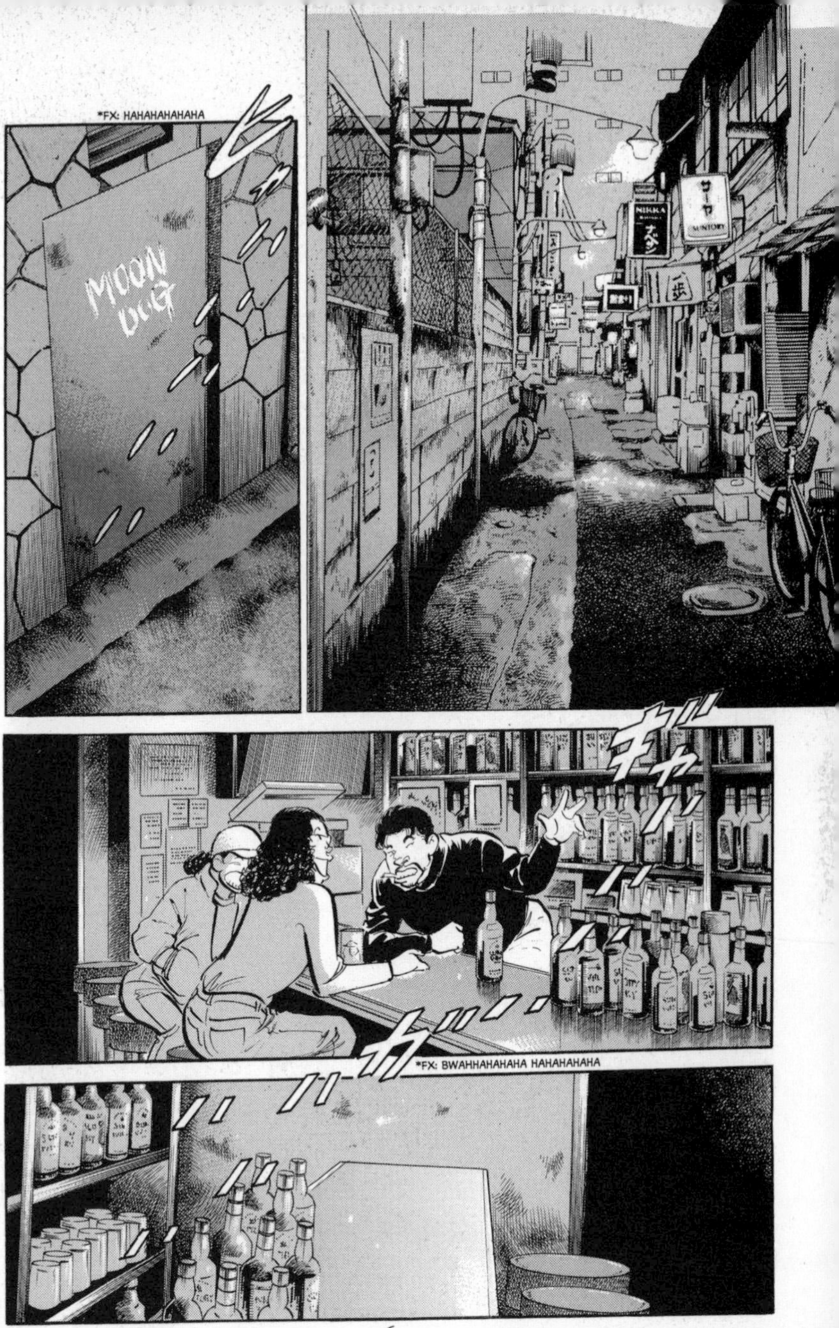
NIKKA
SUNTORY
*FX: HAHAHAHAHAHA
MOON DOG
*FX: BWAHHAHAHAHA HAHAHAHAHA

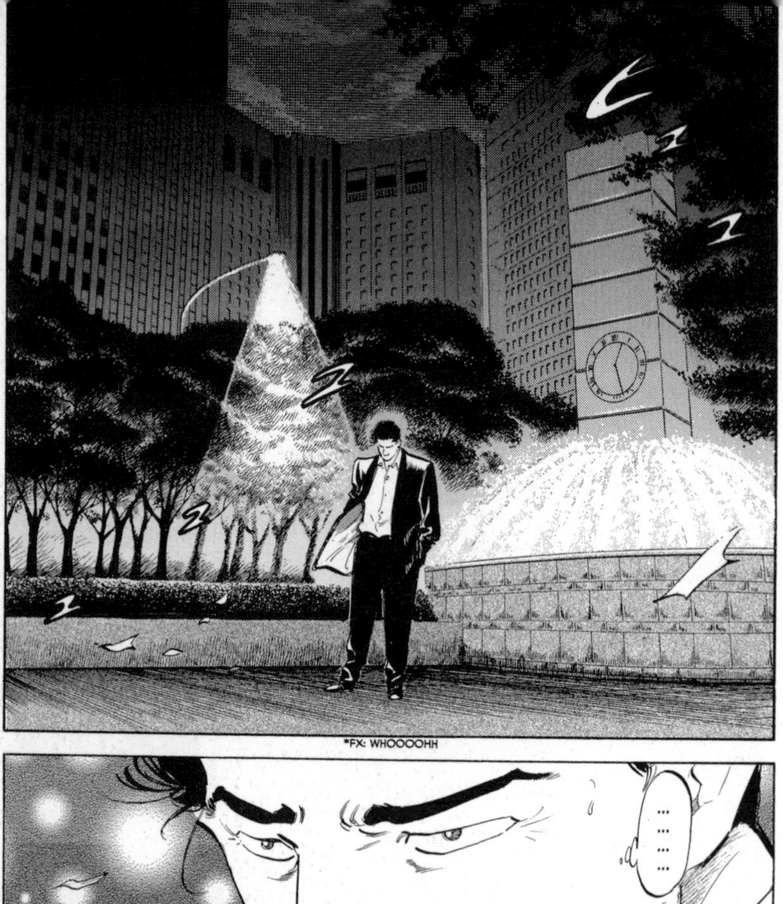

*FX: WHOOOOHH

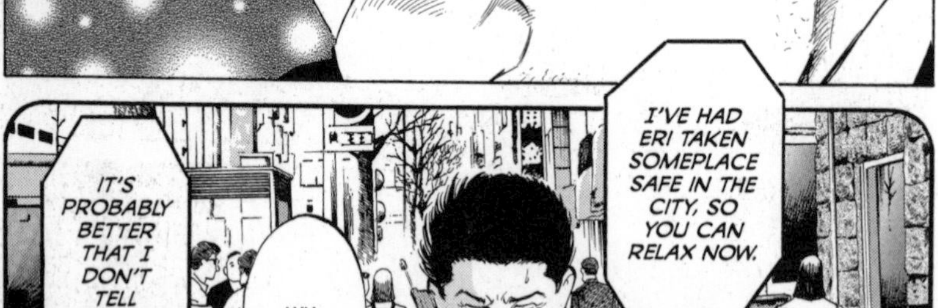

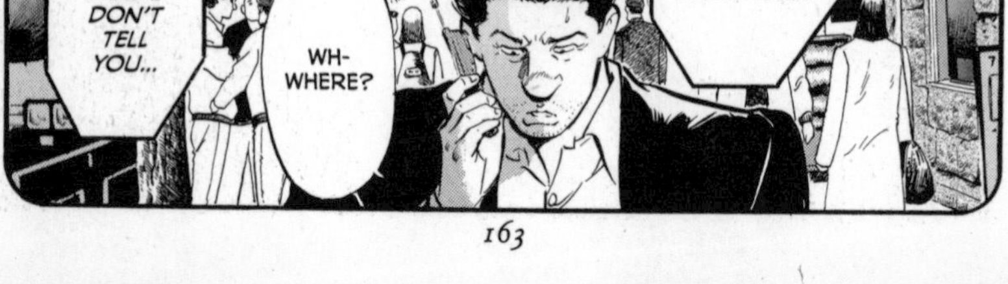
I'VE HAD ERI TAKEN SOMEPLACE SAFE IN THE CITY, SO YOU CAN RELAX NOW.
WH- WHERE?
IT'S PROBABLY BETTER THAT I DON'T TELL YOU...

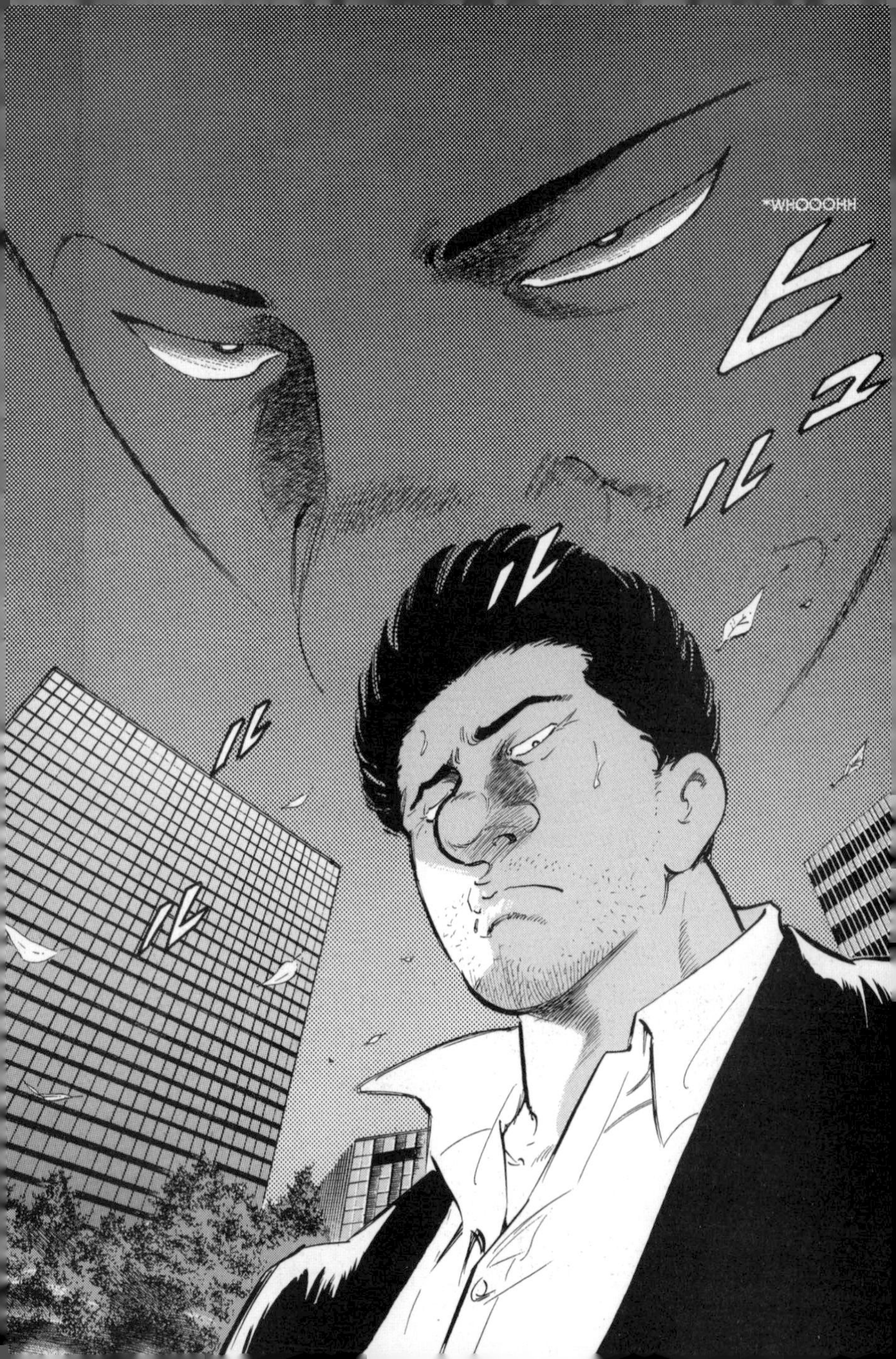
*WHOOOHH
ヒュルルルル

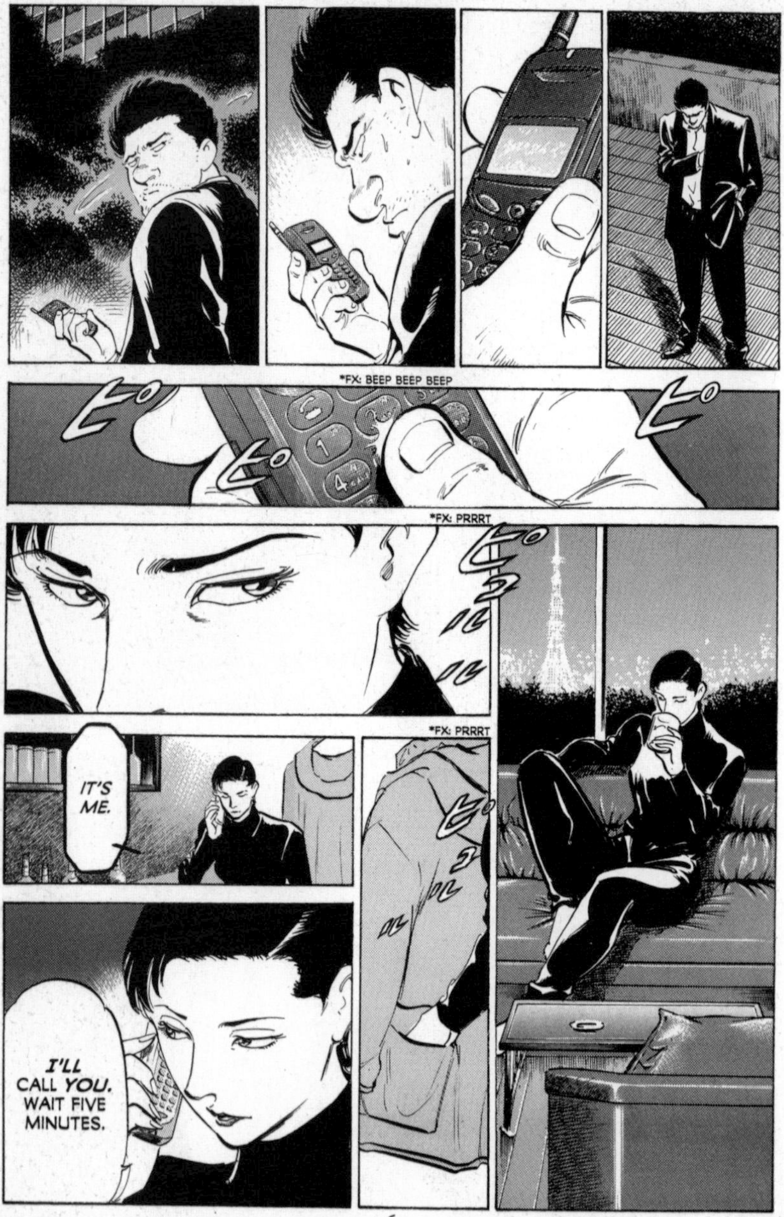
*FX: BEEP BEEP BEEP
*FX: PRRRT
*FX: PRRRT
IT'S ME.
I'LL CALL YOU. WAIT FIVE MINUTES.

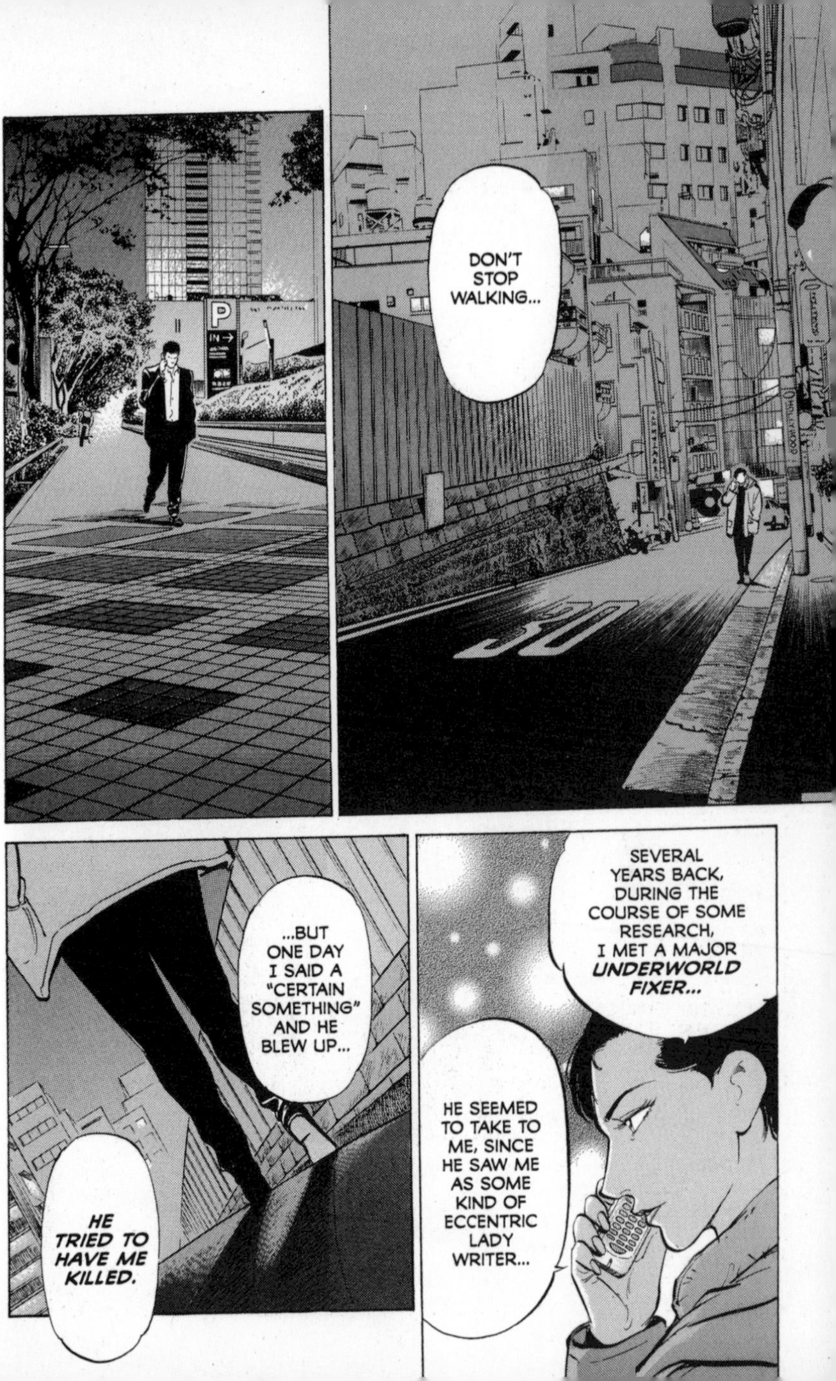
DON'T STOP WALKING...
SEVERAL YEARS BACK, DURING THE COURSE OF SOME RESEARCH, I MET A MAJOR ***UNDERWORLD FIXER...***
HE SEEMED TO TAKE TO ME, SINCE HE SAW ME AS SOME KIND OF ECCENTRIC LADY WRITER...
...BUT ONE DAY I SAID A "CERTAIN SOMETHING" AND HE BLEW UP...
HE TRIED TO HAVE ME KILLED.

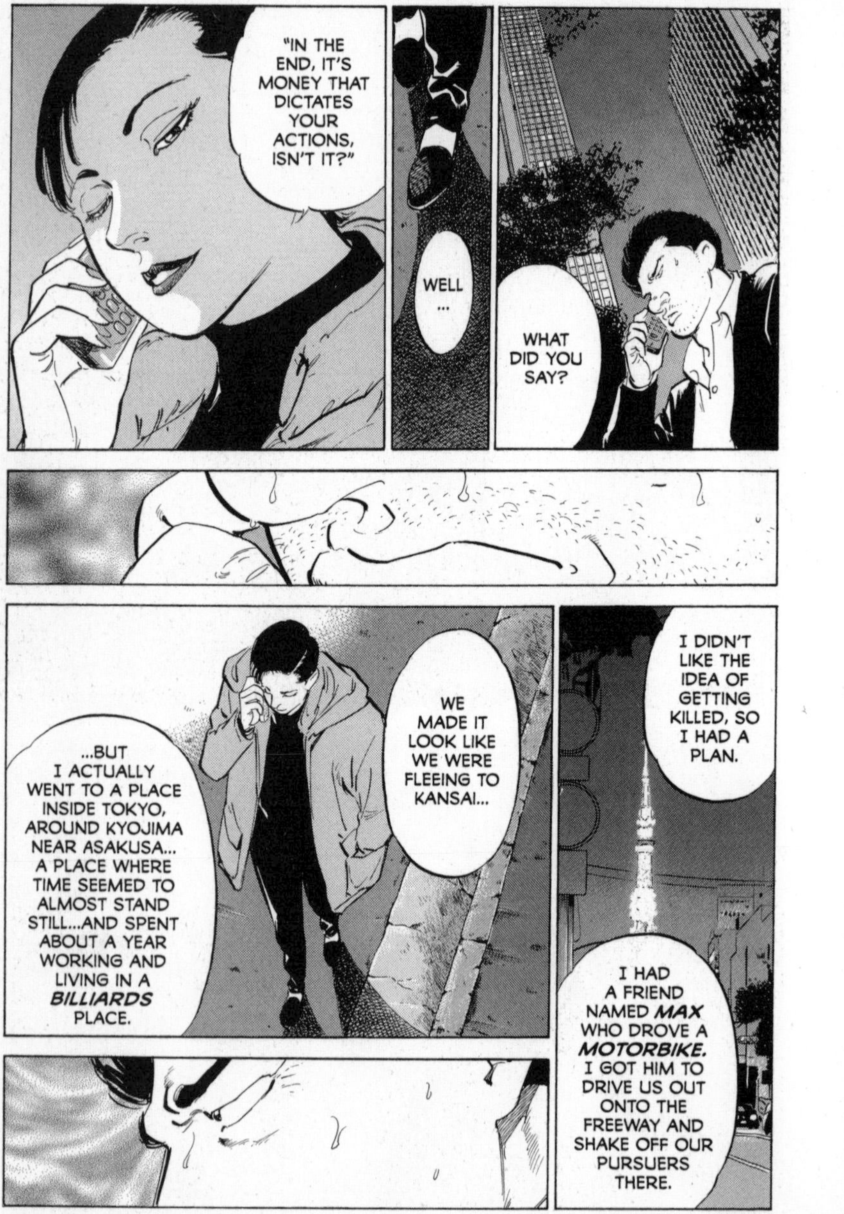
WHAT DID YOU SAY?
WELL ...
"IN THE END, IT'S MONEY THAT DICTATES YOUR ACTIONS, ISN'T IT?"
I DIDN'T LIKE THE IDEA OF GETTING KILLED, SO I HAD A PLAN.
I HAD A FRIEND NAMED ***MAX*** WHO DROVE A ***MOTORBIKE.*** I GOT HIM TO DRIVE US OUT ONTO THE FREEWAY AND SHAKE OFF OUR PURSUERS THERE.
WE MADE IT LOOK LIKE WE WERE FLEEING TO KANSAI...
...BUT I ACTUALLY WENT TO A PLACE INSIDE TOKYO, AROUND KYOJIMA NEAR ASAKUSA... A PLACE WHERE TIME SEEMED TO ALMOST STAND STILL...AND SPENT ABOUT A YEAR WORKING AND LIVING IN A ***BILLIARDS*** PLACE.

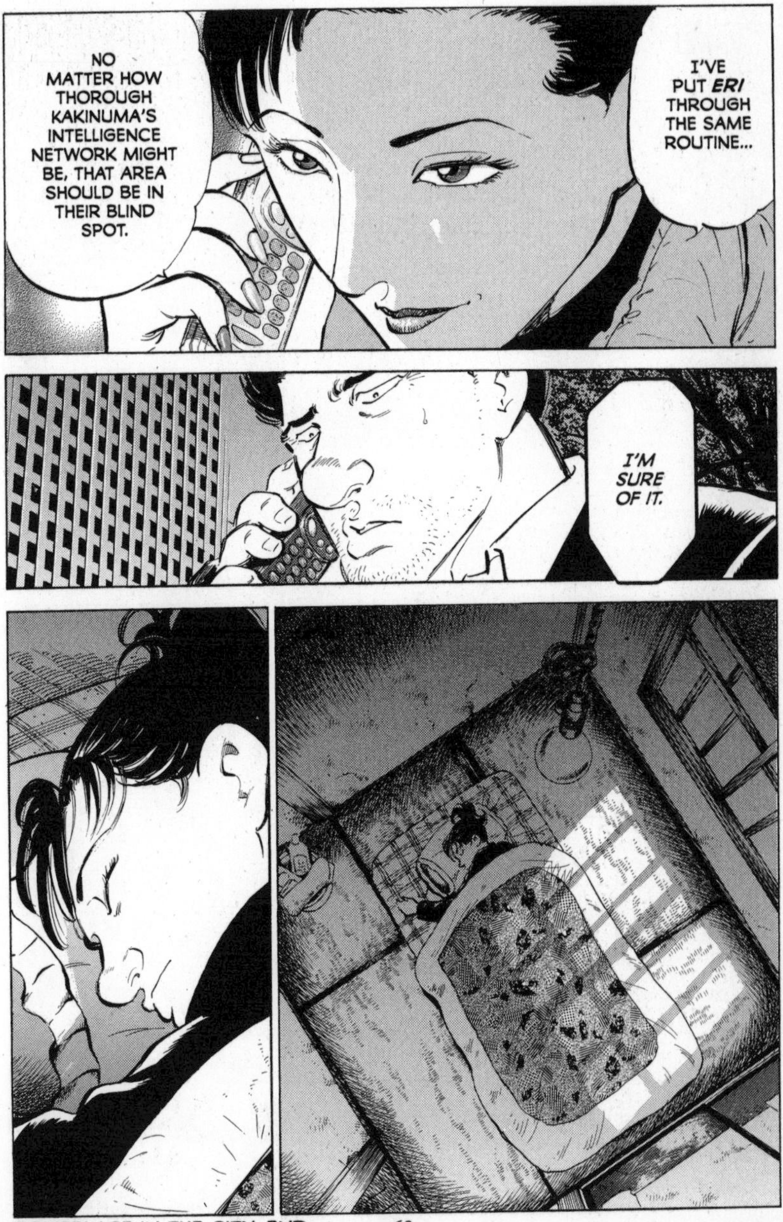
I'VE PUT ERI THROUGH THE SAME ROUTINE...
NO MATTER HOW THOROUGH KAKINUMA'S INTELLIGENCE NETWORK MIGHT BE, THAT AREA SHOULD BE IN THEIR BLIND SPOT.
I'M SURE OF IT.

SOMEPLACE IN THE CITY: END

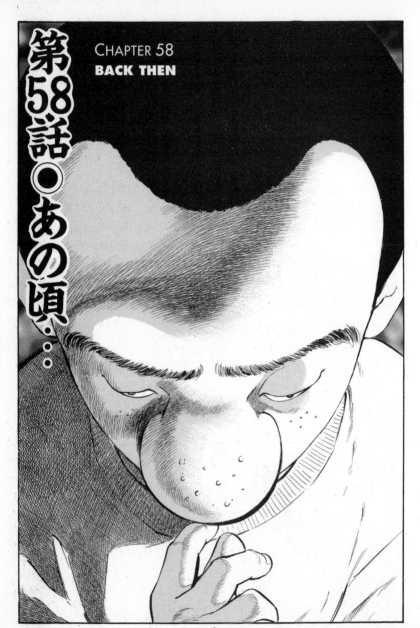

CHAPTER 58
BACK THEN

第58話●あの頃…

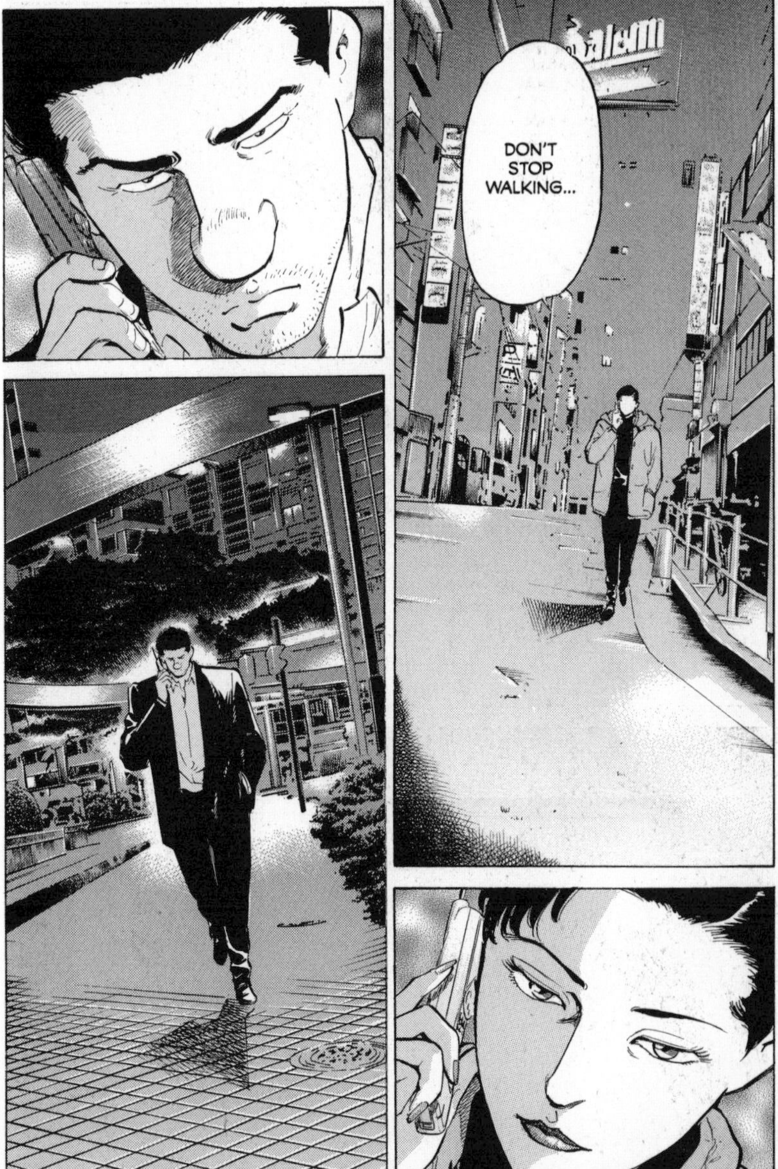
DON'T STOP WALKING...

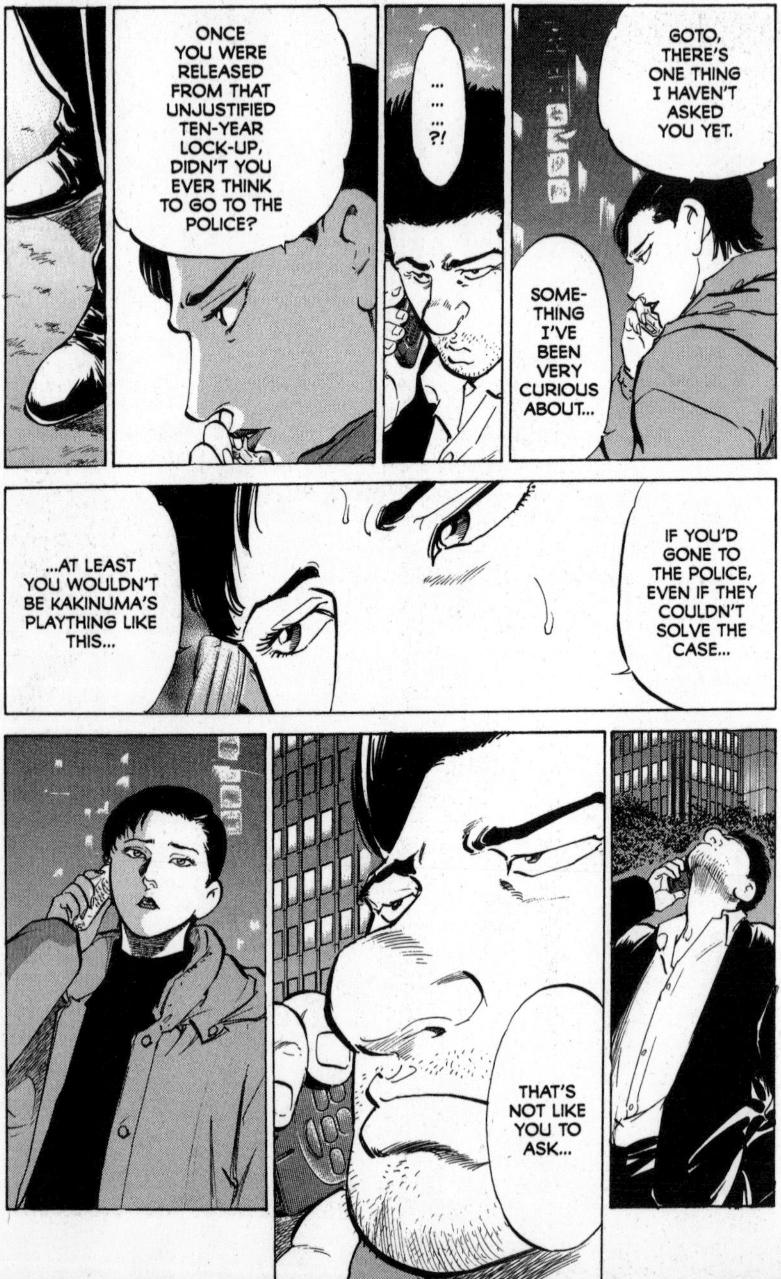
GOTO, THERE'S ONE THING I HAVEN'T ASKED YOU YET.
SOME-THING I'VE BEEN VERY CURIOUS ABOUT...
... ... ?!
ONCE YOU WERE RELEASED FROM THAT UNJUSTIFIED TEN-YEAR LOCK-UP, DIDN'T YOU EVER THINK TO GO TO THE POLICE?
IF YOU'D GONE TO THE POLICE, EVEN IF THEY COULDN'T SOLVE THE CASE...
...AT LEAST YOU WOULDN'T BE KAKINUMA'S PLAYTHING LIKE THIS...
THAT'S NOT LIKE YOU TO ASK...

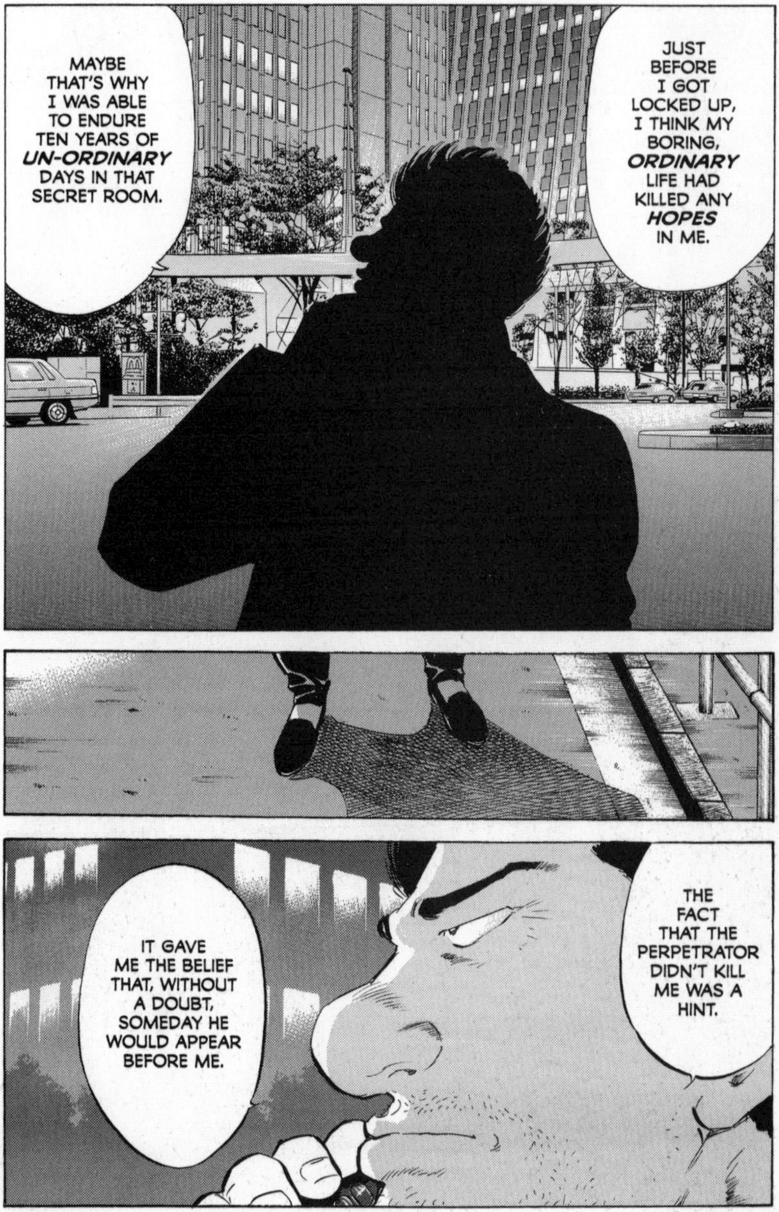
JUST BEFORE I GOT LOCKED UP, I THINK MY BORING, ORDINARY LIFE HAD KILLED ANY HOPES IN ME.
MAYBE THAT'S WHY I WAS ABLE TO ENDURE TEN YEARS OF UN-ORDINARY DAYS IN THAT SECRET ROOM.
THE FACT THAT THE PERPETRATOR DIDN'T KILL ME WAS A HINT.
IT GAVE ME THE BELIEF THAT, WITHOUT A DOUBT, SOMEDAY HE WOULD APPEAR BEFORE ME.

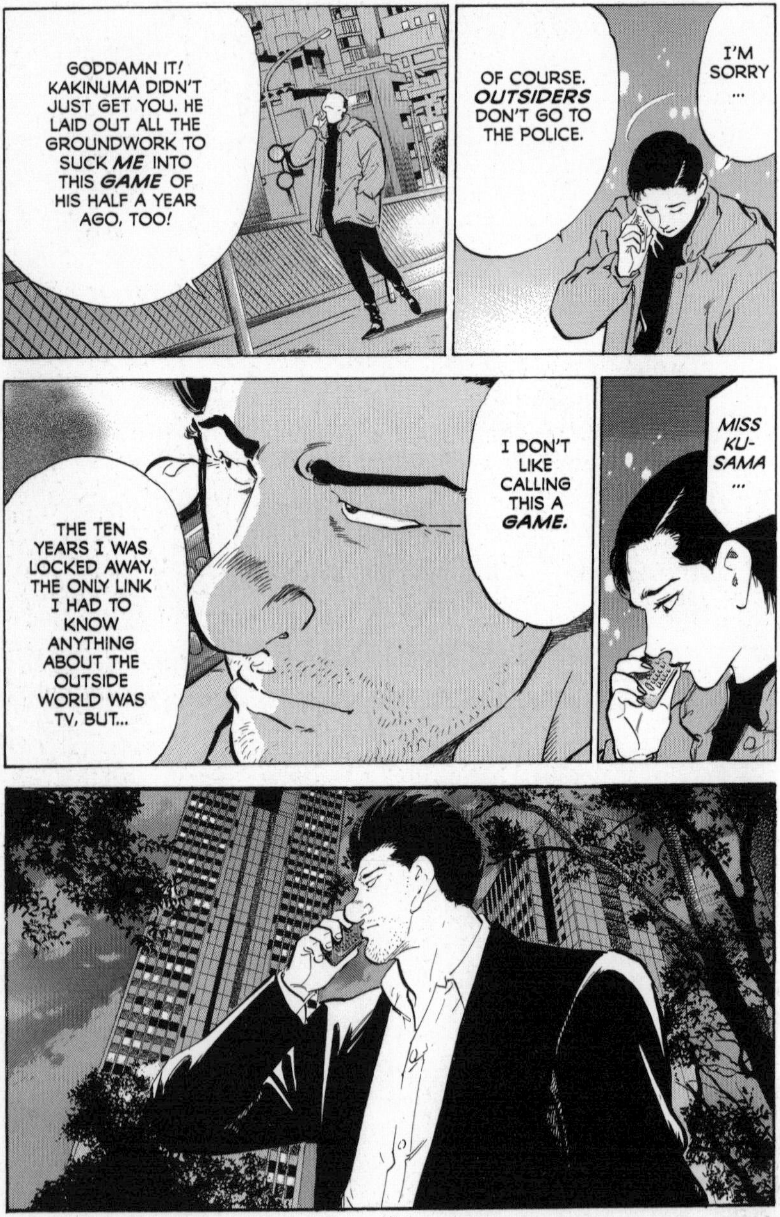
I'M SORRY ...
OF COURSE. OUTSIDERS DON'T GO TO THE POLICE.
GODDAMN IT! KAKINUMA DIDN'T JUST GET YOU. HE LAID OUT ALL THE GROUNDWORK TO SUCK ME INTO THIS GAME OF HIS HALF A YEAR AGO, TOO!
MISS KU-SAMA ...
I DON'T LIKE CALLING THIS A GAME.
THE TEN YEARS I WAS LOCKED AWAY, THE ONLY LINK I HAD TO KNOW ANYTHING ABOUT THE OUTSIDE WORLD WAS TV, BUT...

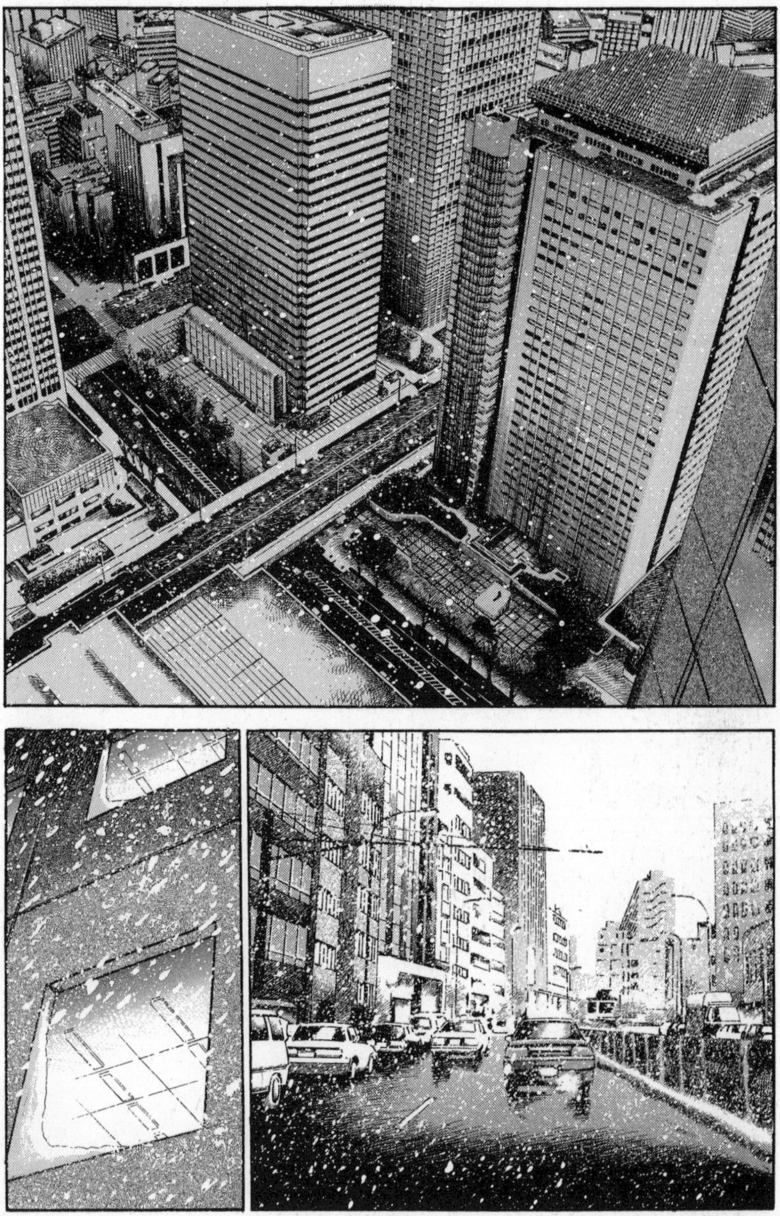

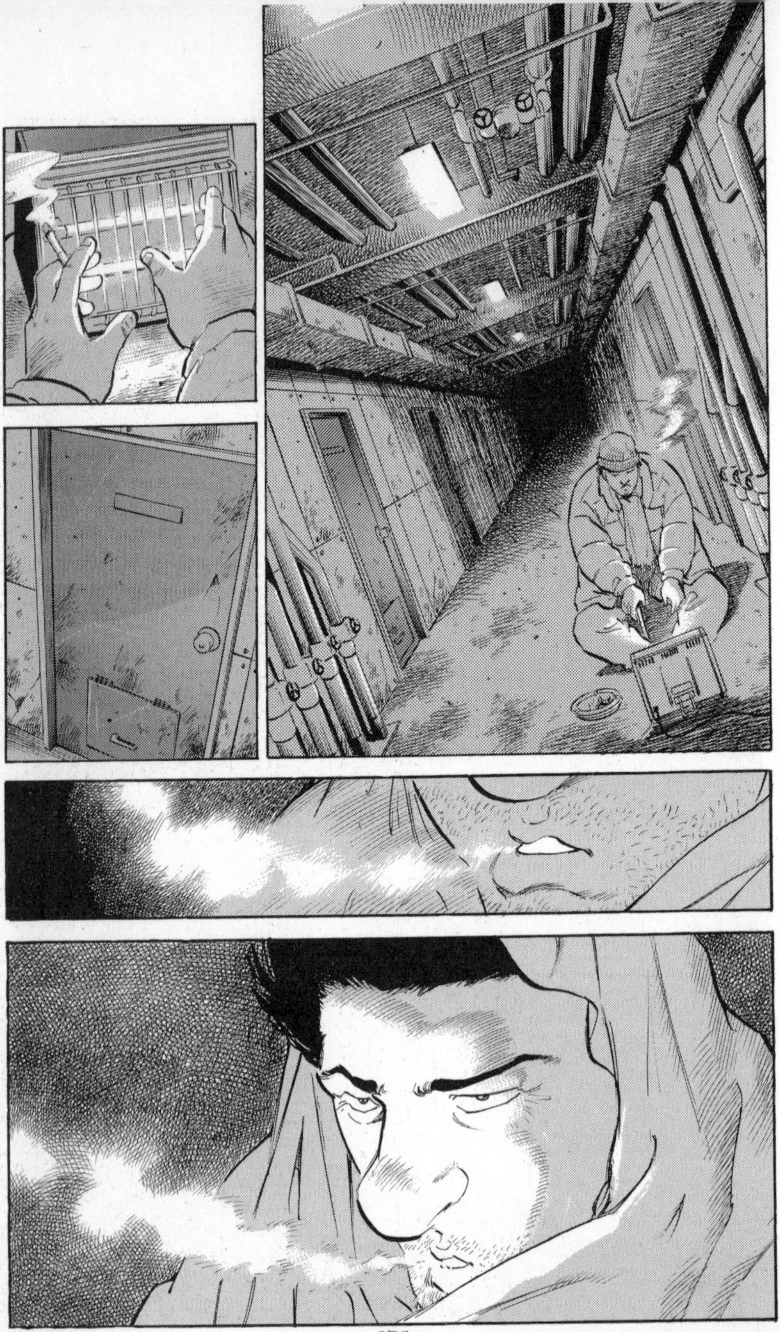

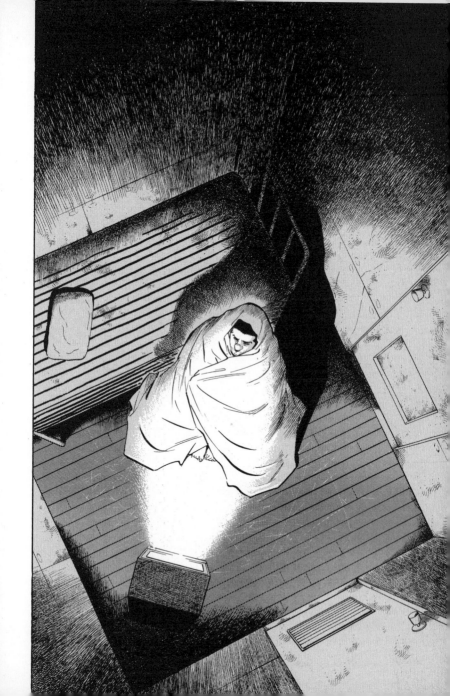

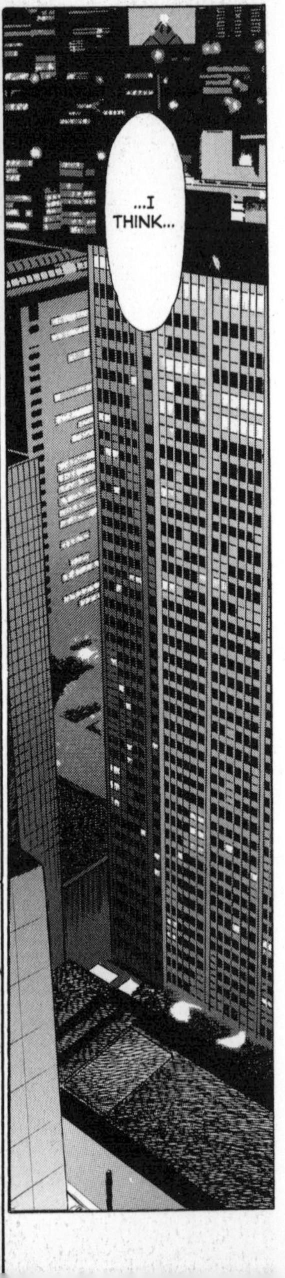
...I THINK...
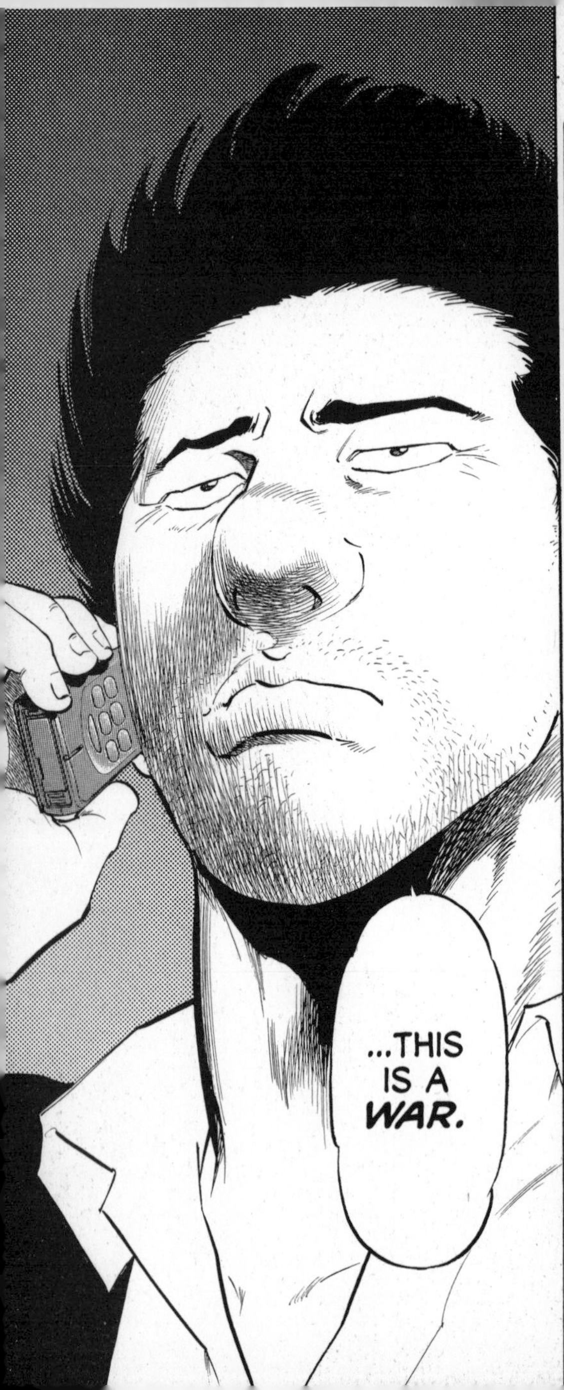
...THIS IS A *WAR.*

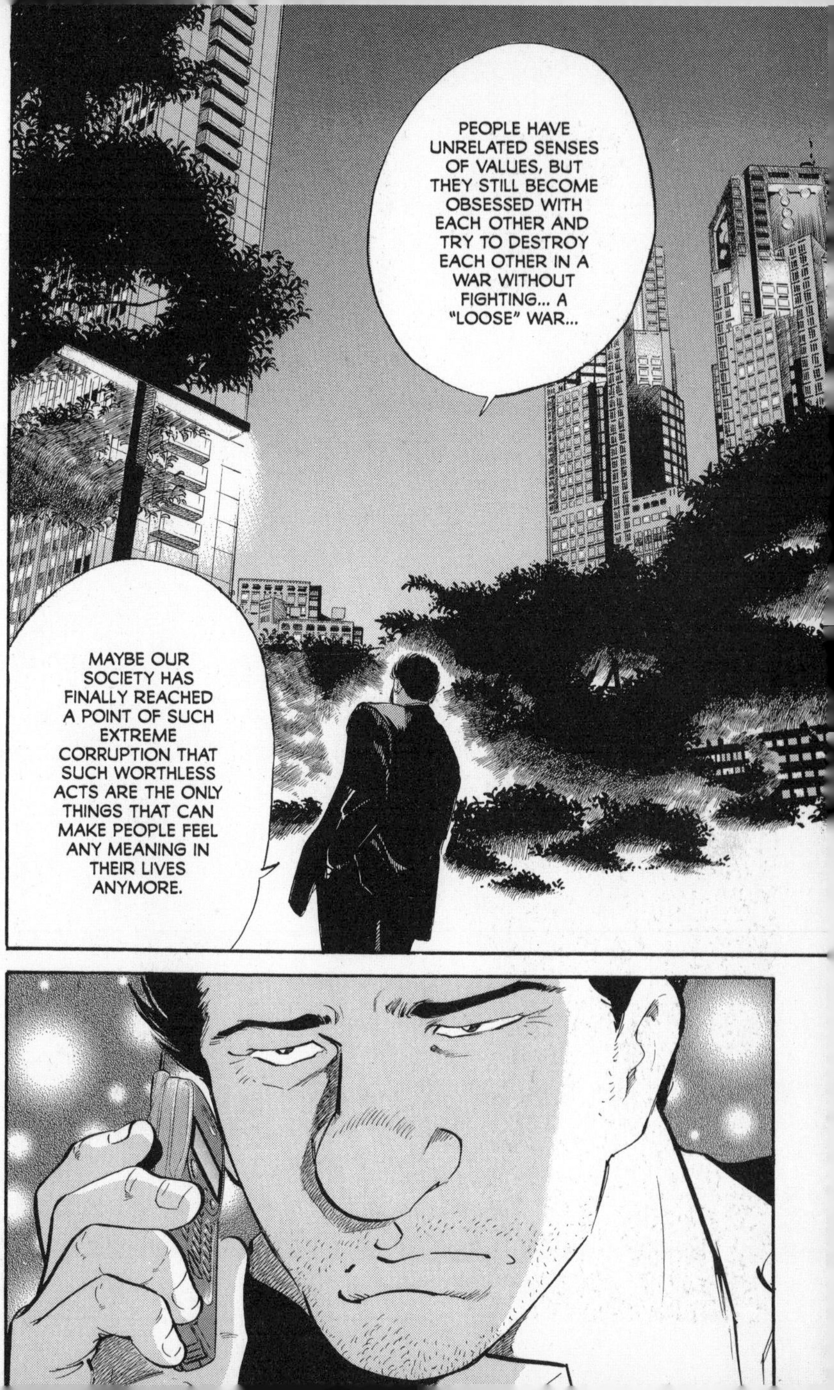
PEOPLE HAVE UNRELATED SENSES OF VALUES, BUT THEY STILL BECOME OBSESSED WITH EACH OTHER AND TRY TO DESTROY EACH OTHER IN A WAR WITHOUT FIGHTING... A "LOOSE" WAR...
MAYBE OUR SOCIETY HAS FINALLY REACHED A POINT OF SUCH EXTREME CORRUPTION THAT SUCH WORTHLESS ACTS ARE THE ONLY THINGS THAT CAN MAKE PEOPLE FEEL ANY MEANING IN THEIR LIVES ANYMORE.

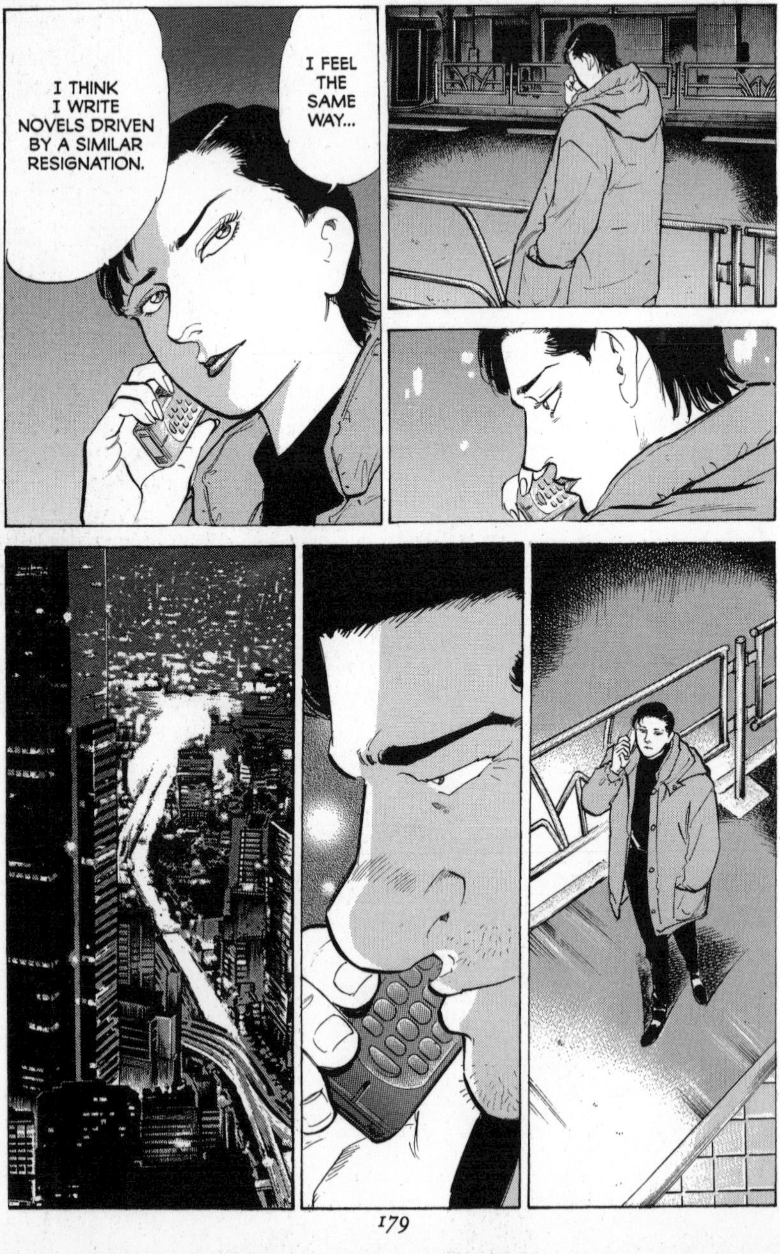
I FEEL THE SAME WAY...
I THINK I WRITE NOVELS DRIVEN BY A SIMILAR RESIGNATION.

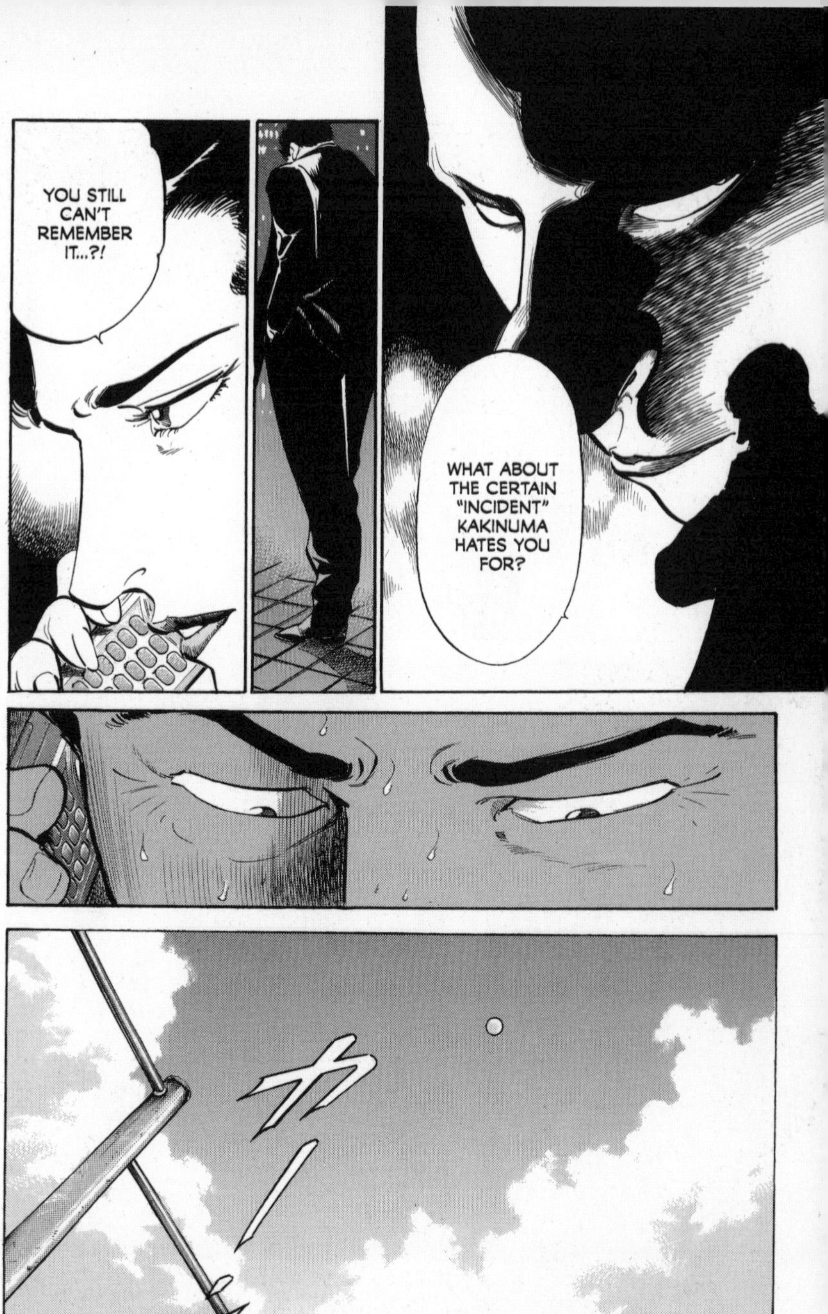
WHAT ABOUT THE CERTAIN "INCIDENT" KAKINUMA HATES YOU FOR?
YOU STILL CAN'T REMEMBER IT...?!
*FX: KRAK

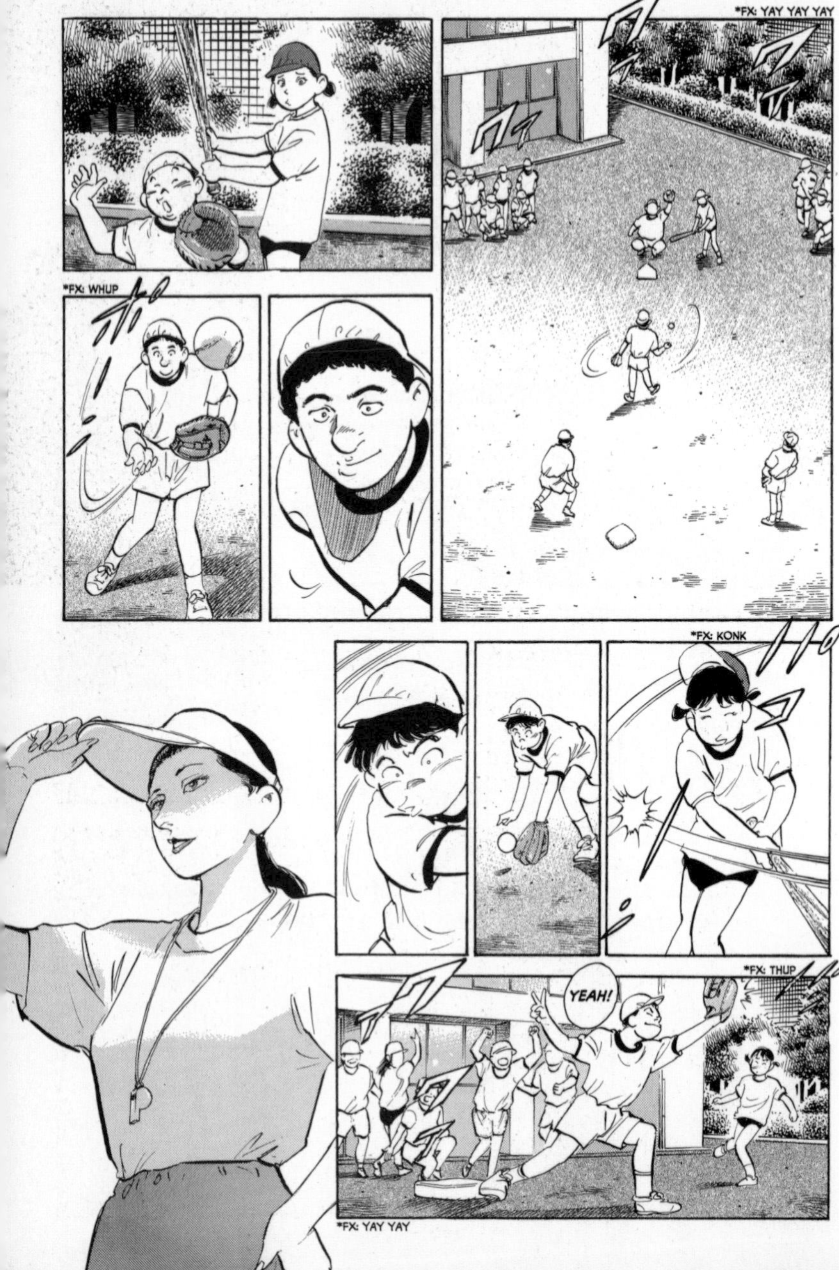
*FX: YAY YAY YAY
*FX: WHUP
*FX: KONK
*FX: THUP
YEAH!
*FX: YAY YAY

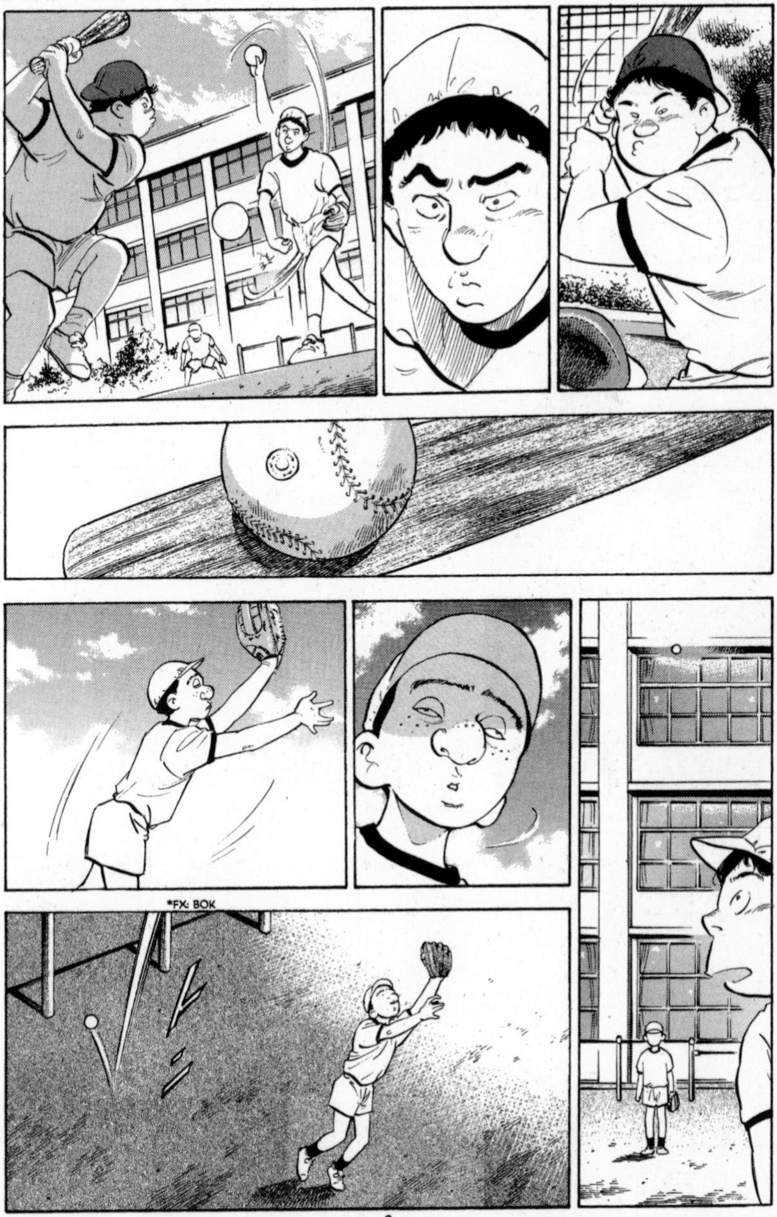
*FX: BOK

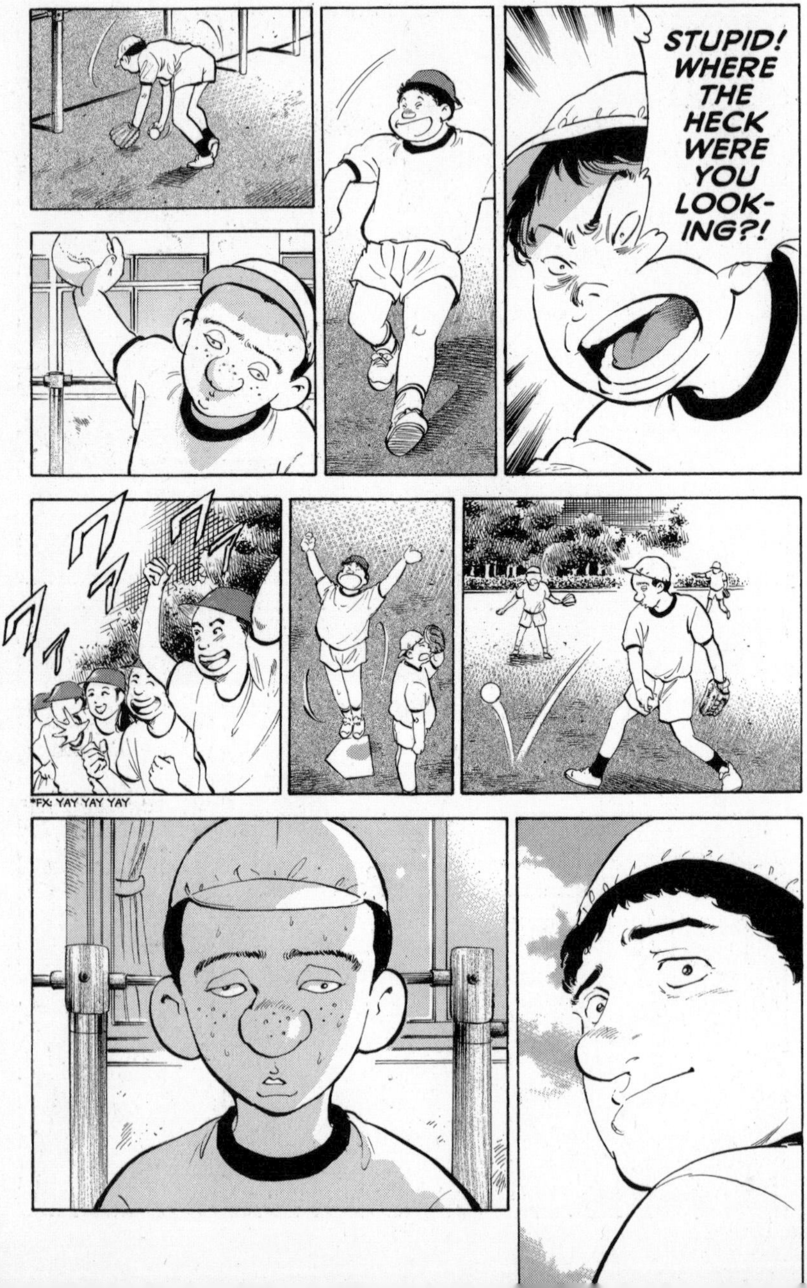
STUPID! WHERE THE HECK WERE YOU LOOKING?!
*FX: YAY YAY YAY

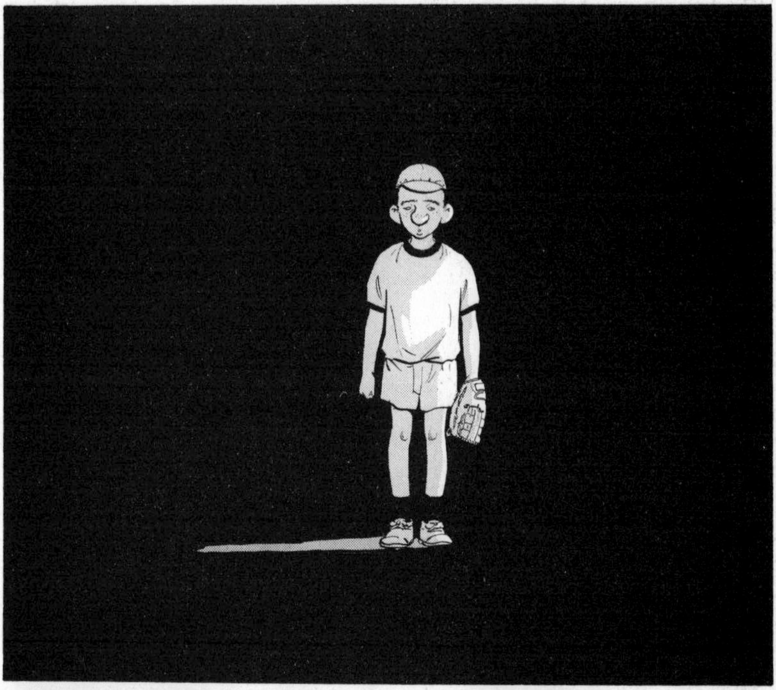

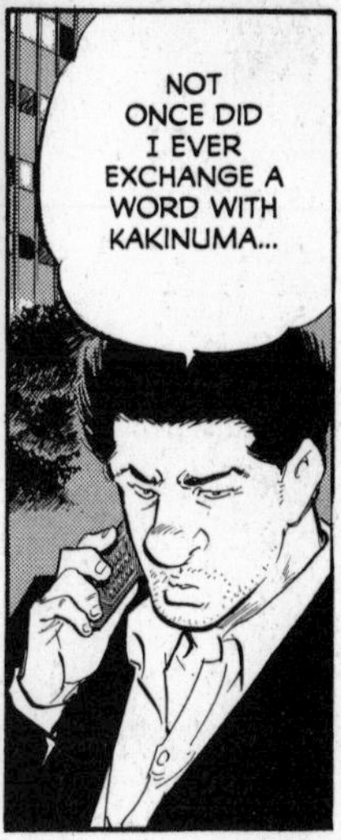
NOT ONCE DID I EVER EXCHANGE A WORD WITH KAKINUMA...

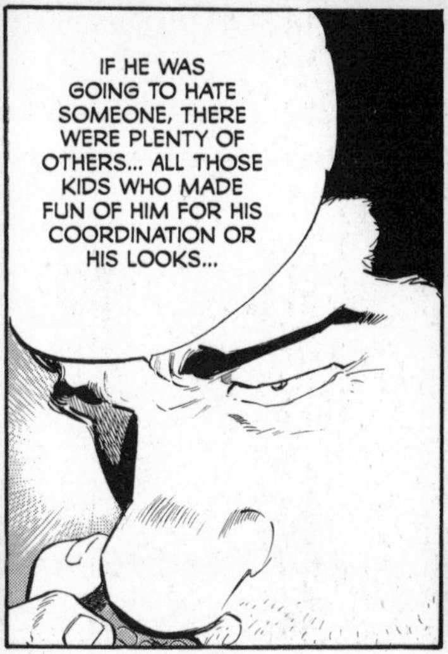
IF HE WAS GOING TO HATE SOMEONE, THERE WERE PLENTY OF OTHERS... ALL THOSE KIDS WHO MADE FUN OF HIM FOR HIS COORDINATION OR HIS LOOKS...

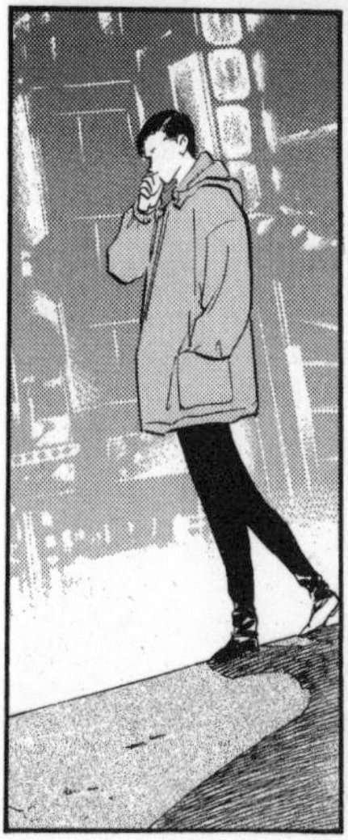

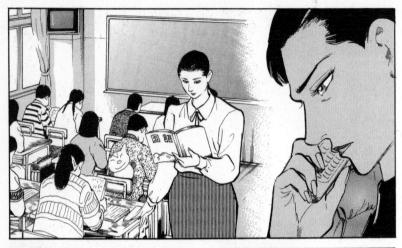

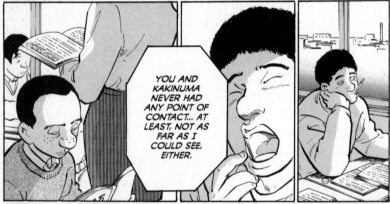

YOU AND KAKINUMA NEVER HAD ANY POINT OF CONTACT... AT LEAST, NOT AS FAR AS I COULD SEE, EITHER.

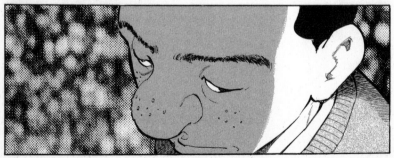

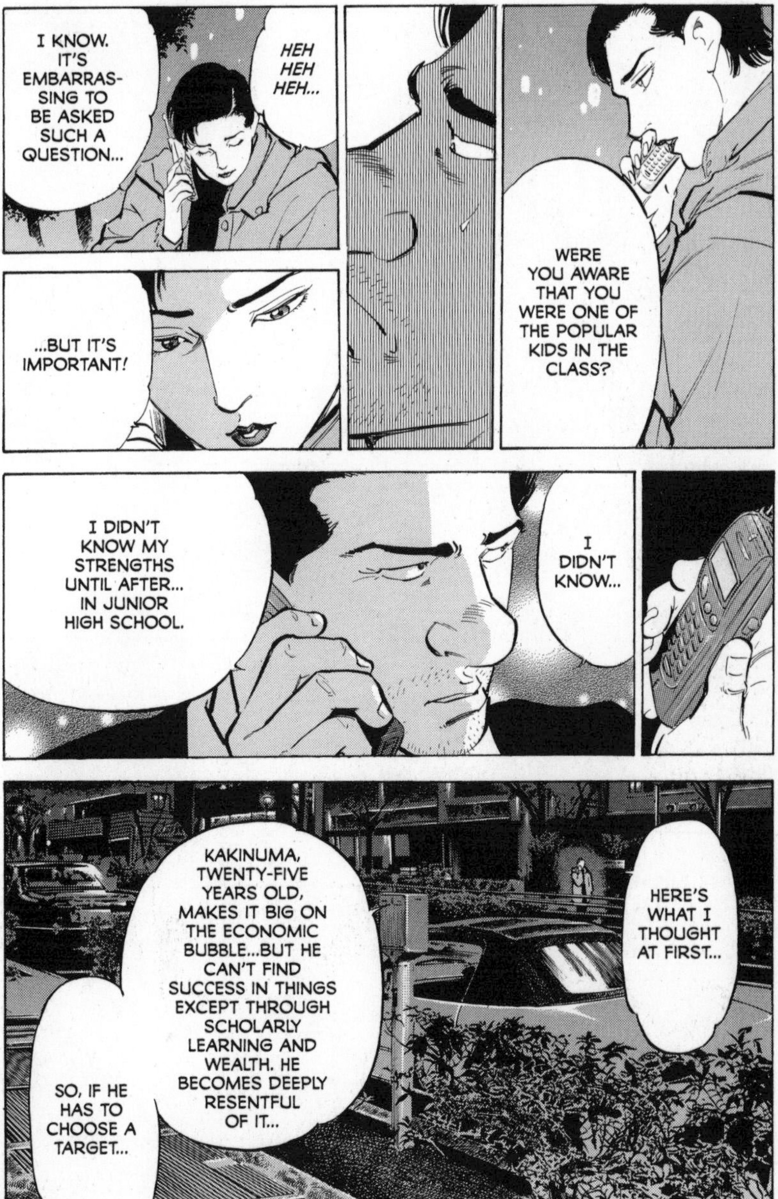
WERE YOU AWARE THAT YOU WERE ONE OF THE POPULAR KIDS IN THE CLASS?
HEH HEH HEH...
I KNOW. IT'S EMBARRAS-SING TO BE ASKED SUCH A QUESTION...
...BUT IT'S IMPORTANT!
I DIDN'T KNOW...
I DIDN'T KNOW MY STRENGTHS UNTIL AFTER... IN JUNIOR HIGH SCHOOL.
HERE'S WHAT I THOUGHT AT FIRST...
KAKINUMA, TWENTY-FIVE YEARS OLD, MAKES IT BIG ON THE ECONOMIC BUBBLE...BUT HE CAN'T FIND SUCCESS IN THINGS EXCEPT THROUGH SCHOLARLY LEARNING AND WEALTH. HE BECOMES DEEPLY RESENTFUL OF IT...
SO, IF HE HAS TO CHOOSE A TARGET...

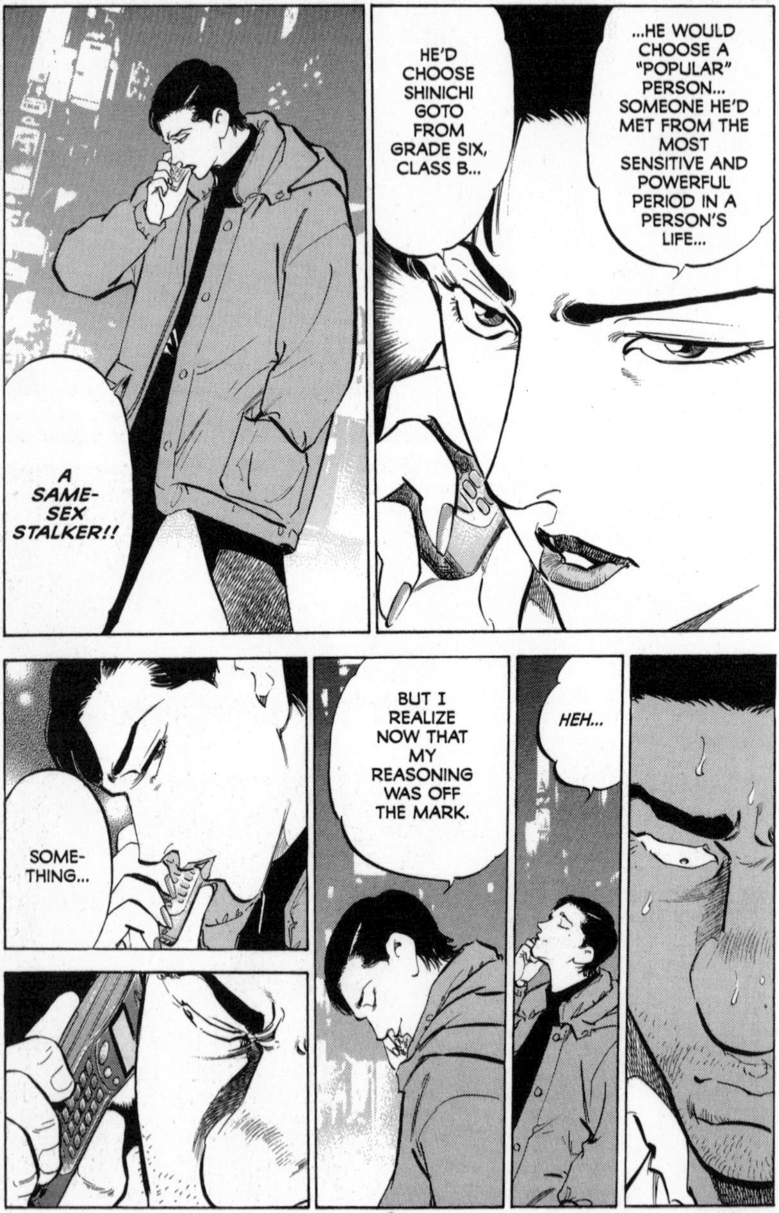
HE'D CHOOSE SHINICHI GOTO FROM GRADE SIX, CLASS B...
...HE WOULD CHOOSE A "POPULAR" PERSON... SOMEONE HE'D MET FROM THE MOST SENSITIVE AND POWERFUL PERIOD IN A PERSON'S LIFE...
A SAME-SEX STALKER!!
HEH...
BUT I REALIZE NOW THAT MY REASONING WAS OFF THE MARK.
SOME-THING...

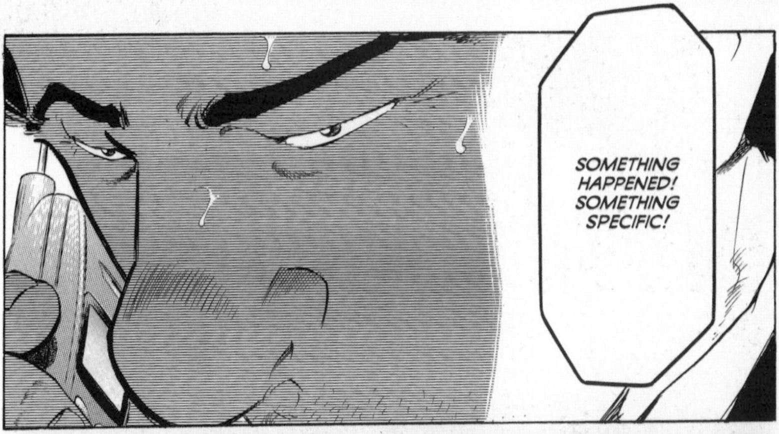
SOMETHING HAPPENED! SOMETHING SPECIFIC!
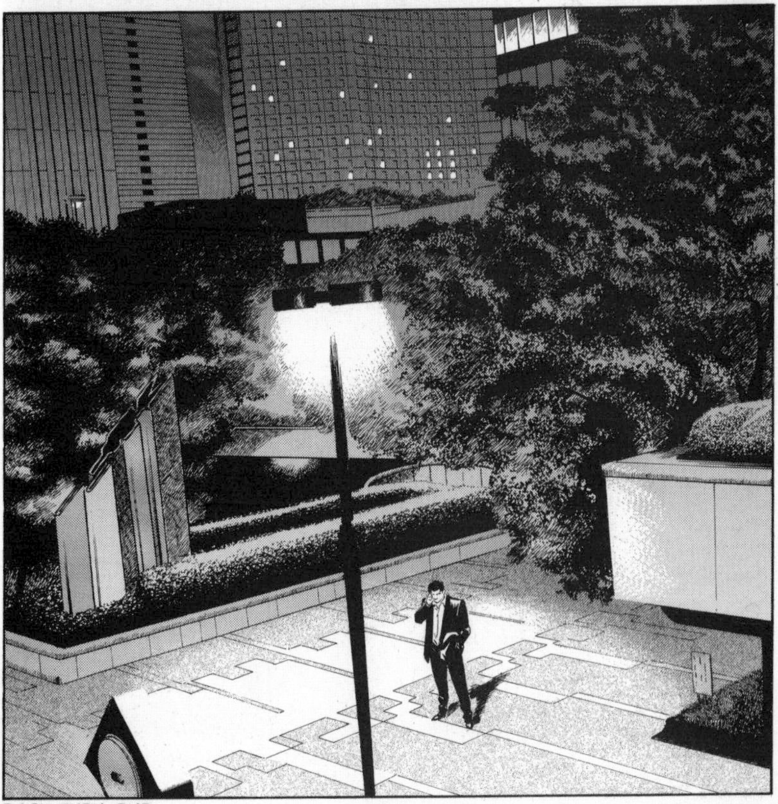
BACK THEN: END

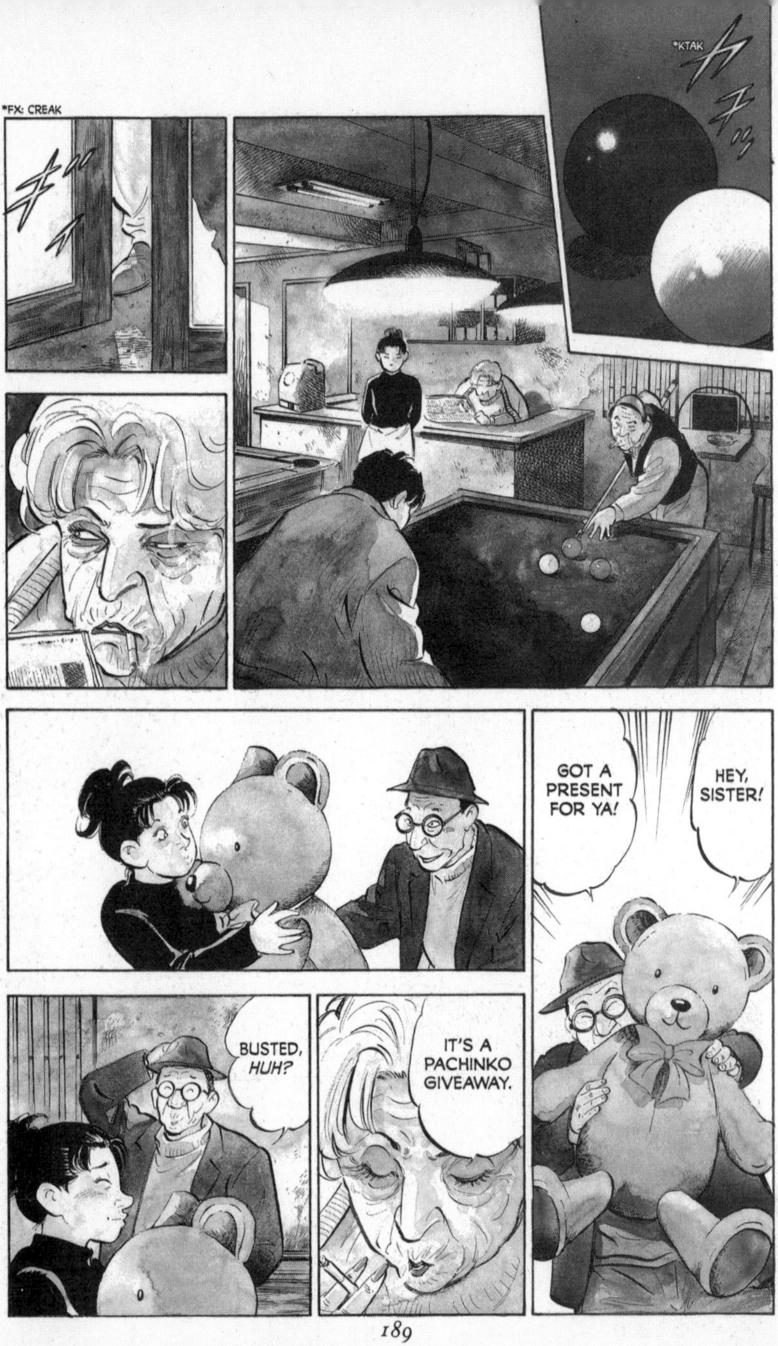
*KTAK
*FX: CREAK
HEY, SISTER!
GOT A PRESENT FOR YA!
IT'S A PACHINKO GIVEAWAY.
BUSTED, *HUH?*

Chapter 59
Around Kyojima, Sumida Ward

第59話◎墨田区京島あたり

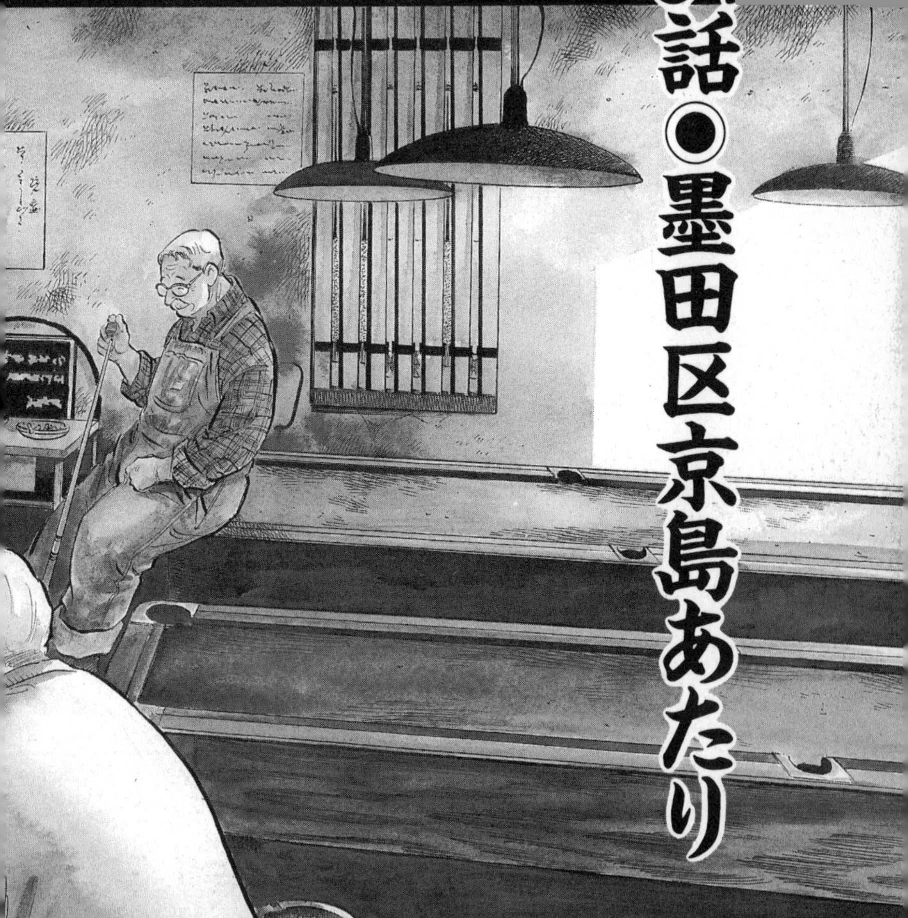

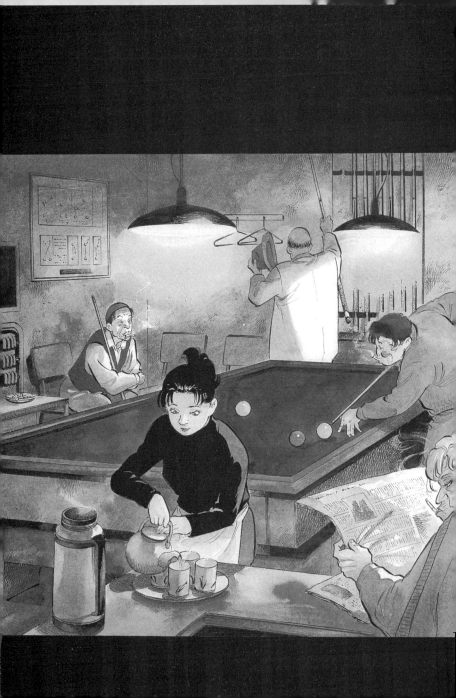

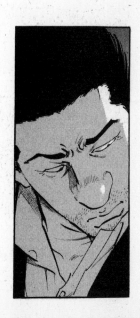

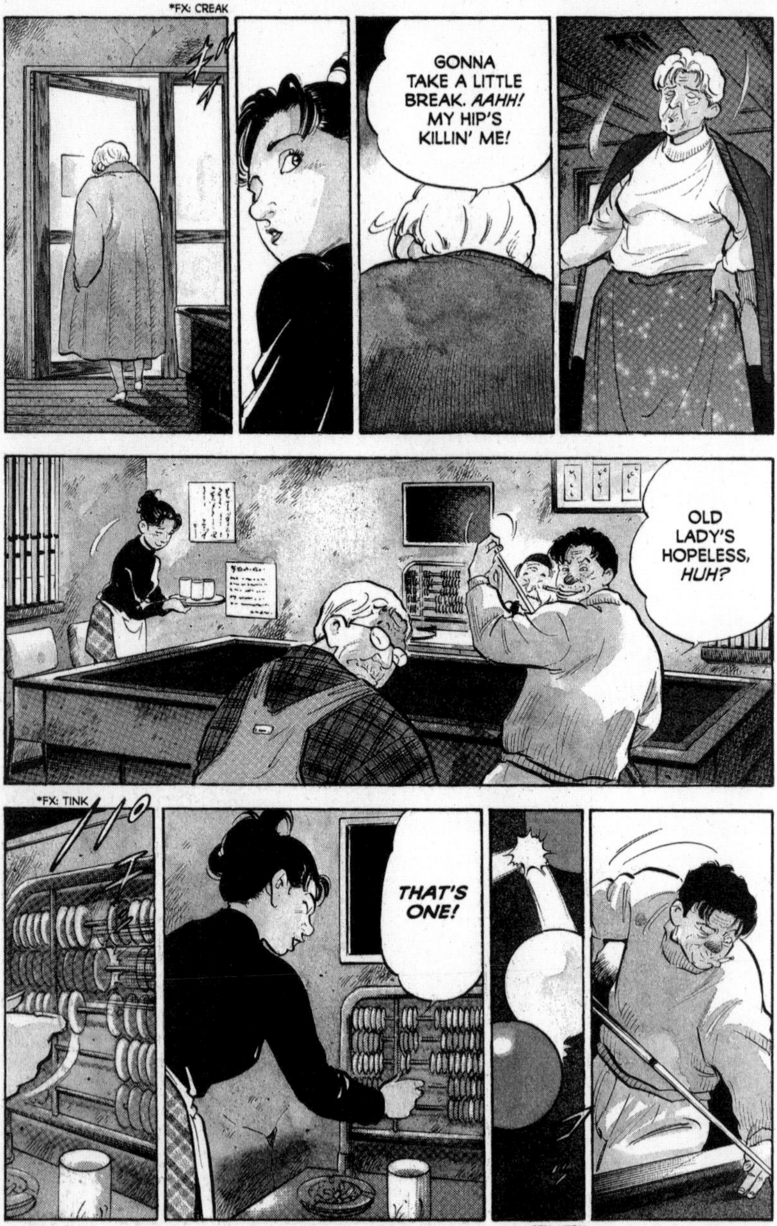
GONNA TAKE A LITTLE BREAK. *AAHH!* MY HIP'S KILLIN' ME!
*FX: CREAK
OLD LADY'S HOPELESS, *HUH?*
*FX: KTOK
THAT'S ONE!
*FX: TINK

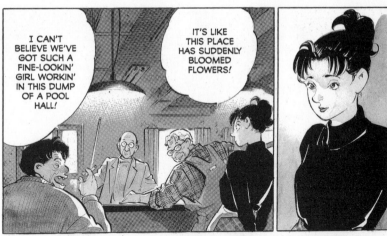

I CAN'T BELIEVE WE'VE GOT SUCH A FINE-LOOKIN' GIRL WORKIN' IN THIS DUMP OF A POOL HALL!

IT'S LIKE THIS PLACE HAS SUDDENLY BLOOMED FLOWERS!

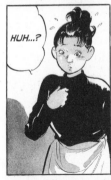

HUH...?

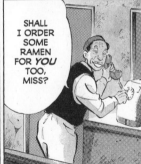

SHALL I ORDER SOME RAMEN FOR *YOU* TOO, MISS?

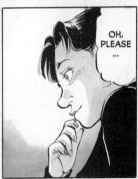

OH, PLEASE ...

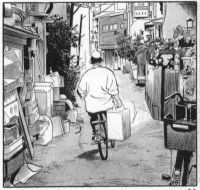

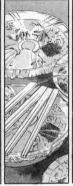

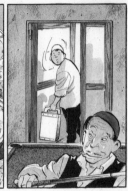

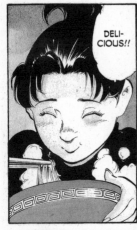

DELI-
CIOUS!!

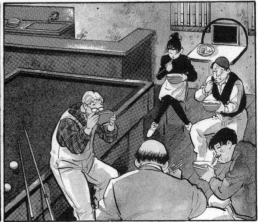

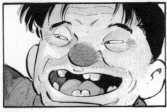

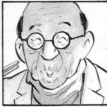

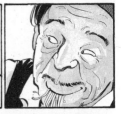

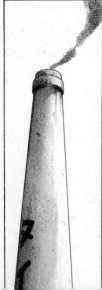

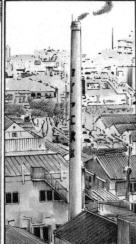

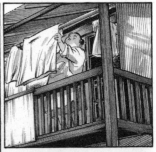

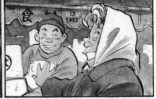

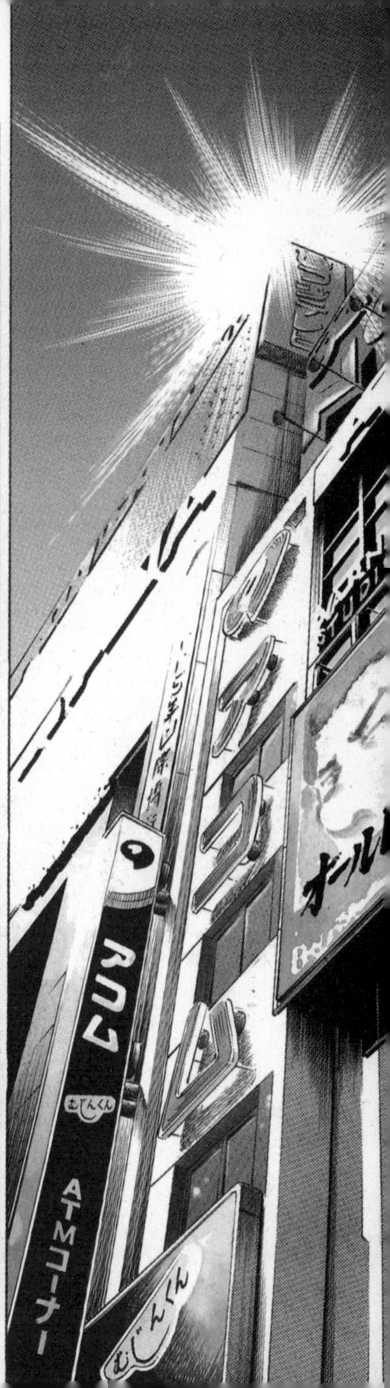
アコム
むじんくん
ATMコーナー
むじんくん
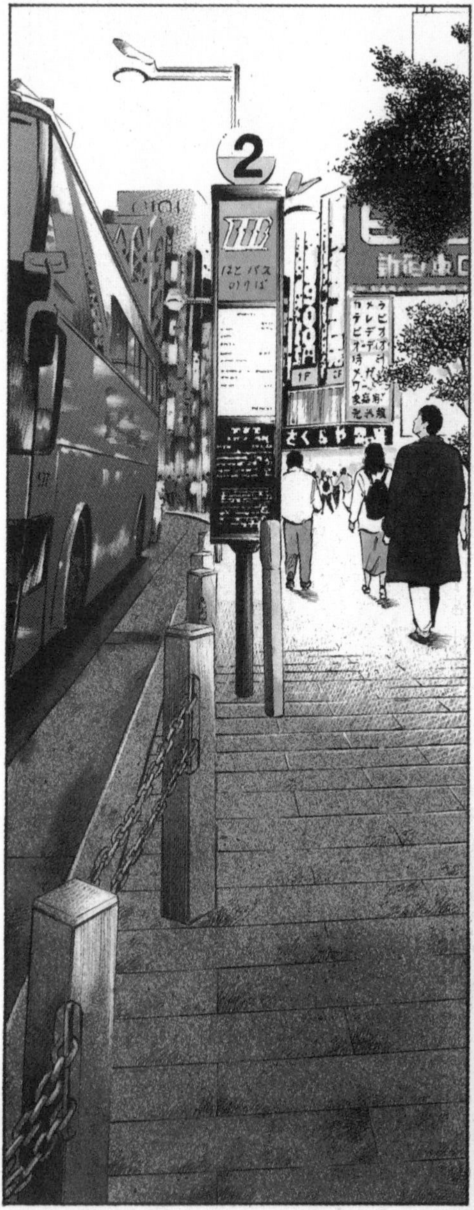
2
はとバス
のりば
さくらや

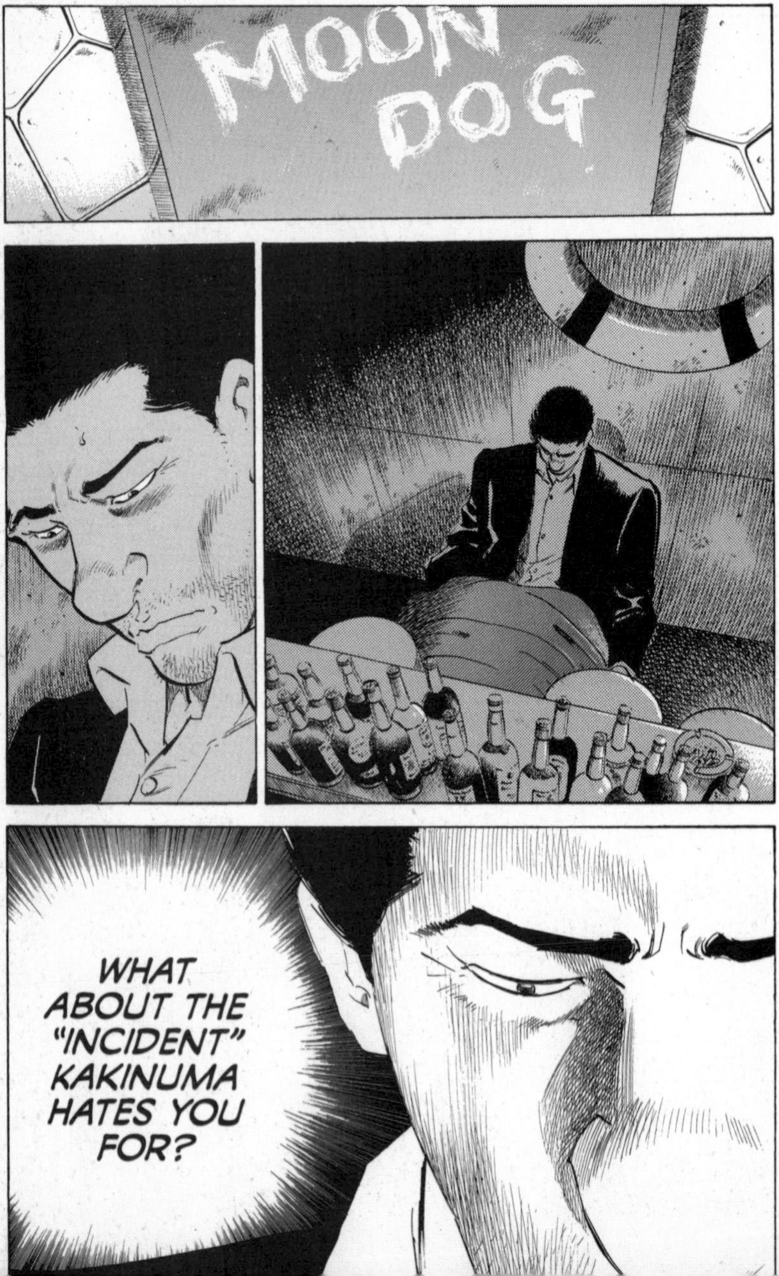
MOON DOG
WHAT ABOUT THE "INCIDENT" KAKINUMA HATES YOU FOR?

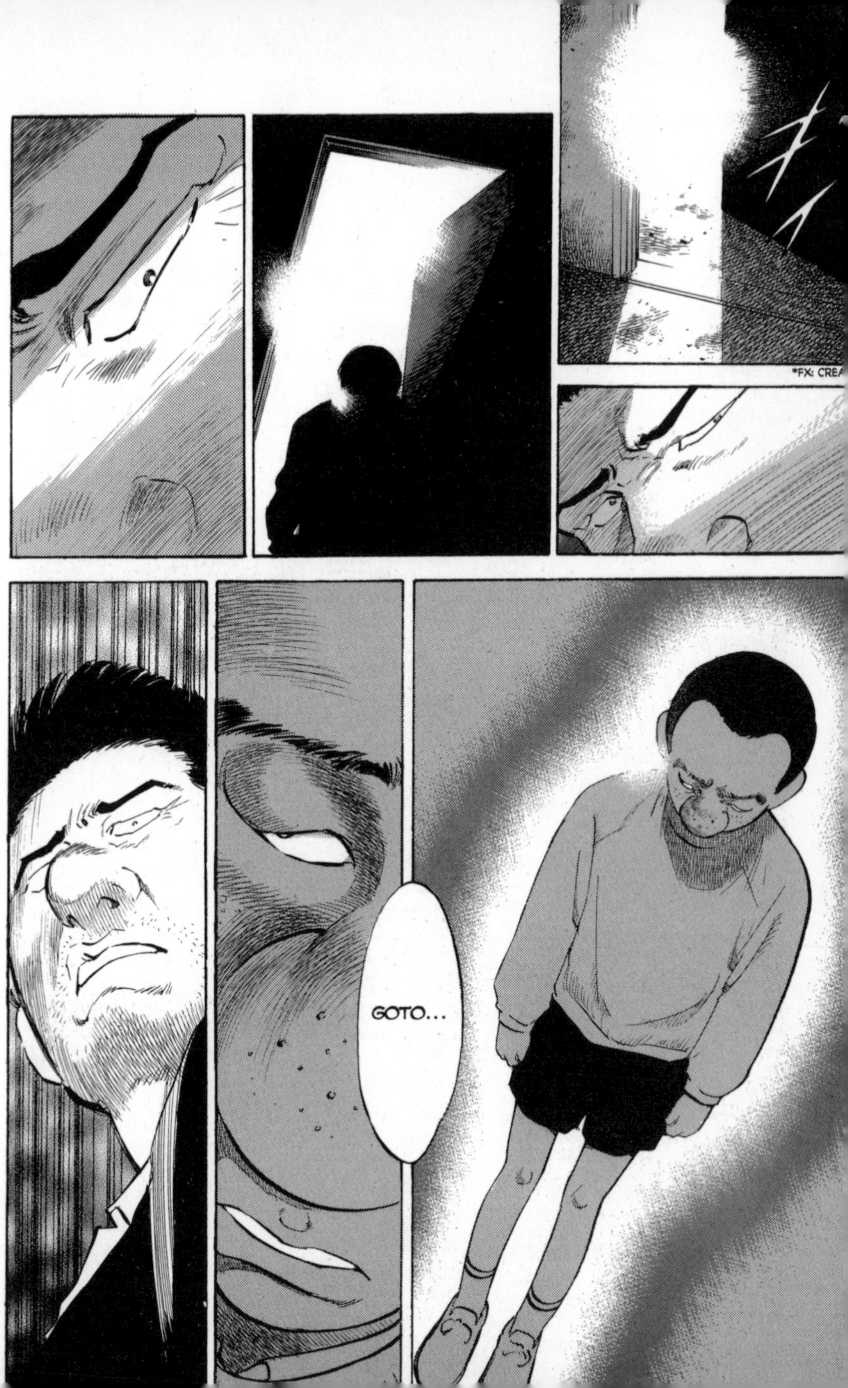
*FX: CREA
GOTO...

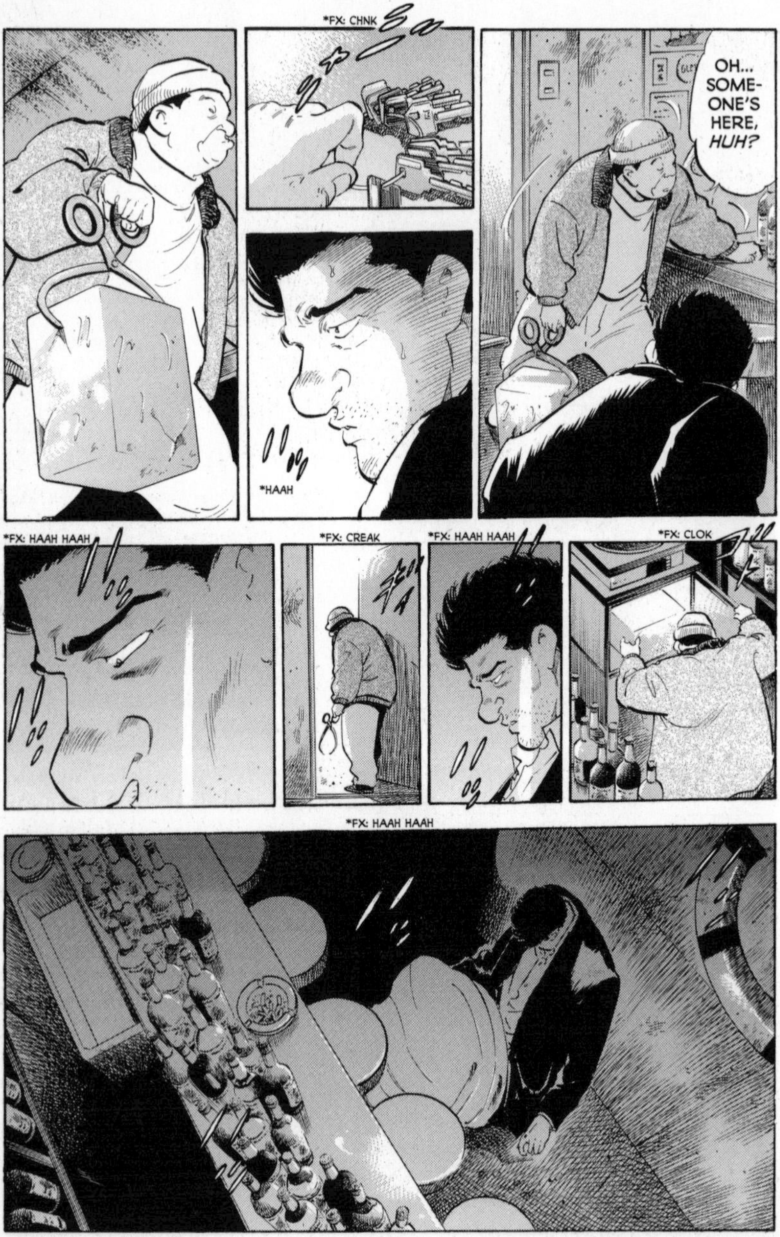
OH... SOME-ONE'S HERE, HUH?
*FX: CHNK
*HAAH
*FX: CLOK
*FX: HAAH HAAH
*FX: CREAK
*FX: HAAH HAAH
*FX: HAAH HAAH

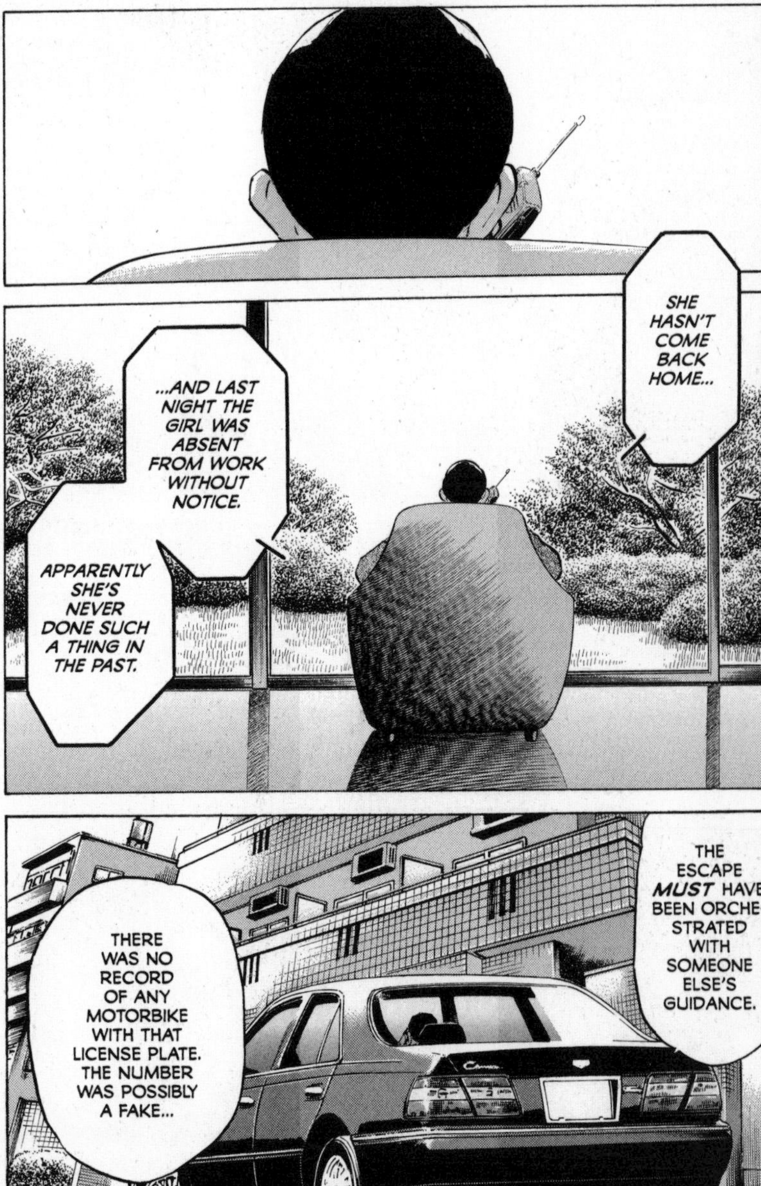
SHE HASN'T COME BACK HOME...
...AND LAST NIGHT THE GIRL WAS ABSENT FROM WORK WITHOUT NOTICE.
APPARENTLY SHE'S NEVER DONE SUCH A THING IN THE PAST.
THE ESCAPE *MUST* HAVE BEEN ORCHE-STRATED WITH SOMEONE ELSE'S GUIDANCE.
THERE WAS NO RECORD OF ANY MOTORBIKE WITH THAT LICENSE PLATE. THE NUMBER WAS POSSIBLY A FAKE...

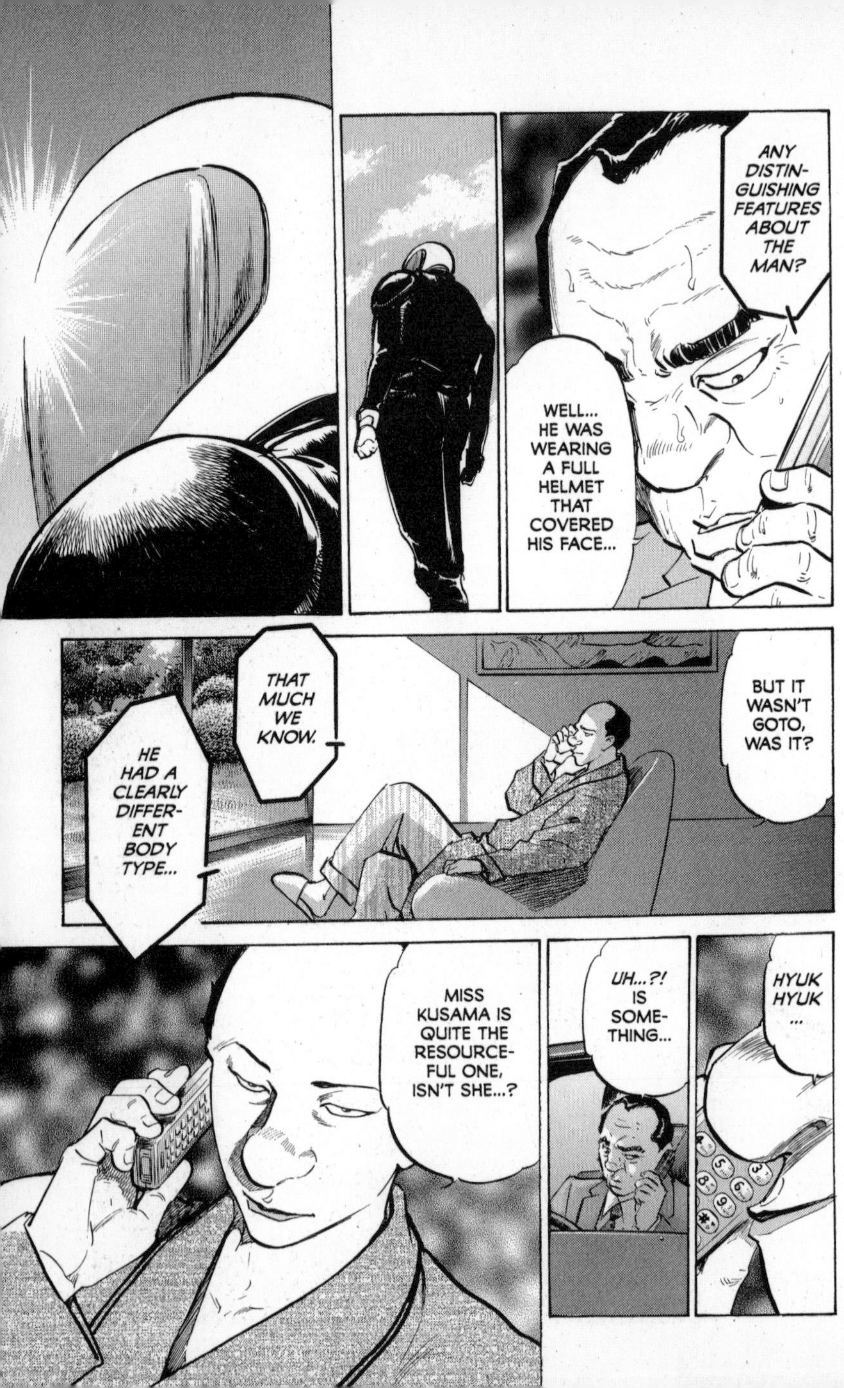
ANY DISTINGUISHING FEATURES ABOUT THE MAN?
WELL... HE WAS WEARING A FULL HELMET THAT COVERED HIS FACE...
BUT IT WASN'T GOTO, WAS IT?
THAT MUCH WE KNOW.
HE HAD A CLEARLY DIFFERENT BODY TYPE...
HYUK HYUK ...
UH...?! IS SOMETHING...
MISS KUSAMA IS QUITE THE RESOURCEFUL ONE, ISN'T SHE...?

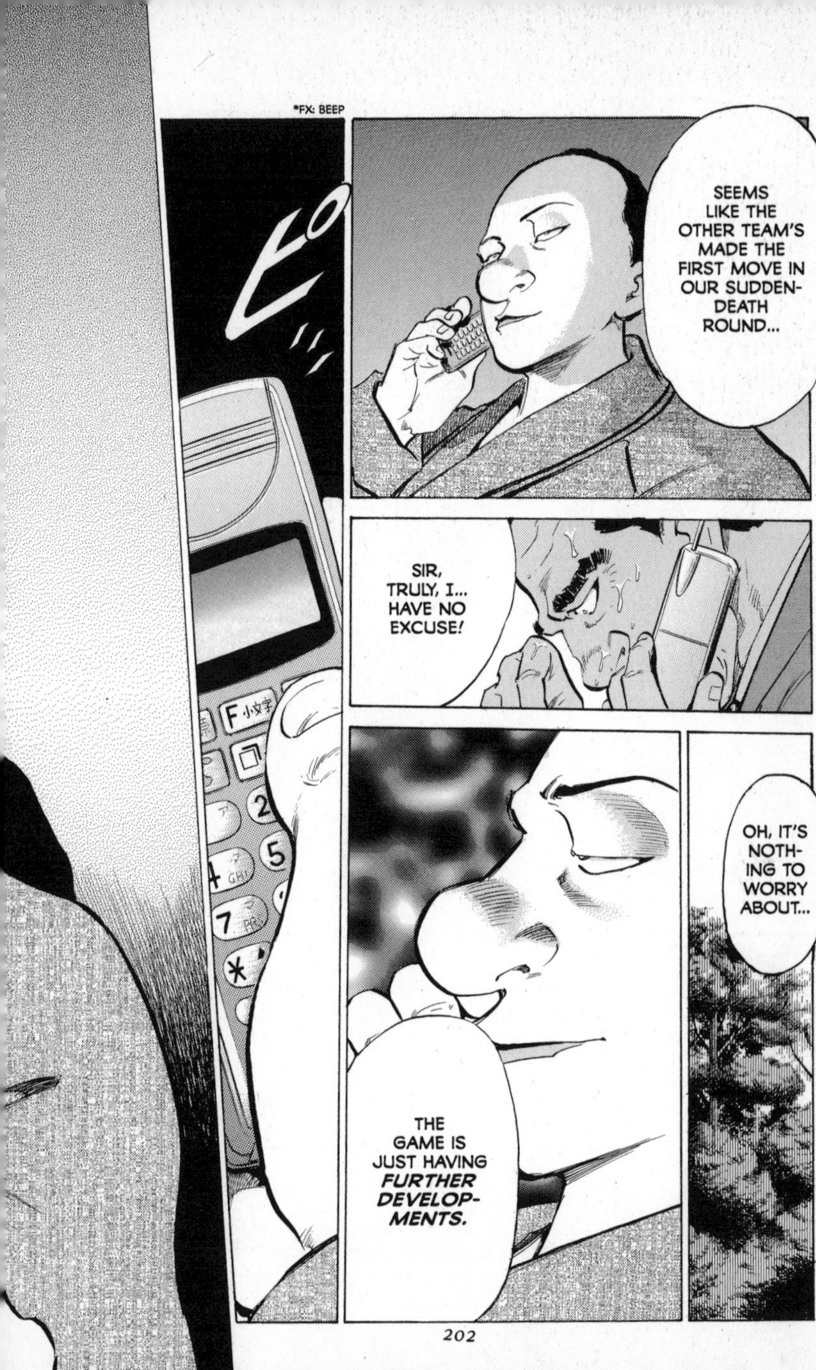
SEEMS LIKE THE OTHER TEAM'S MADE THE FIRST MOVE IN OUR SUDDEN-DEATH ROUND...
SIR, TRULY, I... HAVE NO EXCUSE!
OH, IT'S NOTHING TO WORRY ABOUT...
THE GAME IS JUST HAVING *FURTHER DEVELOPMENTS.*
*FX: BEEP

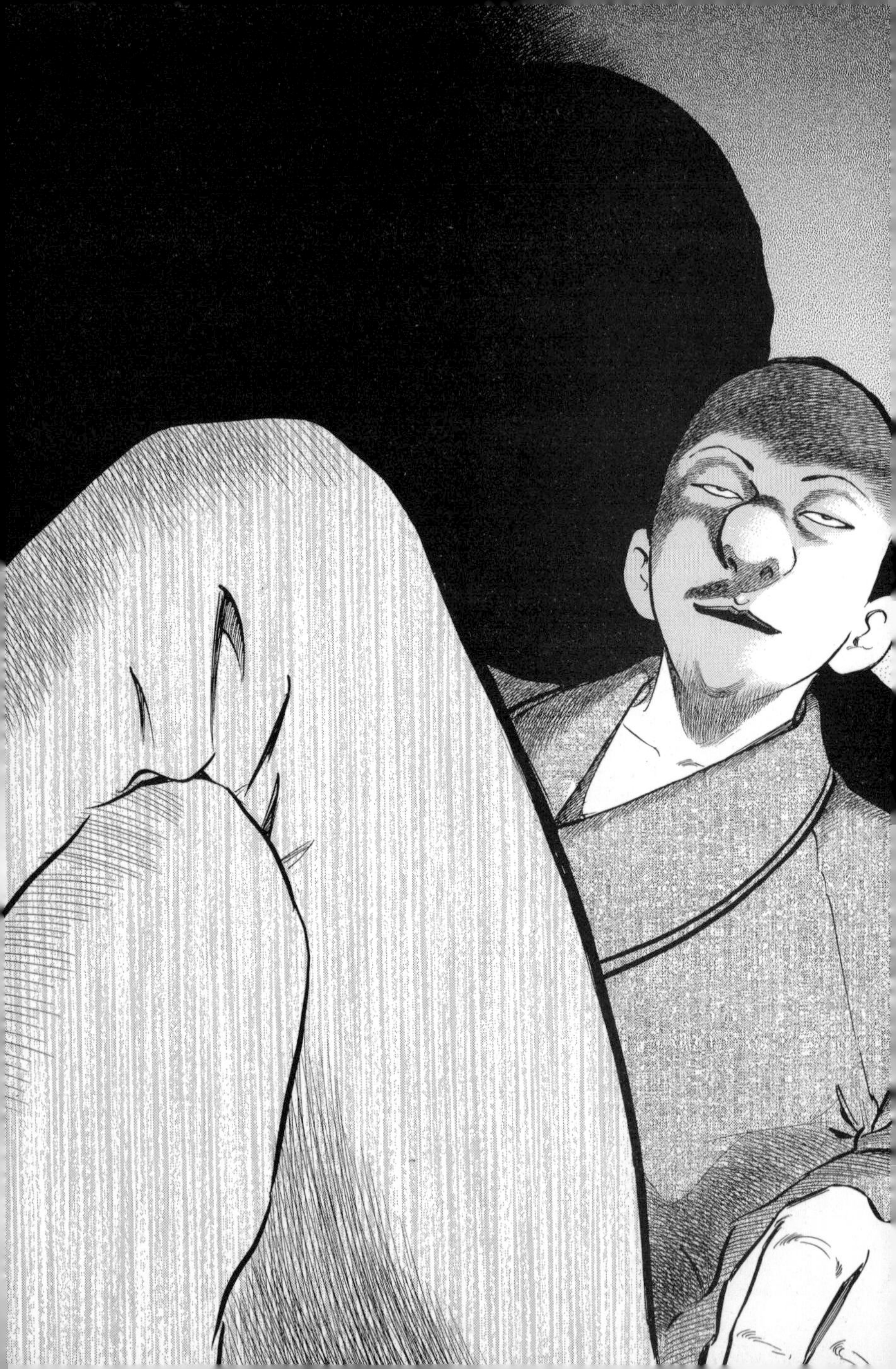

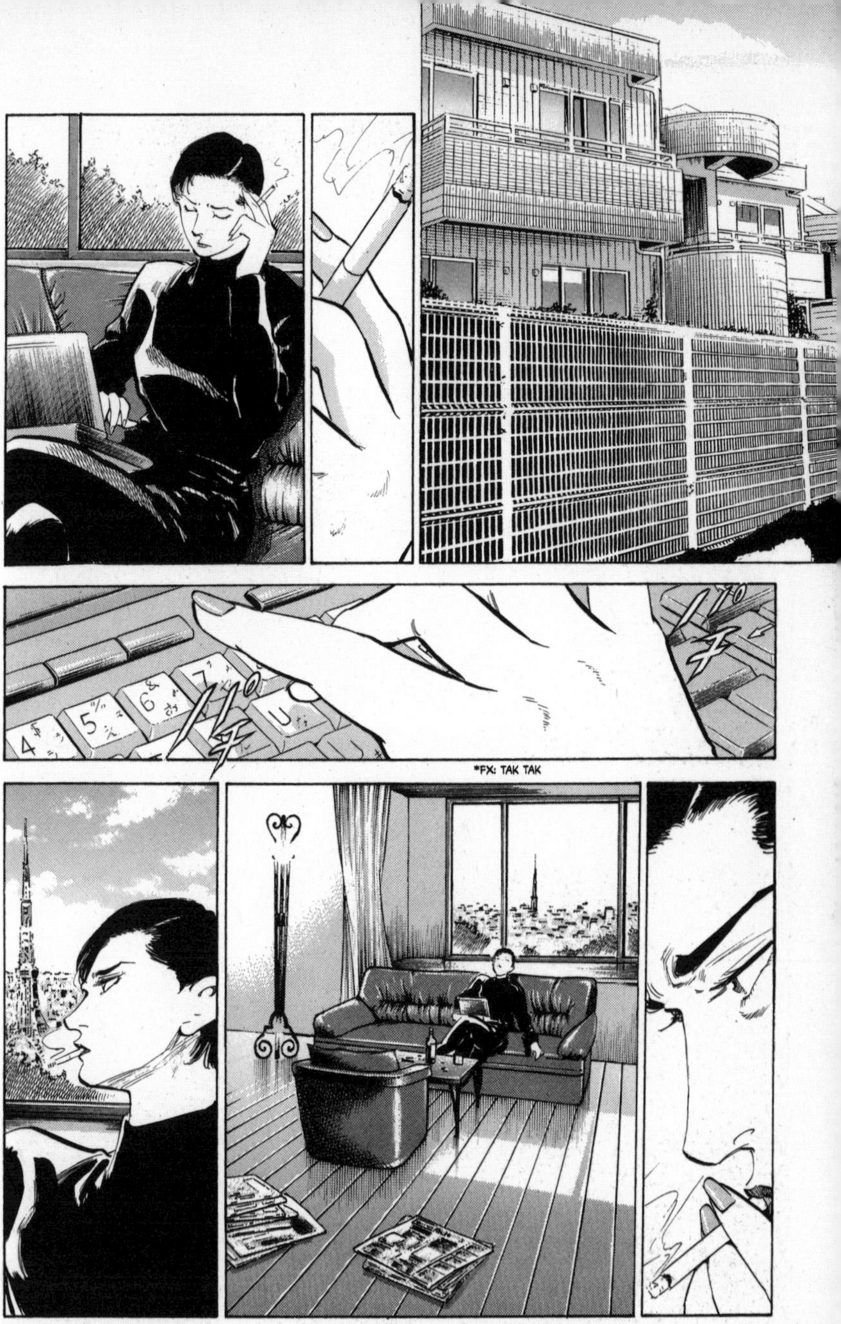
*FX: TAK TAK

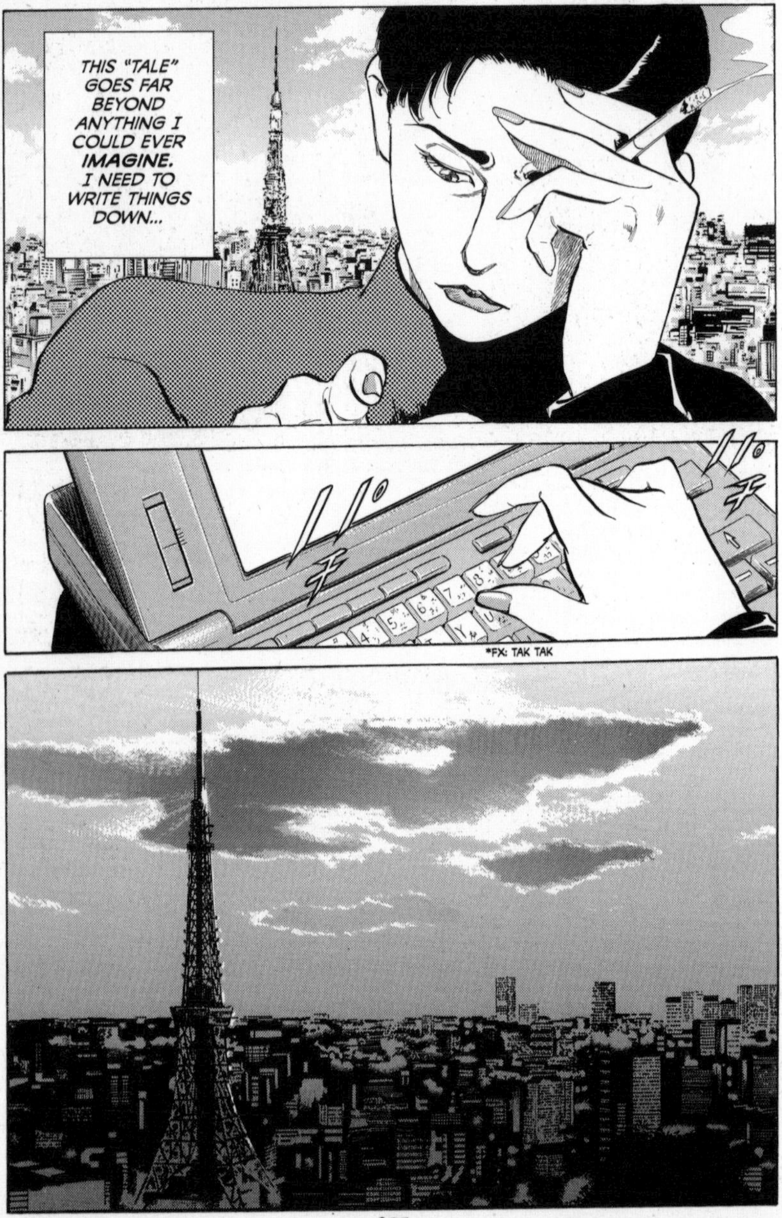
THIS "TALE" GOES FAR BEYOND ANYTHING I COULD EVER IMAGINE. I NEED TO WRITE THINGS DOWN...
*FX: TAK TAK

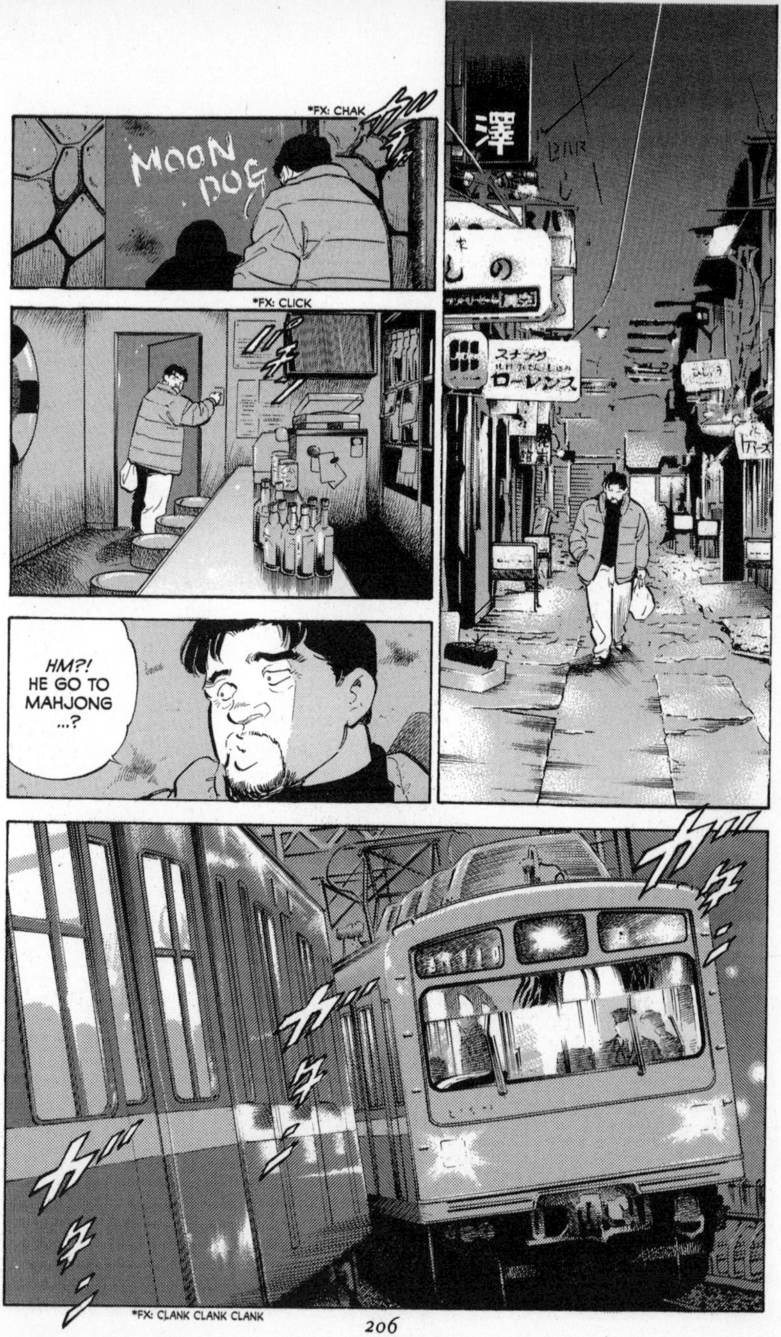
*FX: CHAK
MOON DOG
*FX: CLICK
HM?! HE GO TO MAHJONG ...?
*FX: CLANK CLANK CLANK

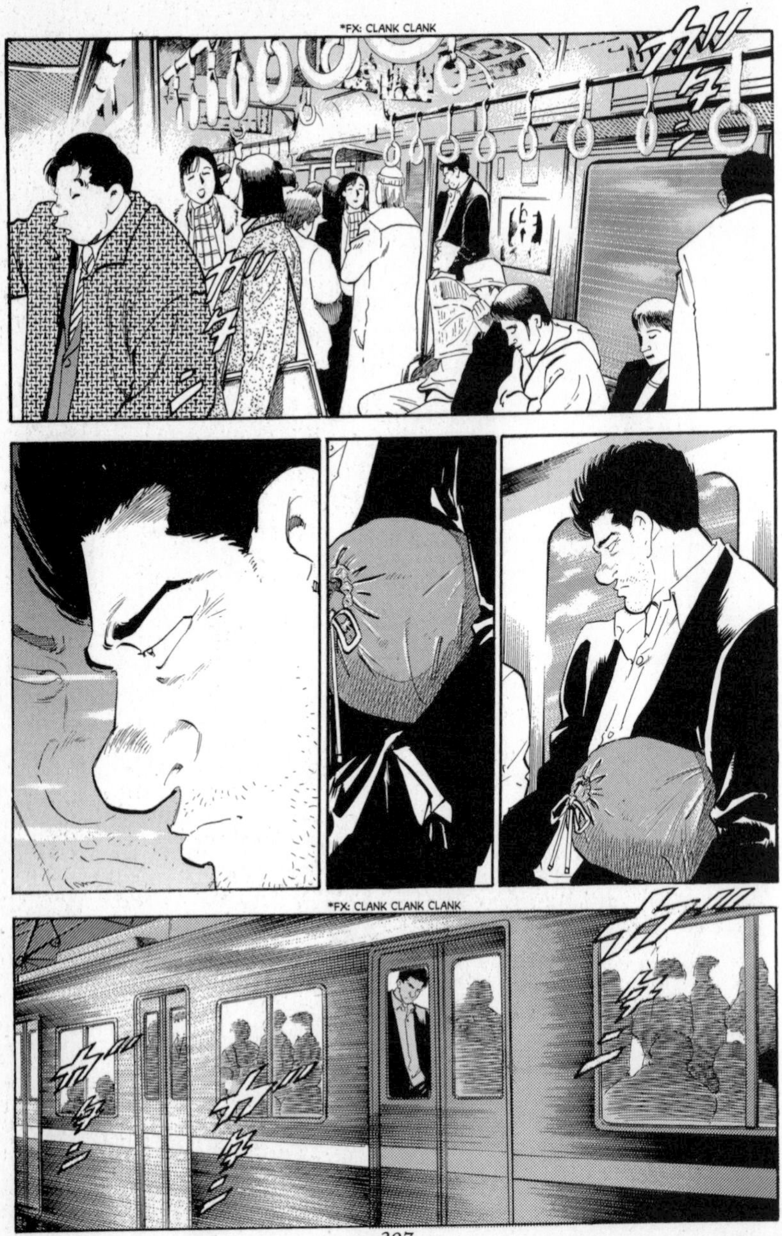
*FX: CLANK CLANK
*FX: CLANK CLANK CLANK

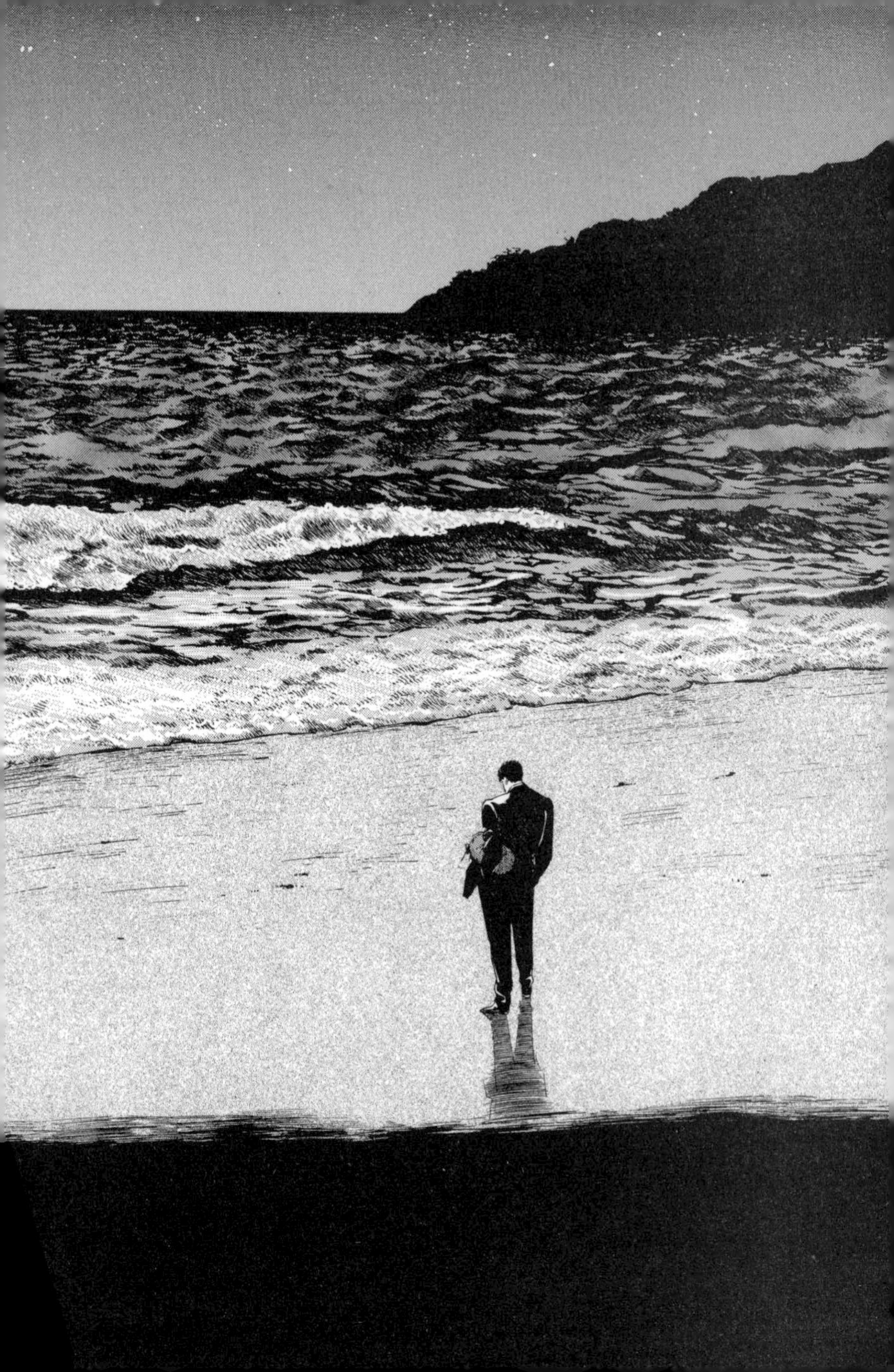

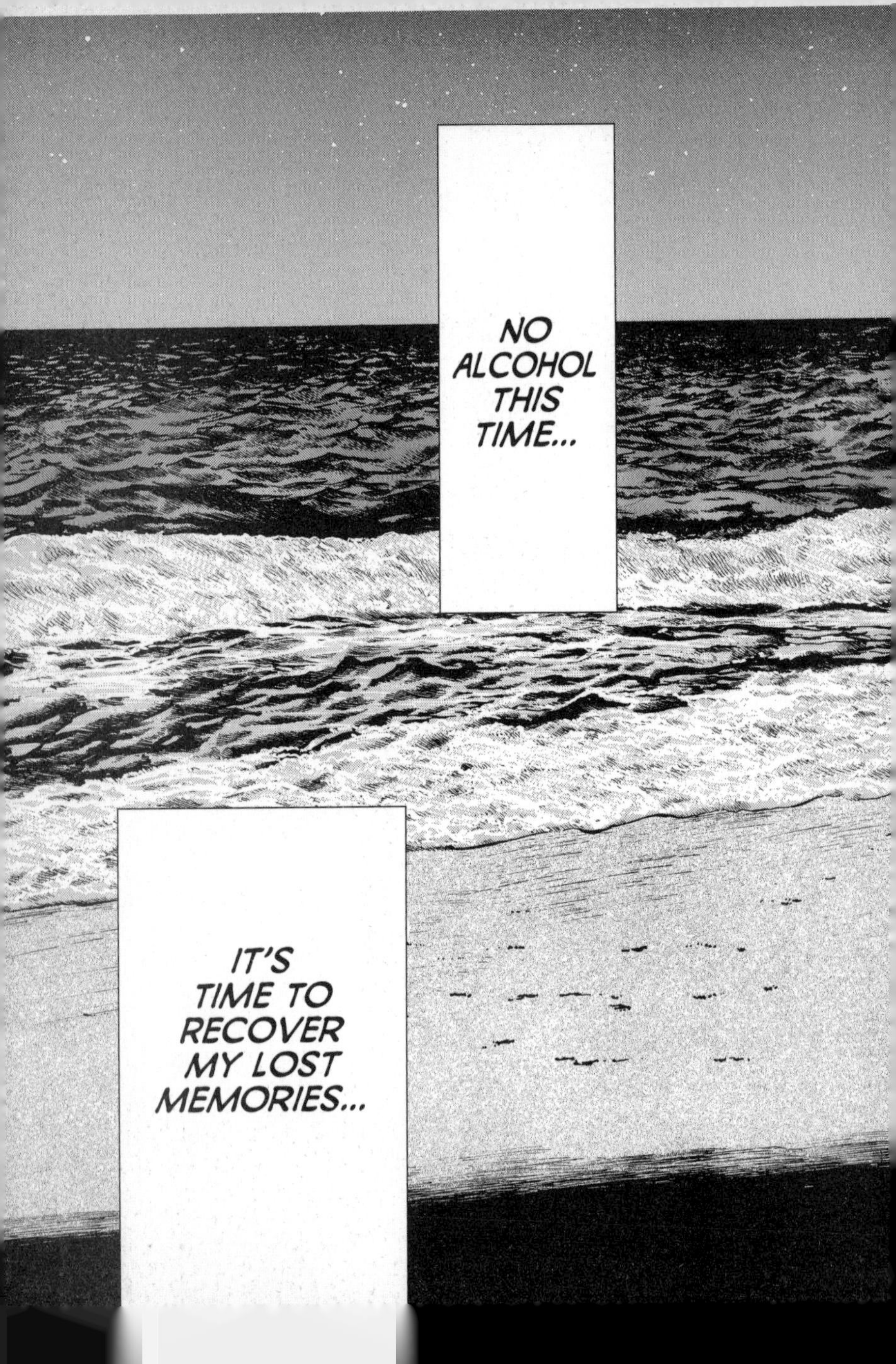
NO ALCOHOL THIS TIME...
IT'S TIME TO RECOVER MY LOST MEMORIES...

*FX: FWAASHH

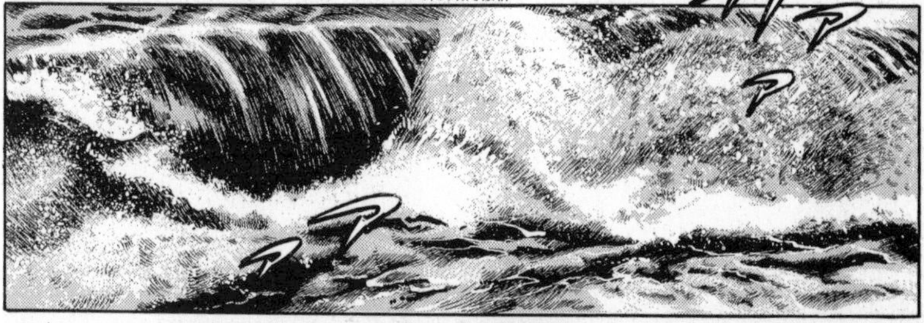

*FX: FWSH FWSH FWSH FWSH

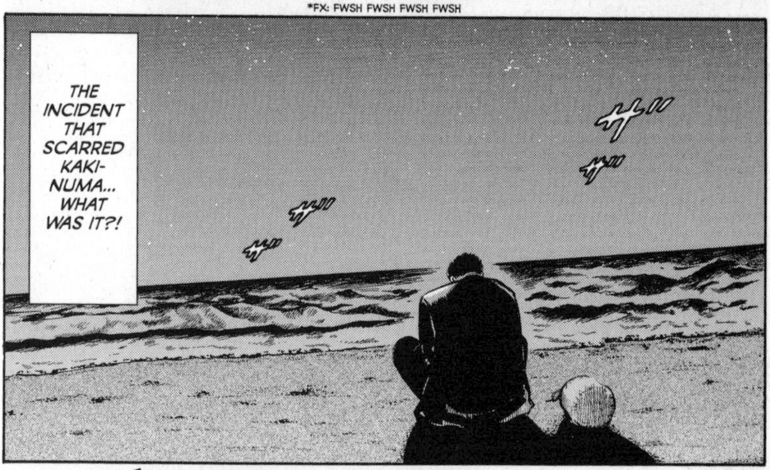
THE INCIDENT THAT SCARRED KAKI-NUMA... WHAT WAS IT?!

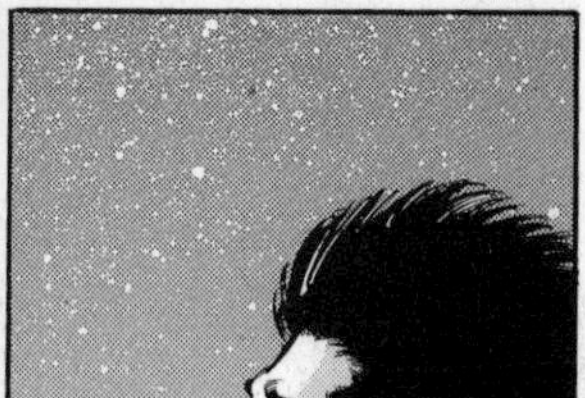

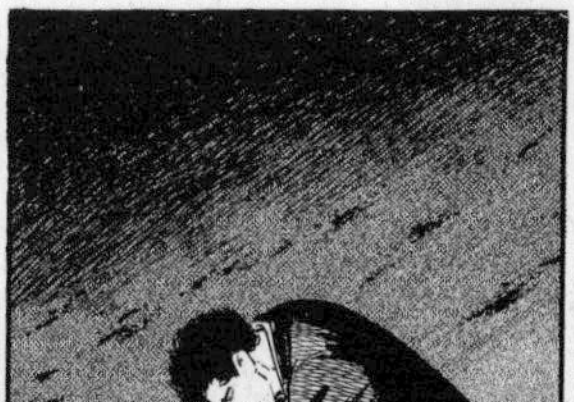

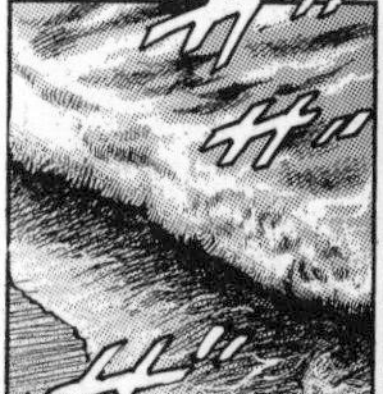

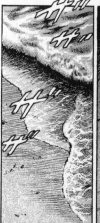

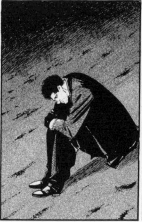

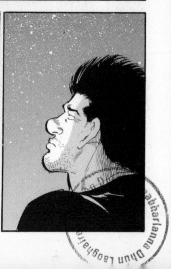

*FX: FWAASH FWAASH

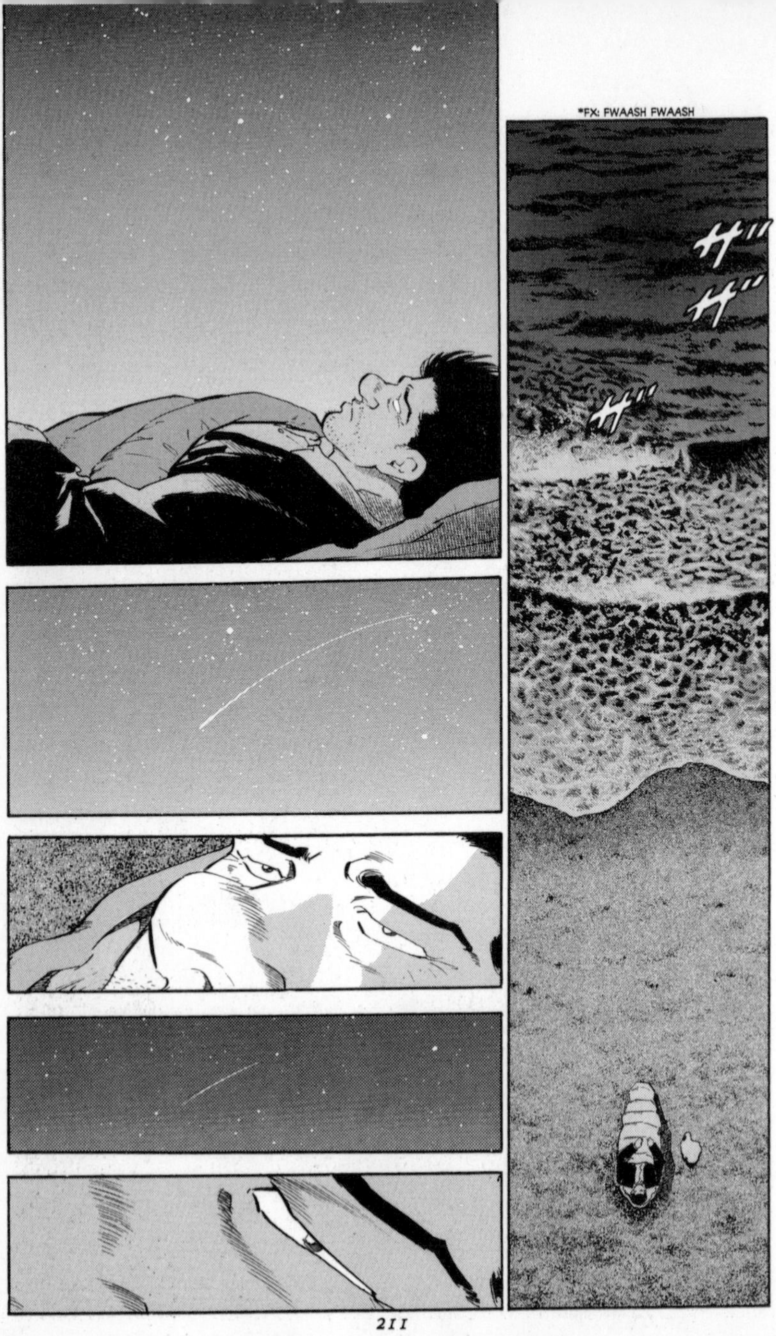
*FX: FWAASH FWAASH
ザッ
ザッ
ザッ

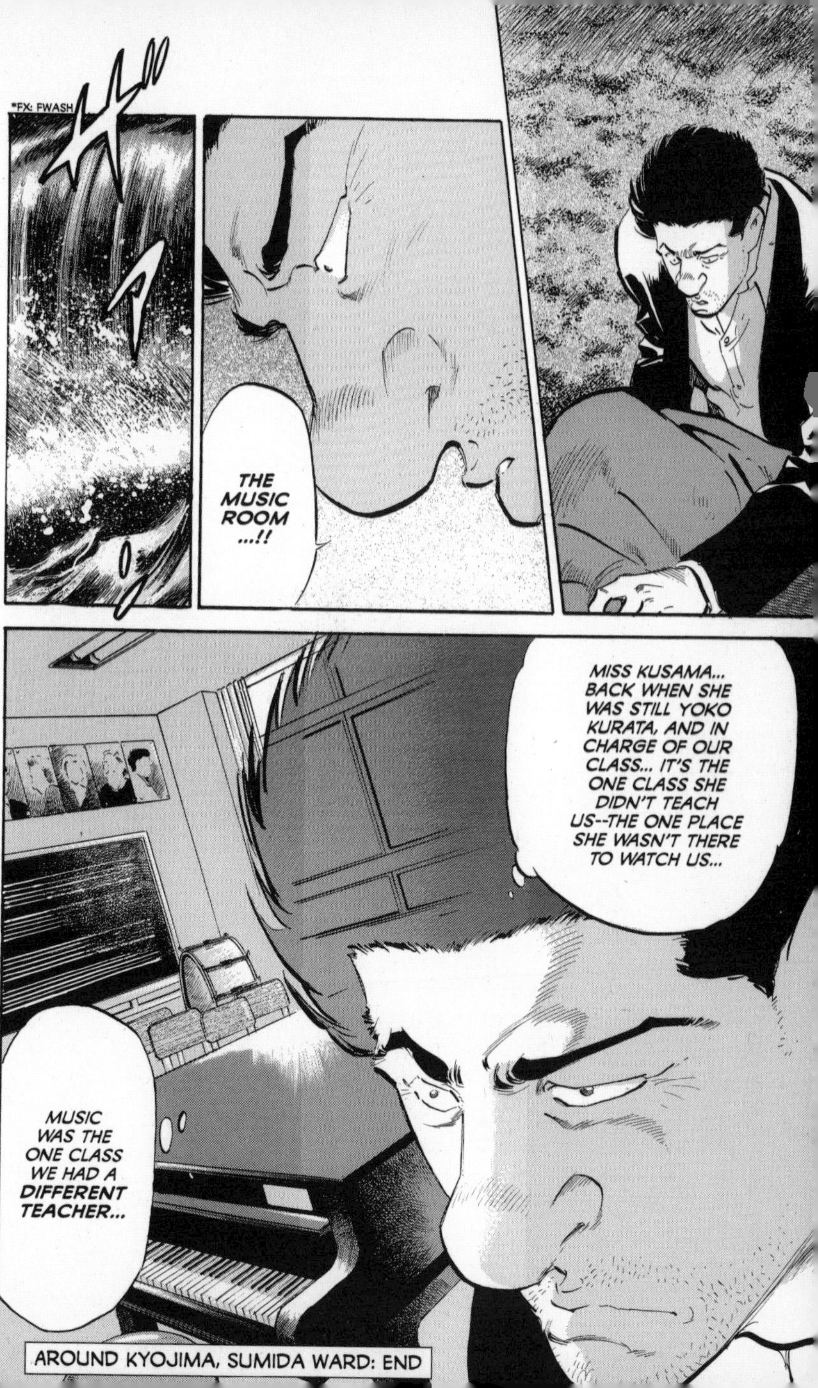
THE MUSIC ROOM ...!!
*FX: FWASH
MISS KUSAMA... BACK WHEN SHE WAS STILL YOKO KURATA, AND IN CHARGE OF OUR CLASS... IT'S THE ONE CLASS SHE DIDN'T TEACH US--THE ONE PLACE SHE WASN'T THERE TO WATCH US...
MUSIC WAS THE ONE CLASS WE HAD A DIFFERENT TEACHER...
AROUND KYOJIMA, SUMIDA WARD: END

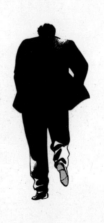

Ten years ago, he was abducted and confined to a private prison. He was never told why he was there, or who put him there. Suddenly his incarceration has ended, again without explanation. He is sedated, stuffed inside a trunk, and dumped in a park. When he awakes, he is free to reclaim what's left of his life . . . and what's left is revenge.

This series is the inspiration of the *Oldboy* film directed by Chan-wook Park, which was awarded the Grand Jury prize at the 2004 Cannes Film Festival!

Winner of the 2007 Eisner Award for Best U.S. Edition of International Material—Japan!

VOLUME 1:
ISBN-10: 1-59307-568-5
ISBN-13: 978-1-59307-568-2

VOLUME 2:
ISBN-10: 1-59307-569-3
ISBN-13: 978-1-59307-569-9

VOLUME 3:
ISBN-10: 1-59307-570-7
ISBN-13: 978-1-59307-570-5

VOLUME 4:
ISBN-10: 1-59307-703-3
ISBN-13: 978-1-59307-703-7

VOLUME 5:
ISBN-10: 1-59307-714-9
ISBN-13: 978-1-59307-714-3

VOLUME 6:
ISBN-10: 1-59307-720-3
ISBN-13: 978-1-59307-720-4

VOLUME 7:
ISBN-10: 1-59307-721-1
ISBN-13: 978-1-59307-721-1

VOLUME 8:
ISBN-10: 1-59307-722-X
ISBN-13: 978-1-59307-722-8

$12.95 EACH!

GARON TSUCHIYA AND NOBUAKI MINEGISHI'S

OLDBOY

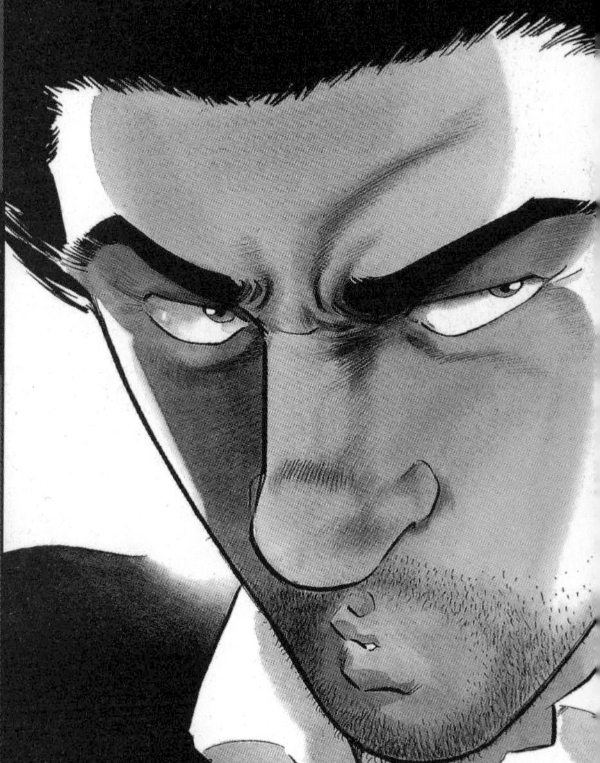

AVAILABLE AT YOUR LOCAL COMICS SHOP OR BOOKSTORE!

To find a comics shop in your area, call 1-888-266-4226.

For more information or to order direct visit darkhorse.com or call 1-800-862-0052
Mon.–Fri. 9 A.M. to 5 P.M. Pacific Time. Prices and availability subject to change without notice.

DARK HORSE MANGA

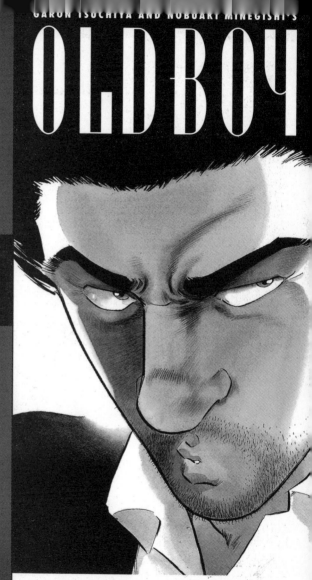

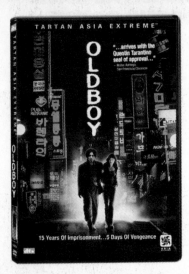
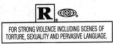
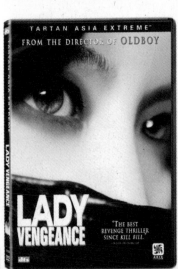
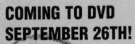
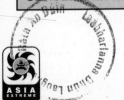

STOP! THIS IS THE BACK OF THE BOOK!

This manga collection is translated into English, but arranged in right-to-left reading format to maintain the artwork's visual orientation as originally drawn and published in Japan. If you've never read comics this way before, take a look at the diagram below to give yourself an idea of how to go about it. Basically, you'll be starting in the upper right-hand corner, and will read each word balloon and panel moving right-to-left. It may take a little getting used to, but you should get the hang of it very quickly. Have fun!

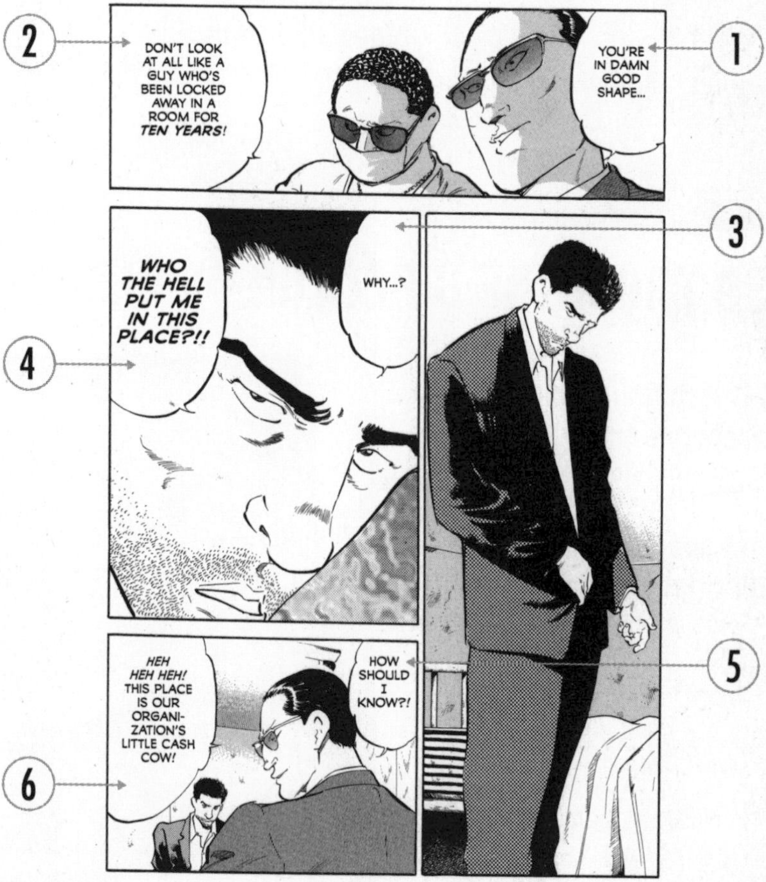
1
YOU'RE IN DAMN GOOD SHAPE...
2
DON'T LOOK AT ALL LIKE A GUY WHO'S BEEN LOCKED AWAY IN A ROOM FOR *TEN YEARS!*
3
WHY...?
4
WHO THE HELL PUT ME IN THIS PLACE?!!
5
HOW SHOULD I KNOW?!
6
HEH HEH HEH! THIS PLACE IS OUR ORGANIZATION'S LITTLE CASH COW!